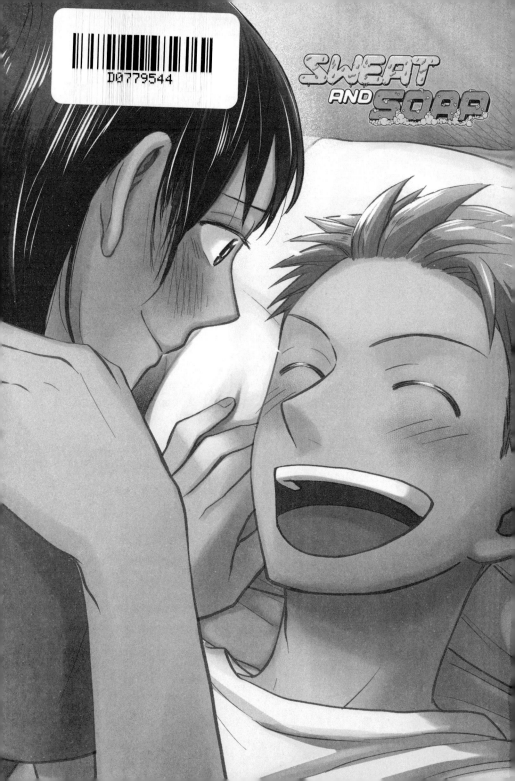

SWEAT AND SOAP

CONTENTS

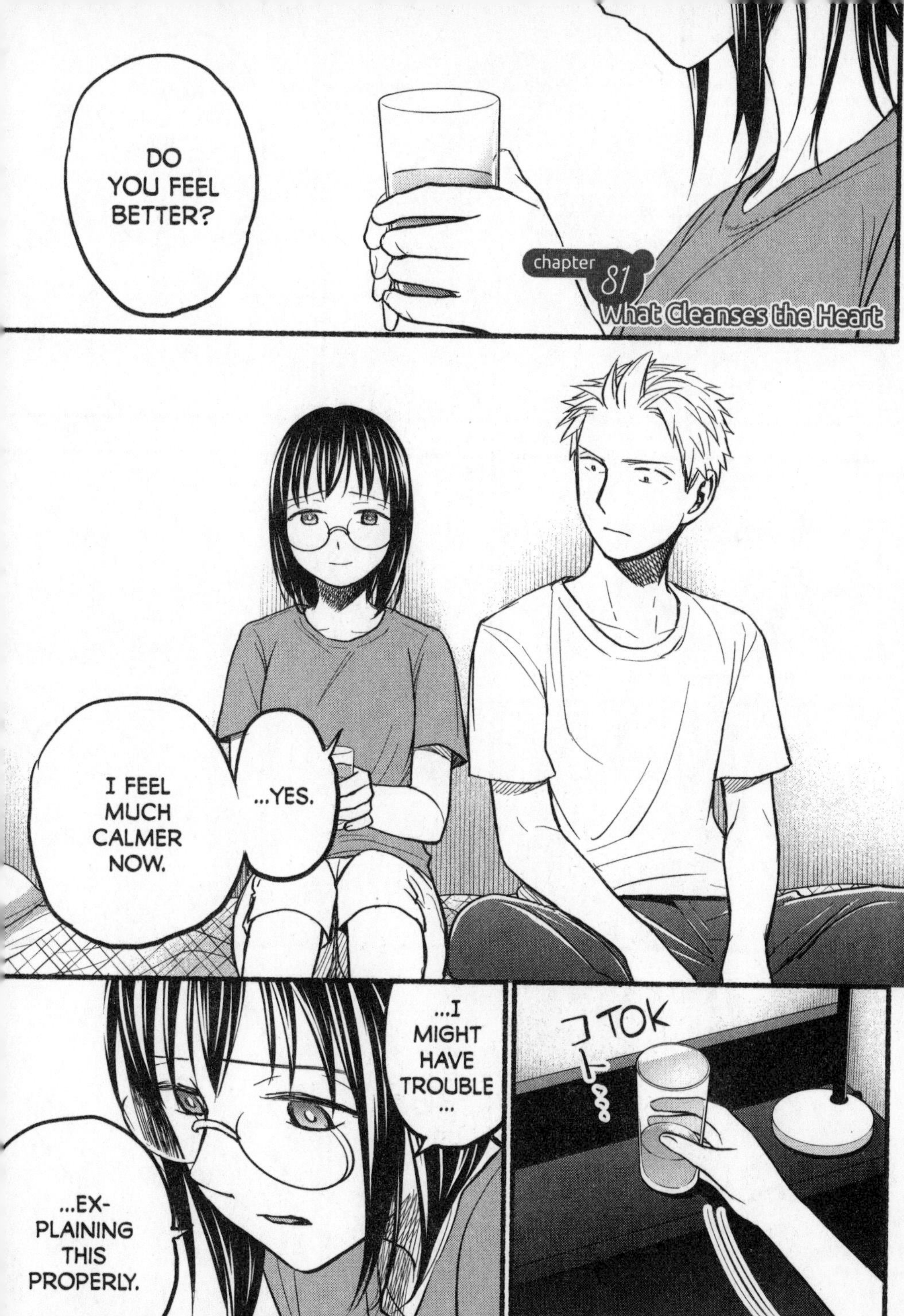
chapter 81
What Cleanses the Heart
DO YOU FEEL BETTER?
...YES.
I FEEL MUCH CALMER NOW.
TOK
...I MIGHT HAVE TROUBLE ...
...EX-PLAINING THIS PROPERLY.

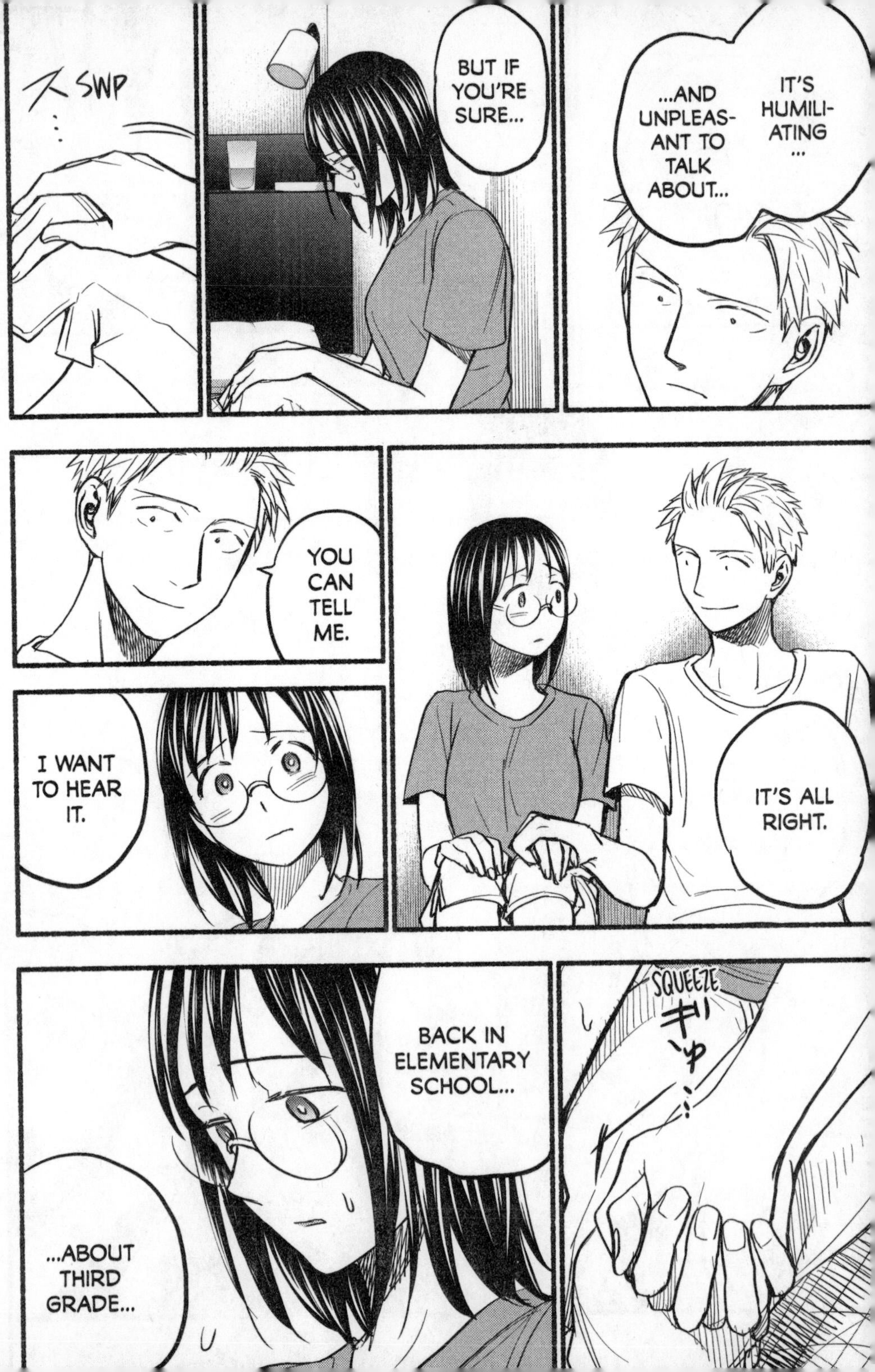
IT'S HUMILIATING...
...AND UNPLEASANT TO TALK ABOUT...
BUT IF YOU'RE SURE...
SWP
IT'S ALL RIGHT.
YOU CAN TELL ME.
I WANT TO HEAR IT.
SQUEEZE
ギュッ
BACK IN ELEMENTARY SCHOOL...
...ABOUT THIRD GRADE...

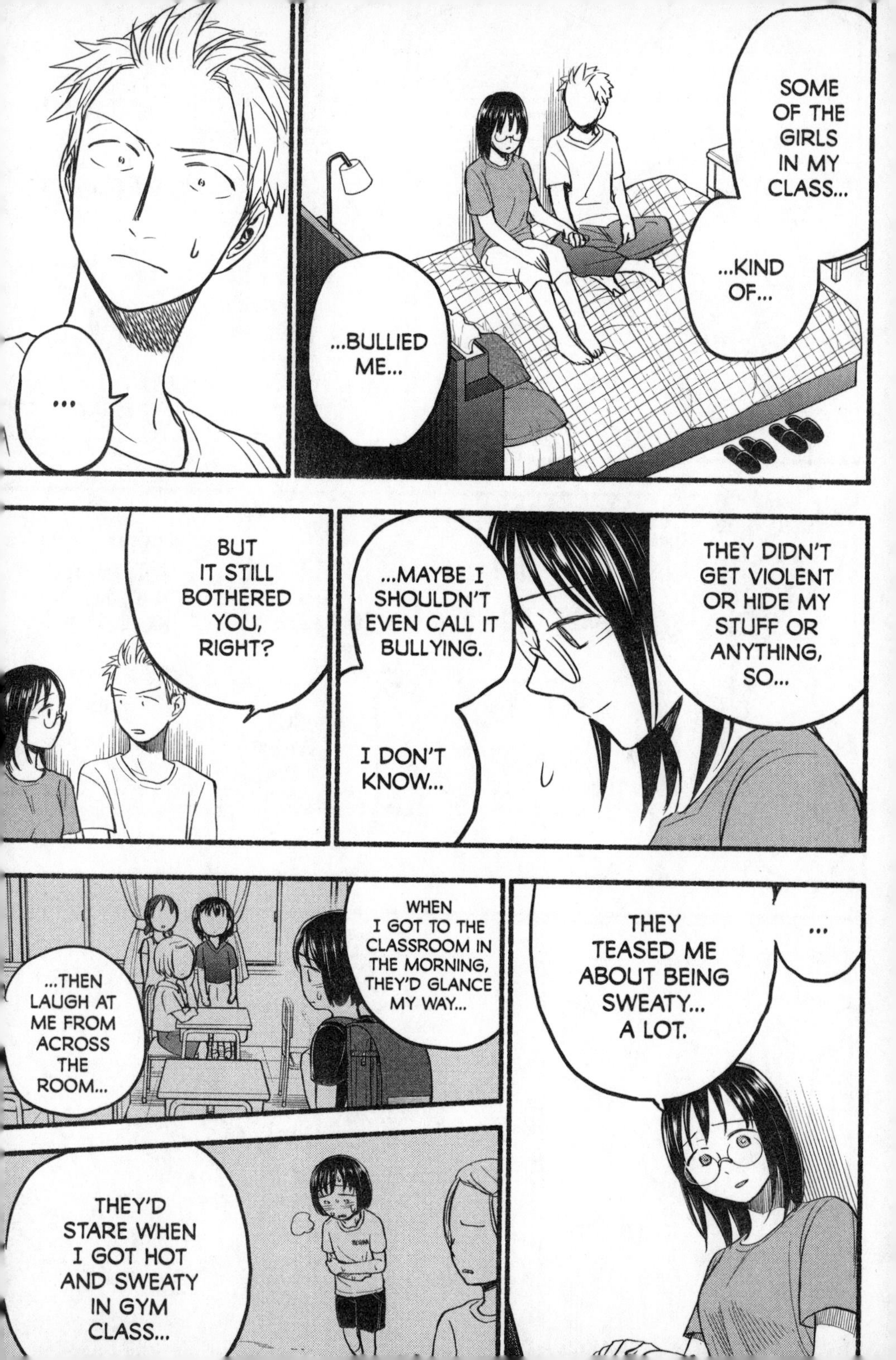
SOME OF THE GIRLS IN MY CLASS...
...KIND OF...
...BULLIED ME...
...
THEY DIDN'T GET VIOLENT OR HIDE MY STUFF OR ANYTHING, SO...
...MAYBE I SHOULDN'T EVEN CALL IT BULLYING.
I DON'T KNOW...
BUT IT STILL BOTHERED YOU, RIGHT?
...
THEY TEASED ME ABOUT BEING SWEATY... A LOT.
WHEN I GOT TO THE CLASSROOM IN THE MORNING, THEY'D GLANCE MY WAY...
...THEN LAUGH AT ME FROM ACROSS THE ROOM...
THEY'D STARE WHEN I GOT HOT AND SWEATY IN GYM CLASS...

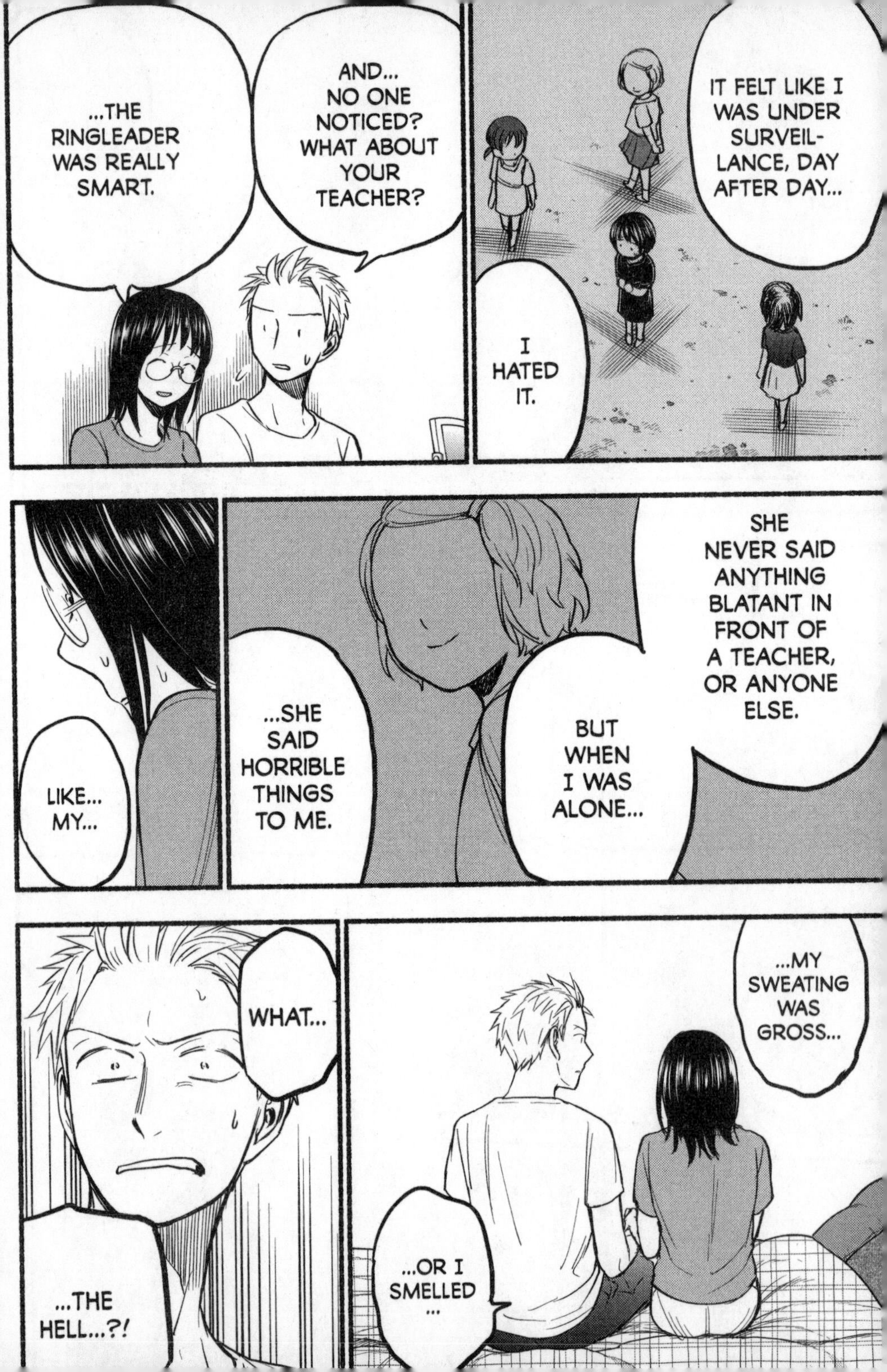
IT FELT LIKE I WAS UNDER SURVEIL-LANCE, DAY AFTER DAY...
I HATED IT.
AND... NO ONE NOTICED? WHAT ABOUT YOUR TEACHER?
...THE RINGLEADER WAS REALLY SMART.
SHE NEVER SAID ANYTHING BLATANT IN FRONT OF A TEACHER, OR ANYONE ELSE.
BUT WHEN I WAS ALONE...
...SHE SAID HORRIBLE THINGS TO ME.
LIKE... MY...
...MY SWEATING WAS GROSS...
...OR I SMELLED ...
WHAT...
...THE HELL...?!

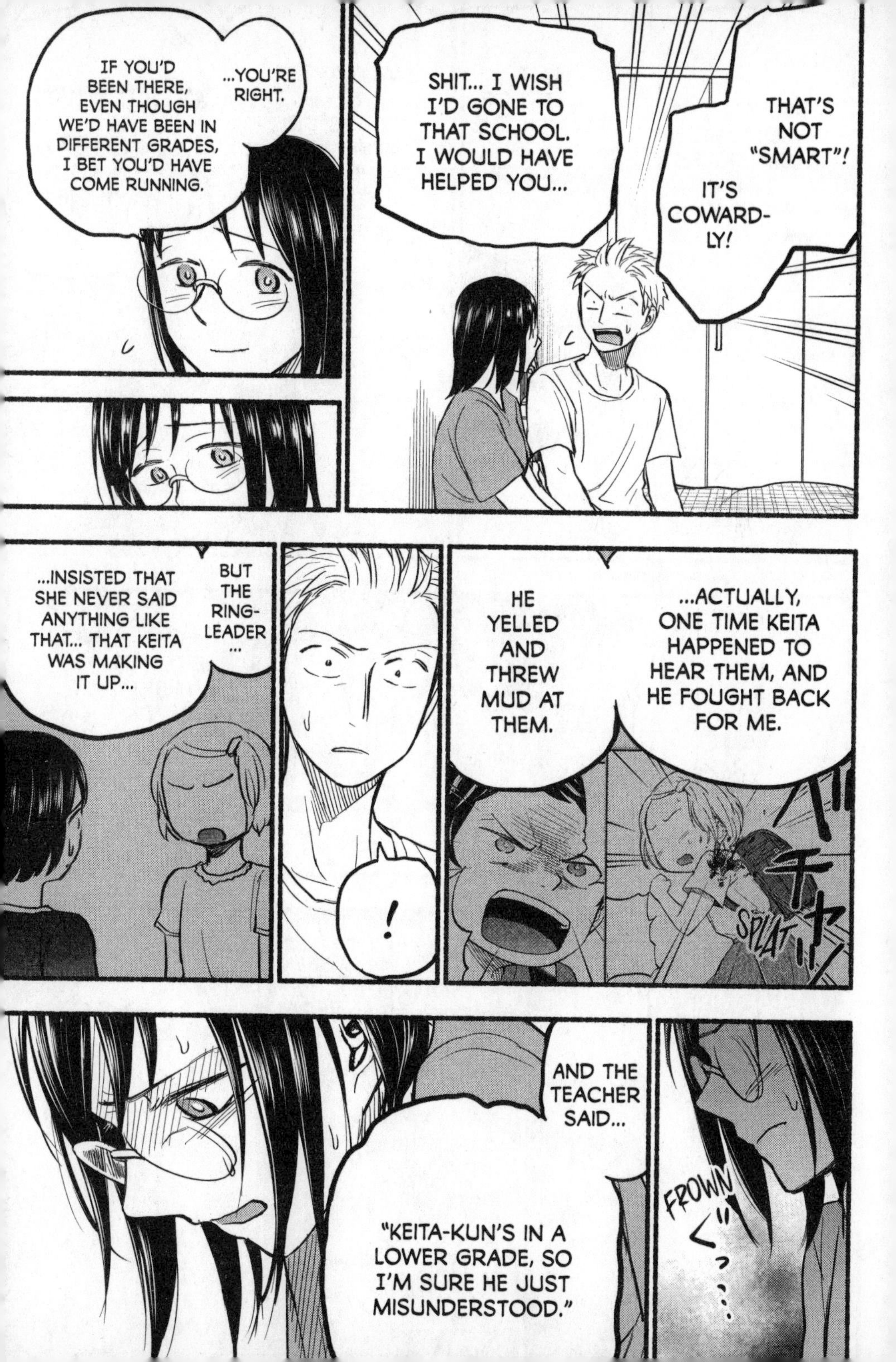
THAT'S NOT "SMART"!
IT'S COWARD-LY!
SHIT... I WISH I'D GONE TO THAT SCHOOL. I WOULD HAVE HELPED YOU...
...YOU'RE RIGHT.
IF YOU'D BEEN THERE, EVEN THOUGH WE'D HAVE BEEN IN DIFFERENT GRADES, I BET YOU'D HAVE COME RUNNING.
...ACTUALLY, ONE TIME KEITA HAPPENED TO HEAR THEM, AND HE FOUGHT BACK FOR ME.
HE YELLED AND THREW MUD AT THEM.
SPLAT
!
BUT THE RING-LEADER...
...INSISTED THAT SHE NEVER SAID ANYTHING LIKE THAT... THAT KEITA WAS MAKING IT UP...
FROWN
AND THE TEACHER SAID...
"KEITA-KUN'S IN A LOWER GRADE, SO I'M SURE HE JUST MISUNDERSTOOD."

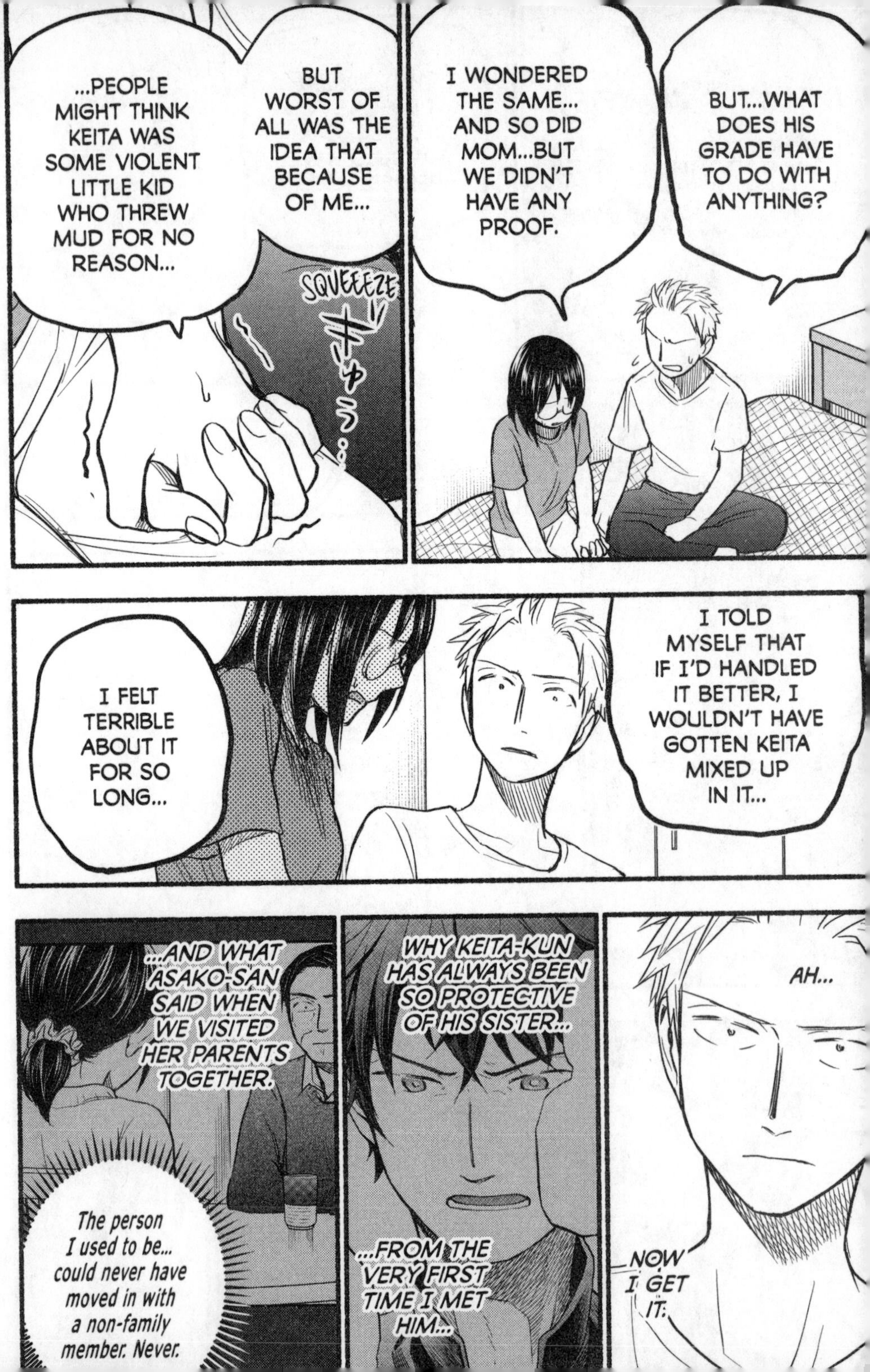
BUT...WHAT DOES HIS GRADE HAVE TO DO WITH ANYTHING?
I WONDERED THE SAME... AND SO DID MOM...BUT WE DIDN'T HAVE ANY PROOF.
BUT WORST OF ALL WAS THE IDEA THAT BECAUSE OF ME...
...PEOPLE MIGHT THINK KEITA WAS SOME VIOLENT LITTLE KID WHO THREW MUD FOR NO REASON...
SQUEEEZE
I TOLD MYSELF THAT IF I'D HANDLED IT BETTER, I WOULDN'T HAVE GOTTEN KEITA MIXED UP IN IT...
I FELT TERRIBLE ABOUT IT FOR SO LONG...
AH...
NOW I GET IT.
WHY KEITA-KUN HAS ALWAYS BEEN SO PROTECTIVE OF HIS SISTER...
...FROM THE VERY FIRST TIME I MET HIM...
...AND WHAT ASAKO-SAN SAID WHEN WE VISITED HER PARENTS TOGETHER.
The person I used to be... could never have moved in with a non-family member. Never.

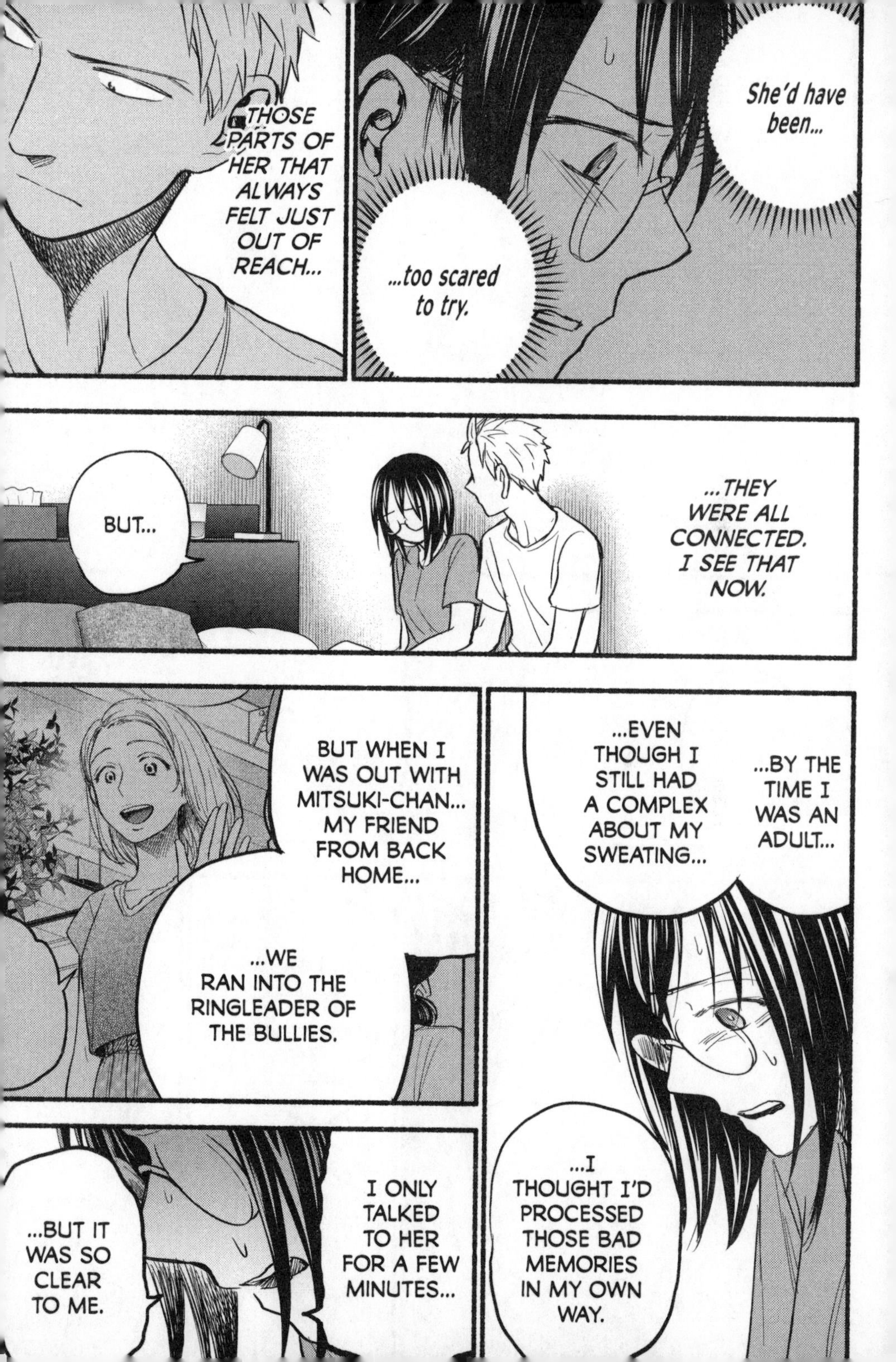

She'd have been...
...too scared to try.
THOSE PARTS OF HER THAT ALWAYS FELT JUST OUT OF REACH...
...THEY WERE ALL CONNECTED. I SEE THAT NOW.
BUT...
...BY THE TIME I WAS AN ADULT...
...EVEN THOUGH I STILL HAD A COMPLEX ABOUT MY SWEATING...
...I THOUGHT I'D PROCESSED THOSE BAD MEMORIES IN MY OWN WAY.
BUT WHEN I WAS OUT WITH MITSUKI-CHAN... MY FRIEND FROM BACK HOME...
...WE RAN INTO THE RINGLEADER OF THE BULLIES.
I ONLY TALKED TO HER FOR A FEW MINUTES...
...BUT IT WAS SO CLEAR TO ME.

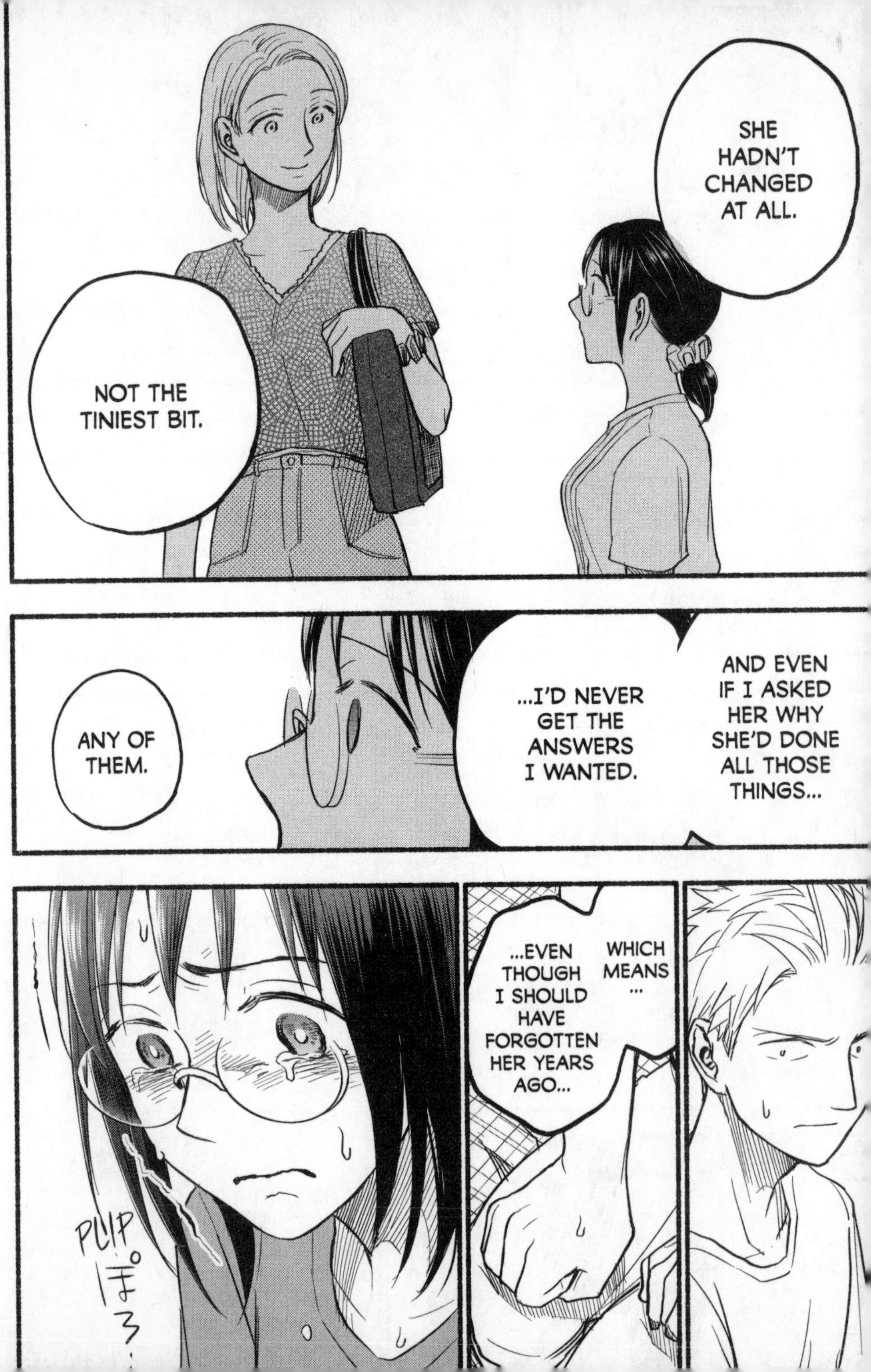
SHE HADN'T CHANGED AT ALL.
NOT THE TINIEST BIT.
AND EVEN IF I ASKED HER WHY SHE'D DONE ALL THOSE THINGS...
...I'D NEVER GET THE ANSWERS I WANTED.
ANY OF THEM.
WHICH MEANS ...
...EVEN THOUGH I SHOULD HAVE FORGOTTEN HER YEARS AGO...
PLIP

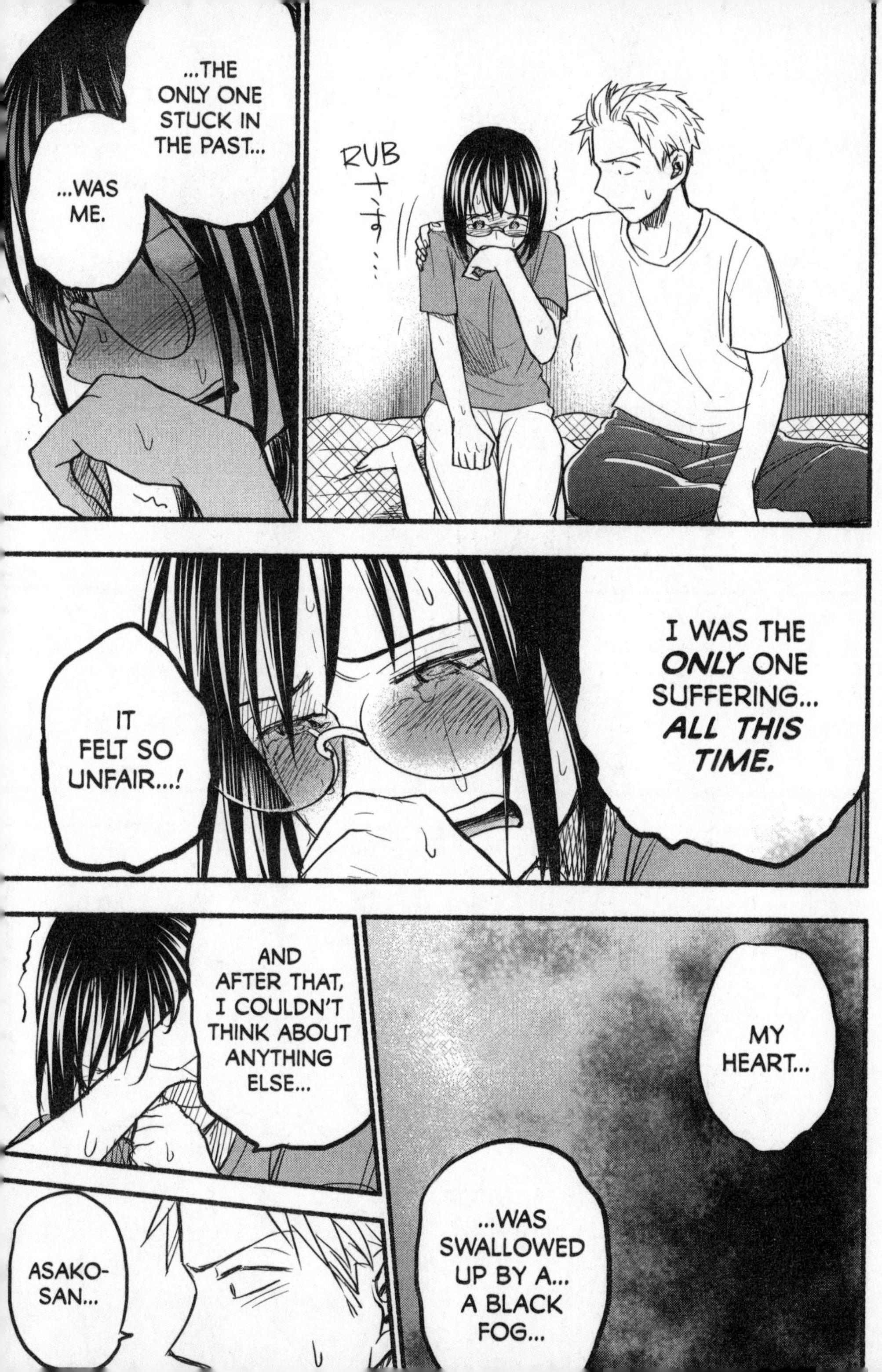
RUB さす…
...THE ONLY ONE STUCK IN THE PAST...
...WAS ME.
I WAS THE *ONLY* ONE SUFFERING... ***ALL THIS TIME.***
IT FELT SO UNFAIR...!
MY HEART...
...WAS SWALLOWED UP BY A... A BLACK FOG...
AND AFTER THAT, I COULDN'T THINK ABOUT ANYTHING ELSE...
ASAKO-SAN...

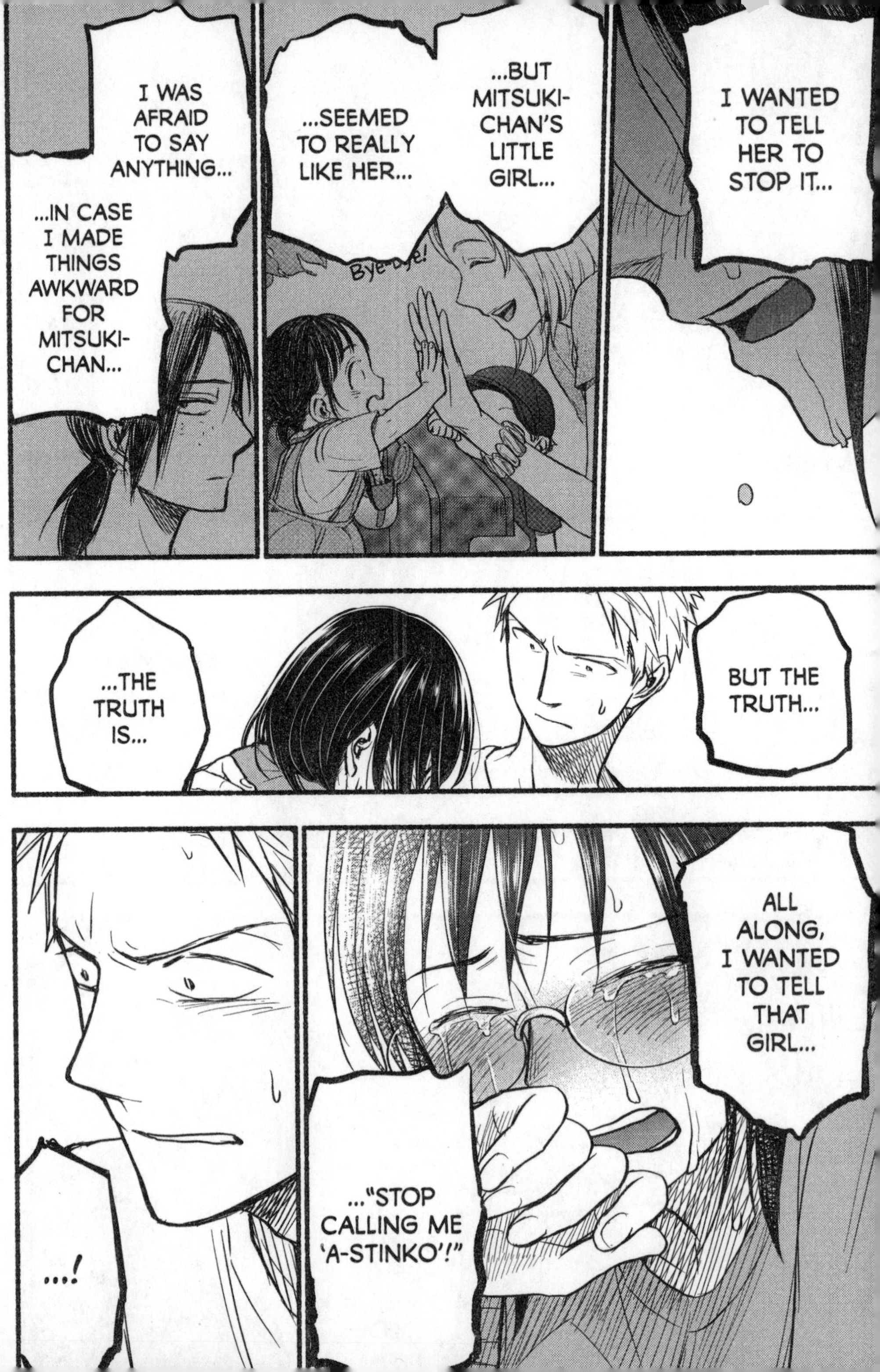
I WANTED TO TELL HER TO STOP IT...
...BUT MITSUKI-CHAN'S LITTLE GIRL...
...SEEMED TO REALLY LIKE HER...
Bye-bye!
I WAS AFRAID TO SAY ANYTHING...
...IN CASE I MADE THINGS AWKWARD FOR MITSUKI-CHAN...
BUT THE TRUTH...
...THE TRUTH IS...
ALL ALONG, I WANTED TO TELL THAT GIRL...
..."STOP CALLING ME 'A-STINKO'!"
...!

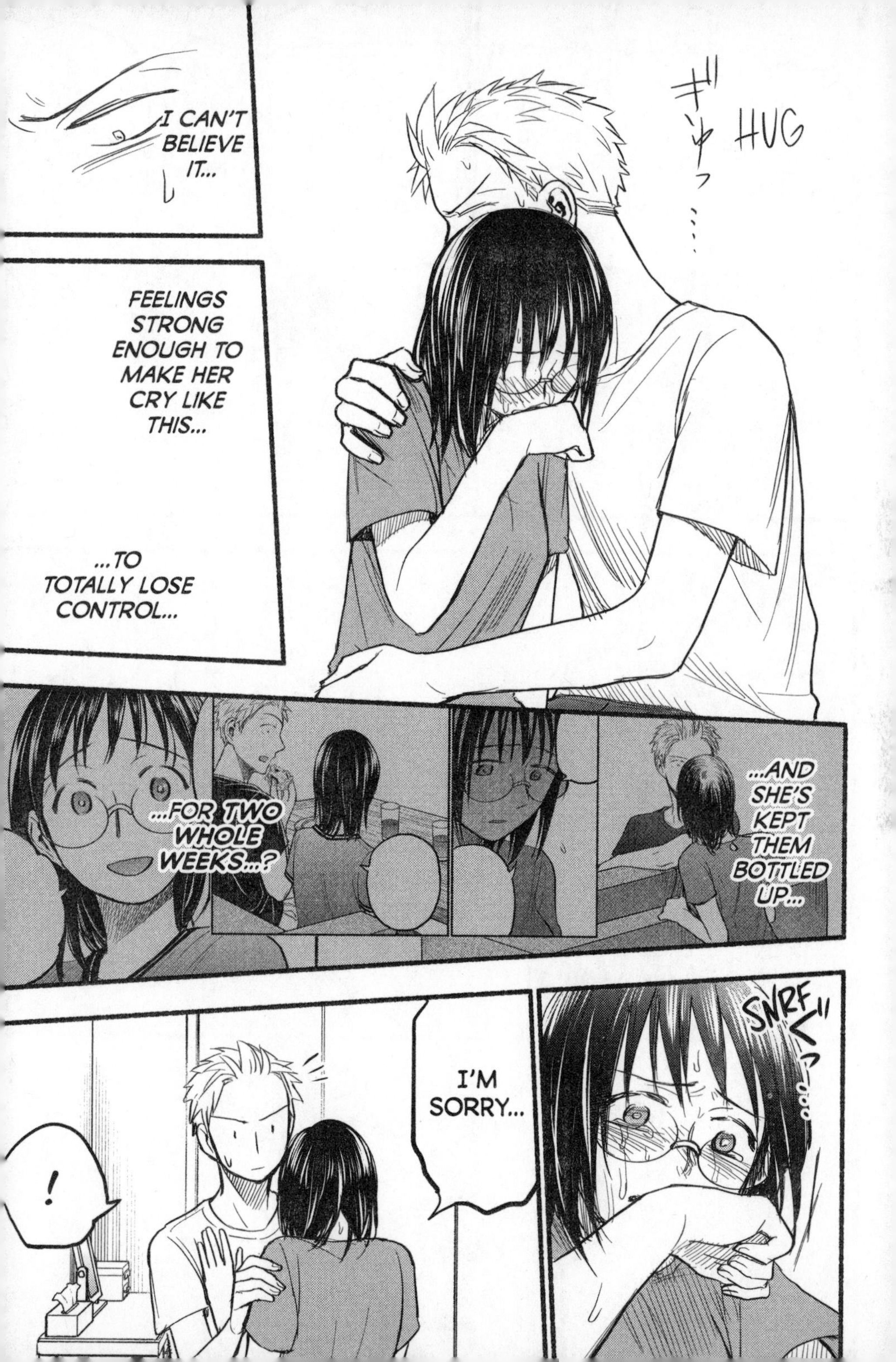
ギュッ…
HUG
I CAN'T BELIEVE IT...
FEELINGS STRONG ENOUGH TO MAKE HER CRY LIKE THIS...
...TO TOTALLY LOSE CONTROL...
...AND SHE'S KEPT THEM BOTTLED UP...
...FOR TWO WHOLE WEEKS...?
SNRF
I'M SORRY...
!

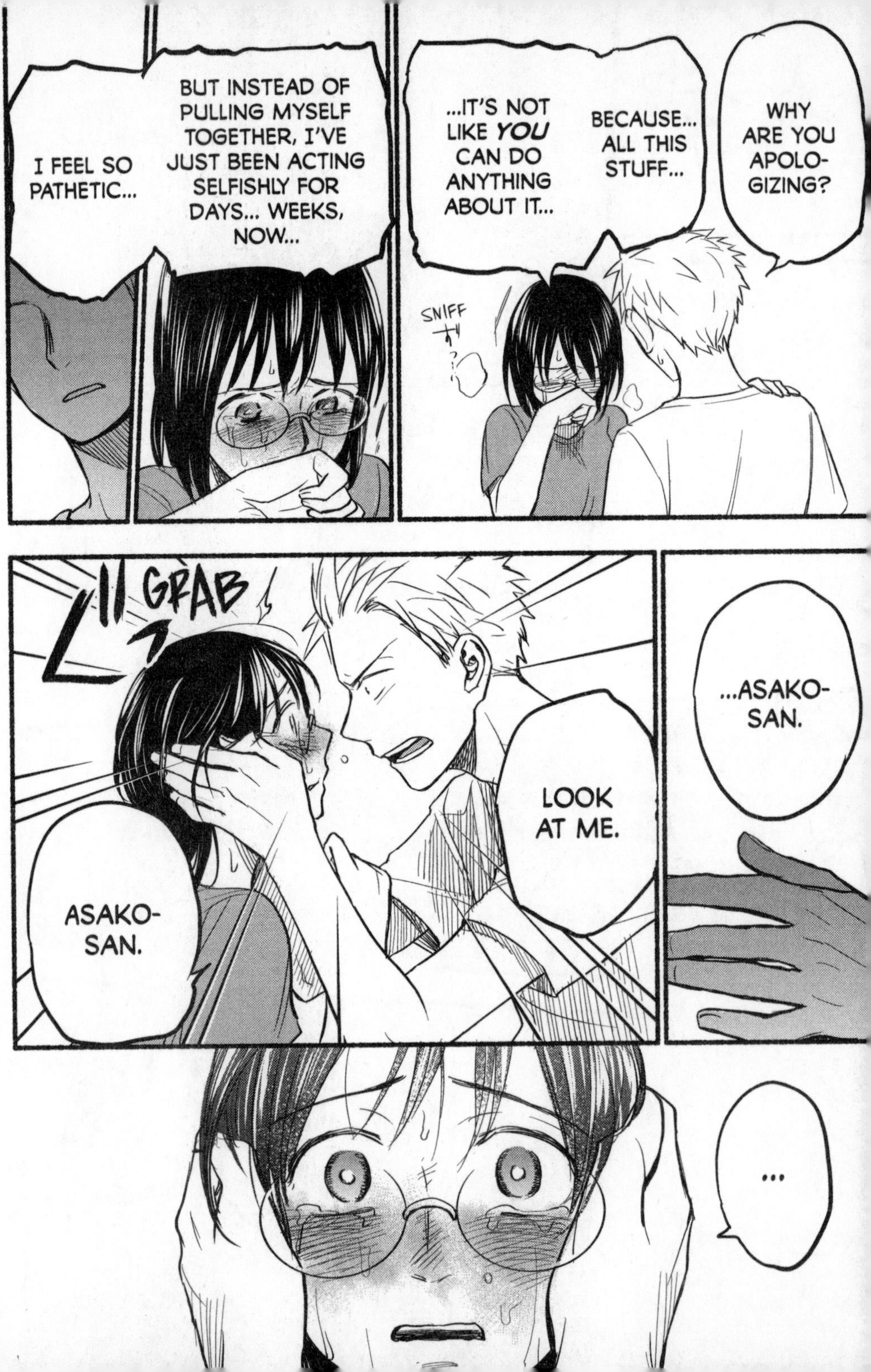
WHY ARE YOU APOLOGIZING?
BECAUSE... ALL THIS STUFF...
...IT'S NOT LIKE *YOU* CAN DO ANYTHING ABOUT IT...
SNIFF
BUT INSTEAD OF PULLING MYSELF TOGETHER, I'VE JUST BEEN ACTING SELFISHLY FOR DAYS... WEEKS, NOW...
I FEEL SO PATHETIC...
...ASAKO-SAN.
GRAB
LOOK AT ME.
ASAKO-SAN.
...

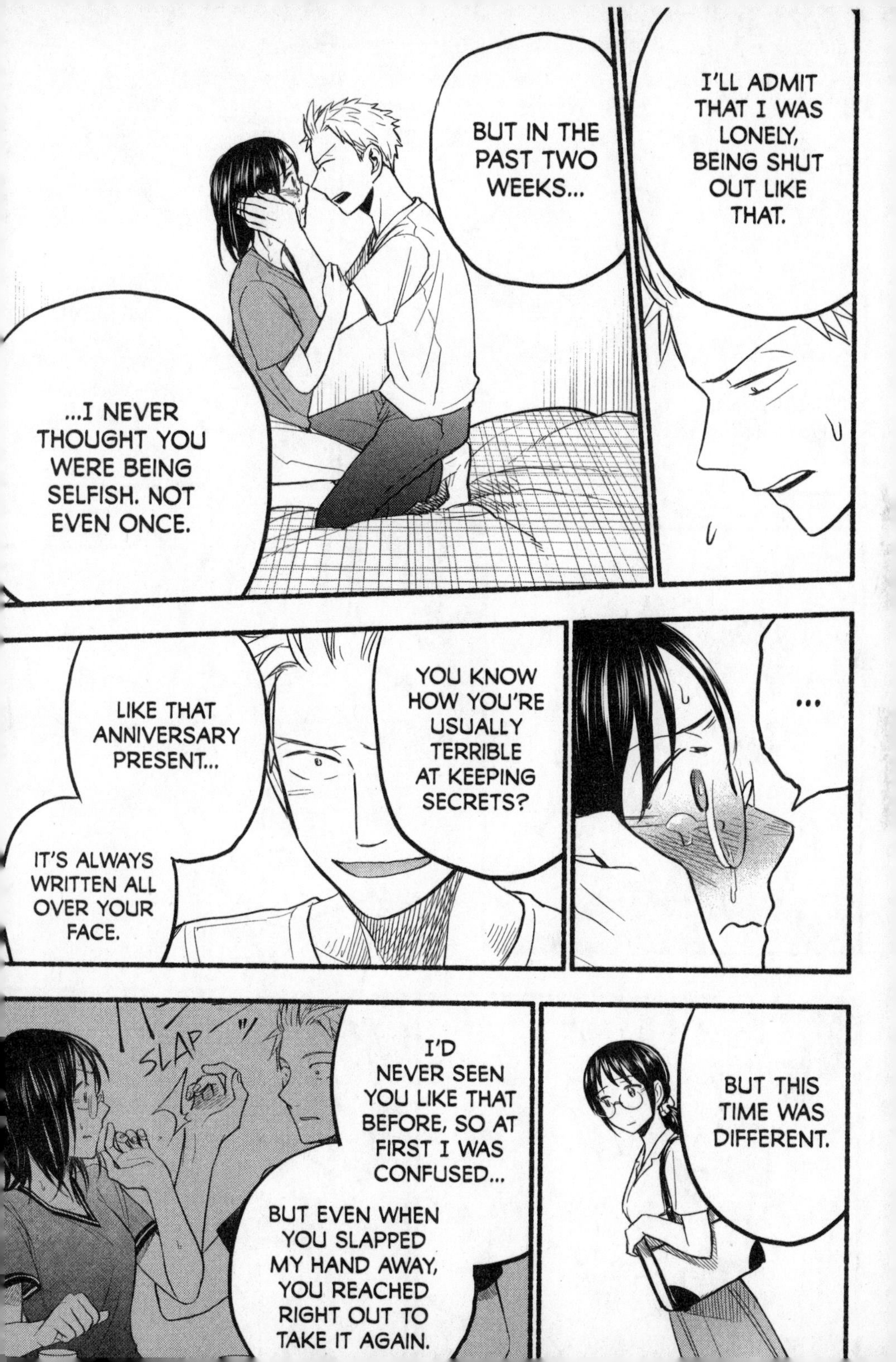
I'LL ADMIT THAT I WAS LONELY, BEING SHUT OUT LIKE THAT.
BUT IN THE PAST TWO WEEKS...
...I NEVER THOUGHT YOU WERE BEING SELFISH. NOT EVEN ONCE.
...
YOU KNOW HOW YOU'RE USUALLY TERRIBLE AT KEEPING SECRETS?
LIKE THAT ANNIVERSARY PRESENT...
IT'S ALWAYS WRITTEN ALL OVER YOUR FACE.
BUT THIS TIME WAS DIFFERENT.
I'D NEVER SEEN YOU LIKE THAT BEFORE, SO AT FIRST I WAS CONFUSED...
SLAP
BUT EVEN WHEN YOU SLAPPED MY HAND AWAY, YOU REACHED RIGHT OUT TO TAKE IT AGAIN.

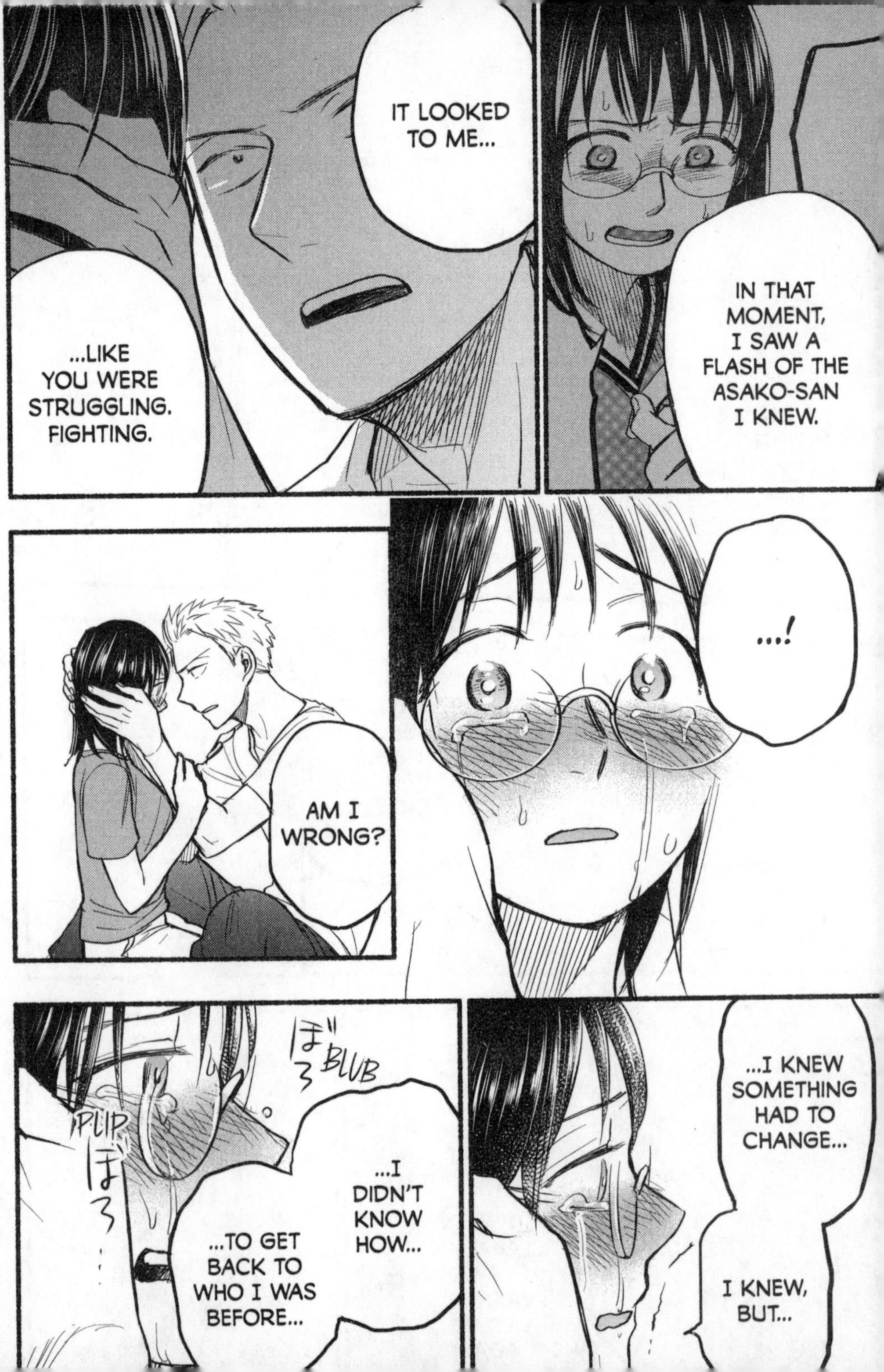
IN THAT MOMENT, I SAW A FLASH OF THE ASAKO-SAN I KNEW.
IT LOOKED TO ME...
...LIKE YOU WERE STRUGGLING. FIGHTING.
...!
AM I WRONG?
...I KNEW SOMETHING HAD TO CHANGE...
I KNEW, BUT...
ぽろ BLUB
PLIP ぽろ
...I DIDN'T KNOW HOW...
...TO GET BACK TO WHO I WAS BEFORE...

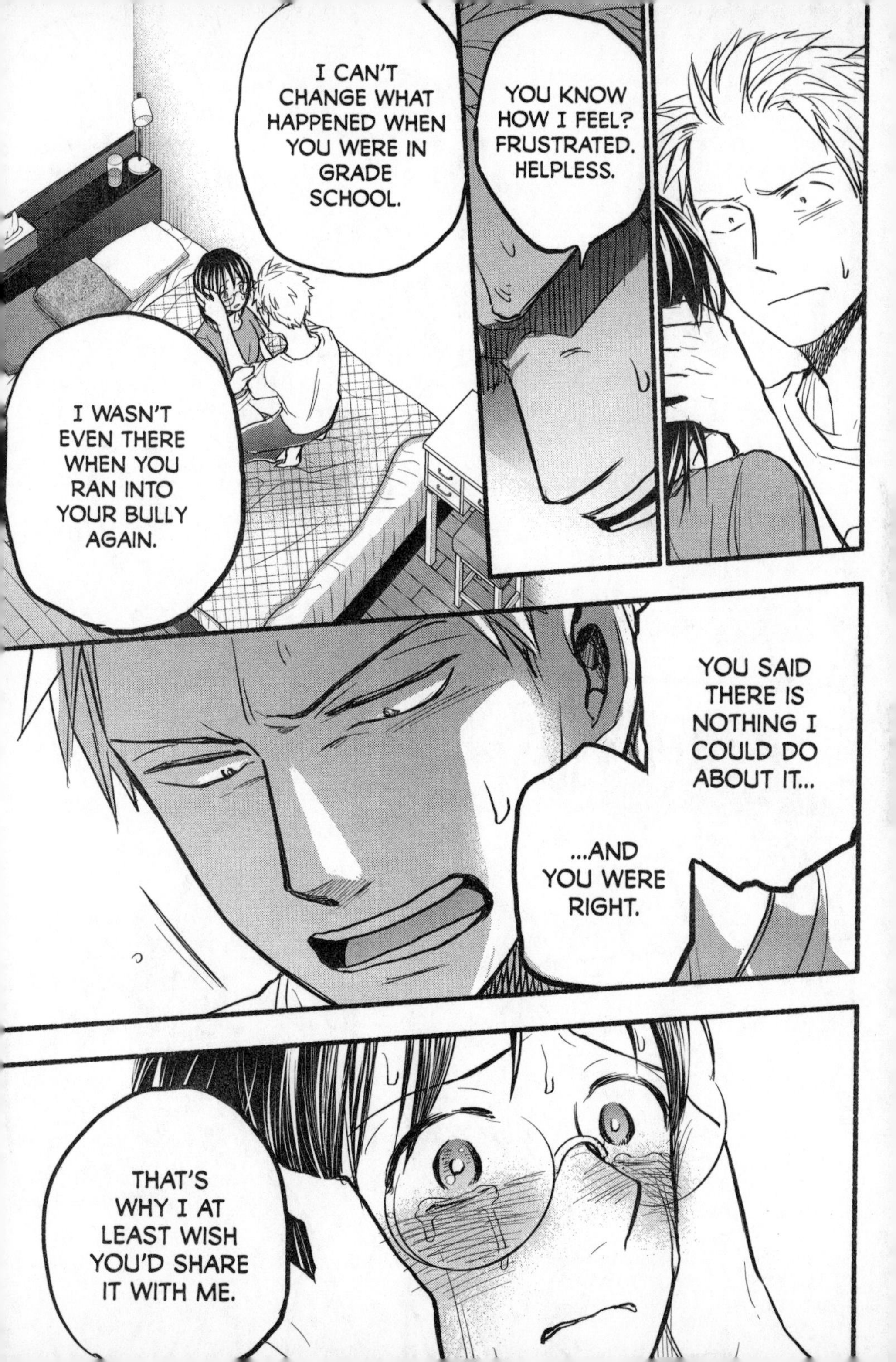
YOU KNOW HOW I FEEL? FRUSTRATED. HELPLESS.
I CAN'T CHANGE WHAT HAPPENED WHEN YOU WERE IN GRADE SCHOOL.
I WASN'T EVEN THERE WHEN YOU RAN INTO YOUR BULLY AGAIN.
YOU SAID THERE IS NOTHING I COULD DO ABOUT IT...
...AND YOU WERE RIGHT.
THAT'S WHY I AT LEAST WISH YOU'D SHARE IT WITH ME.

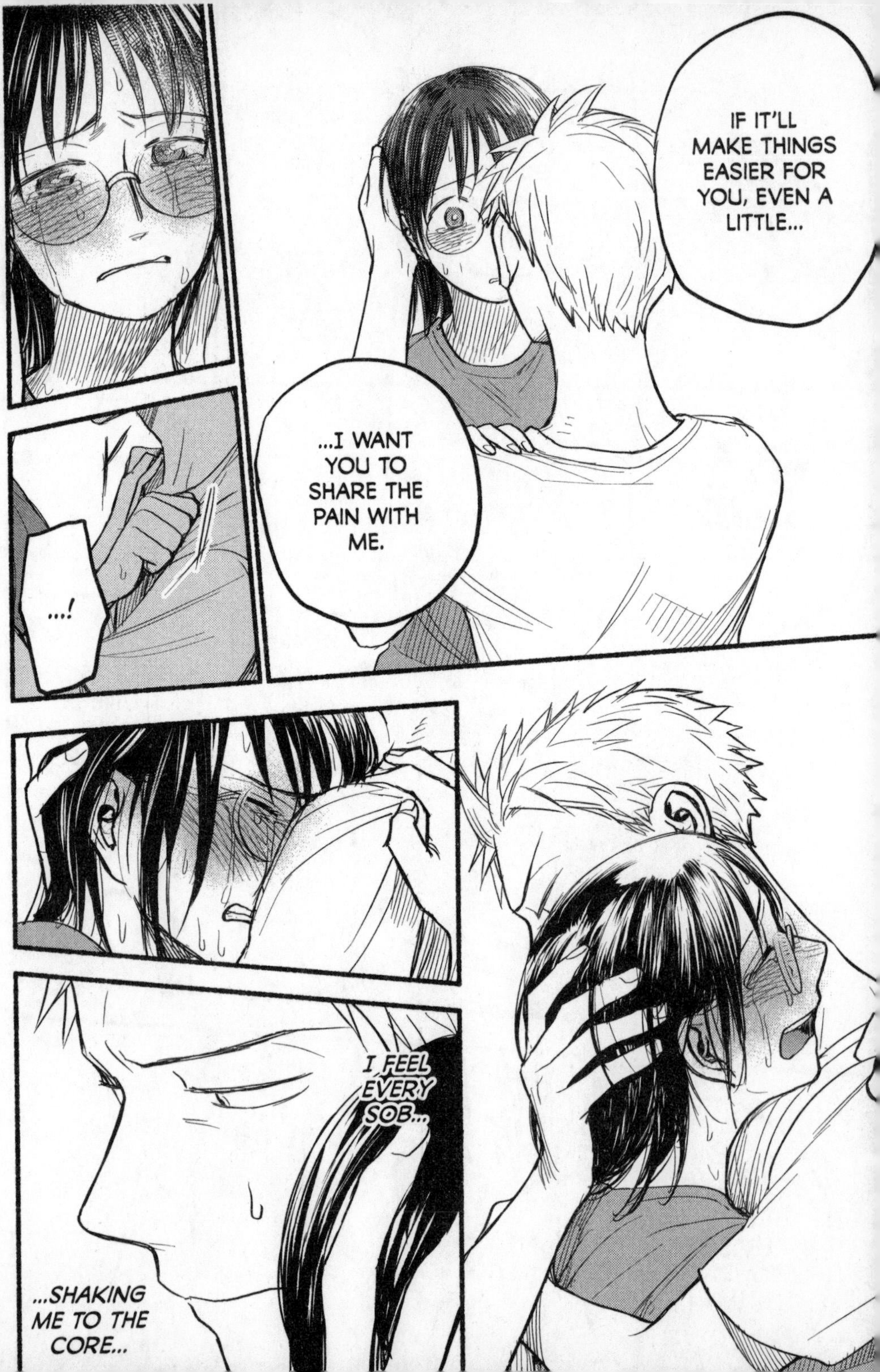
IF IT'LL MAKE THINGS EASIER FOR YOU, EVEN A LITTLE...
...I WANT YOU TO SHARE THE PAIN WITH ME.
...!
I FEEL EVERY SOB...
...SHAKING ME TO THE CORE...

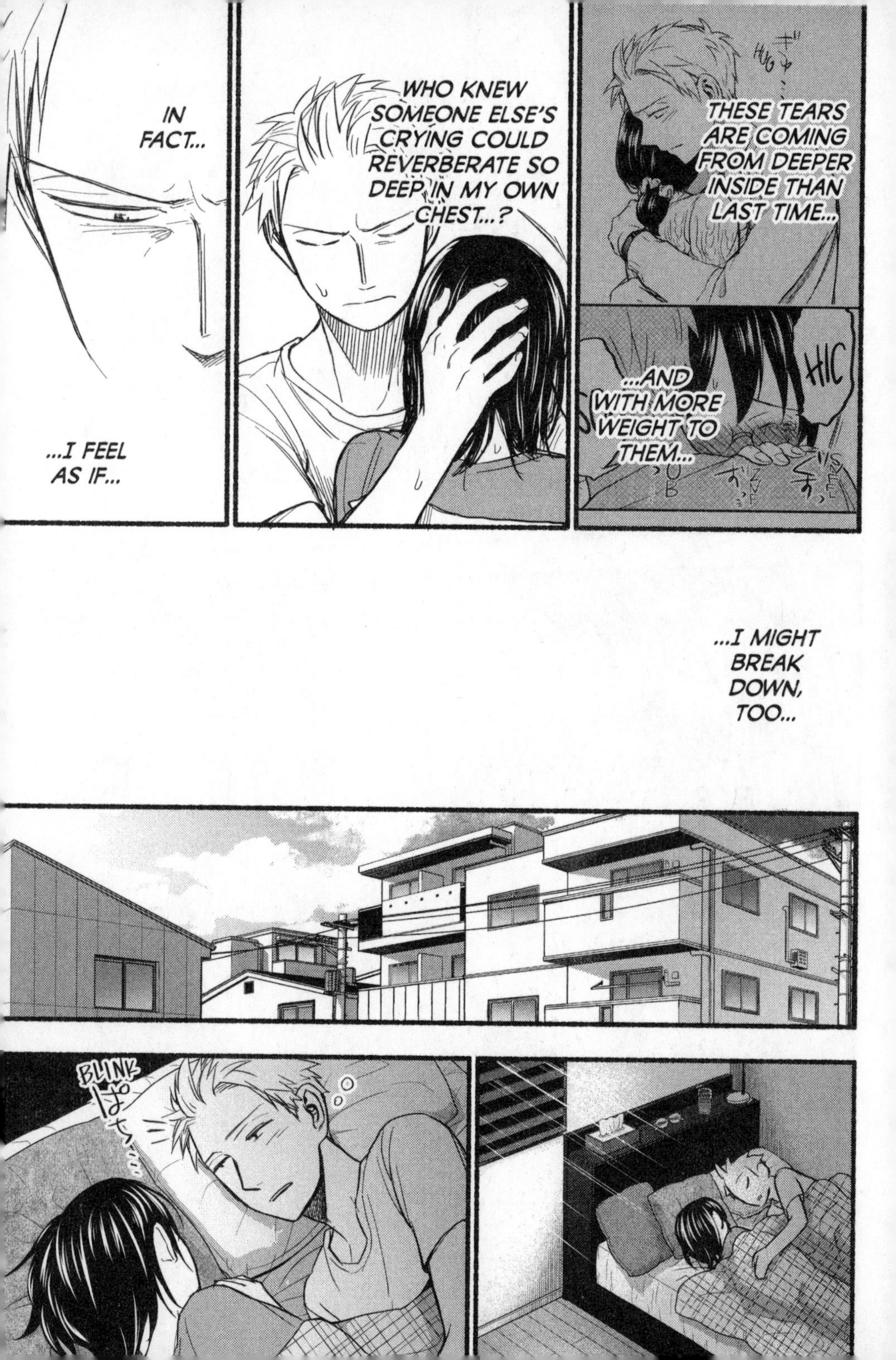
HUG
THESE TEARS ARE COMING FROM DEEPER INSIDE THAN LAST TIME...
HIC
...AND WITH MORE WEIGHT TO THEM...
SOB
SNIF
WHO KNEW SOMEONE ELSE'S CRYING COULD REVERBERATE SO DEEP IN MY OWN CHEST...?
IN FACT...
...I FEEL AS IF...
...I MIGHT BREAK DOWN, TOO...
BLINK

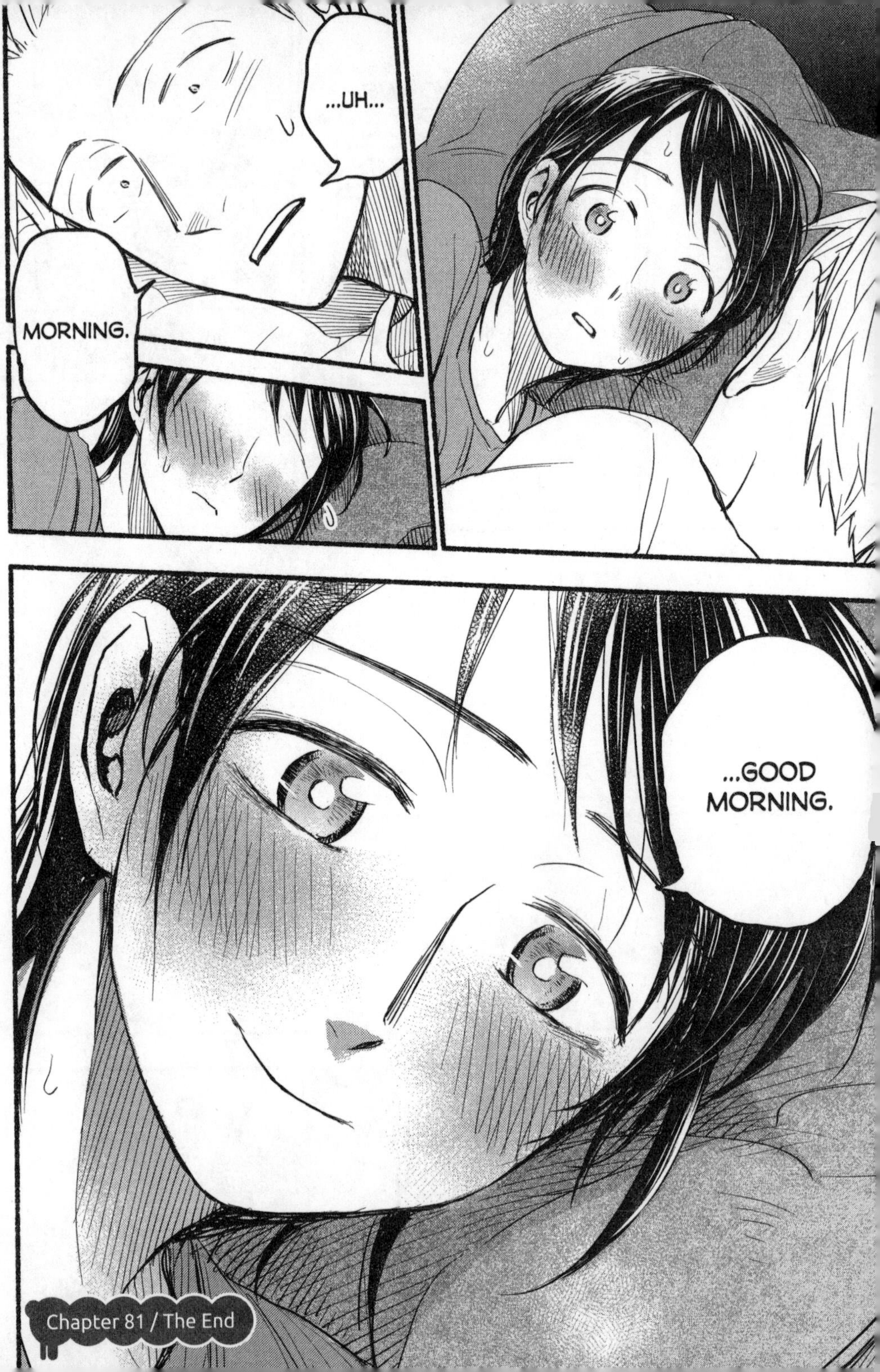
...UH...
MORNING.
...GOOD MORNING.
Chapter 81 / The End

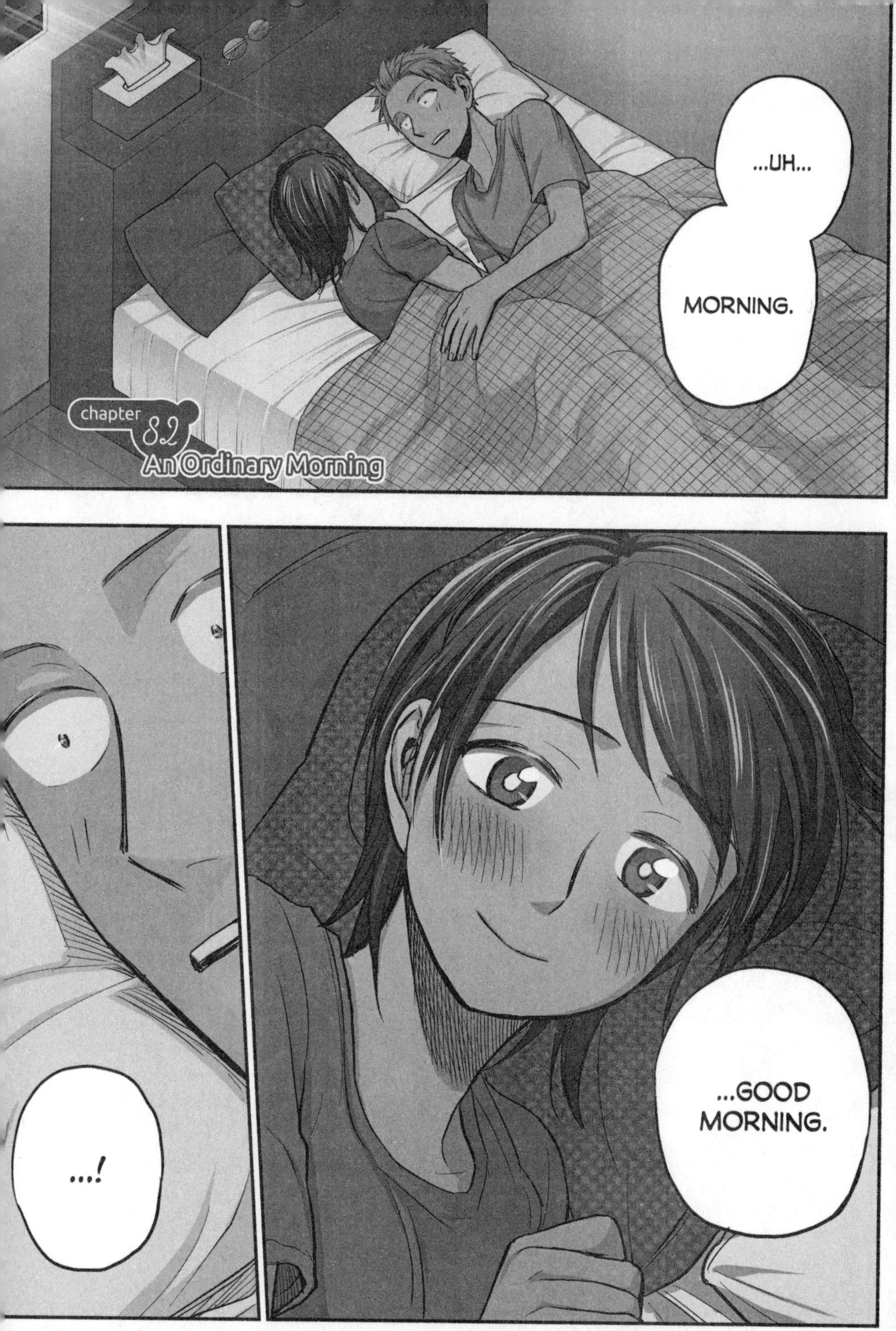
...UH...
MORNING.
chapter 82
An Ordinary Morning
...GOOD MORNING.
...!

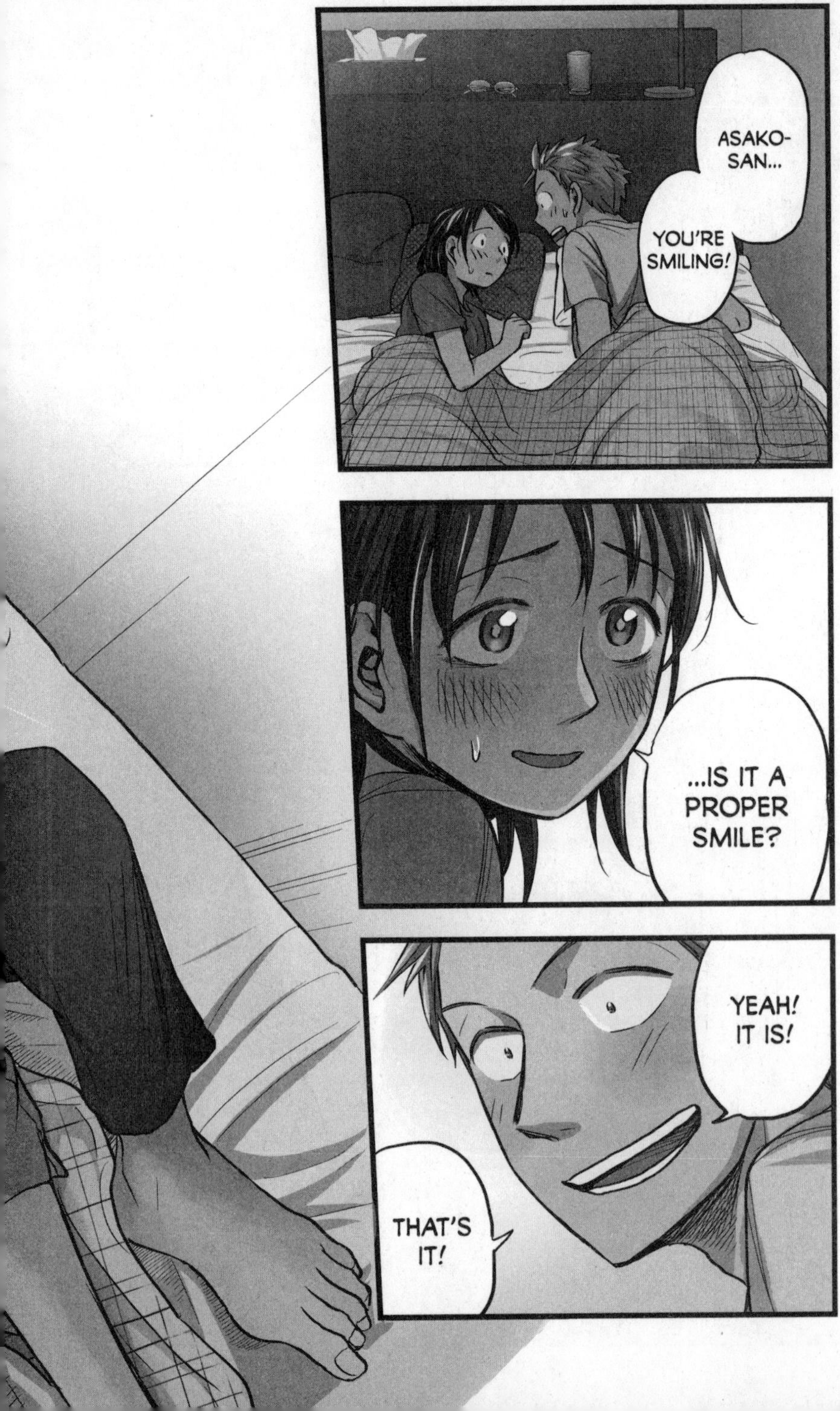
ASAKO-SAN...
YOU'RE SMILING!
...IS IT A PROPER SMILE?
YEAH! IT IS!
THAT'S IT!

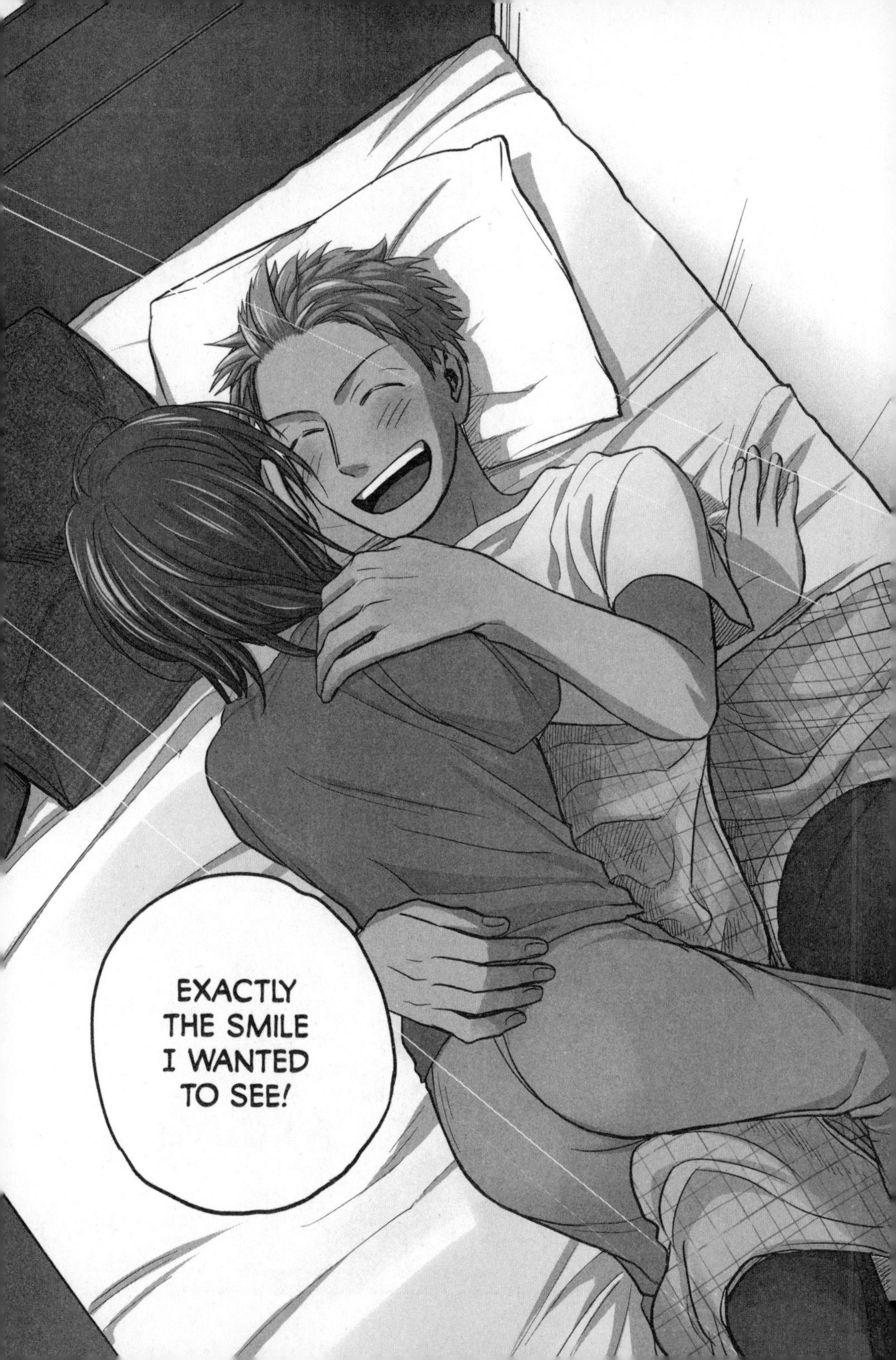
EXACTLY THE SMILE I WANTED TO SEE!

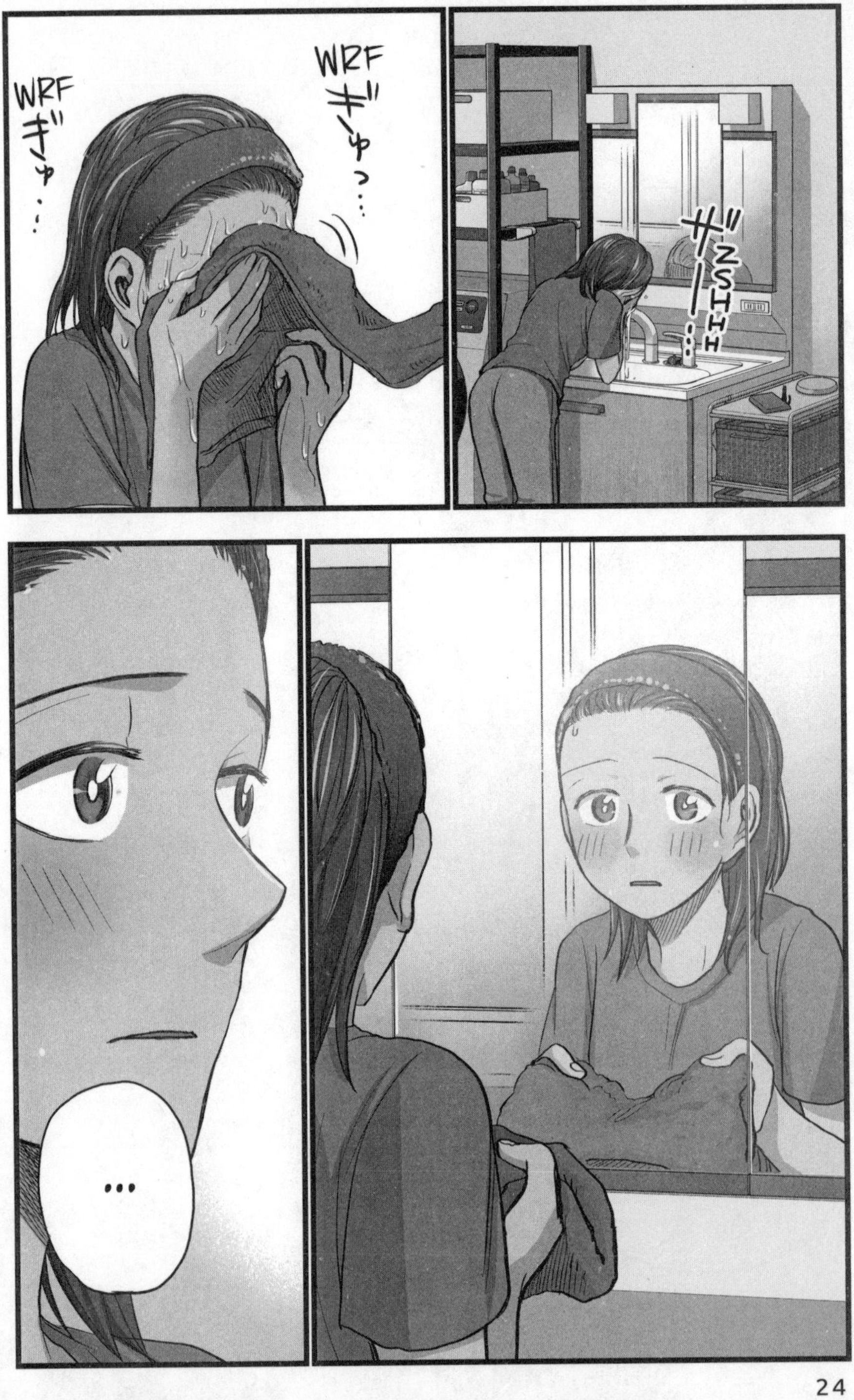
ZSHHH
ザー…
WRF
ぎゅっ…
WRF
ぎゅ…
...

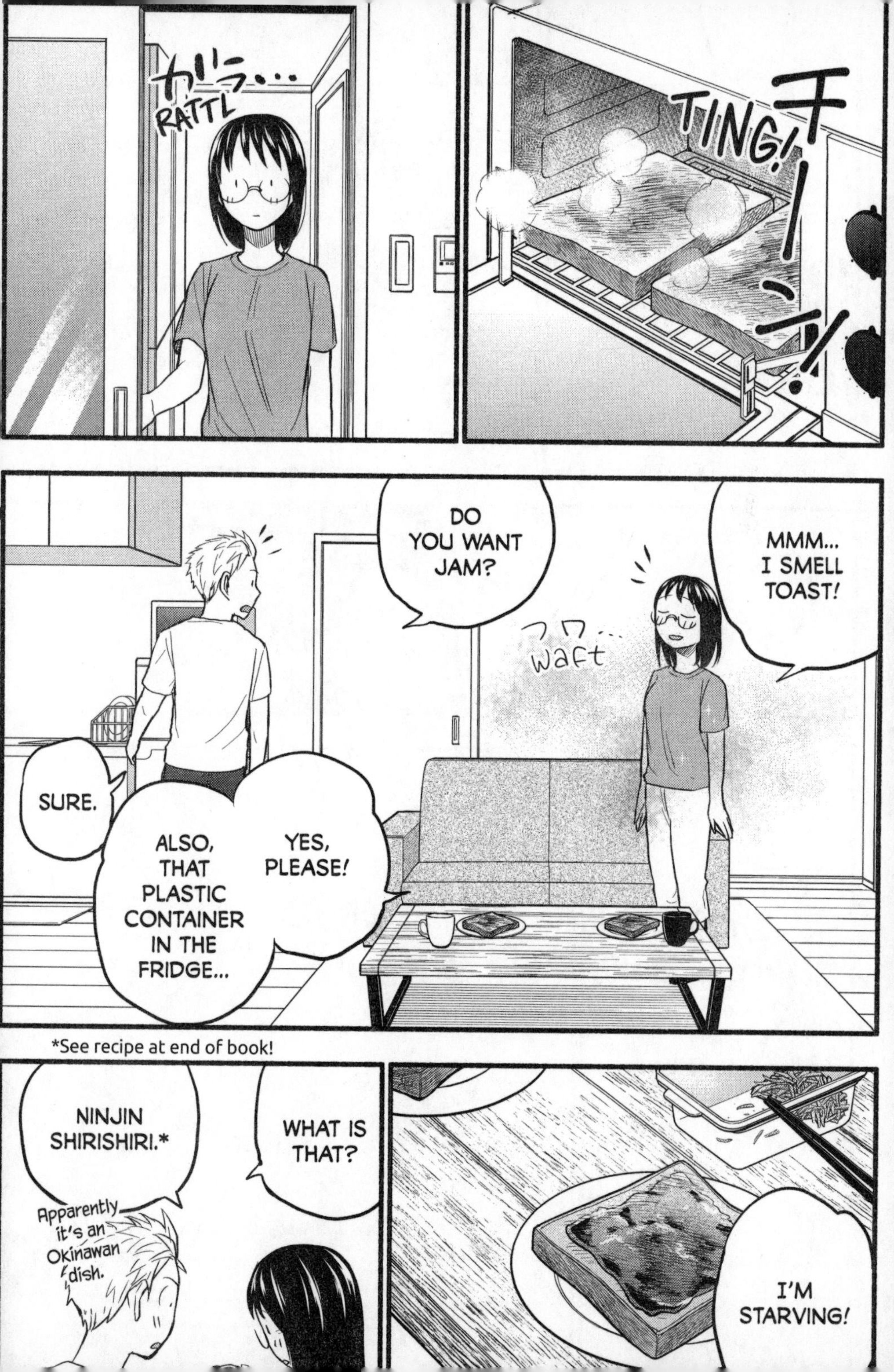

TING! チーン!!
カラ… RATTL
MMM... I SMELL TOAST!
フワ… waft
DO YOU WANT JAM?
YES, PLEASE!
ALSO, THAT PLASTIC CONTAINER IN THE FRIDGE...
SURE.
I'M STARVING!
WHAT IS THAT?
NINJIN SHIRISHIRI.*
Apparently it's an Okinawan dish.

*See recipe at end of book!

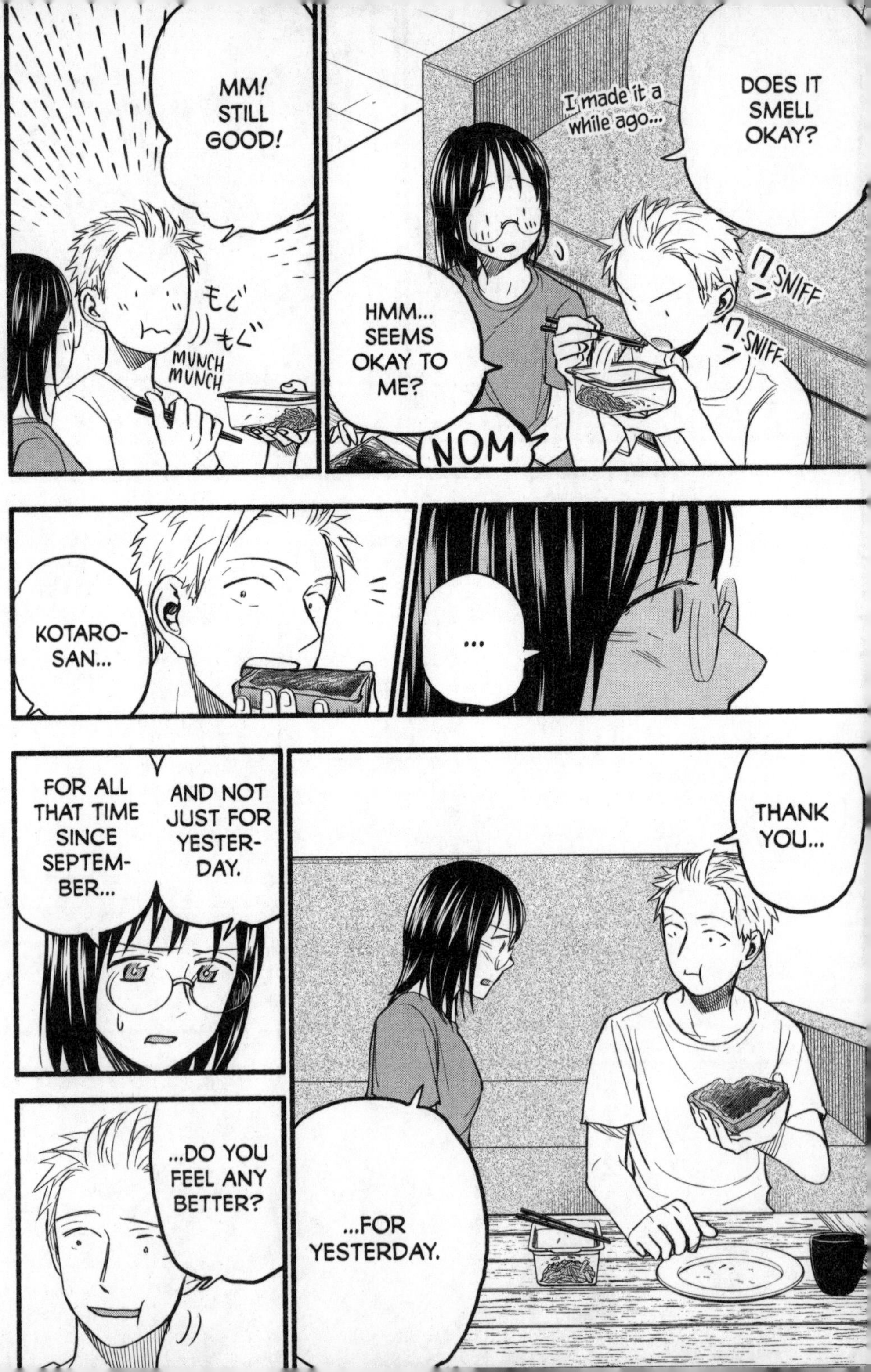
DOES IT SMELL OKAY?
I made it a while ago...
SNIFF
SNIFF
HMM... SEEMS OKAY TO ME?
NOM
MM! STILL GOOD!
もぐもぐ
MUNCH MUNCH
...
KOTARO-SAN...
THANK YOU...
...FOR YESTERDAY.
AND NOT JUST FOR YESTERDAY.
FOR ALL THAT TIME SINCE SEPTEMBER...
...DO YOU FEEL ANY BETTER?

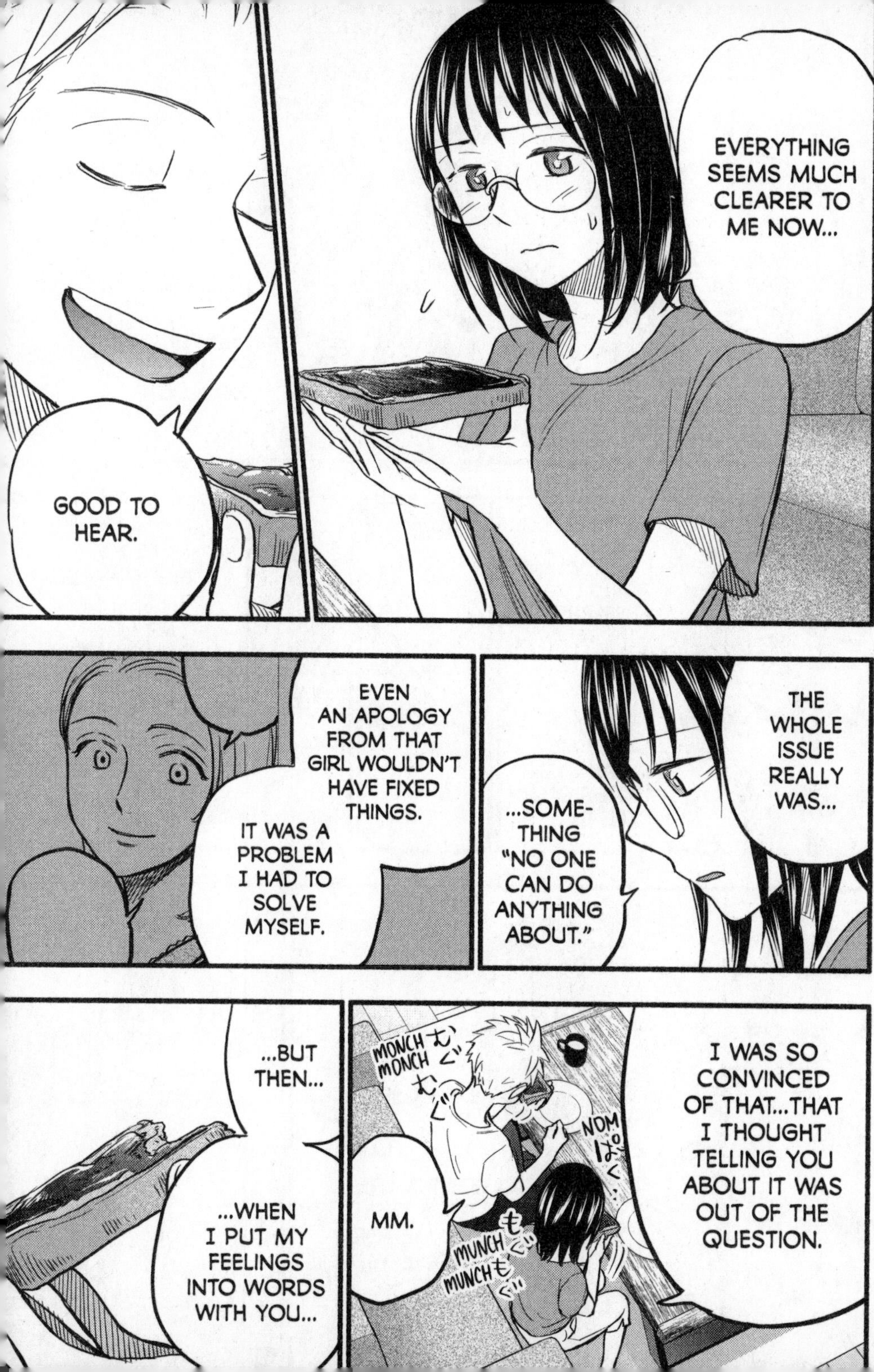
EVERYTHING SEEMS MUCH CLEARER TO ME NOW...
GOOD TO HEAR.
THE WHOLE ISSUE REALLY WAS...
...SOME-THING "NO ONE CAN DO ANYTHING ABOUT."
EVEN AN APOLOGY FROM THAT GIRL WOULDN'T HAVE FIXED THINGS.
IT WAS A PROBLEM I HAD TO SOLVE MYSELF.
I WAS SO CONVINCED OF THAT...THAT I THOUGHT TELLING YOU ABOUT IT WAS OUT OF THE QUESTION.
MONCH MONCH むぐむぐ
NOM ぱく…
MM.
MUNCH MUNCH もぐもぐ
...BUT THEN...
...WHEN I PUT MY FEELINGS INTO WORDS WITH YOU...

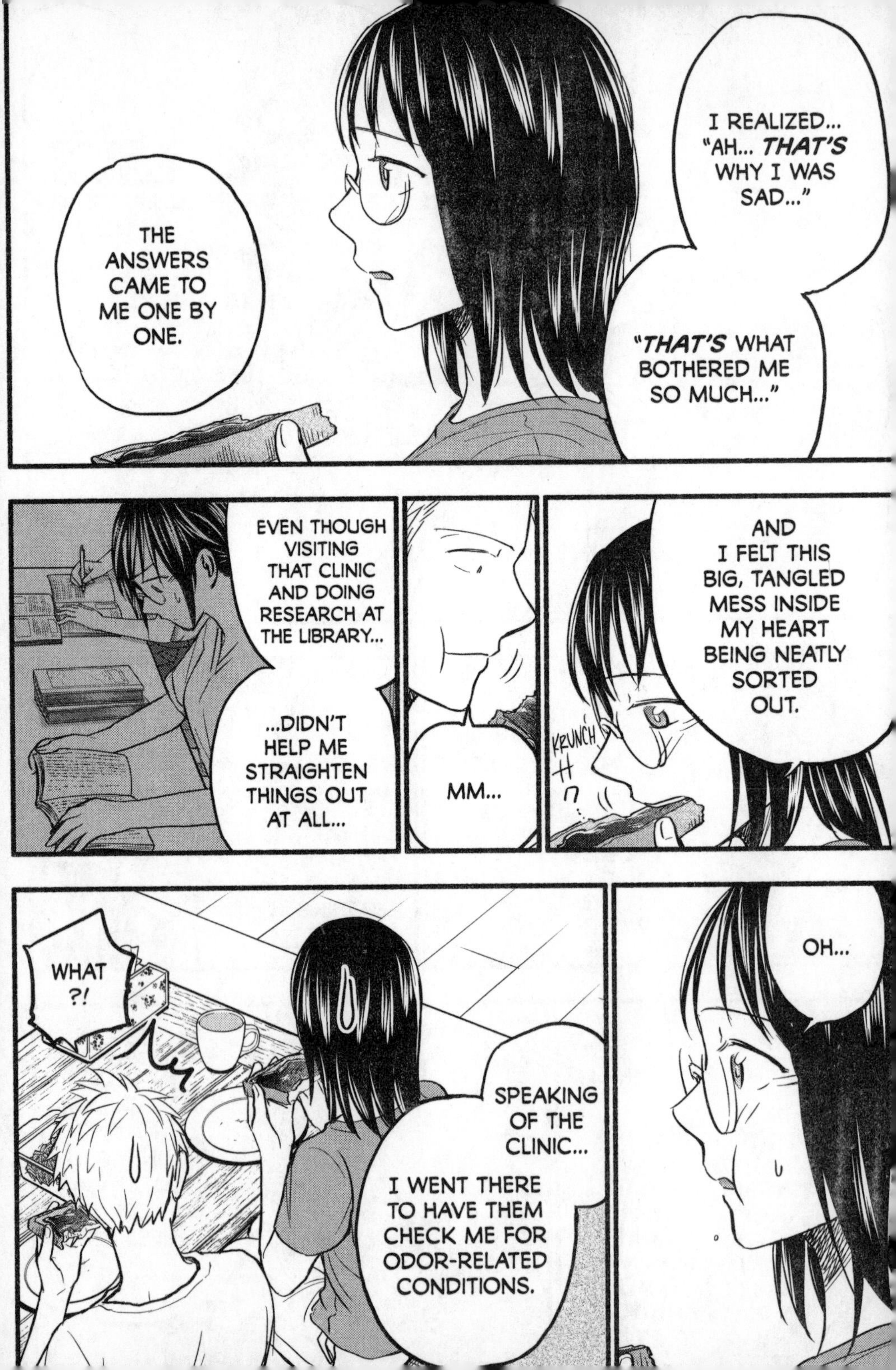
I REALIZED... "AH... *THAT'S* WHY I WAS SAD..."
"*THAT'S* WHAT BOTHERED ME SO MUCH..."
THE ANSWERS CAME TO ME ONE BY ONE.
AND I FELT THIS BIG, TANGLED MESS INSIDE MY HEART BEING NEATLY SORTED OUT.
KRUNCH
MM...
EVEN THOUGH VISITING THAT CLINIC AND DOING RESEARCH AT THE LIBRARY...
...DIDN'T HELP ME STRAIGHTEN THINGS OUT AT ALL...
OH...
SPEAKING OF THE CLINIC...
I WENT THERE TO HAVE THEM CHECK ME FOR ODOR-RELATED CONDITIONS.
WHAT ?!

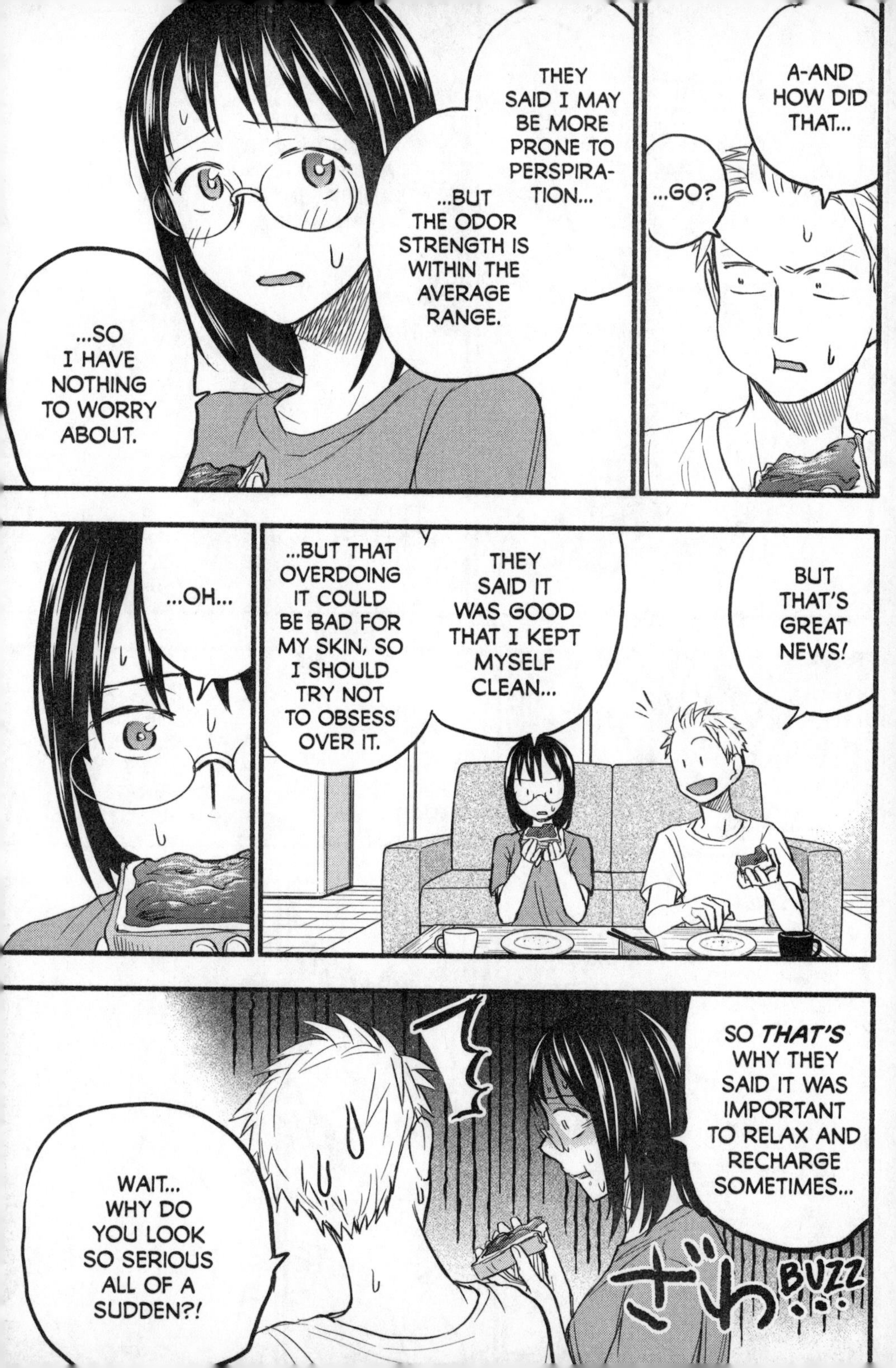
A-AND HOW DID THAT...
...GO?
THEY SAID I MAY BE MORE PRONE TO PERSPIRATION...
...BUT THE ODOR STRENGTH IS WITHIN THE AVERAGE RANGE.
...SO I HAVE NOTHING TO WORRY ABOUT.
BUT THAT'S GREAT NEWS!
THEY SAID IT WAS GOOD THAT I KEPT MYSELF CLEAN...
...BUT THAT OVERDOING IT COULD BE BAD FOR MY SKIN, SO I SHOULD TRY NOT TO OBSESS OVER IT.
...OH...
SO *THAT'S* WHY THEY SAID IT WAS IMPORTANT TO RELAX AND RECHARGE SOMETIMES...
ざわ BUZZ
WAIT... WHY DO YOU LOOK SO SERIOUS ALL OF A SUDDEN?!

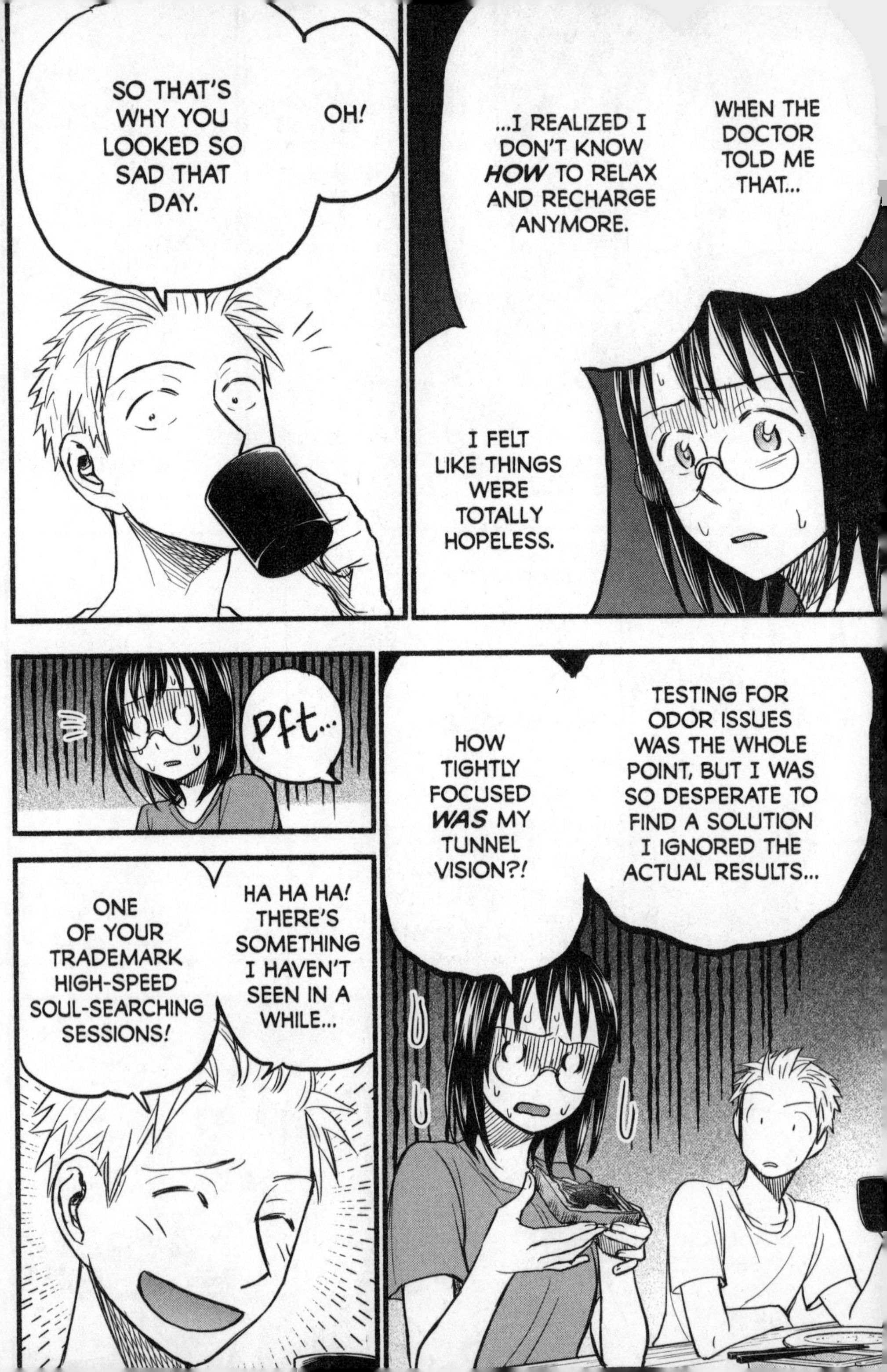
WHEN THE DOCTOR TOLD ME THAT...
...I REALIZED I DON'T KNOW *HOW* TO RELAX AND RECHARGE ANYMORE.
I FELT LIKE THINGS WERE TOTALLY HOPELESS.
OH!
SO THAT'S WHY YOU LOOKED SO SAD THAT DAY.
TESTING FOR ODOR ISSUES WAS THE WHOLE POINT, BUT I WAS SO DESPERATE TO FIND A SOLUTION I IGNORED THE ACTUAL RESULTS...
HOW TIGHTLY FOCUSED *WAS* MY TUNNEL VISION?!
Pft...
HA HA HA! THERE'S SOMETHING I HAVEN'T SEEN IN A WHILE...
ONE OF YOUR TRADEMARK HIGH-SPEED SOUL-SEARCHING SESSIONS!

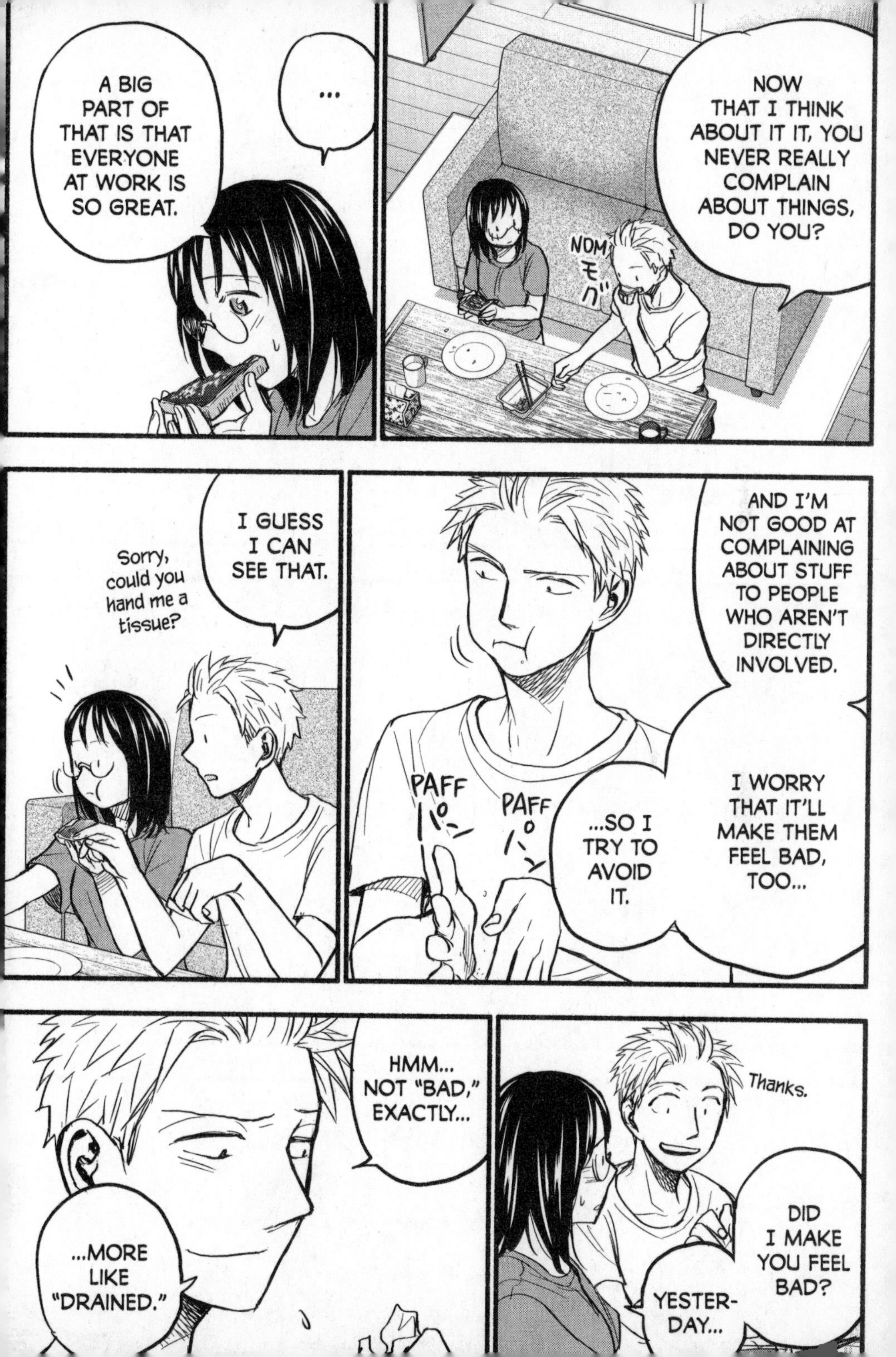
NOW THAT I THINK ABOUT IT IT, YOU NEVER REALLY COMPLAIN ABOUT THINGS, DO YOU?
NOM
モグ
...
A BIG PART OF THAT IS THAT EVERYONE AT WORK IS SO GREAT.
AND I'M NOT GOOD AT COMPLAINING ABOUT STUFF TO PEOPLE WHO AREN'T DIRECTLY INVOLVED.
I WORRY THAT IT'LL MAKE THEM FEEL BAD, TOO...
...SO I TRY TO AVOID IT.
PAFF
PAFF
I GUESS I CAN SEE THAT.
Sorry, could you hand me a tissue?
Thanks.
DID I MAKE YOU FEEL BAD?
YESTER-DAY...
HMM... NOT "BAD," EXACTLY...
...MORE LIKE "DRAINED."

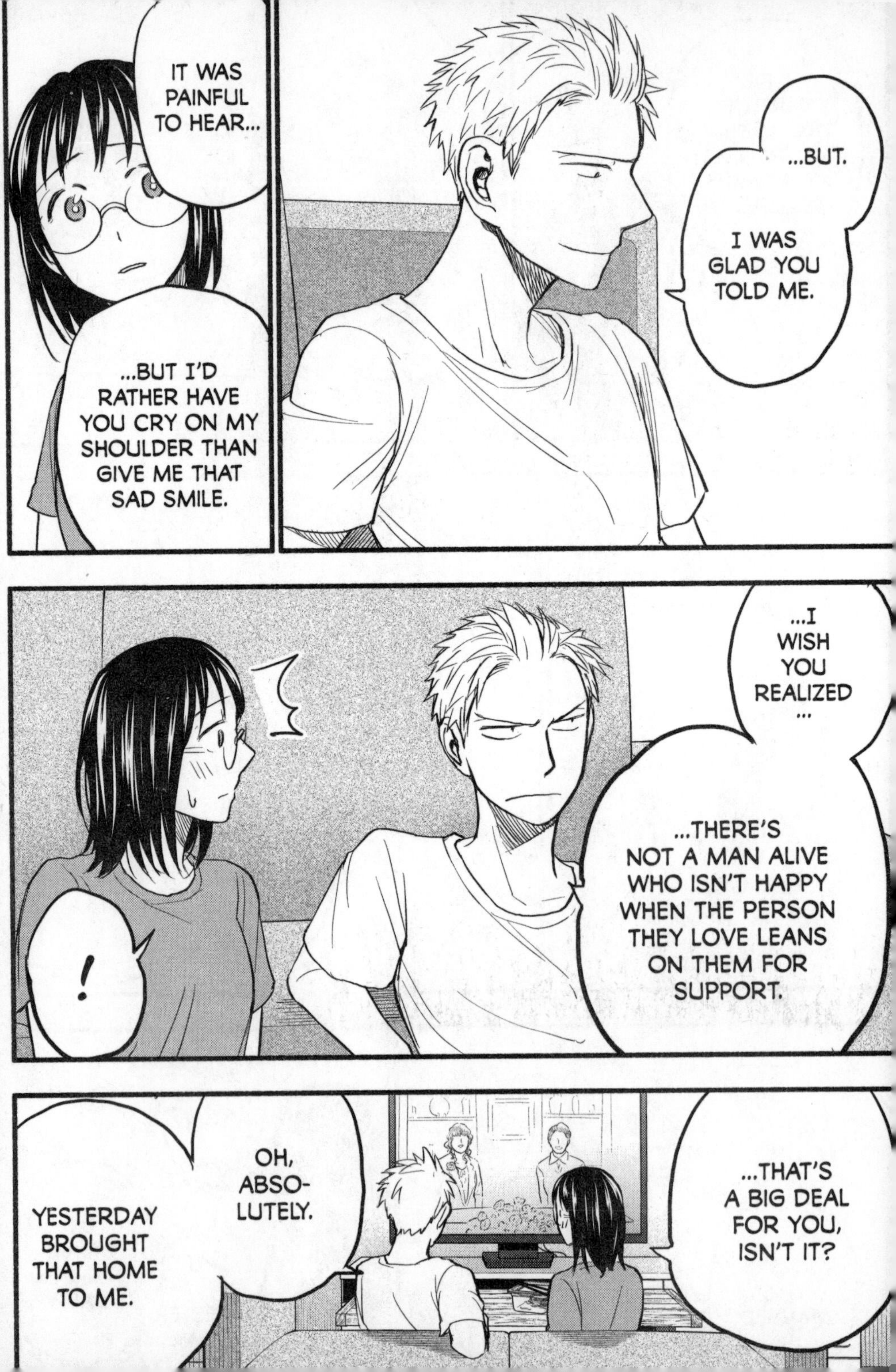
...BUT.
I WAS GLAD YOU TOLD ME.
IT WAS PAINFUL TO HEAR...
...BUT I'D RATHER HAVE YOU CRY ON MY SHOULDER THAN GIVE ME THAT SAD SMILE.
...I WISH YOU REALIZED ...
...THERE'S NOT A MAN ALIVE WHO ISN'T HAPPY WHEN THE PERSON THEY LOVE LEANS ON THEM FOR SUPPORT.
!
...THAT'S A BIG DEAL FOR YOU, ISN'T IT?
OH, ABSO-LUTELY.
YESTERDAY BROUGHT THAT HOME TO ME.

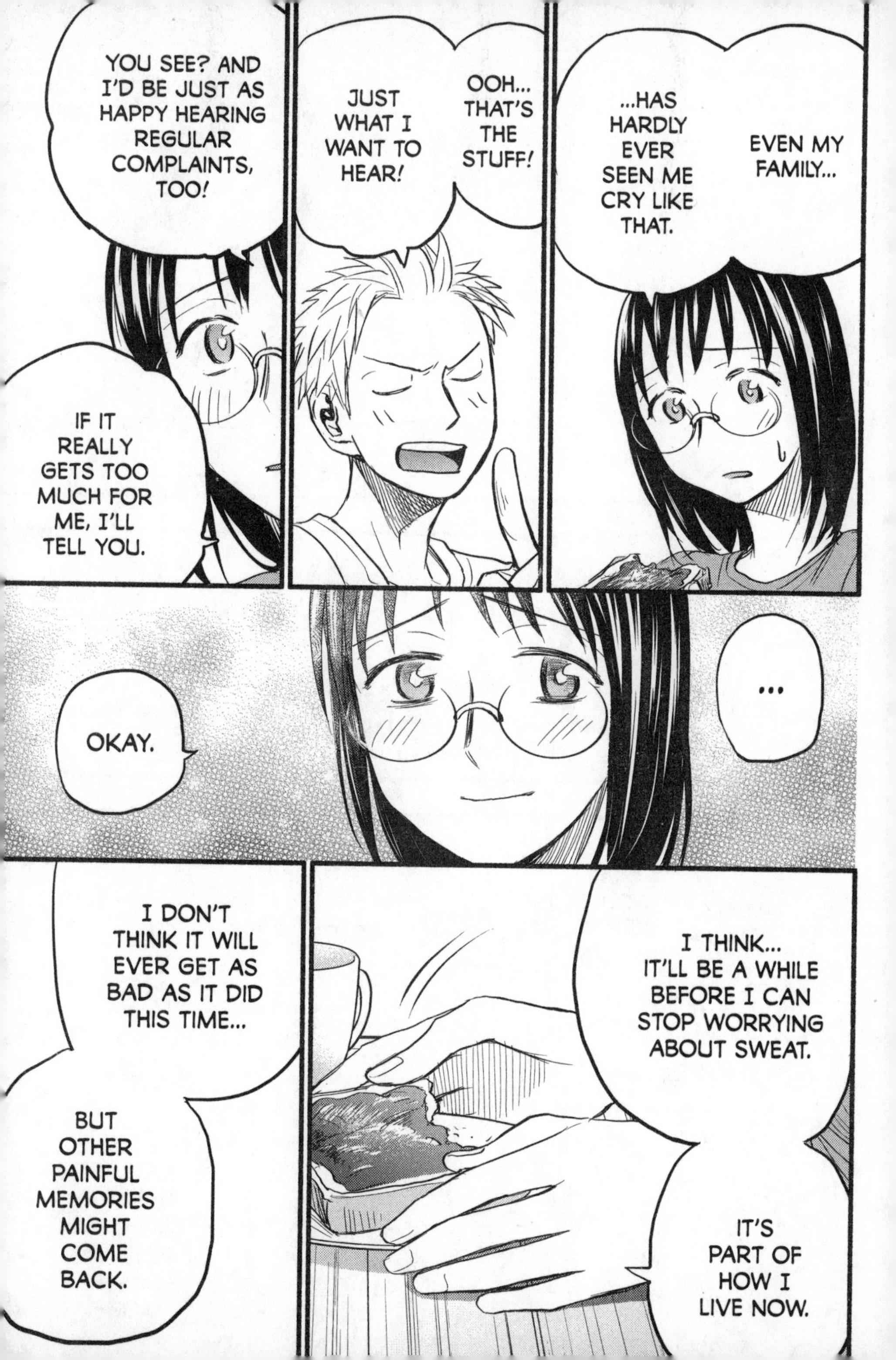
EVEN MY FAMILY...
...HAS HARDLY EVER SEEN ME CRY LIKE THAT.
OOH... THAT'S THE STUFF!
JUST WHAT I WANT TO HEAR!
YOU SEE? AND I'D BE JUST AS HAPPY HEARING REGULAR COMPLAINTS, TOO!
IF IT REALLY GETS TOO MUCH FOR ME, I'LL TELL YOU.
...
OKAY.
I THINK... IT'LL BE A WHILE BEFORE I CAN STOP WORRYING ABOUT SWEAT.
IT'S PART OF HOW I LIVE NOW.
I DON'T THINK IT WILL EVER GET AS BAD AS IT DID THIS TIME...
BUT OTHER PAINFUL MEMORIES MIGHT COME BACK.

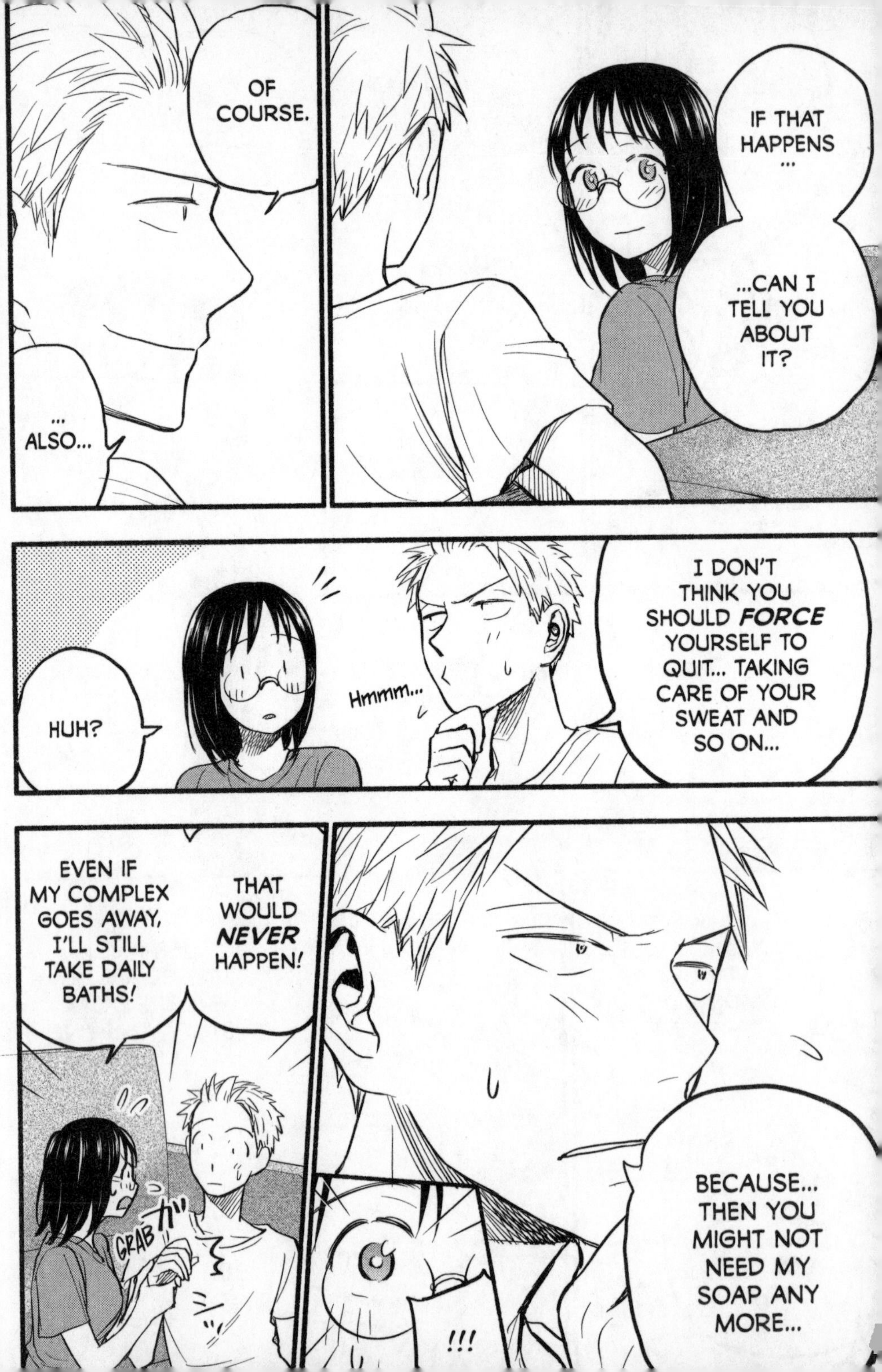
IF THAT HAPPENS ...
...CAN I TELL YOU ABOUT IT?
OF COURSE.
... ALSO...
I DON'T THINK YOU SHOULD *FORCE* YOURSELF TO QUIT... TAKING CARE OF YOUR SWEAT AND SO ON...
Hmmm...
HUH?
BECAUSE... THEN YOU MIGHT NOT NEED MY SOAP ANY MORE...
!!!
THAT WOULD *NEVER* HAPPEN!
EVEN IF MY COMPLEX GOES AWAY, I'LL STILL TAKE DAILY BATHS!
GRAB ガ

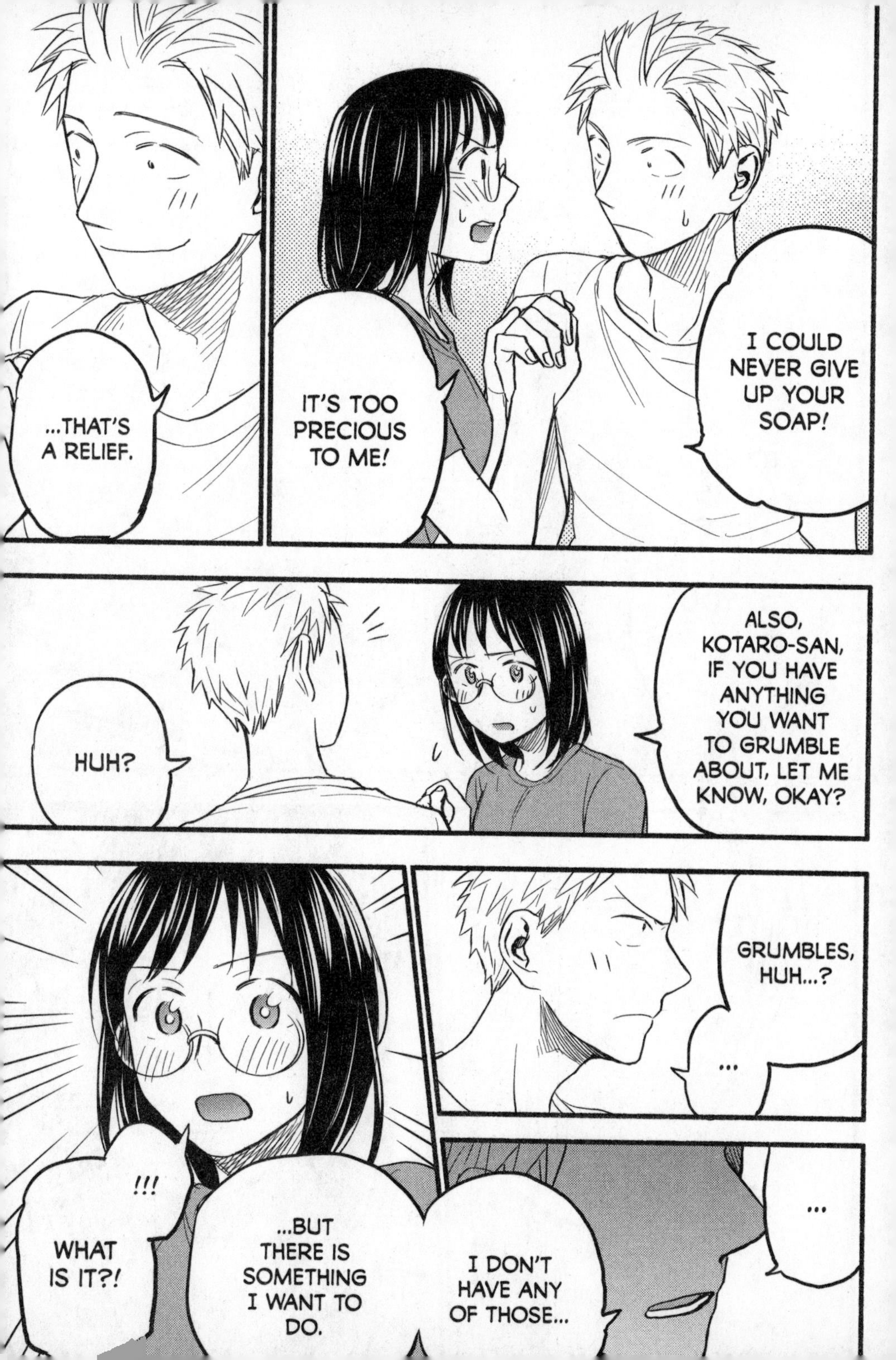
I COULD NEVER GIVE UP YOUR SOAP!
IT'S TOO PRECIOUS TO ME!
...THAT'S A RELIEF.
ALSO, KOTARO-SAN, IF YOU HAVE ANYTHING YOU WANT TO GRUMBLE ABOUT, LET ME KNOW, OKAY?
HUH?
GRUMBLES, HUH...?
...
...
I DON'T HAVE ANY OF THOSE...
...BUT THERE IS SOMETHING I WANT TO DO.
!!!
WHAT IS IT?!

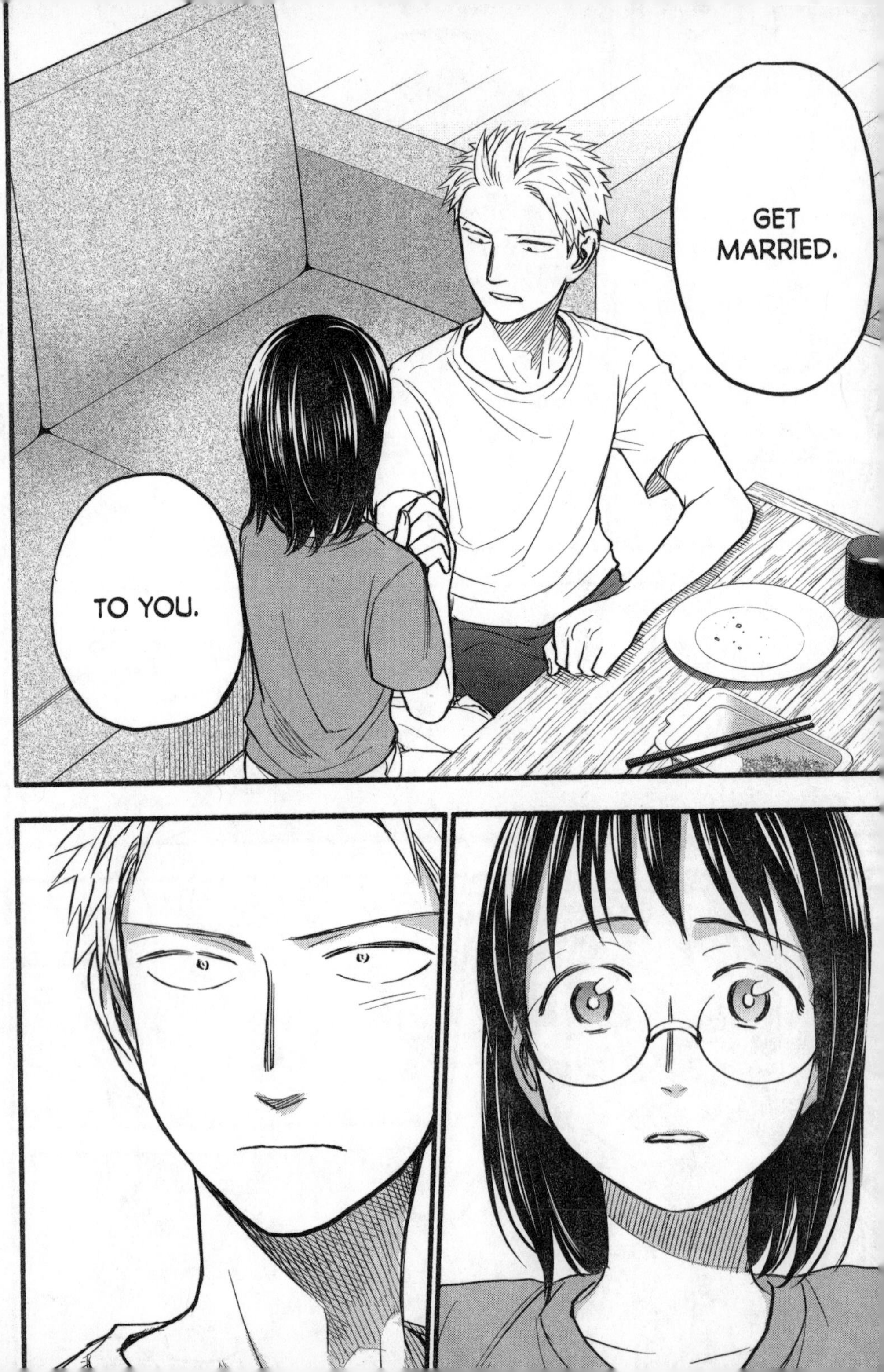
GET MARRIED.
TO YOU.

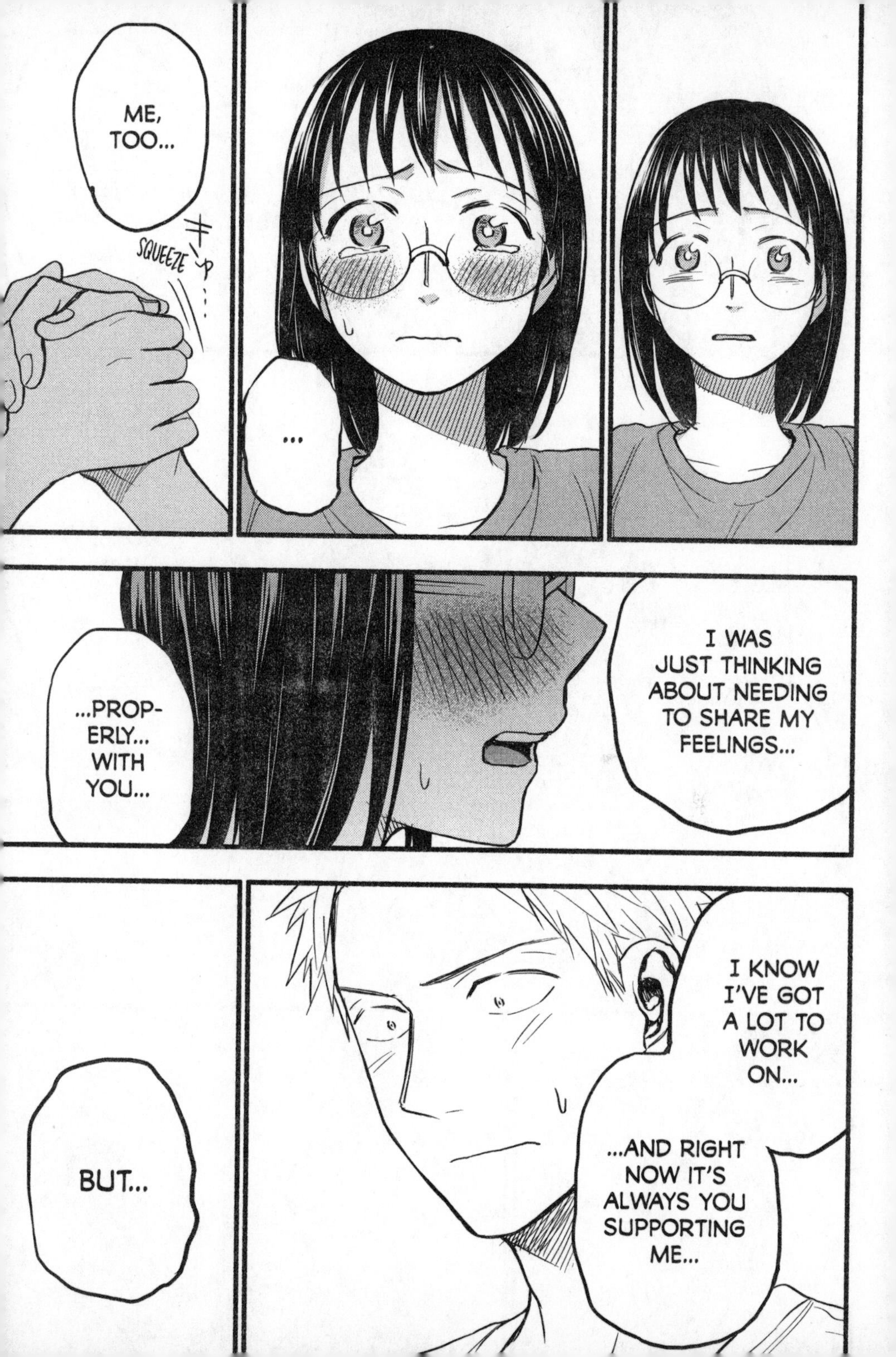
...
ME, TOO...
SQUEEZE
I WAS JUST THINKING ABOUT NEEDING TO SHARE MY FEELINGS...
...PROP-ERLY... WITH YOU...
I KNOW I'VE GOT A LOT TO WORK ON...
...AND RIGHT NOW IT'S ALWAYS YOU SUPPORTING ME...
BUT...

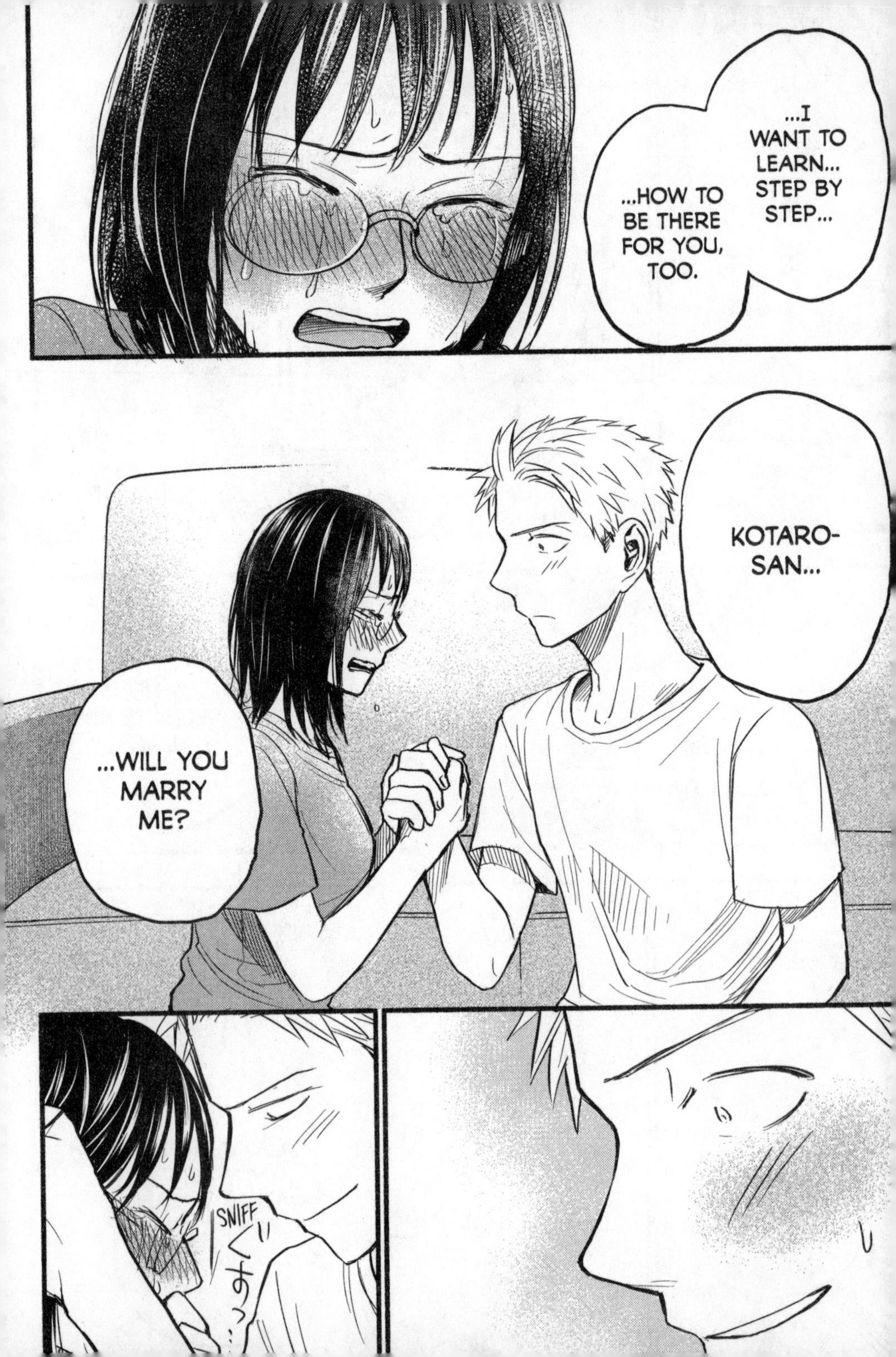
...I WANT TO LEARN... STEP BY STEP...
...HOW TO BE THERE FOR YOU, TOO.
KOTARO-SAN...
...WILL YOU MARRY ME?
SNIFF

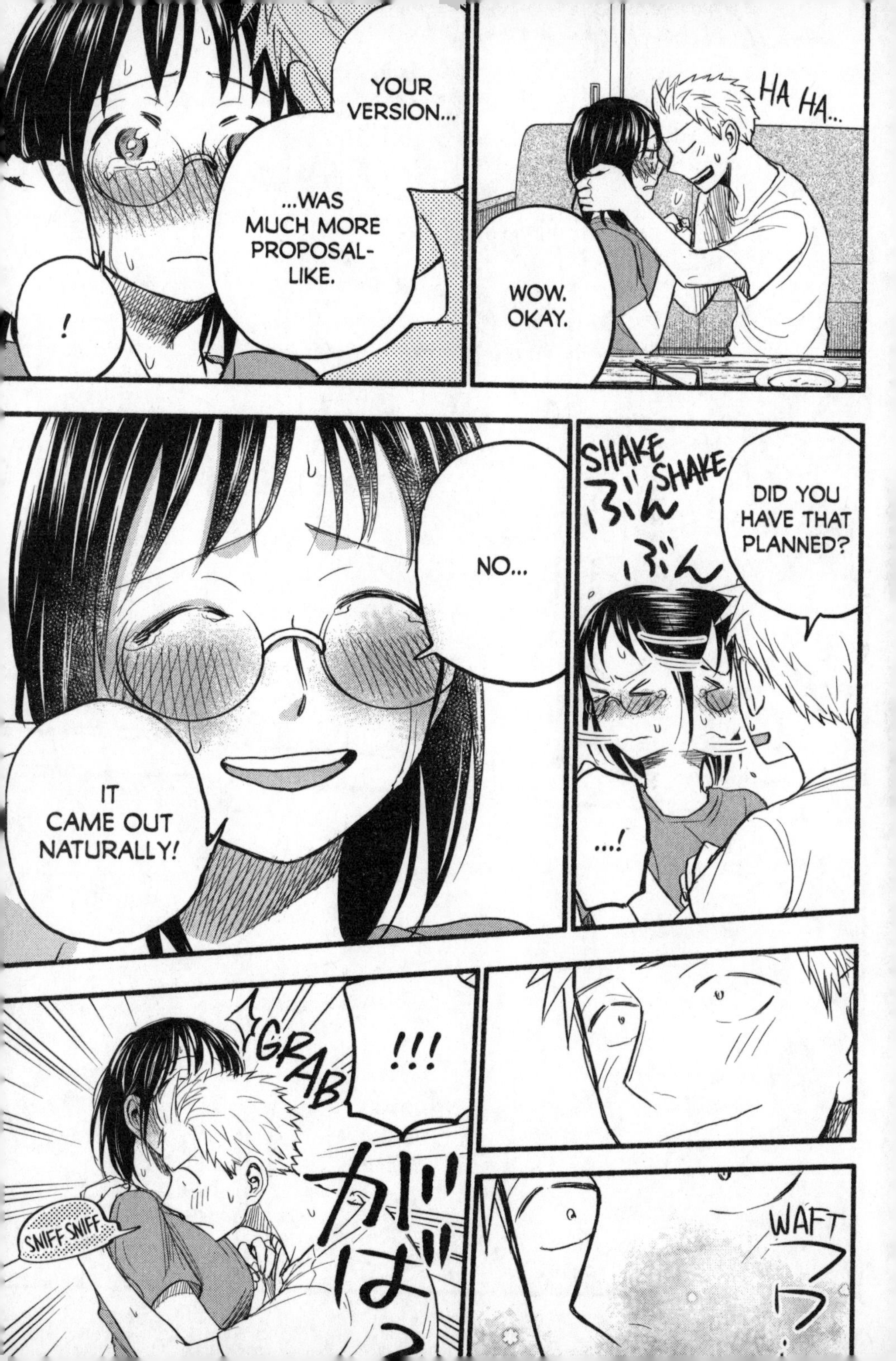
HA HA...
WOW. OKAY.
YOUR VERSION...
...WAS MUCH MORE PROPOSAL-LIKE.
!
DID YOU HAVE THAT PLANNED?
SHAKE SHAKE
ぶん ぶん
...!
NO...
IT CAME OUT NATURALLY!
WAFT
GRAB
がばっ
!!!
SNIFF SNIFF

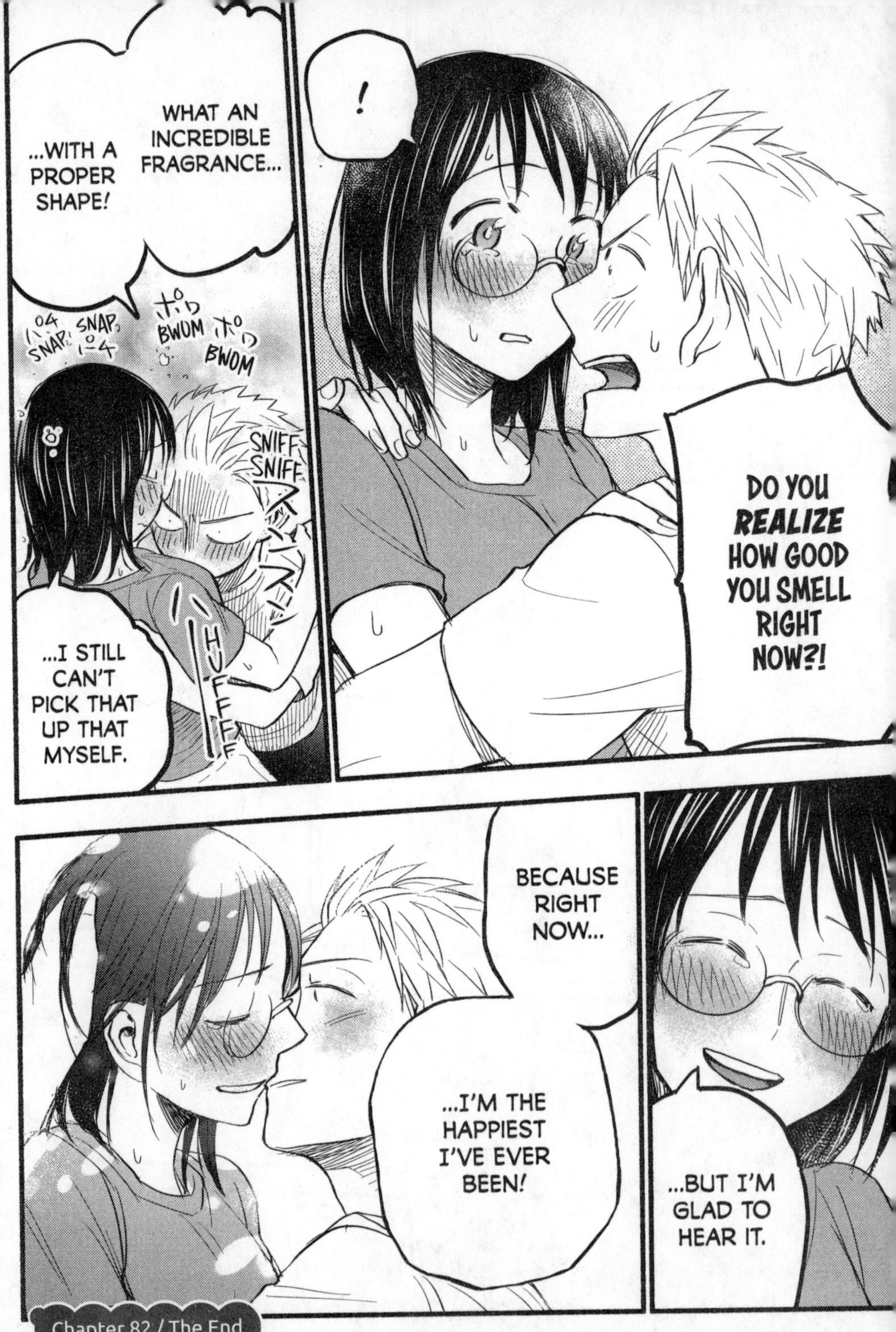
!
DO YOU REALIZE HOW GOOD YOU SMELL RIGHT NOW?!
WHAT AN INCREDIBLE FRAGRANCE...
...WITH A PROPER SHAPE!
SNAP SNAP
BWOM BWOM
SNIFF SNIFF
HUFFFFF
...I STILL CAN'T PICK THAT UP THAT MYSELF.
...BUT I'M GLAD TO HEAR IT.
BECAUSE RIGHT NOW...
...I'M THE HAPPIEST I'VE EVER BEEN!

Chapter 82 / The End

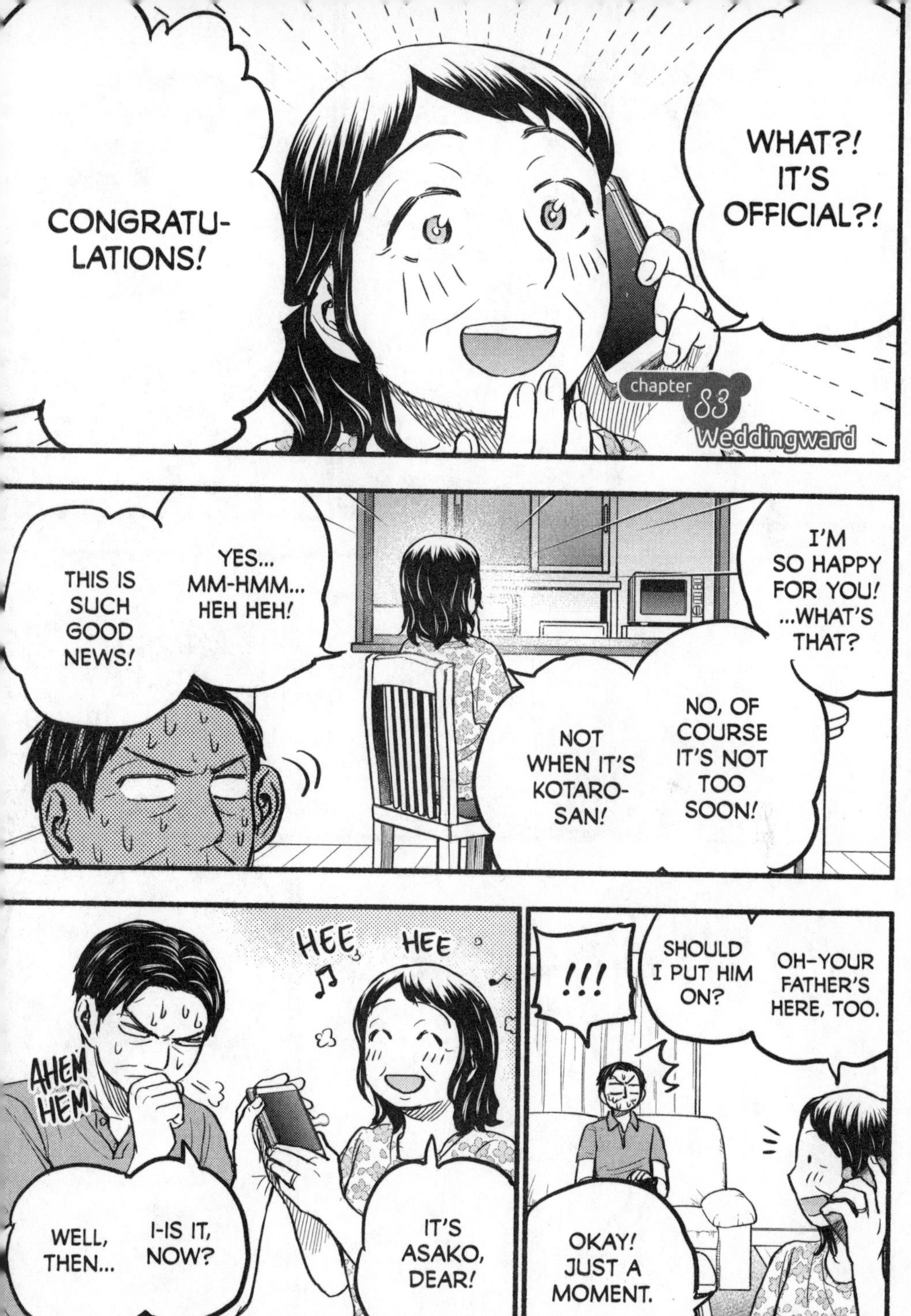

WHAT?! IT'S OFFICIAL?!
CONGRATU-LATIONS!
chapter 83
Weddingward
I'M SO HAPPY FOR YOU! ...WHAT'S THAT?
NO, OF COURSE IT'S NOT TOO SOON!
NOT WHEN IT'S KOTARO-SAN!
YES... MM-HMM... HEH HEH!
THIS IS SUCH GOOD NEWS!
OH—YOUR FATHER'S HERE, TOO.
SHOULD I PUT HIM ON?
!!!
OKAY! JUST A MOMENT.
HEE HEE
IT'S ASAKO, DEAR!
AHEM HEM
I-IS IT, NOW?
WELL, THEN...

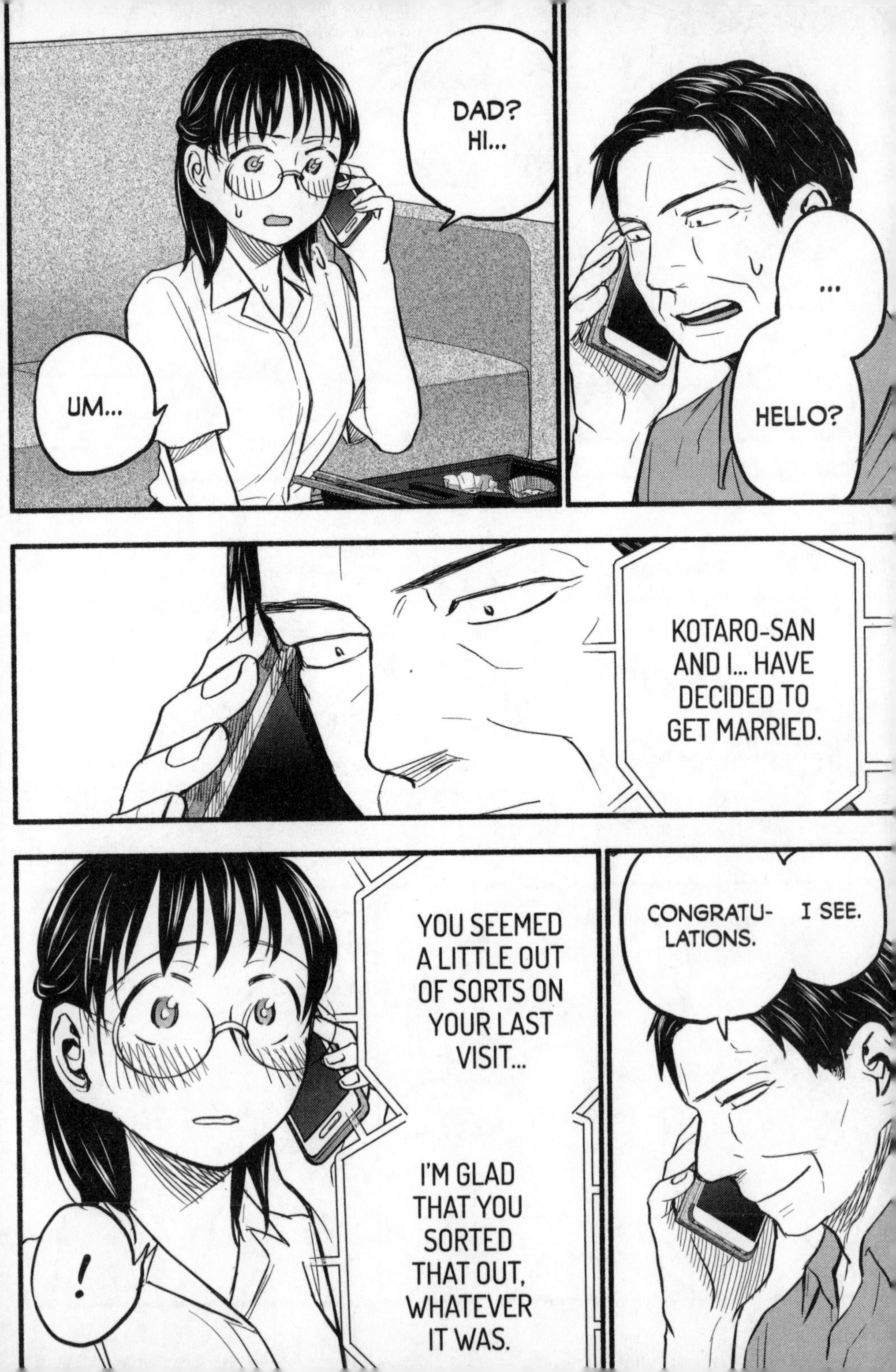
...
HELLO?
DAD? HI...
UM...
KOTARO-SAN AND I... HAVE DECIDED TO GET MARRIED.
I SEE.
CONGRATU-LATIONS.
YOU SEEMED A LITTLE OUT OF SORTS ON YOUR LAST VISIT...
I'M GLAD THAT YOU SORTED THAT OUT, WHATEVER IT WAS.
!

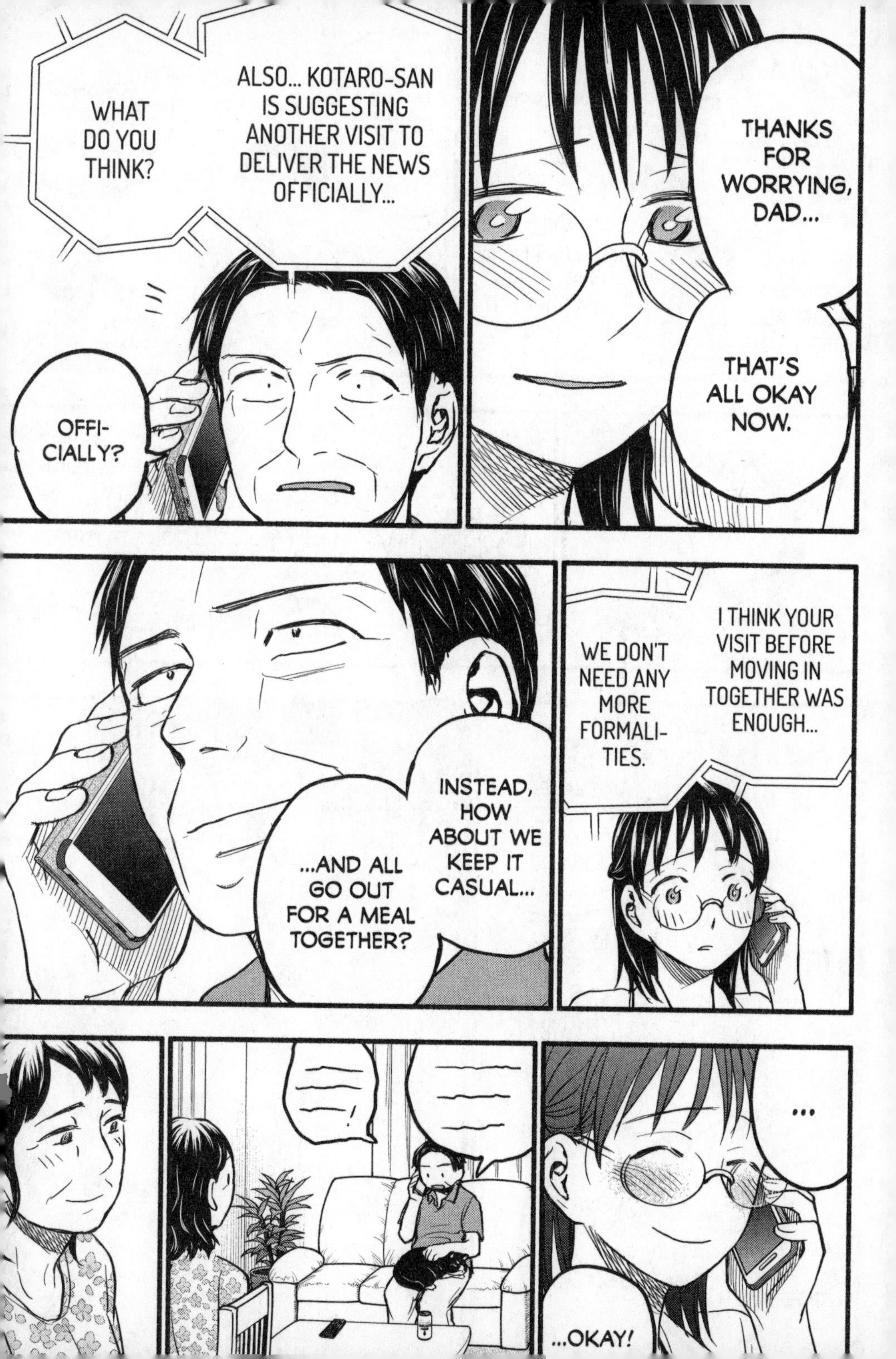
THANKS FOR WORRYING, DAD...
THAT'S ALL OKAY NOW.
ALSO... KOTARO-SAN IS SUGGESTING ANOTHER VISIT TO DELIVER THE NEWS OFFICIALLY...
WHAT DO YOU THINK?
OFFI-CIALLY?
I THINK YOUR VISIT BEFORE MOVING IN TOGETHER WAS ENOUGH...
WE DON'T NEED ANY MORE FORMALI-TIES.
INSTEAD, HOW ABOUT WE KEEP IT CASUAL...
...AND ALL GO OUT FOR A MEAL TOGETHER?
...
...OKAY!

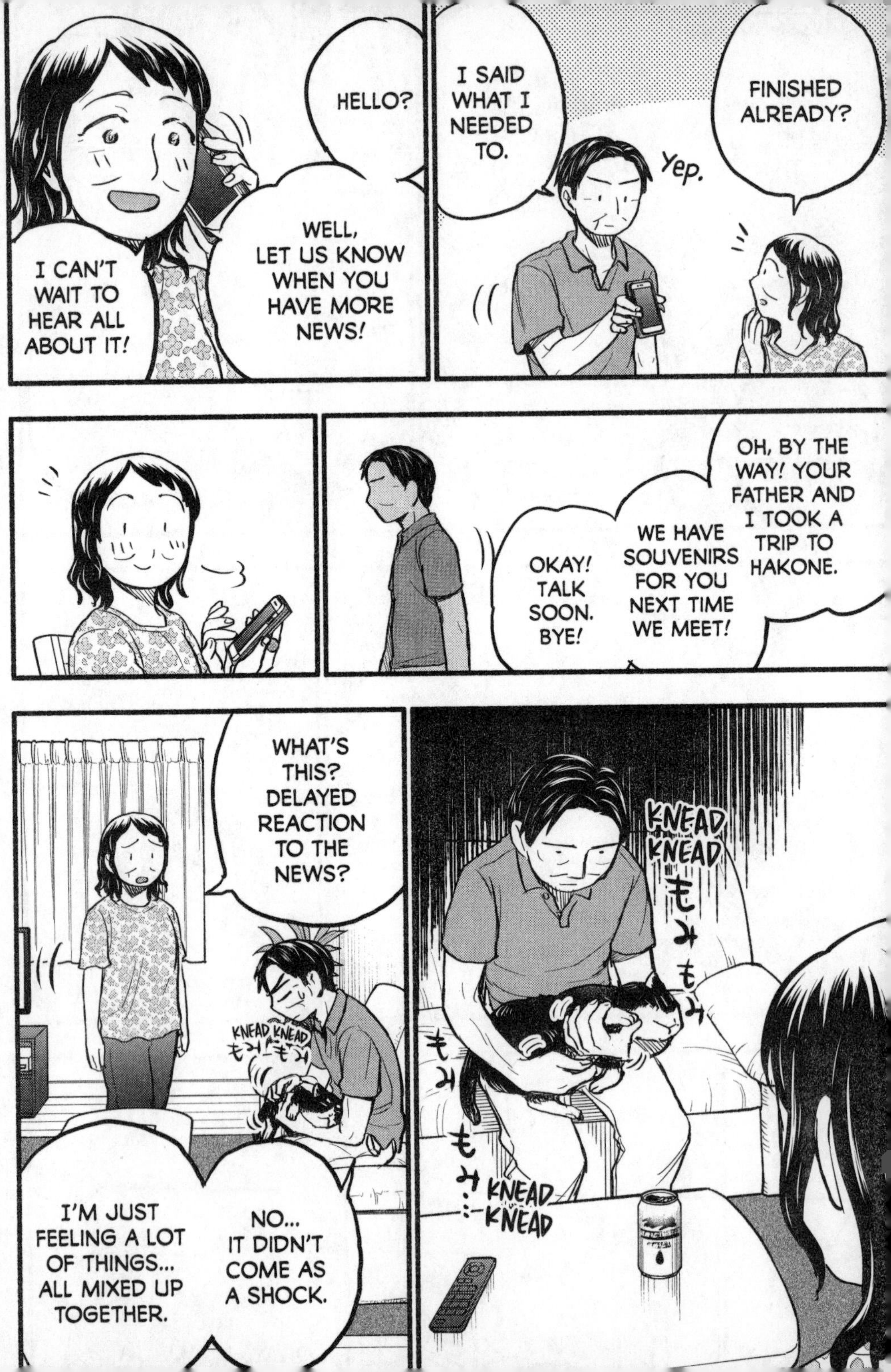
FINISHED ALREADY?
I SAID WHAT I NEEDED TO.
Yep.
HELLO?
WELL, LET US KNOW WHEN YOU HAVE MORE NEWS!
I CAN'T WAIT TO HEAR ALL ABOUT IT!
OH, BY THE WAY! YOUR FATHER AND I TOOK A TRIP TO HAKONE.
WE HAVE SOUVENIRS FOR YOU NEXT TIME WE MEET!
OKAY! TALK SOON. BYE!
KNEAD KNEAD
もみもみ
KNEAD KNEAD
もみもみ
WHAT'S THIS? DELAYED REACTION TO THE NEWS?
KNEAD KNEAD
もみもみ
NO... IT DIDN'T COME AS A SHOCK.
I'M JUST FEELING A LOT OF THINGS... ALL MIXED UP TOGETHER.

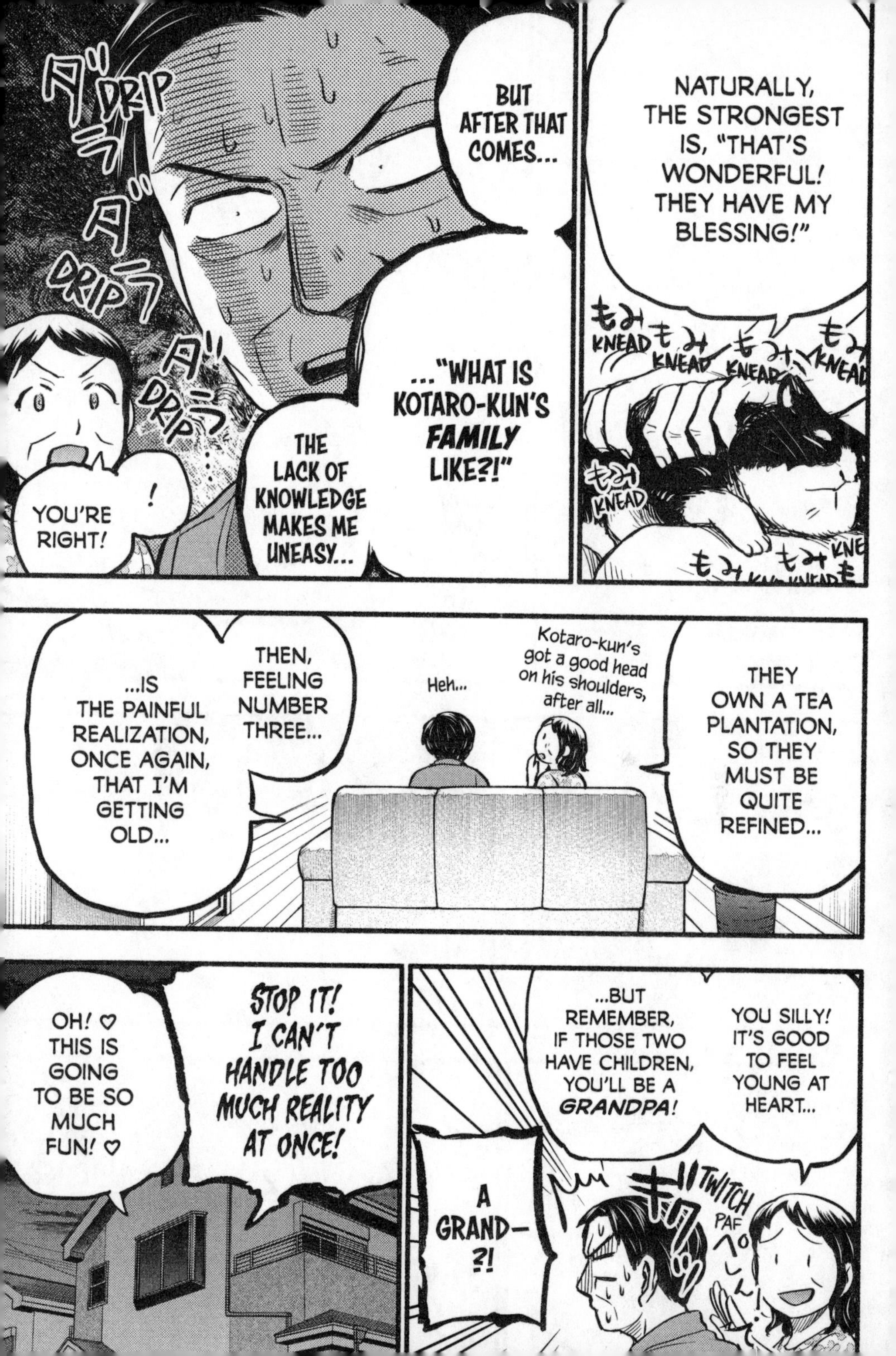
NATURALLY, THE STRONGEST IS, "THAT'S WONDERFUL! THEY HAVE MY BLESSING!"
KNEAD KNEAD KNEAD KNEAD
KNEAD
BUT AFTER THAT COMES...
..."WHAT IS KOTARO-KUN'S FAMILY LIKE?!"
THE LACK OF KNOWLEDGE MAKES ME UNEASY...
DRIP DRIP DRIP
YOU'RE RIGHT!
THEY OWN A TEA PLANTATION, SO THEY MUST BE QUITE REFINED...
Kotaro-kun's got a good head on his shoulders, after all...
Heh...
THEN, FEELING NUMBER THREE...
...IS THE PAINFUL REALIZATION, ONCE AGAIN, THAT I'M GETTING OLD...
YOU SILLY! IT'S GOOD TO FEEL YOUNG AT HEART...
...BUT REMEMBER, IF THOSE TWO HAVE CHILDREN, YOU'LL BE A GRANDPA!
A GRAND-?!
TWITCH
PAF
STOP IT! I CAN'T HANDLE TOO MUCH REALITY AT ONCE!
OH! ♡ THIS IS GOING TO BE SO MUCH FUN! ♡

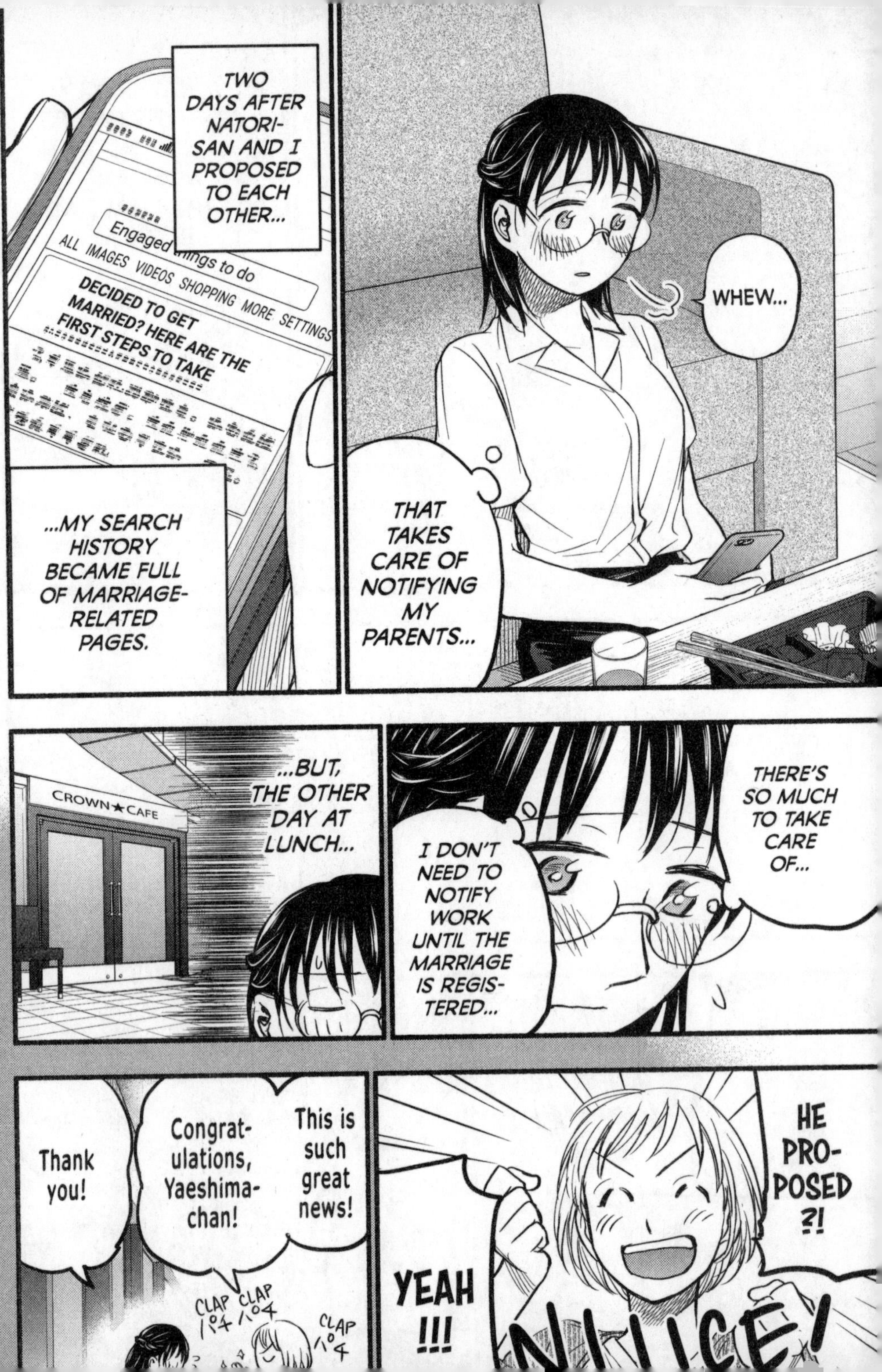
WHEW...
THAT TAKES CARE OF NOTIFYING MY PARENTS...
TWO DAYS AFTER NATORI-SAN AND I PROPOSED TO EACH OTHER...
Engaged things to do
ALL IMAGES VIDEOS SHOPPING MORE SETTINGS
DECIDED TO GET MARRIED? HERE ARE THE FIRST STEPS TO TAKE
...MY SEARCH HISTORY BECAME FULL OF MARRIAGE-RELATED PAGES.
THERE'S SO MUCH TO TAKE CARE OF...
I DON'T NEED TO NOTIFY WORK UNTIL THE MARRIAGE IS REGISTERED...
...BUT, THE OTHER DAY AT LUNCH...
CROWN★CAFE
HE PROPOSED?!
YEAH!!!
NIIICE!
This is such great news!
Congratulations, Yaeshima-chan!
Thank you!
CLAP CLAP
CLAP

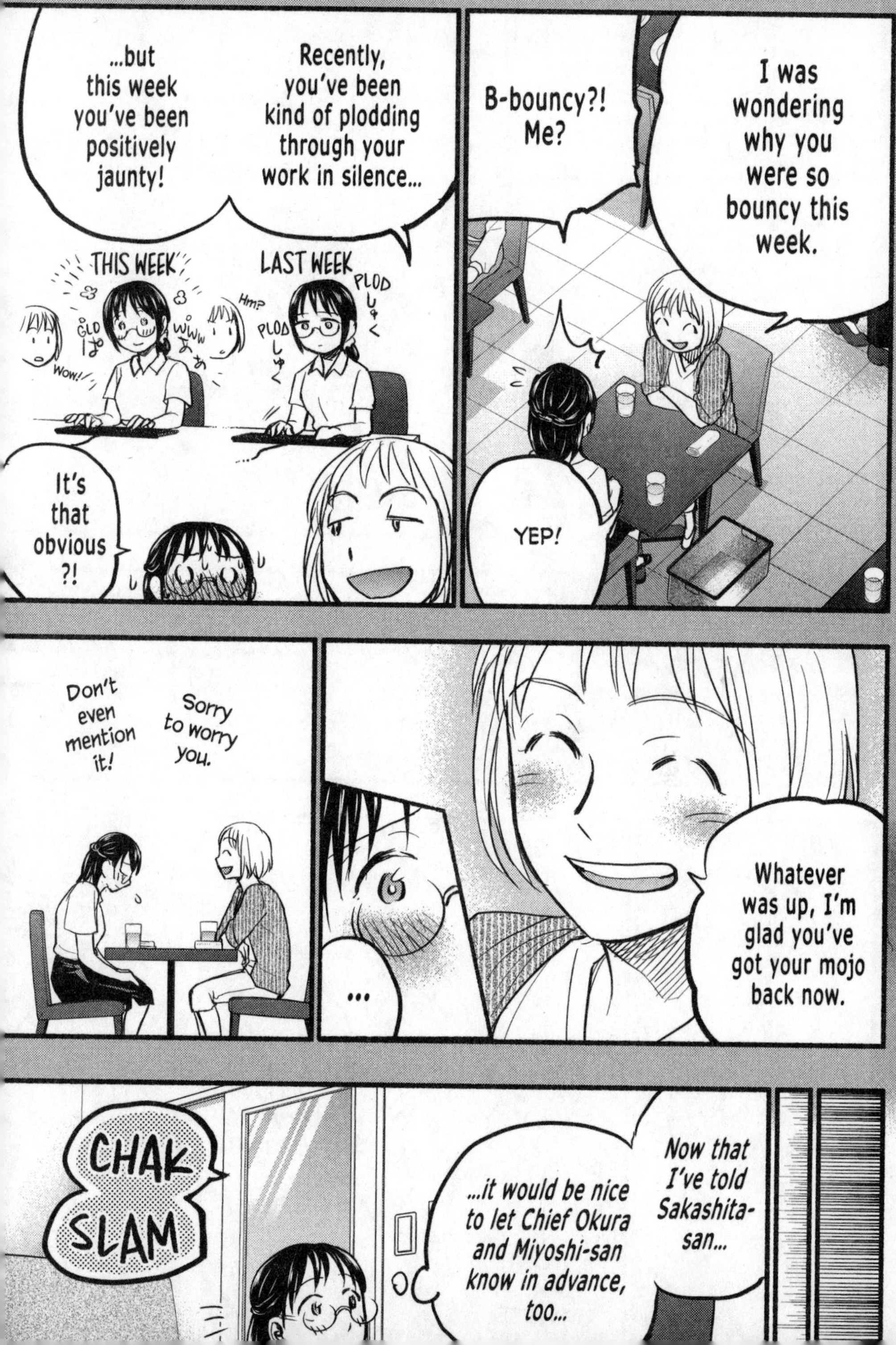
I was wondering why you were so bouncy this week.
B-bouncy?! Me?
YEP!
Recently, you've been kind of plodding through your work in silence...
...but this week you've been positively jaunty!
LAST WEEK
PLOD
PLOD
THIS WEEK
Hm?
WOW!
It's that obvious?!
Whatever was up, I'm glad you've got your mojo back now.
...
Sorry to worry you.
Don't even mention it!
Now that I've told Sakashita-san...
...it would be nice to let Chief Okura and Miyoshi-san know in advance, too...
CHAK SLAM

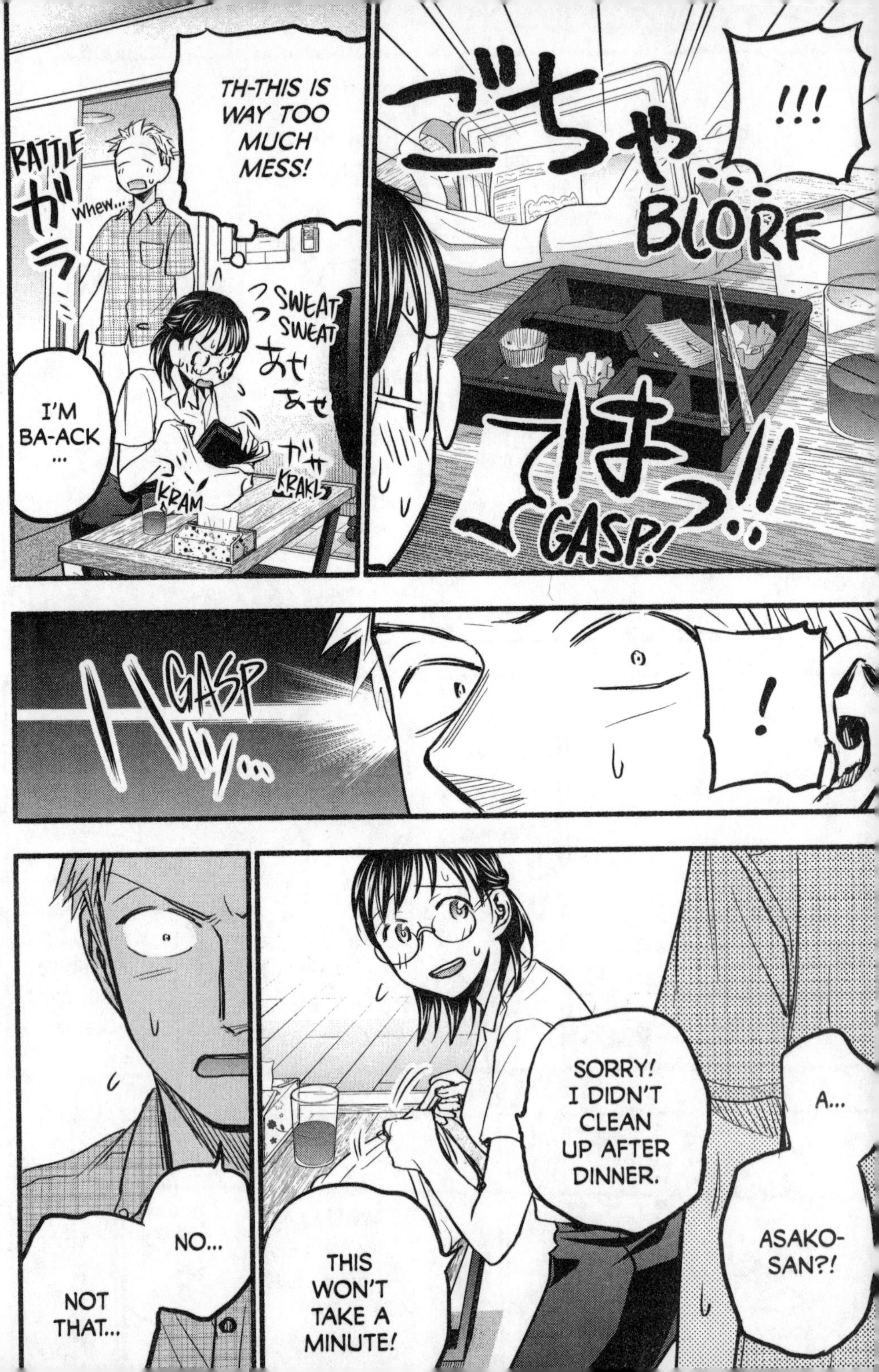
!!!
ごちゃ
BLORF
はっ!!
GASP!
TH-THIS IS WAY TOO MUCH MESS!
RATTLE
ガラ
Whew...
I'M BA-ACK ...
SWEAT SWEAT
あせあせ
ガサ
KRAKL
KRAM
!
GASP
A...
ASAKO-SAN?!
SORRY! I DIDN'T CLEAN UP AFTER DINNER.
THIS WON'T TAKE A MINUTE!
NO...
NOT THAT...

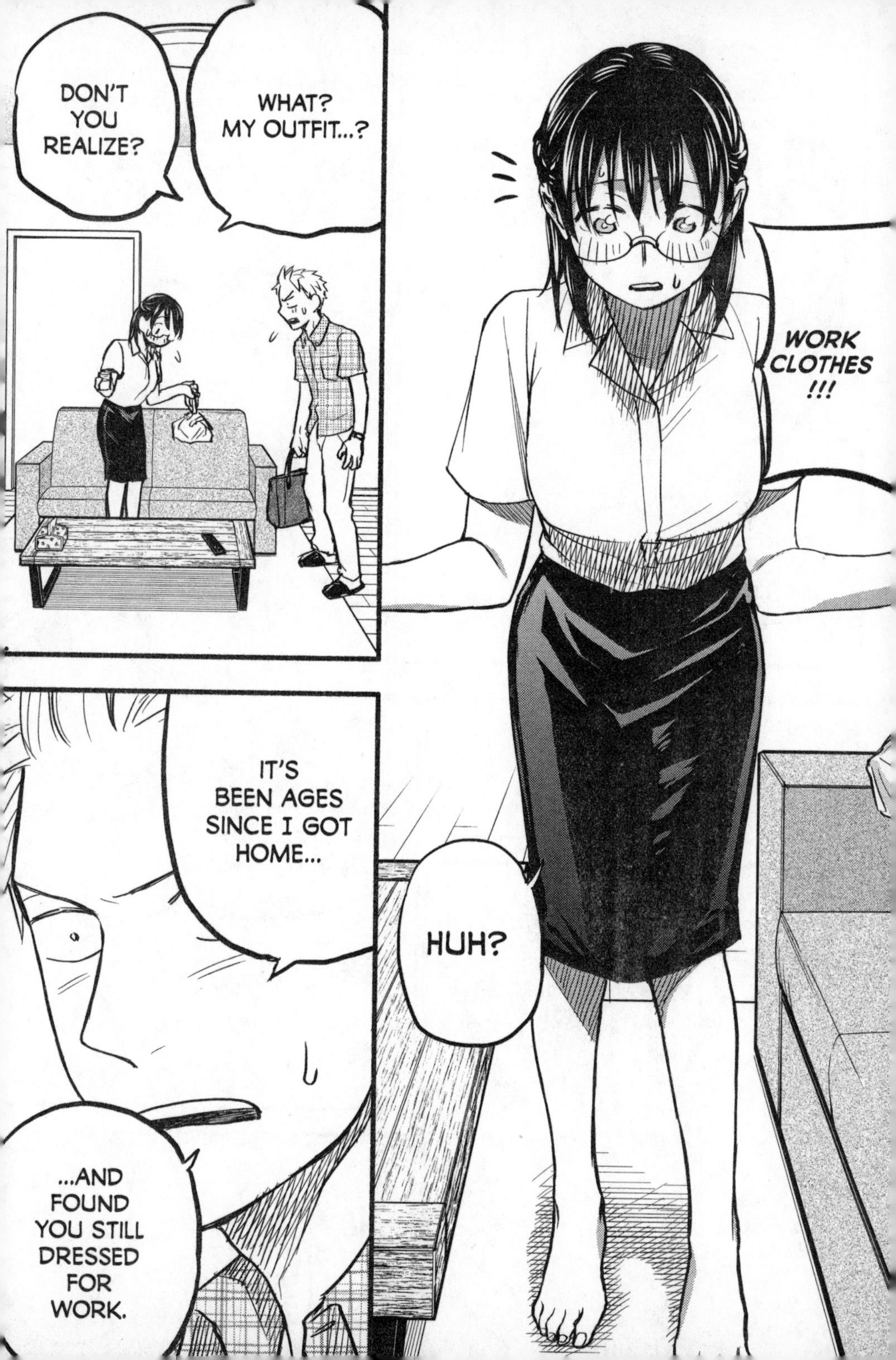
WORK CLOTHES !!!
HUH?
WHAT? MY OUTFIT...?
DON'T YOU REALIZE?
IT'S BEEN AGES SINCE I GOT HOME...
...AND FOUND YOU STILL DRESSED FOR WORK.

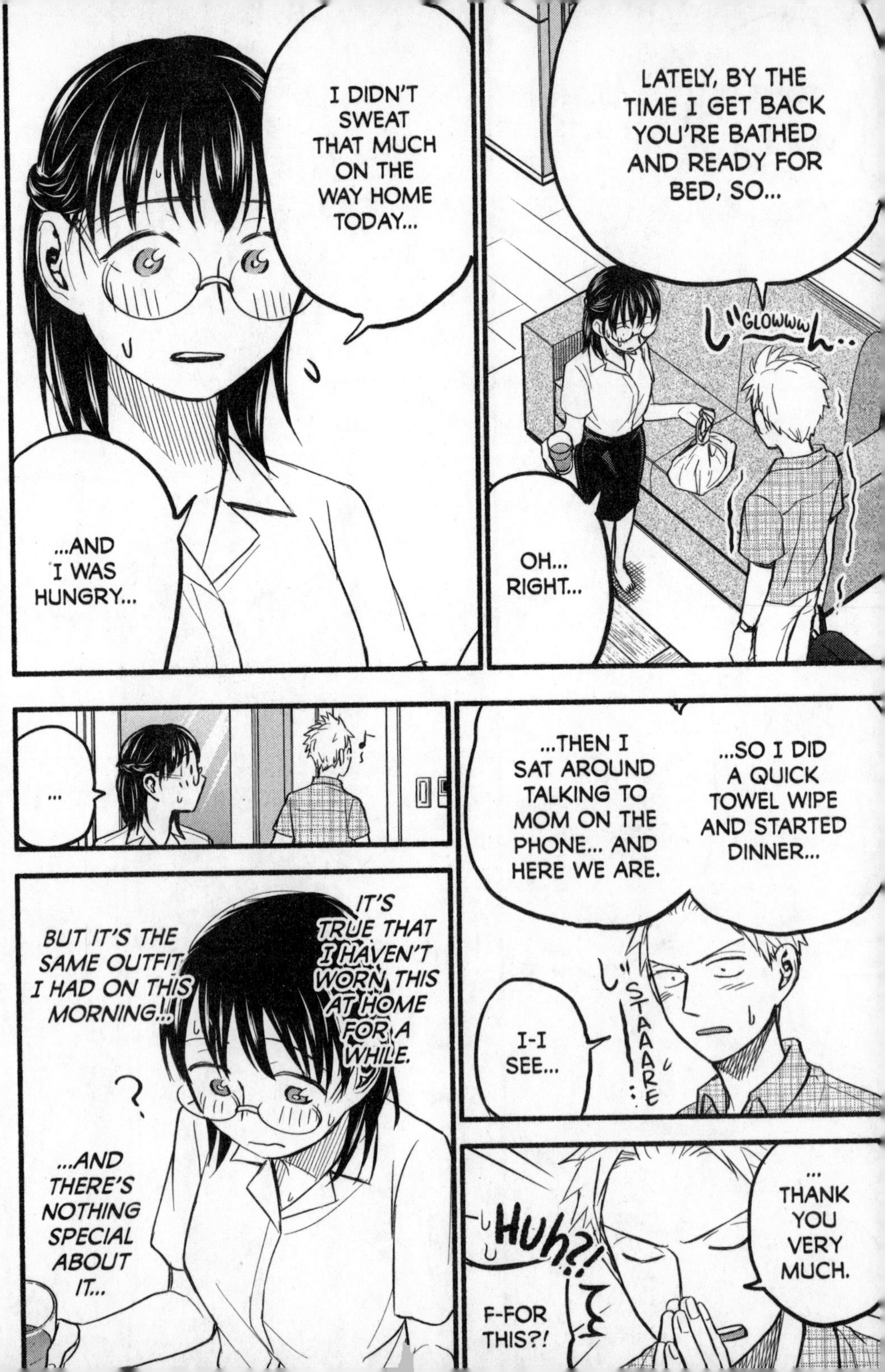
LATELY, BY THE TIME I GET BACK YOU'RE BATHED AND READY FOR BED, SO...
じ GLOWWWん...
OH... RIGHT...
I DIDN'T SWEAT THAT MUCH ON THE WAY HOME TODAY...
...AND I WAS HUNGRY...
...SO I DID A QUICK TOWEL WIPE AND STARTED DINNER...
...THEN I SAT AROUND TALKING TO MOM ON THE PHONE... AND HERE WE ARE.
じ STAAARE
I-I SEE...
...
IT'S TRUE THAT I HAVEN'T WORN THIS AT HOME FOR A WHILE.
BUT IT'S THE SAME OUTFIT I HAD ON THIS MORNING...
?
...AND THERE'S NOTHING SPECIAL ABOUT IT...
... THANK YOU VERY MUCH.
HUH?!
F-FOR THIS?!

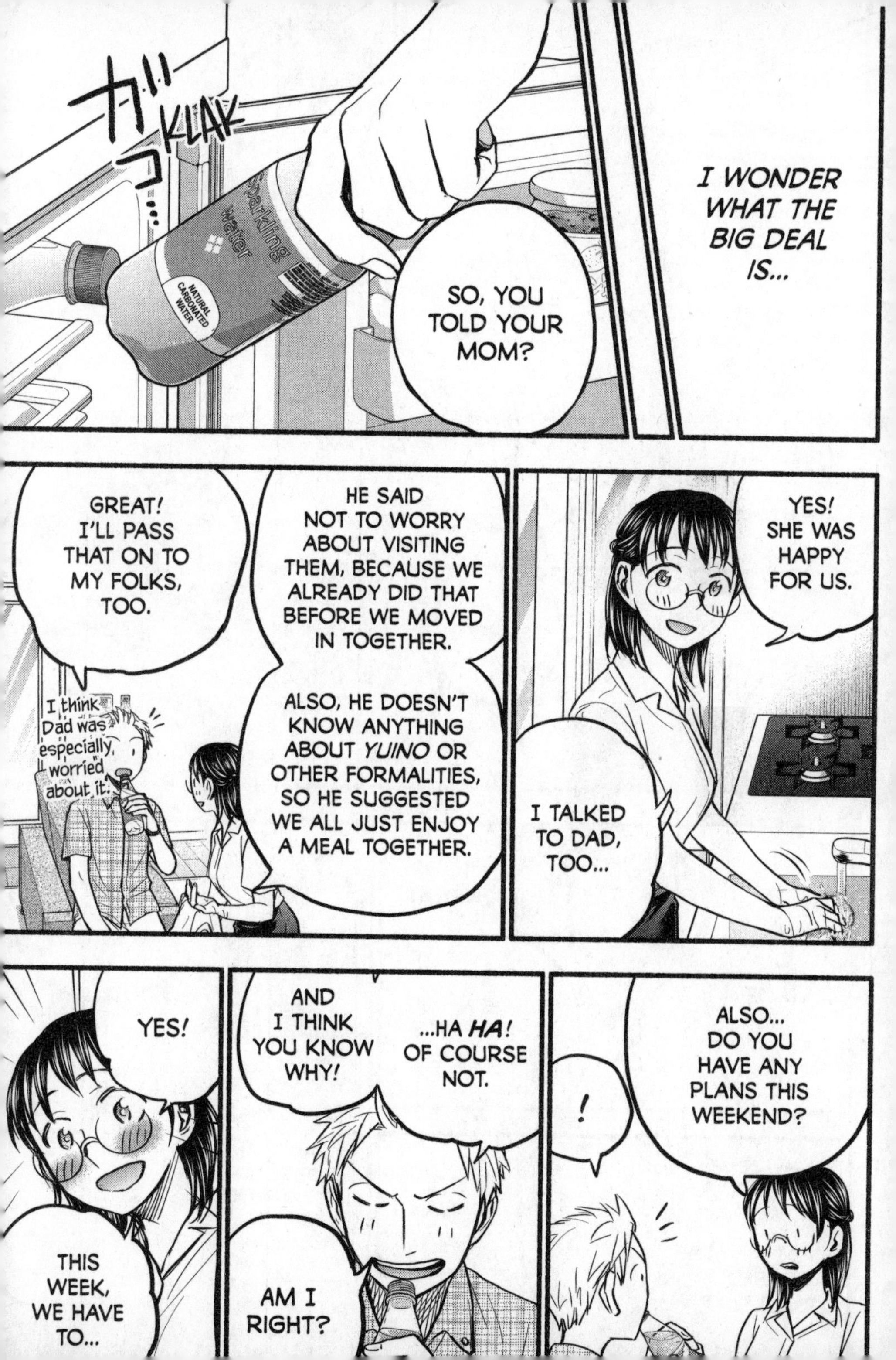
I WONDER WHAT THE BIG DEAL IS...
KLAK
Sparkling water
NATURAL CARBONATED WATER
SO, YOU TOLD YOUR MOM?
YES! SHE WAS HAPPY FOR US.
I TALKED TO DAD, TOO...
HE SAID NOT TO WORRY ABOUT VISITING THEM, BECAUSE WE ALREADY DID THAT BEFORE WE MOVED IN TOGETHER.
ALSO, HE DOESN'T KNOW ANYTHING ABOUT *YUINO* OR OTHER FORMALITIES, SO HE SUGGESTED WE ALL JUST ENJOY A MEAL TOGETHER.
GREAT! I'LL PASS THAT ON TO MY FOLKS, TOO.
I think Dad was especially worried about it.
ALSO... DO YOU HAVE ANY PLANS THIS WEEKEND?
!
...HA ***HA***! OF COURSE NOT.
AND I THINK YOU KNOW WHY!
AM I RIGHT?
YES!
THIS WEEK, WE HAVE TO...

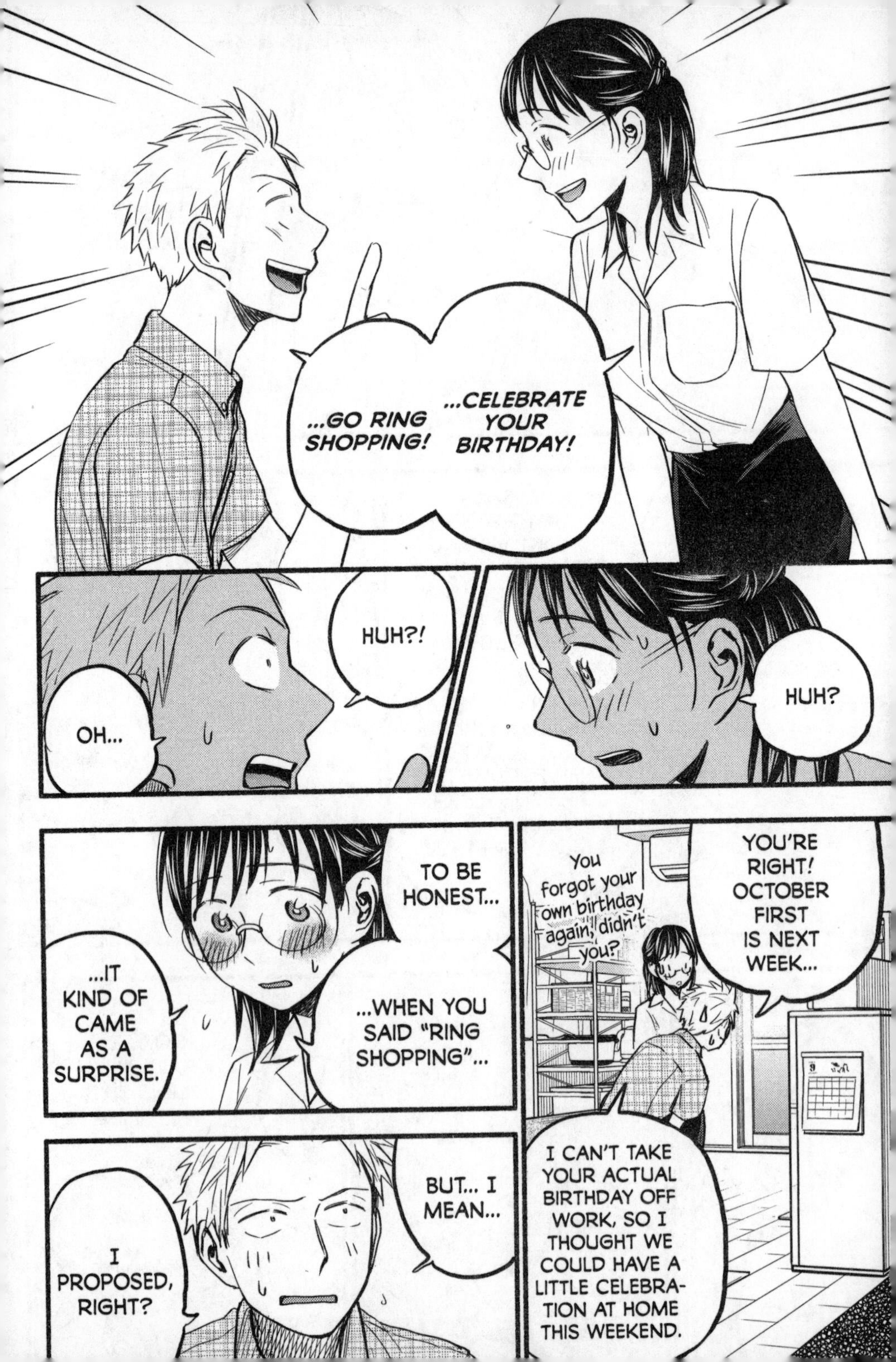
...CELEBRATE YOUR BIRTHDAY!
...GO RING SHOPPING!
HUH?
HUH?!
OH...
YOU'RE RIGHT! OCTOBER FIRST IS NEXT WEEK...
You forgot your own birthday again, didn't you?
I CAN'T TAKE YOUR ACTUAL BIRTHDAY OFF WORK, SO I THOUGHT WE COULD HAVE A LITTLE CELEBRATION AT HOME THIS WEEKEND.
TO BE HONEST...
...WHEN YOU SAID "RING SHOPPING"...
...IT KIND OF CAME AS A SURPRISE.
BUT... I MEAN...
I PROPOSED, RIGHT?

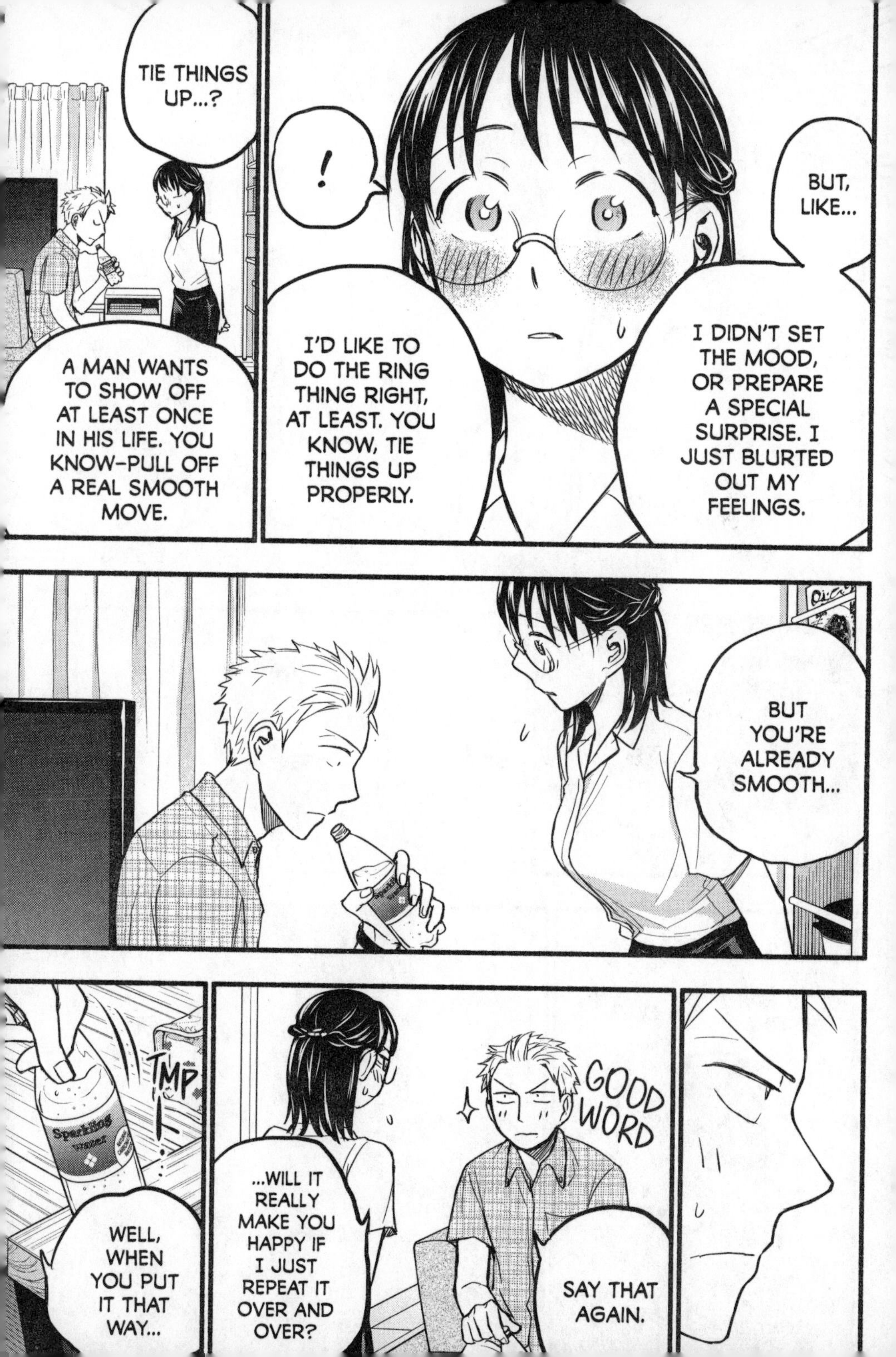
BUT, LIKE...
I DIDN'T SET THE MOOD, OR PREPARE A SPECIAL SURPRISE. I JUST BLURTED OUT MY FEELINGS.
!
I'D LIKE TO DO THE RING THING RIGHT, AT LEAST. YOU KNOW, TIE THINGS UP PROPERLY.
TIE THINGS UP...?
A MAN WANTS TO SHOW OFF AT LEAST ONCE IN HIS LIFE. YOU KNOW–PULL OFF A REAL SMOOTH MOVE.
BUT YOU'RE ALREADY SMOOTH...
GOOD WORD
SAY THAT AGAIN.
...WILL IT REALLY MAKE YOU HAPPY IF I JUST REPEAT IT OVER AND OVER?
TMP
WELL, WHEN YOU PUT IT THAT WAY...

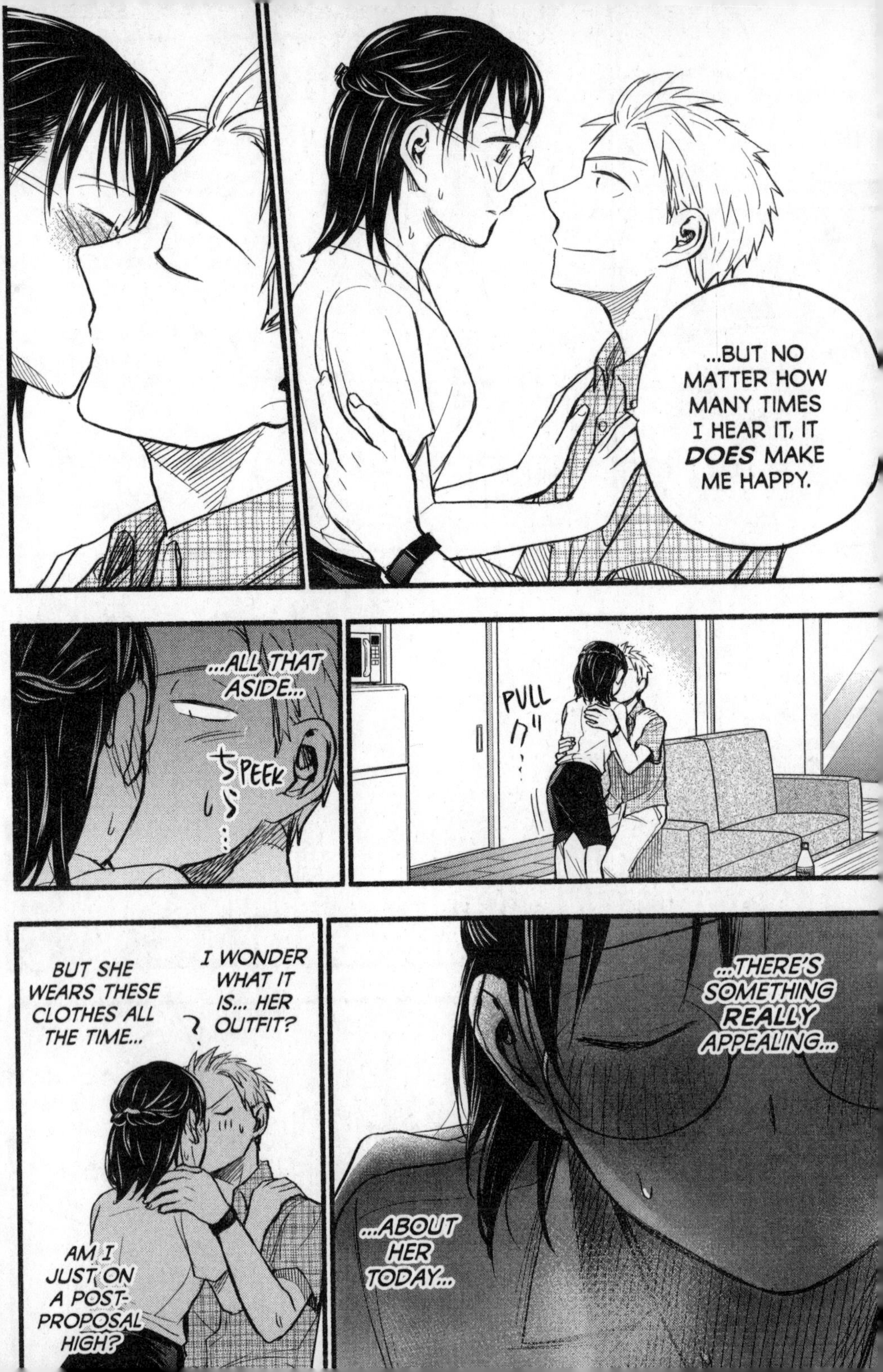
...BUT NO MATTER HOW MANY TIMES I HEAR IT, IT **DOES** MAKE ME HAPPY.
PULL
グ…
...ALL THAT ASIDE...
PEEK
ちら…
...THERE'S SOMETHING **REALLY** APPEALING...
...ABOUT HER TODAY...
I WONDER WHAT IT IS... HER OUTFIT?
BUT SHE WEARS THESE CLOTHES ALL THE TIME...
?
AM I JUST ON A POST-PROPOSAL HIGH?

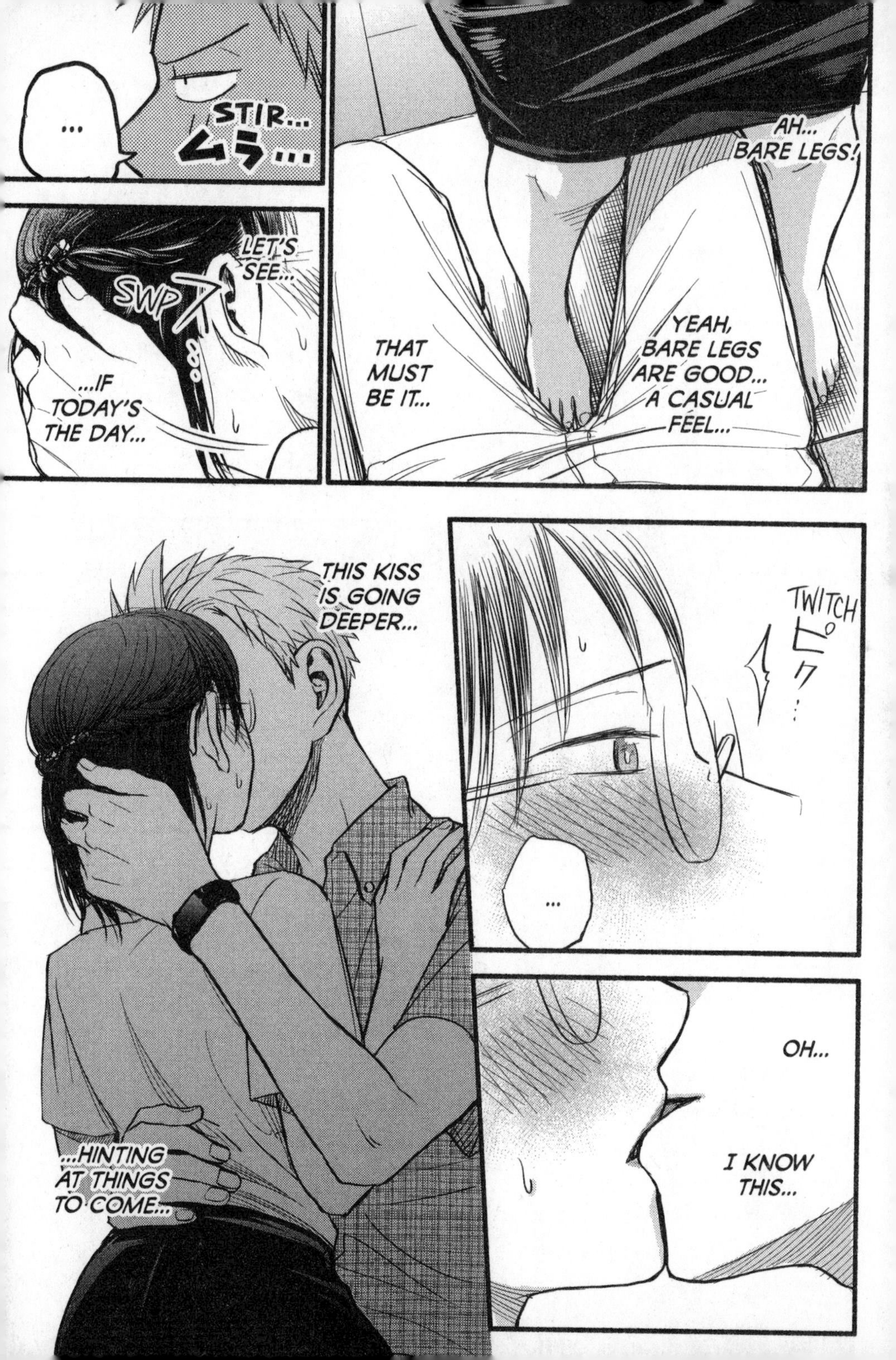
AH... BARE LEGS!
YEAH, BARE LEGS ARE GOOD... A CASUAL FEEL...
THAT MUST BE IT...
...
STIR... ムラ...
LET'S SEE...
SWP
...IF TODAY'S THE DAY...
TWITCH ピク...
...
OH...
I KNOW THIS...
THIS KISS IS GOING DEEPER...
...HINTING AT THINGS TO COME...

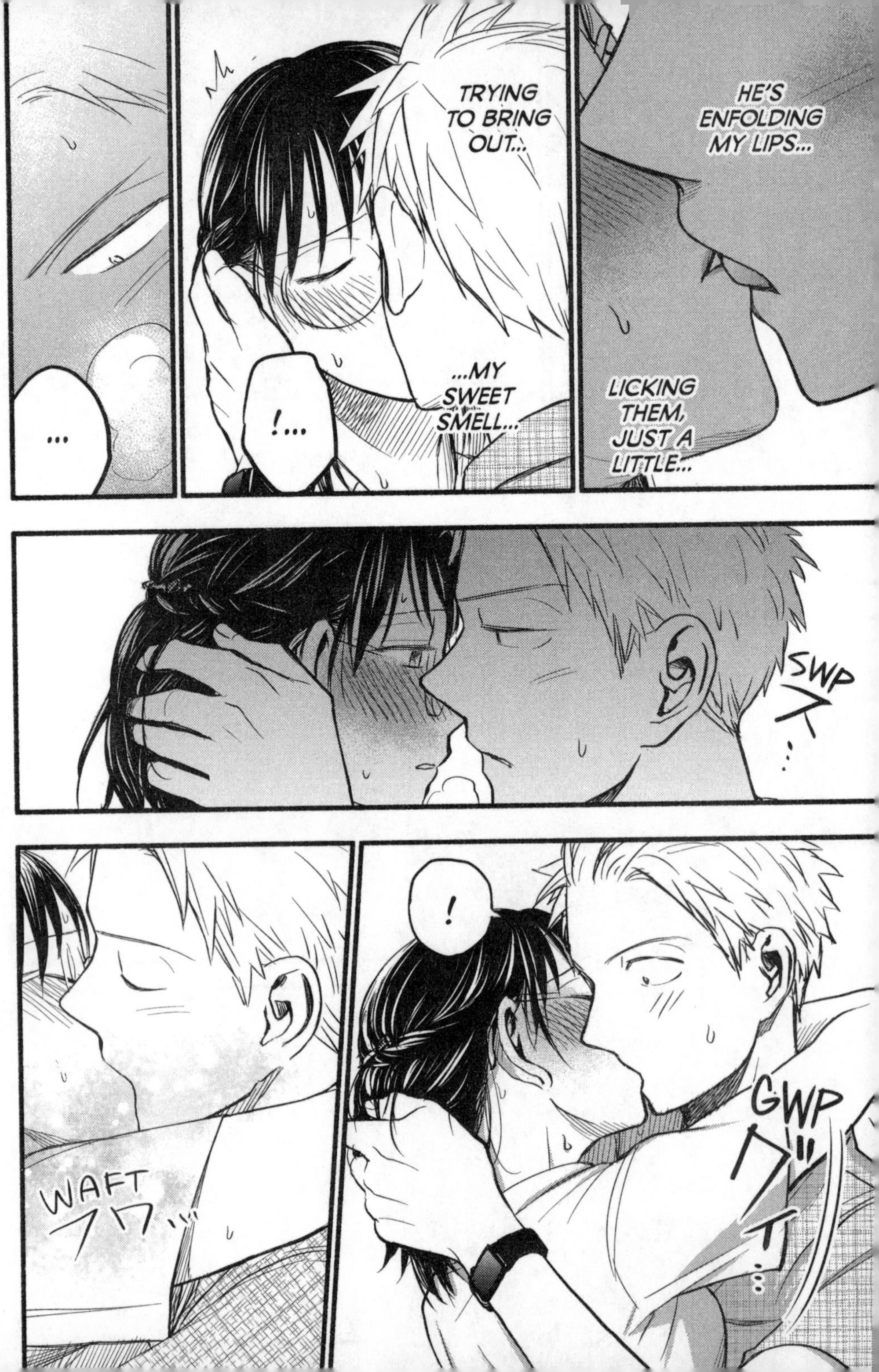
HE'S ENFOLDING MY LIPS...
LICKING THEM, JUST A LITTLE...
TRYING TO BRING OUT...
...MY SWEET SMELL...
!...
...
SWP
!
GWP
WAFT
フワ...

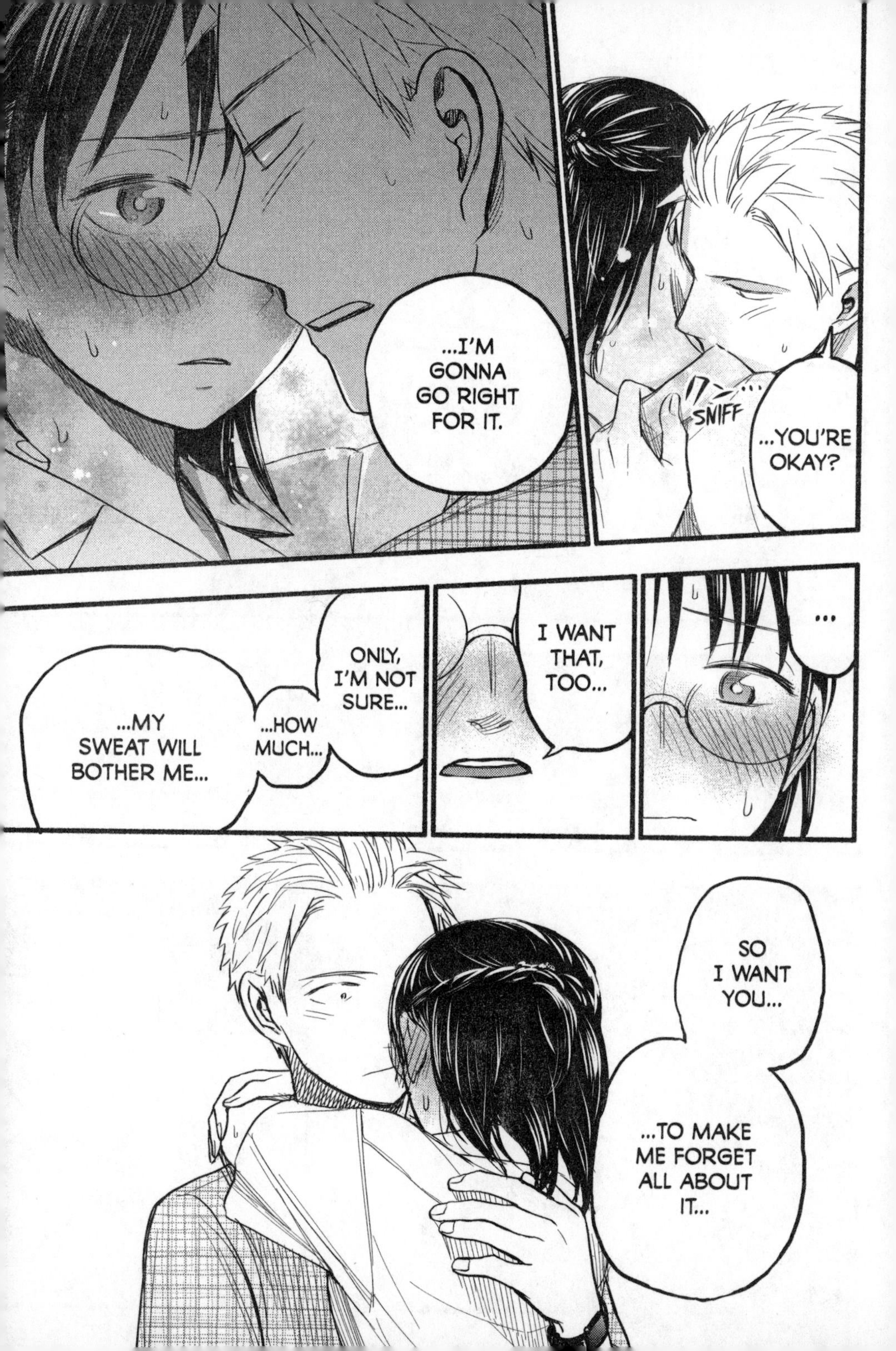

...YOU'RE OKAY?
SNIFF
...I'M GONNA GO RIGHT FOR IT.
...
I WANT THAT, TOO...
ONLY, I'M NOT SURE...
...HOW MUCH...
...MY SWEAT WILL BOTHER ME...
SO I WANT YOU...
...TO MAKE ME FORGET ALL ABOUT IT...

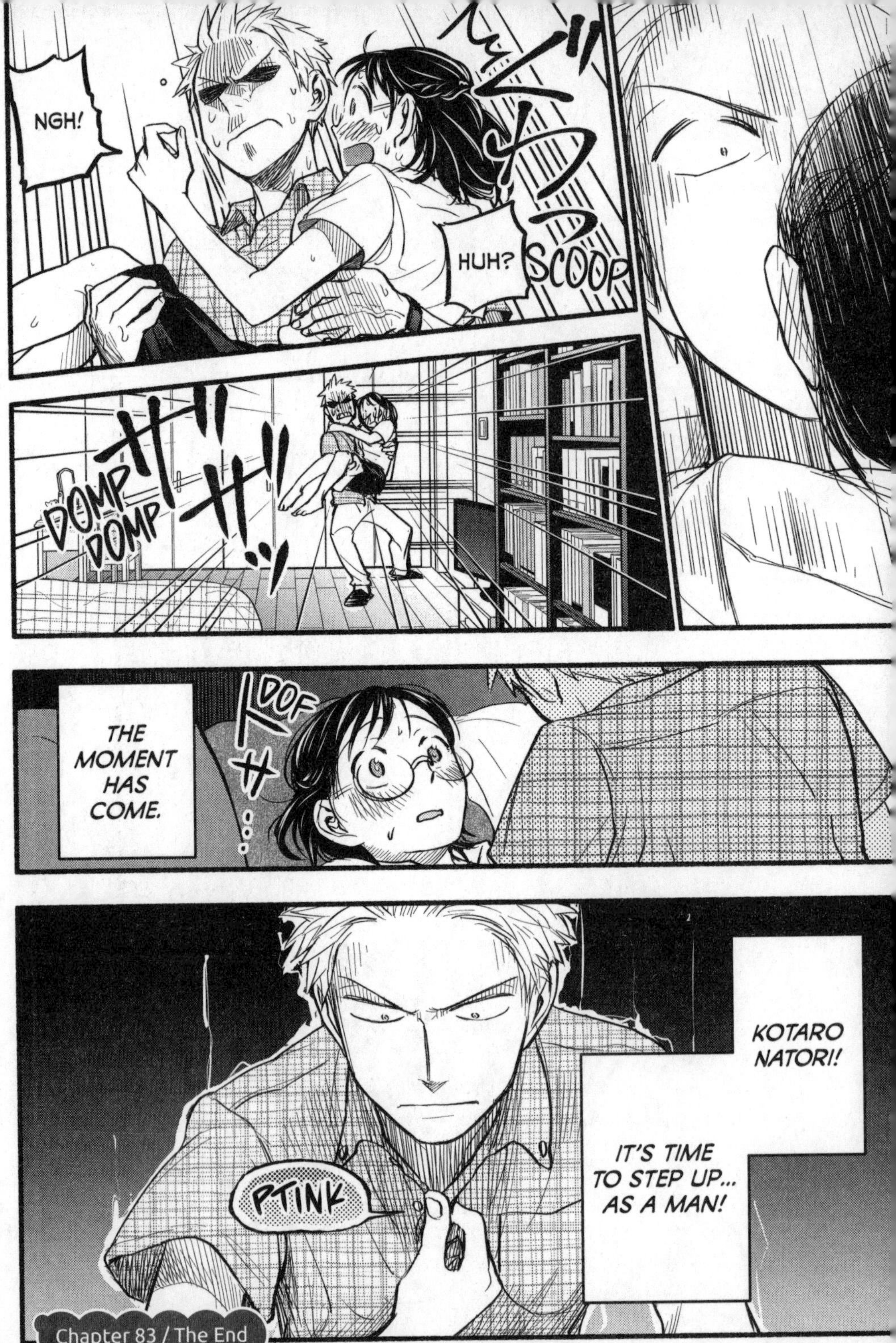
HUH?
SCOOP
NGH!
DOMP DOMP
THE MOMENT HAS COME.
KOTARO NATORI!
IT'S TIME TO STEP UP... AS A MAN!
PTINK
Chapter 83 / The End

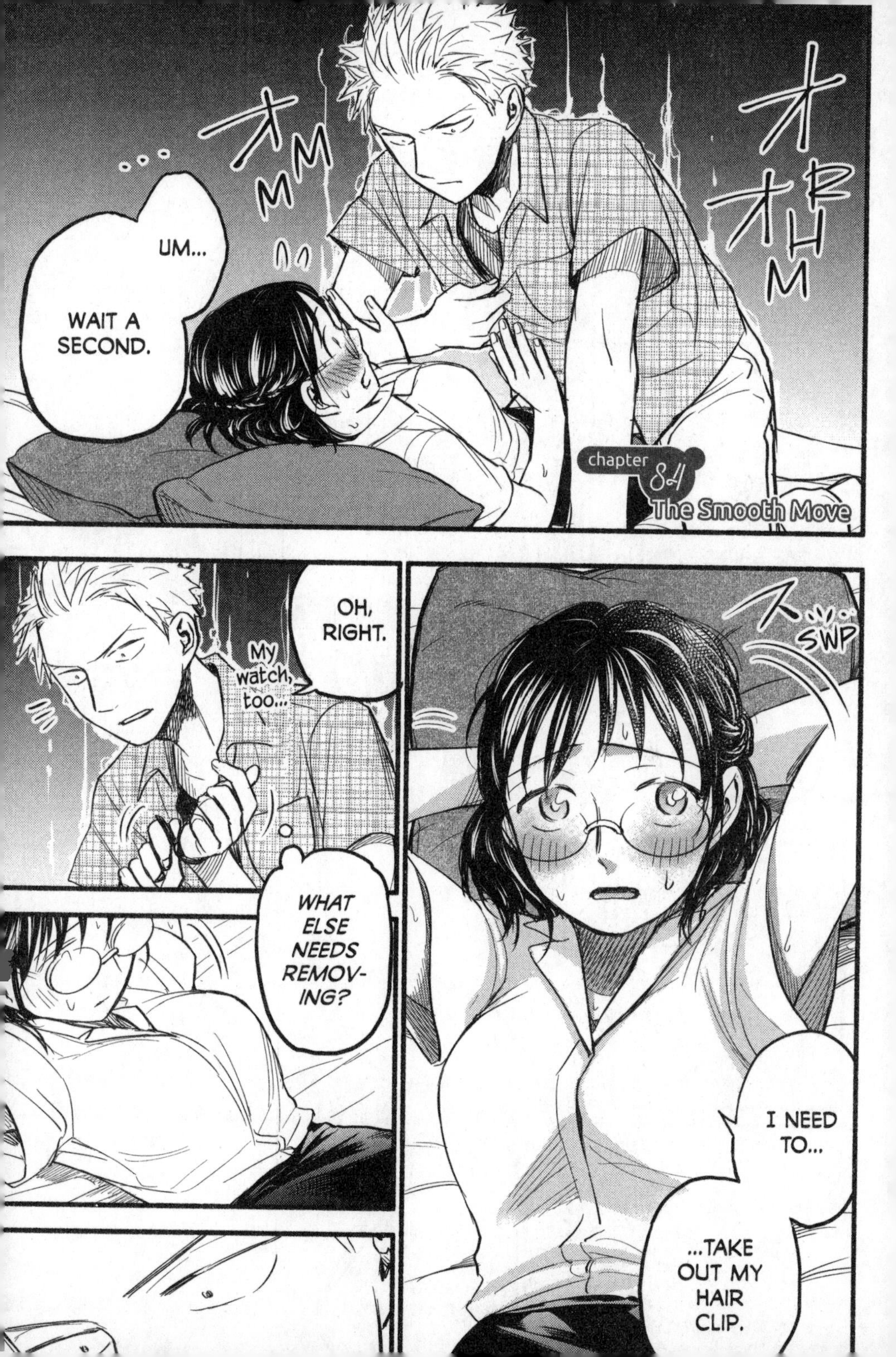

オオ
RHM
オ
MMM
...
UM...
WAIT A SECOND.
chapter 84
The Smooth Move
ス
SWP
I NEED TO...
...TAKE OUT MY HAIR CLIP.
OH, RIGHT.
My watch, too...
WHAT ELSE NEEDS REMOVING?

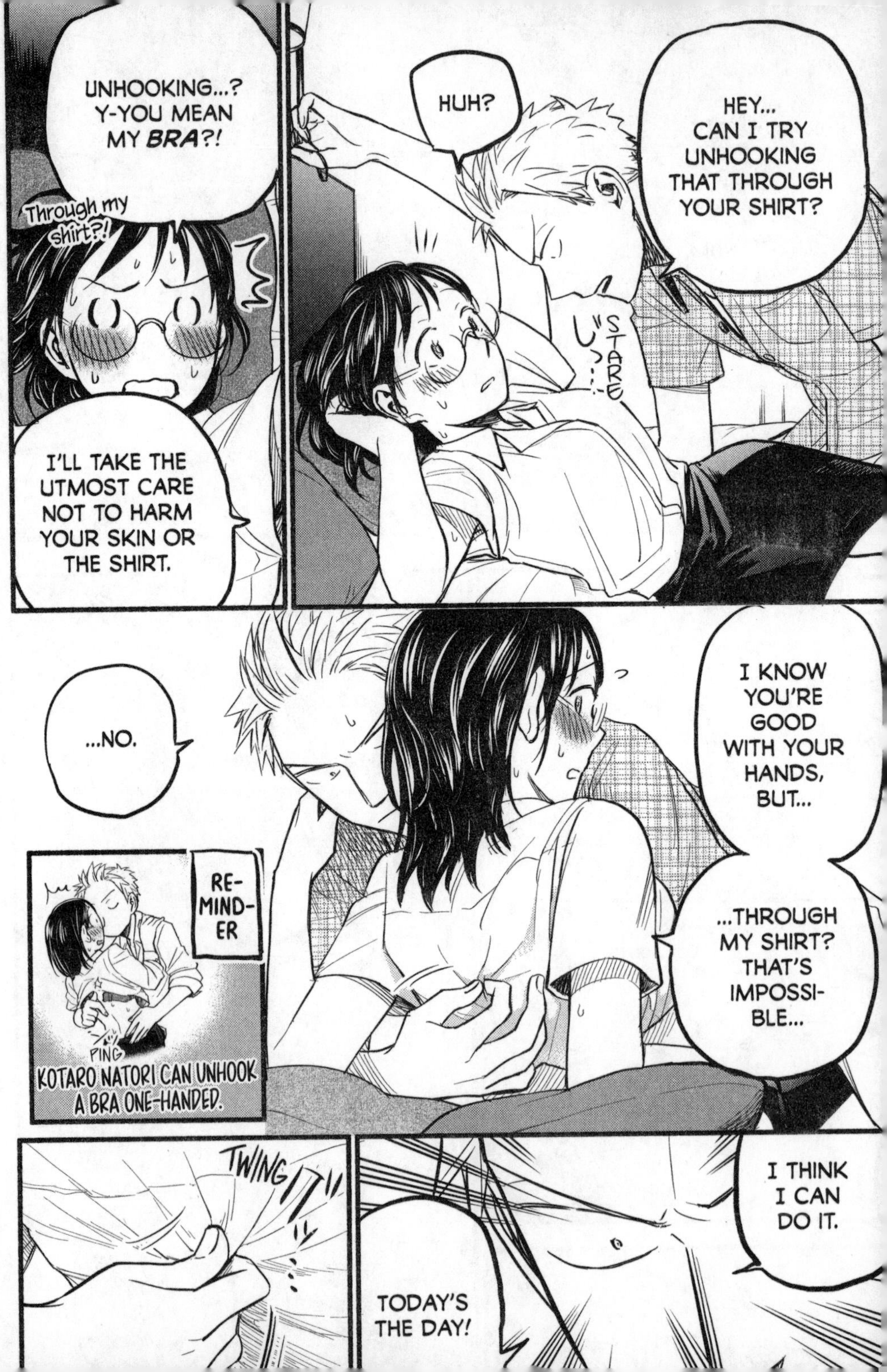

HEY... CAN I TRY UNHOOKING THAT THROUGH YOUR SHIRT?
HUH?
STARE
UNHOOKING...? Y-YOU MEAN MY *BRA*?!
Through my shirt?!
I'LL TAKE THE UTMOST CARE NOT TO HARM YOUR SKIN OR THE SHIRT.
I KNOW YOU'RE GOOD WITH YOUR HANDS, BUT...
...THROUGH MY SHIRT? THAT'S IMPOSSI-BLE...
...NO.
RE-MINDER
PING
KOTARO NATORI CAN UNHOOK A BRA ONE-HANDED.
I THINK I CAN DO IT.
TODAY'S THE DAY!
TWING!!

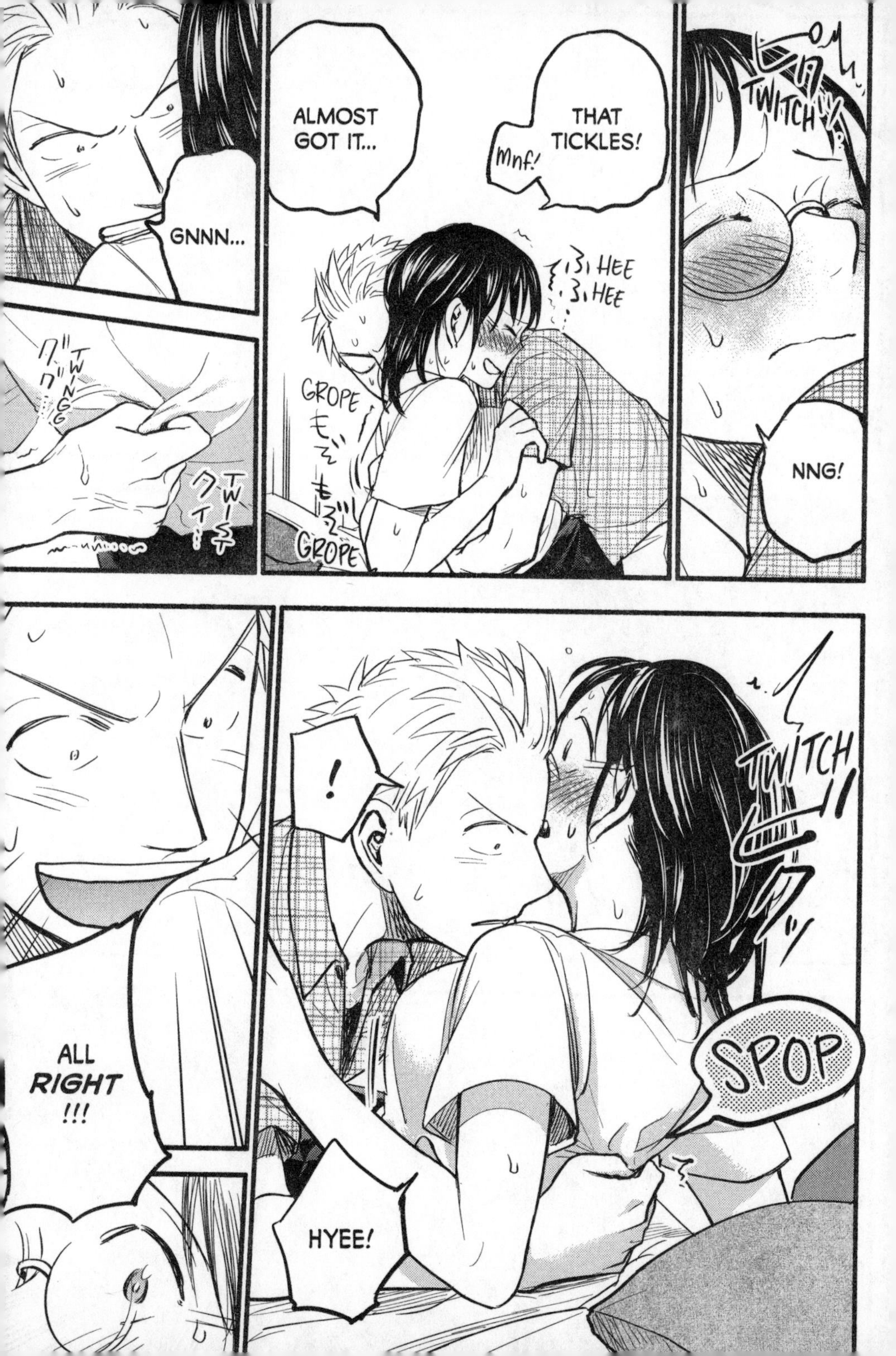
TWITCH
NNG!
THAT TICKLES!
Mnf!
ALMOST GOT IT...
HEE
HEE
GROPE
GROPE
GNNN...
TWINGG
TWIST
TWITCH
SPOP
!
HYEE!
ALL RIGHT!!!

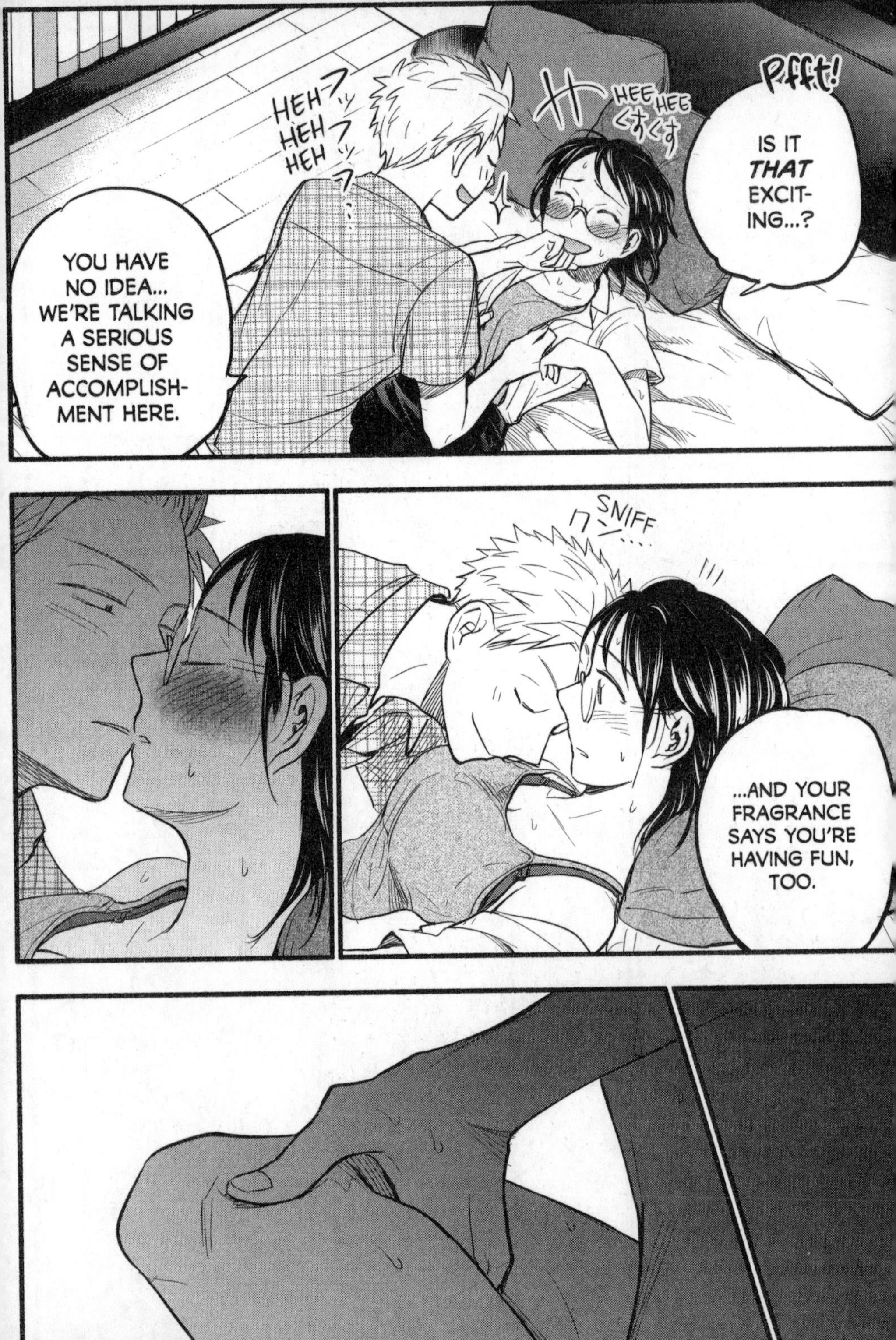
Pfft!
IS IT THAT EXCITING...?
HEE HEE
くすくす
HEH HEH HEH
フッフッフ
YOU HAVE NO IDEA... WE'RE TALKING A SERIOUS SENSE OF ACCOMPLISHMENT HERE.
SNIFF
クン...
...AND YOUR FRAGRANCE SAYS YOU'RE HAVING FUN, TOO.

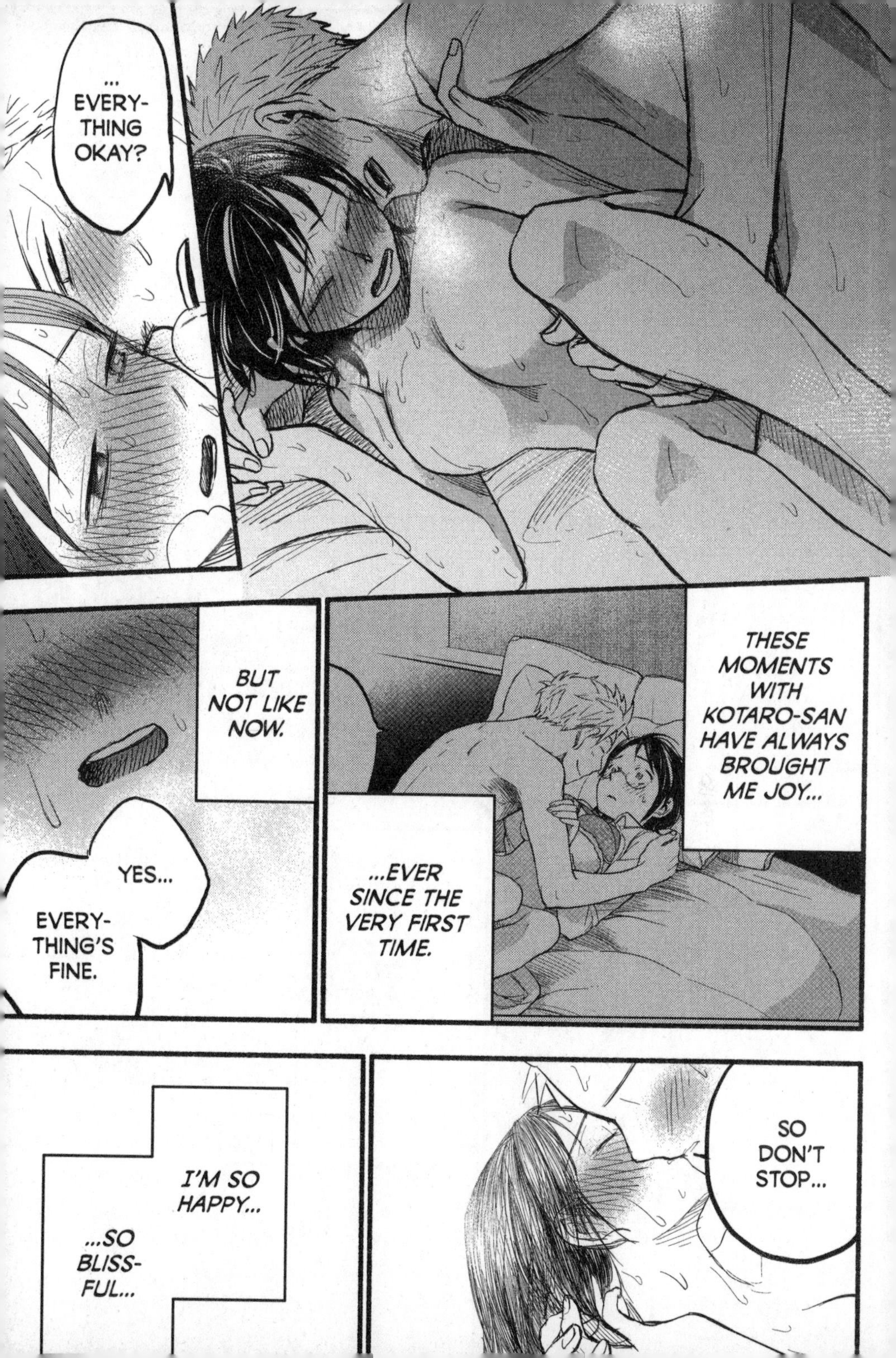
... EVERY-THING OKAY?
THESE MOMENTS WITH KOTARO-SAN HAVE ALWAYS BROUGHT ME JOY...
...EVER SINCE THE VERY FIRST TIME.
BUT NOT LIKE NOW.
YES... EVERY-THING'S FINE.
SO DON'T STOP...
I'M SO HAPPY...
...SO BLISS-FUL...

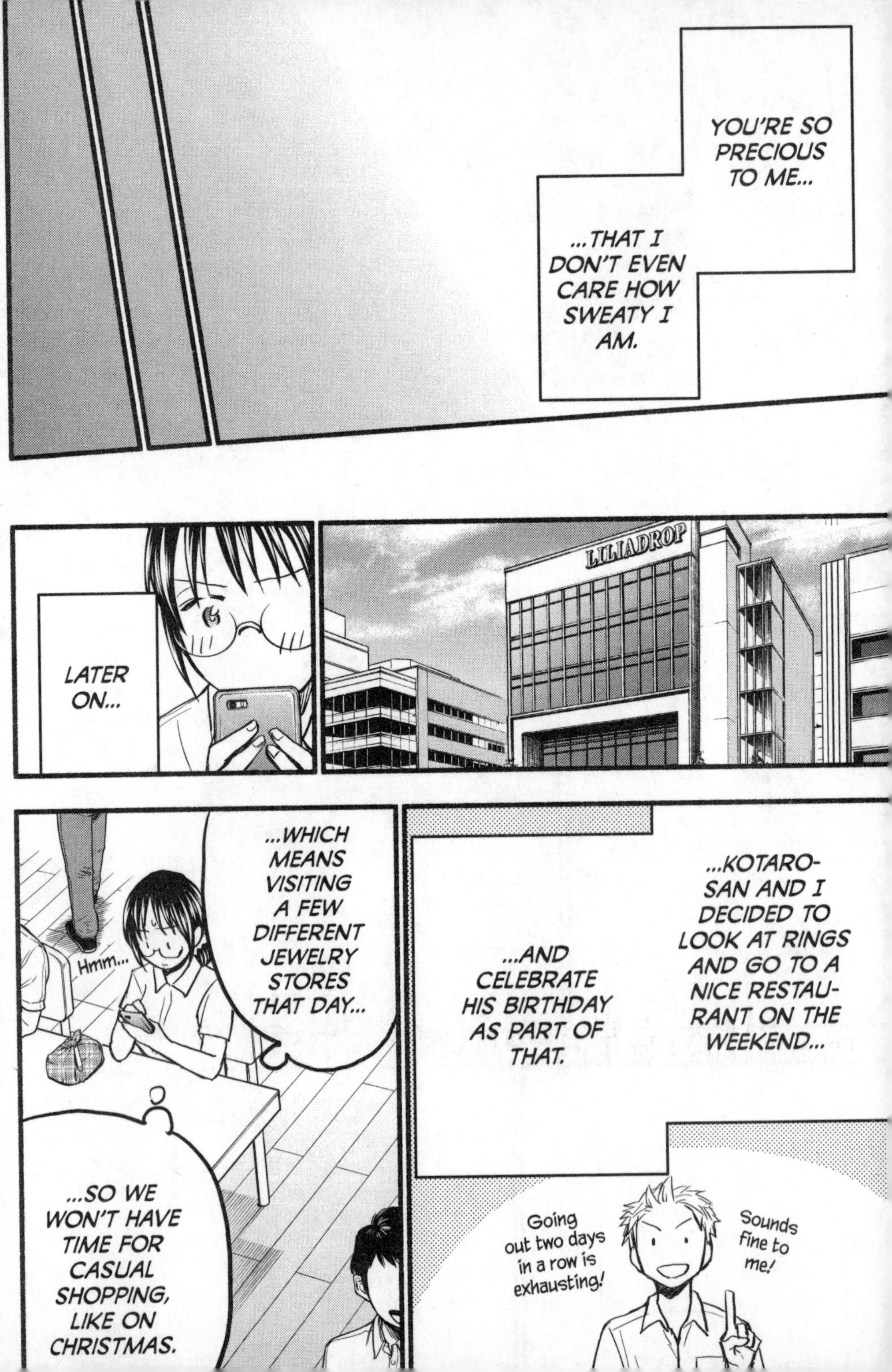

YOU'RE SO PRECIOUS TO ME...
...THAT I DON'T EVEN CARE HOW SWEATY I AM.
LILIADROP
LATER ON...
...KOTARO-SAN AND I DECIDED TO LOOK AT RINGS AND GO TO A NICE RESTAURANT ON THE WEEKEND...
...AND CELEBRATE HIS BIRTHDAY AS PART OF THAT.
Sounds fine to me!
Going out two days in a row is exhausting!
...WHICH MEANS VISITING A FEW DIFFERENT JEWELRY STORES THAT DAY...
Hmm...
...SO WE WON'T HAVE TIME FOR CASUAL SHOPPING, LIKE ON CHRISTMAS.

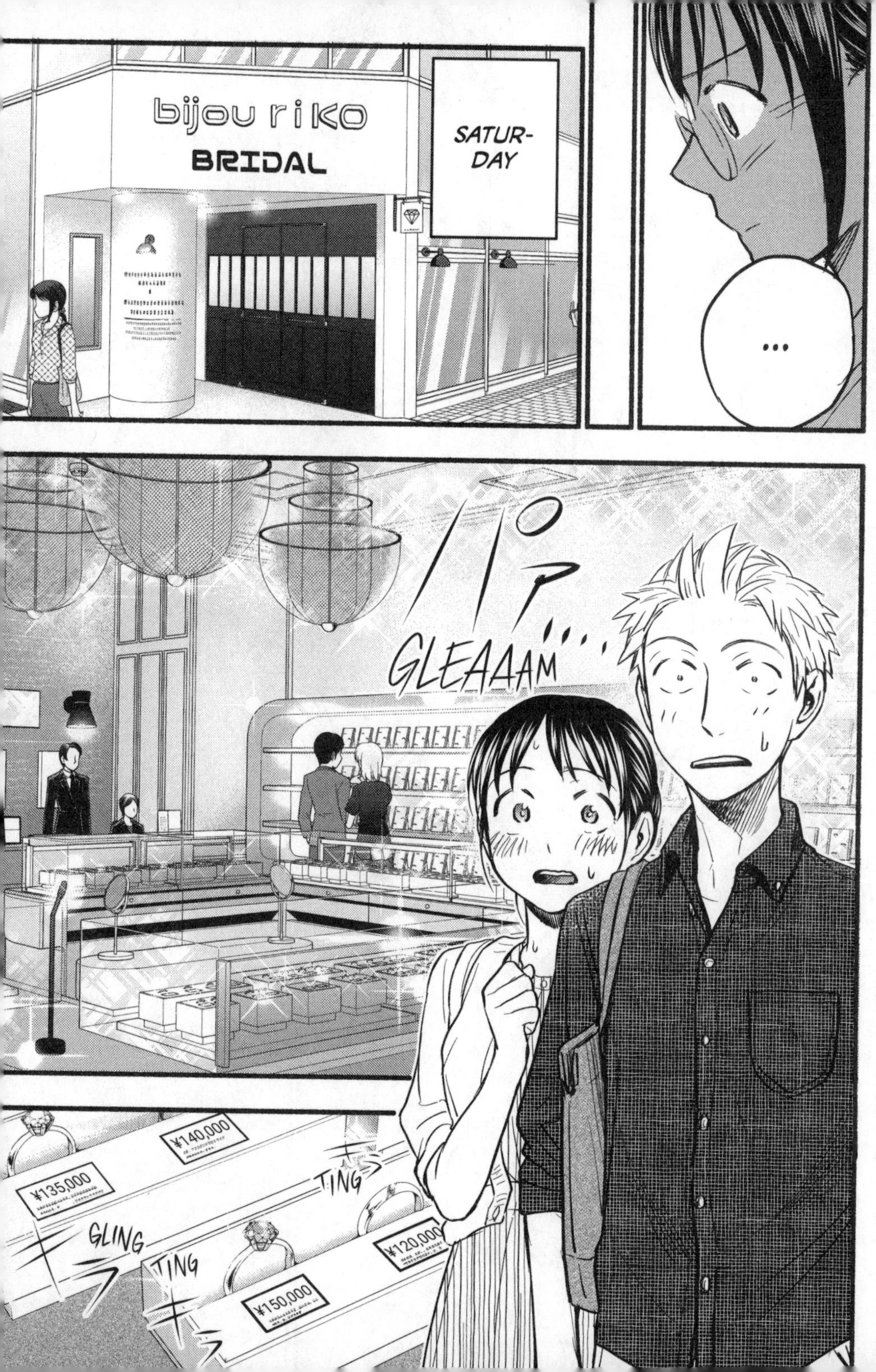
...
SATUR-
DAY
bijou riko
BRIDAL
パ...
GLEAAAM
¥140,000
TING
¥135,000
¥120,000
GLING
TING
¥150,000

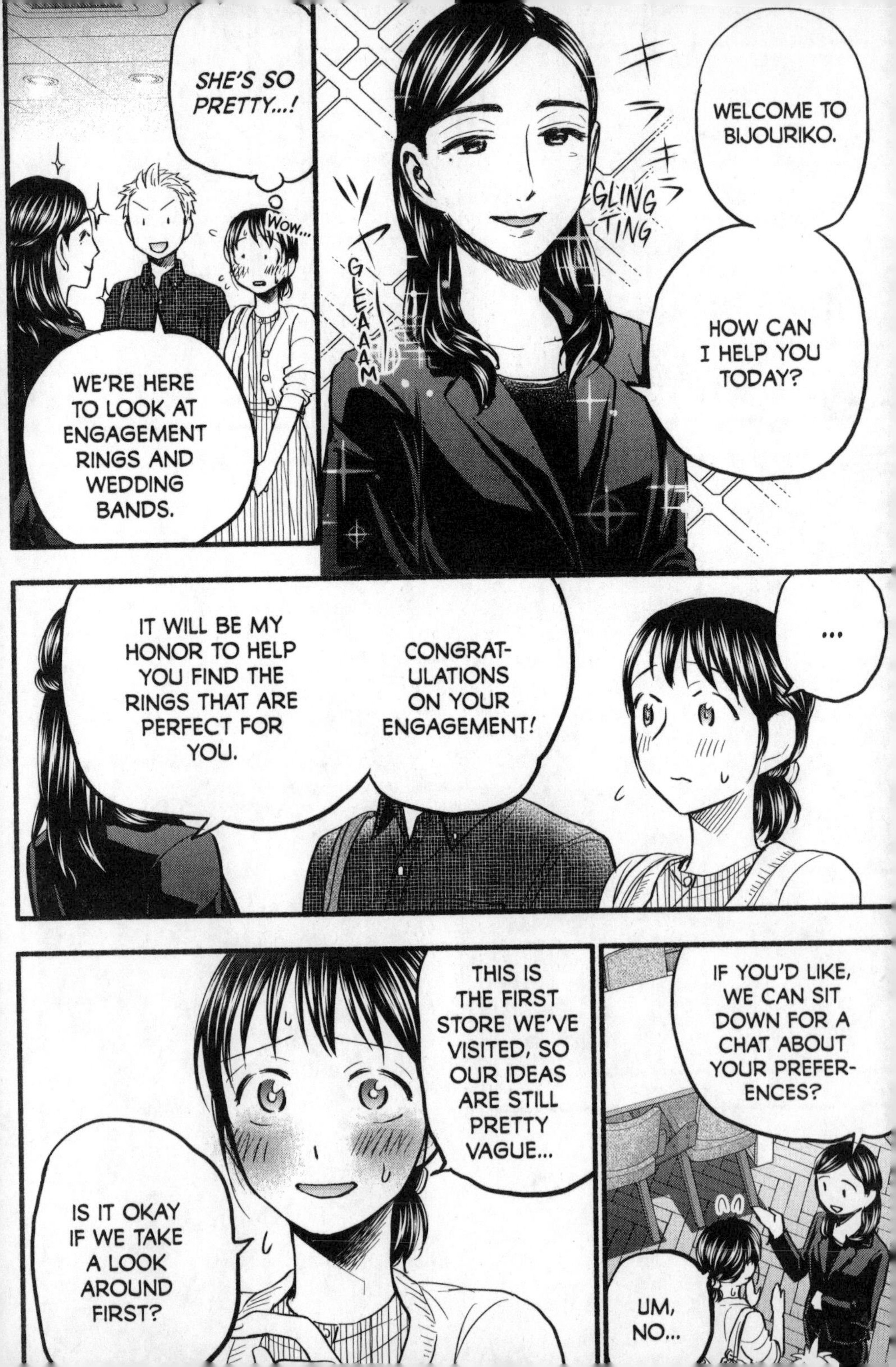
WELCOME TO BIJOURIKO.
GLING TING
GLEAAAM
HOW CAN I HELP YOU TODAY?
SHE'S SO PRETTY...!
WOW...
WE'RE HERE TO LOOK AT ENGAGEMENT RINGS AND WEDDING BANDS.
...
CONGRAT-ULATIONS ON YOUR ENGAGEMENT!
IT WILL BE MY HONOR TO HELP YOU FIND THE RINGS THAT ARE PERFECT FOR YOU.
IF YOU'D LIKE, WE CAN SIT DOWN FOR A CHAT ABOUT YOUR PREFER-ENCES?
UM, NO...
THIS IS THE FIRST STORE WE'VE VISITED, SO OUR IDEAS ARE STILL PRETTY VAGUE...
IS IT OKAY IF WE TAKE A LOOK AROUND FIRST?

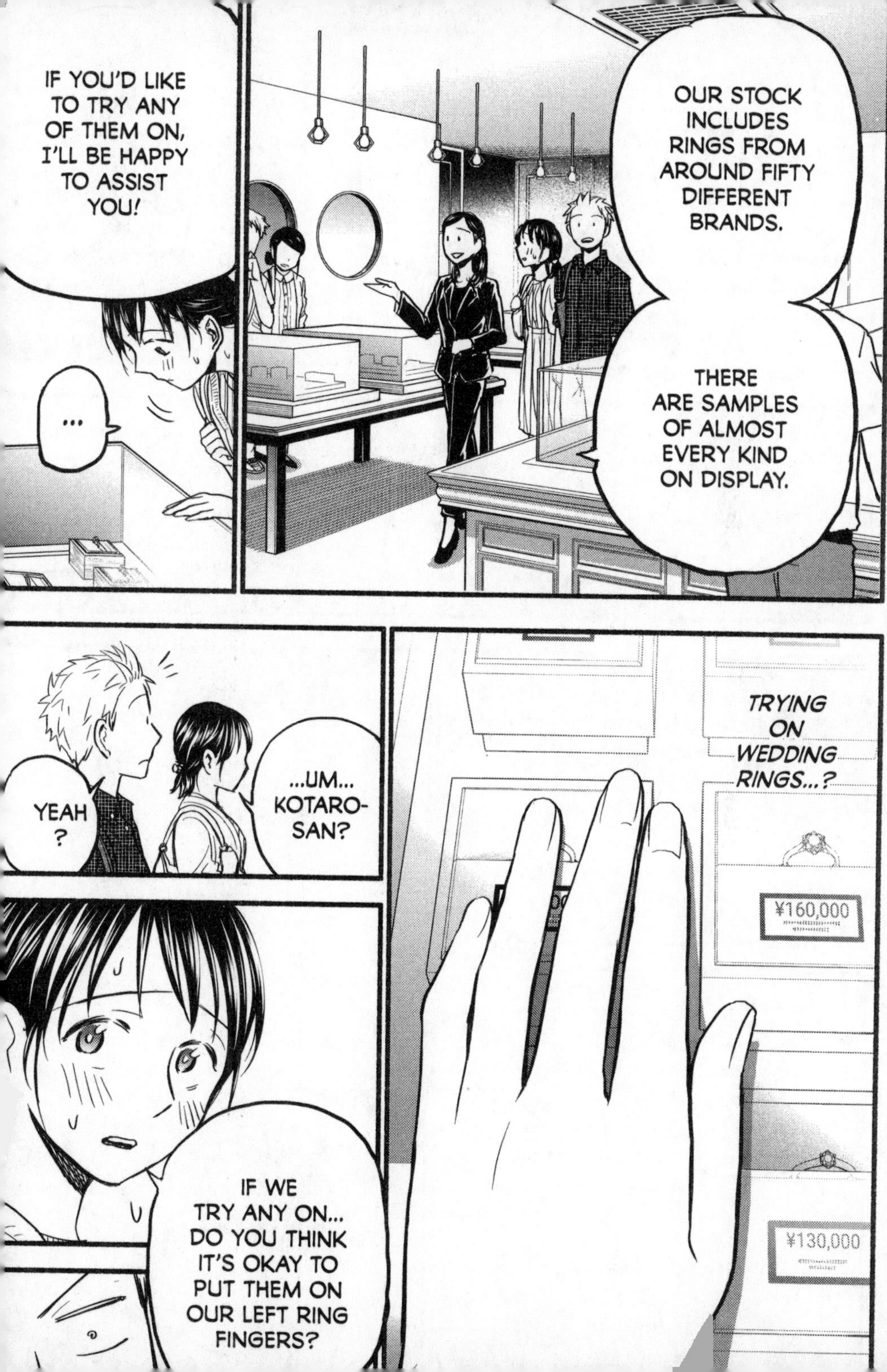
OUR STOCK INCLUDES RINGS FROM AROUND FIFTY DIFFERENT BRANDS.
THERE ARE SAMPLES OF ALMOST EVERY KIND ON DISPLAY.
IF YOU'D LIKE TO TRY ANY OF THEM ON, I'LL BE HAPPY TO ASSIST YOU!
...
TRYING ON WEDDING RINGS...?
¥160,000
¥130,000
...UM... KOTARO-SAN?
YEAH?
IF WE TRY ANY ON... DO YOU THINK IT'S OKAY TO PUT THEM ON OUR LEFT RING FINGERS?

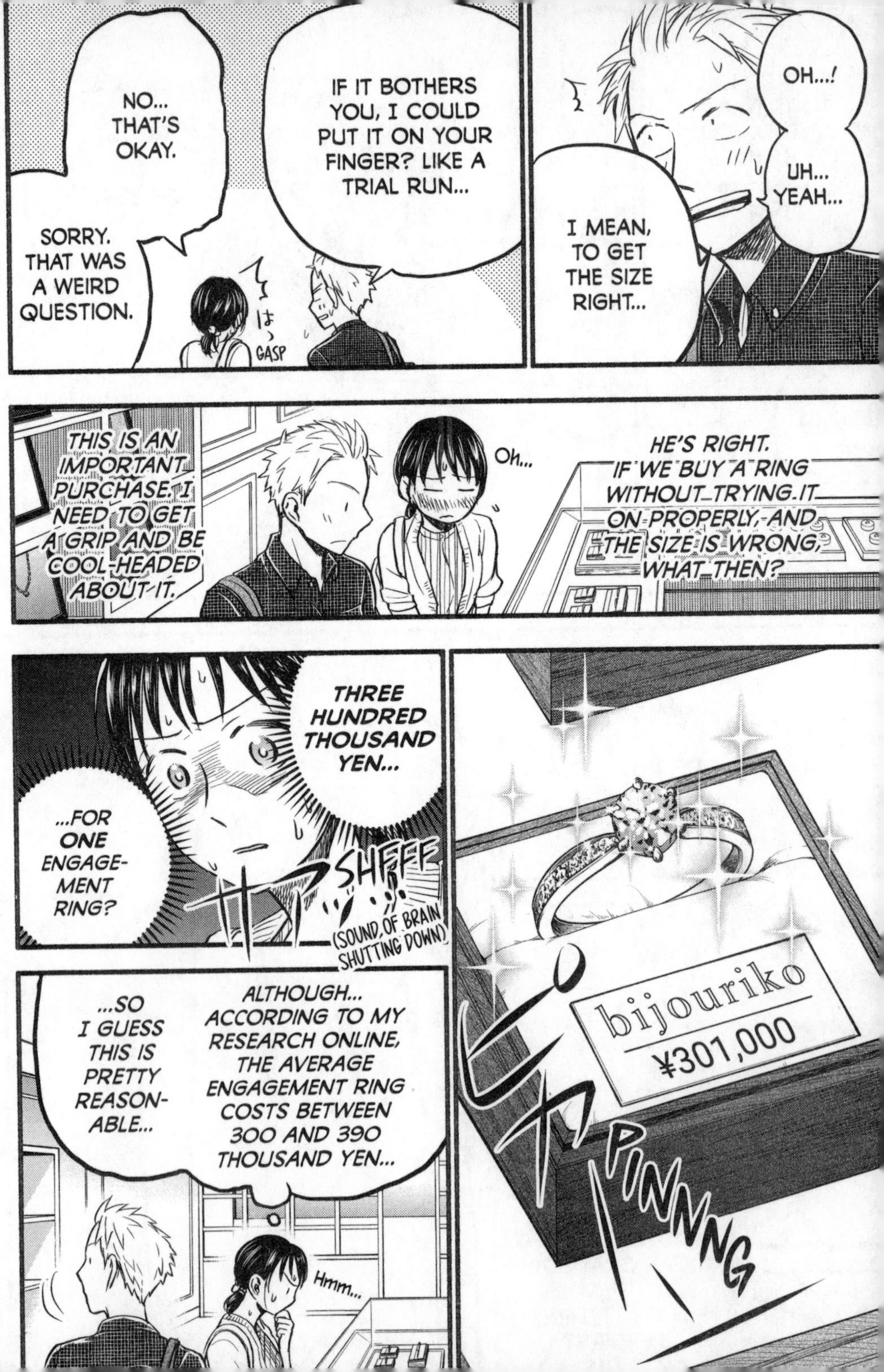
OH...!
UH... YEAH...
I MEAN, TO GET THE SIZE RIGHT...
IF IT BOTHERS YOU, I COULD PUT IT ON YOUR FINGER? LIKE A TRIAL RUN...
GASP
NO... THAT'S OKAY.
SORRY. THAT WAS A WEIRD QUESTION.
HE'S RIGHT. IF WE BUY A RING WITHOUT TRYING IT ON PROPERLY, AND THE SIZE IS WRONG, WHAT THEN?
Oh...
THIS IS AN IMPORTANT PURCHASE. I NEED TO GET A GRIP AND BE COOL-HEADED ABOUT IT.
bijouriko
¥301,000
PINNNG
THREE HUNDRED THOUSAND YEN...
...FOR ONE ENGAGEMENT RING?
SHFFF
(SOUND OF BRAIN SHUTTING DOWN)
ALTHOUGH... ACCORDING TO MY RESEARCH ONLINE, THE AVERAGE ENGAGEMENT RING COSTS BETWEEN 300 AND 390 THOUSAND YEN...
...SO I GUESS THIS IS PRETTY REASONABLE...
Hmm...

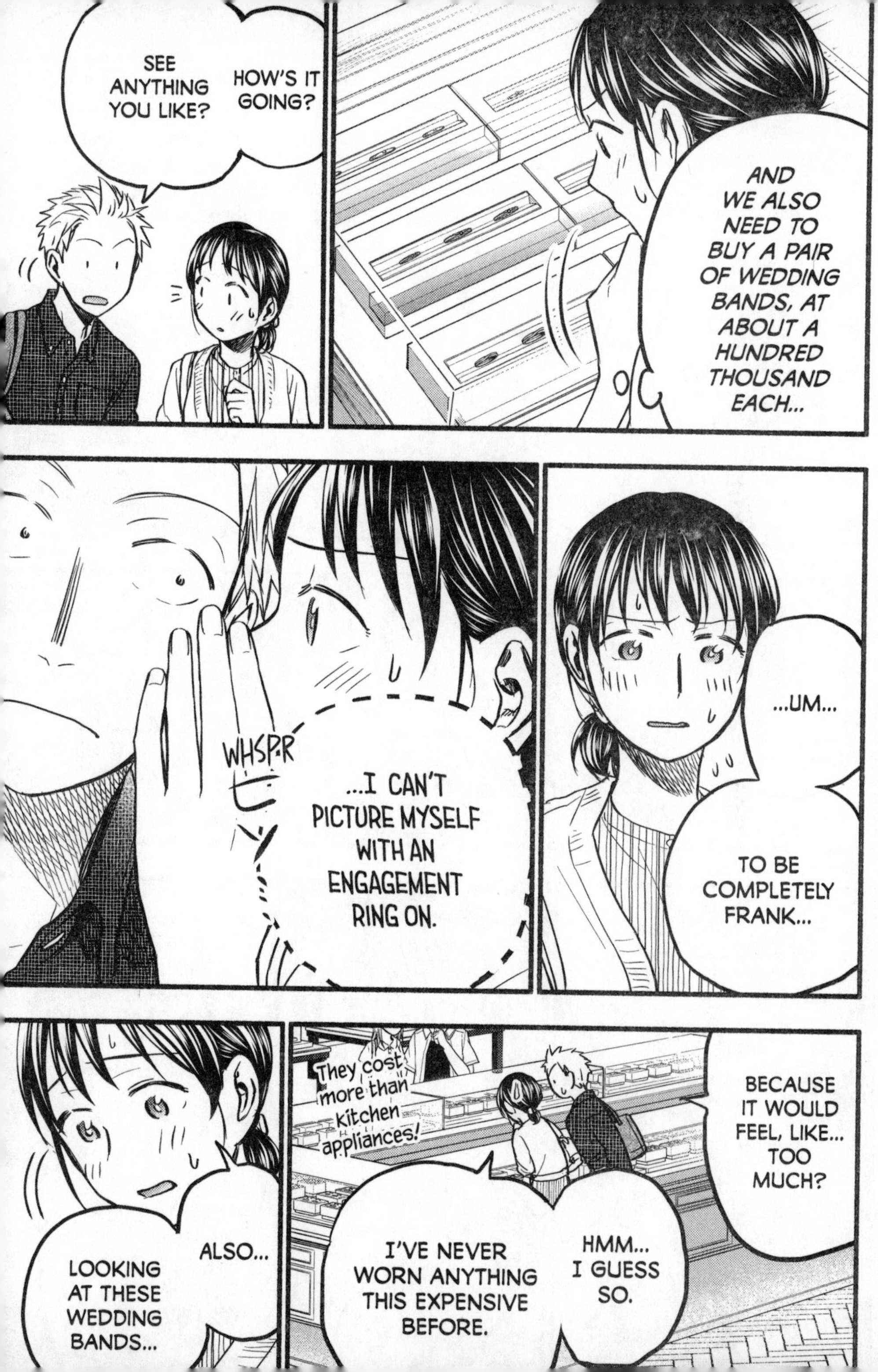
AND WE ALSO NEED TO BUY A PAIR OF WEDDING BANDS, AT ABOUT A HUNDRED THOUSAND EACH...
HOW'S IT GOING?
SEE ANYTHING YOU LIKE?
...UM...
TO BE COMPLETELY FRANK...
WHSP:R
...I CAN'T PICTURE MYSELF WITH AN ENGAGEMENT RING ON.
BECAUSE IT WOULD FEEL, LIKE... TOO MUCH?
They cost more than kitchen appliances!
HMM... I GUESS SO.
I'VE NEVER WORN ANYTHING THIS EXPENSIVE BEFORE.
ALSO...
LOOKING AT THESE WEDDING BANDS...

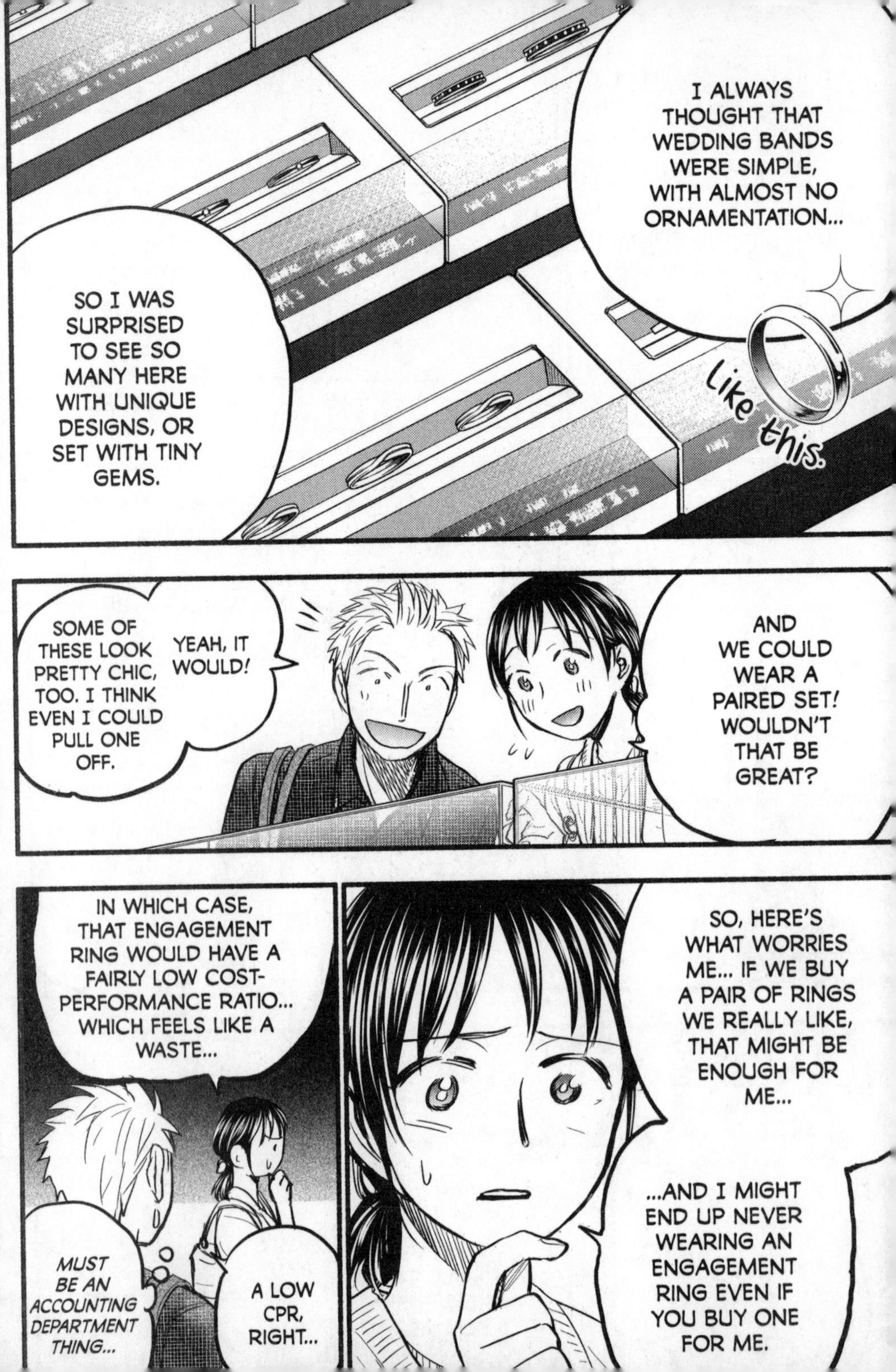
I ALWAYS THOUGHT THAT WEDDING BANDS WERE SIMPLE, WITH ALMOST NO ORNAMENTATION...
Like this.
SO I WAS SURPRISED TO SEE SO MANY HERE WITH UNIQUE DESIGNS, OR SET WITH TINY GEMS.
AND WE COULD WEAR A PAIRED SET! WOULDN'T THAT BE GREAT?
YEAH, IT WOULD!
SOME OF THESE LOOK PRETTY CHIC, TOO. I THINK EVEN I COULD PULL ONE OFF.
SO, HERE'S WHAT WORRIES ME... IF WE BUY A PAIR OF RINGS WE REALLY LIKE, THAT MIGHT BE ENOUGH FOR ME...
...AND I MIGHT END UP NEVER WEARING AN ENGAGEMENT RING EVEN IF YOU BUY ONE FOR ME.
IN WHICH CASE, THAT ENGAGEMENT RING WOULD HAVE A FAIRLY LOW COST-PERFORMANCE RATIO... WHICH FEELS LIKE A WASTE...
A LOW CPR, RIGHT...
MUST BE AN ACCOUNTING DEPARTMENT THING...

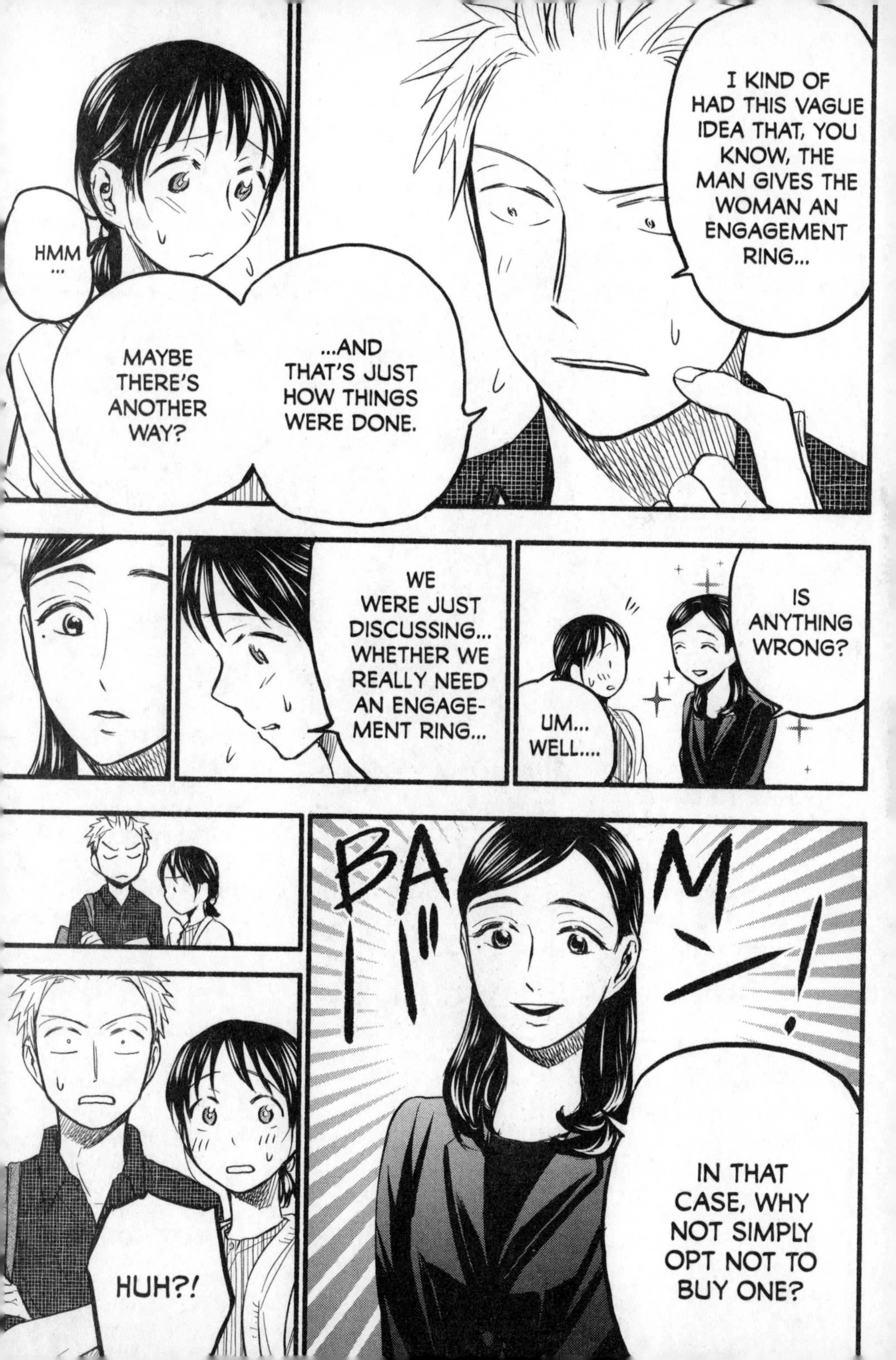
I KIND OF HAD THIS VAGUE IDEA THAT, YOU KNOW, THE MAN GIVES THE WOMAN AN ENGAGEMENT RING...
...AND THAT'S JUST HOW THINGS WERE DONE.
HMM...
MAYBE THERE'S ANOTHER WAY?
IS ANYTHING WRONG?
UM... WELL....
WE WERE JUST DISCUSSING... WHETHER WE REALLY NEED AN ENGAGE-MENT RING...
BAM!
IN THAT CASE, WHY NOT SIMPLY OPT NOT TO BUY ONE?
HUH?!

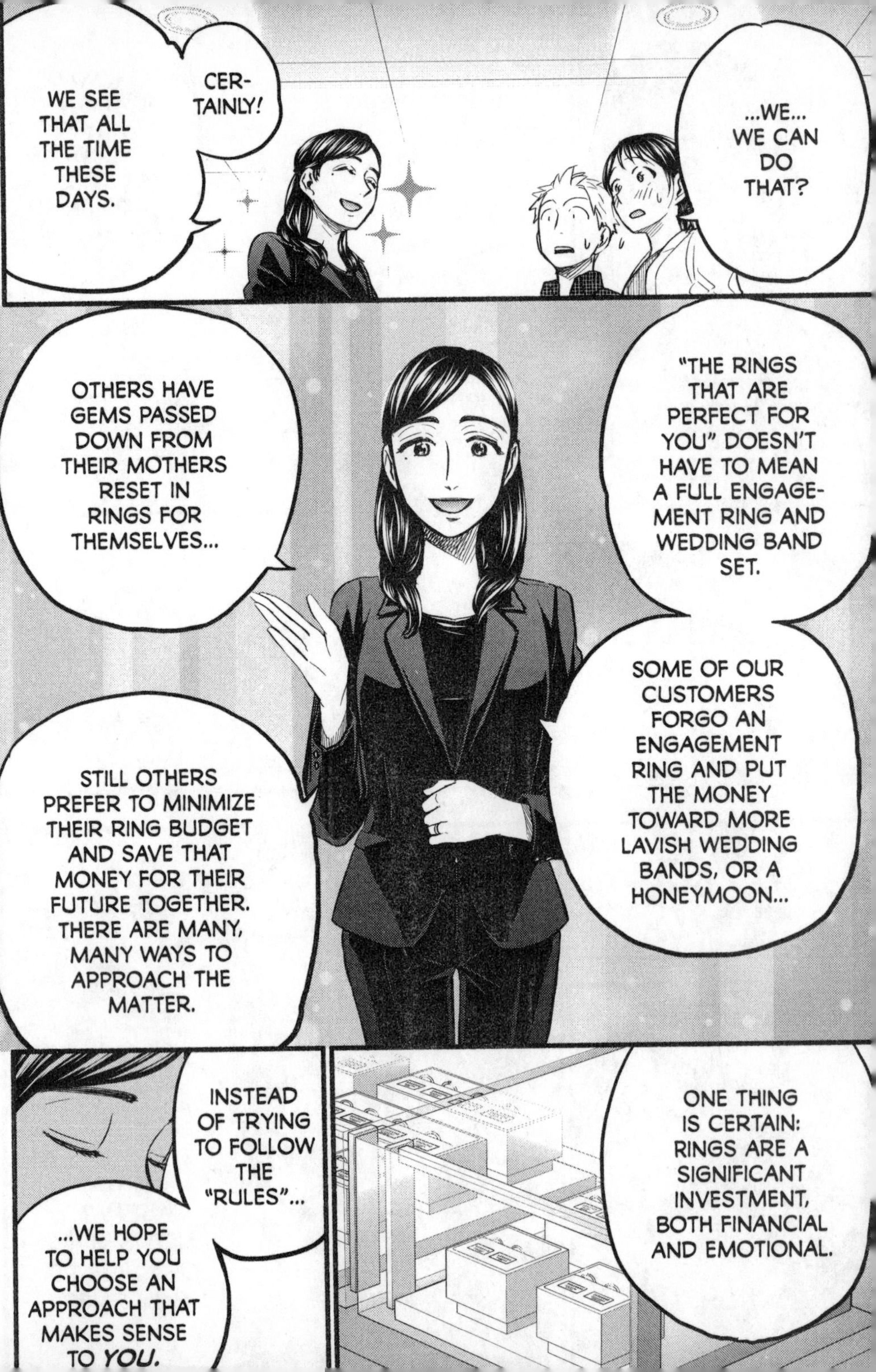
...WE... WE CAN DO THAT?
CER-TAINLY!
WE SEE THAT ALL THE TIME THESE DAYS.
"THE RINGS THAT ARE PERFECT FOR YOU" DOESN'T HAVE TO MEAN A FULL ENGAGE-MENT RING AND WEDDING BAND SET.
SOME OF OUR CUSTOMERS FORGO AN ENGAGEMENT RING AND PUT THE MONEY TOWARD MORE LAVISH WEDDING BANDS, OR A HONEYMOON...
OTHERS HAVE GEMS PASSED DOWN FROM THEIR MOTHERS RESET IN RINGS FOR THEMSELVES...
STILL OTHERS PREFER TO MINIMIZE THEIR RING BUDGET AND SAVE THAT MONEY FOR THEIR FUTURE TOGETHER. THERE ARE MANY, MANY WAYS TO APPROACH THE MATTER.
ONE THING IS CERTAIN: RINGS ARE A SIGNIFICANT INVESTMENT, BOTH FINANCIAL AND EMOTIONAL.
INSTEAD OF TRYING TO FOLLOW THE "RULES"...
...WE HOPE TO HELP YOU CHOOSE AN APPROACH THAT MAKES SENSE TO *YOU*.

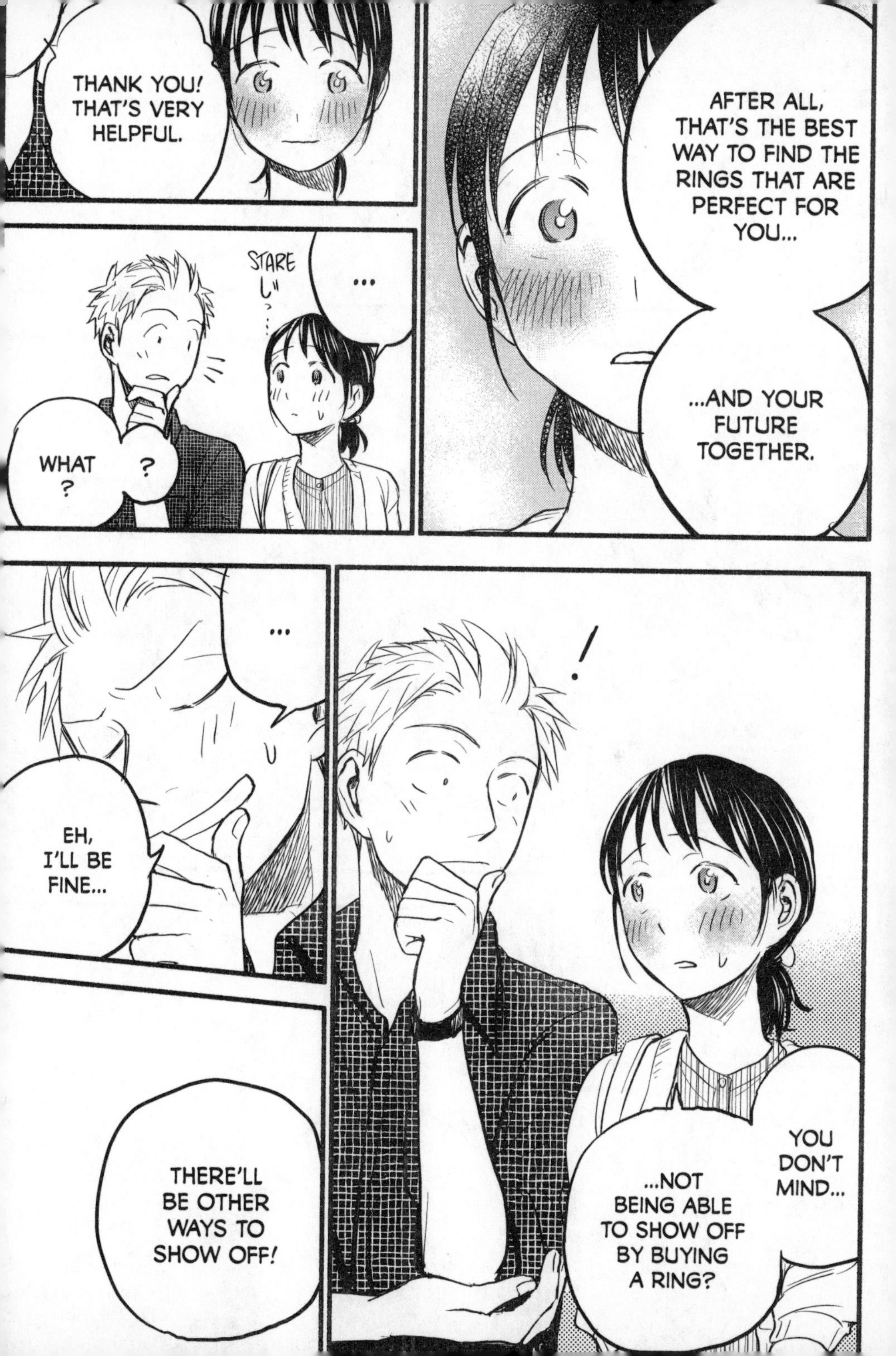
AFTER ALL, THAT'S THE BEST WAY TO FIND THE RINGS THAT ARE PERFECT FOR YOU...
...AND YOUR FUTURE TOGETHER.
THANK YOU! THAT'S VERY HELPFUL.
...
STARE
WHAT ? ?
!
YOU DON'T MIND...
...NOT BEING ABLE TO SHOW OFF BY BUYING A RING?
...
EH, I'LL BE FINE...
THERE'LL BE OTHER WAYS TO SHOW OFF!

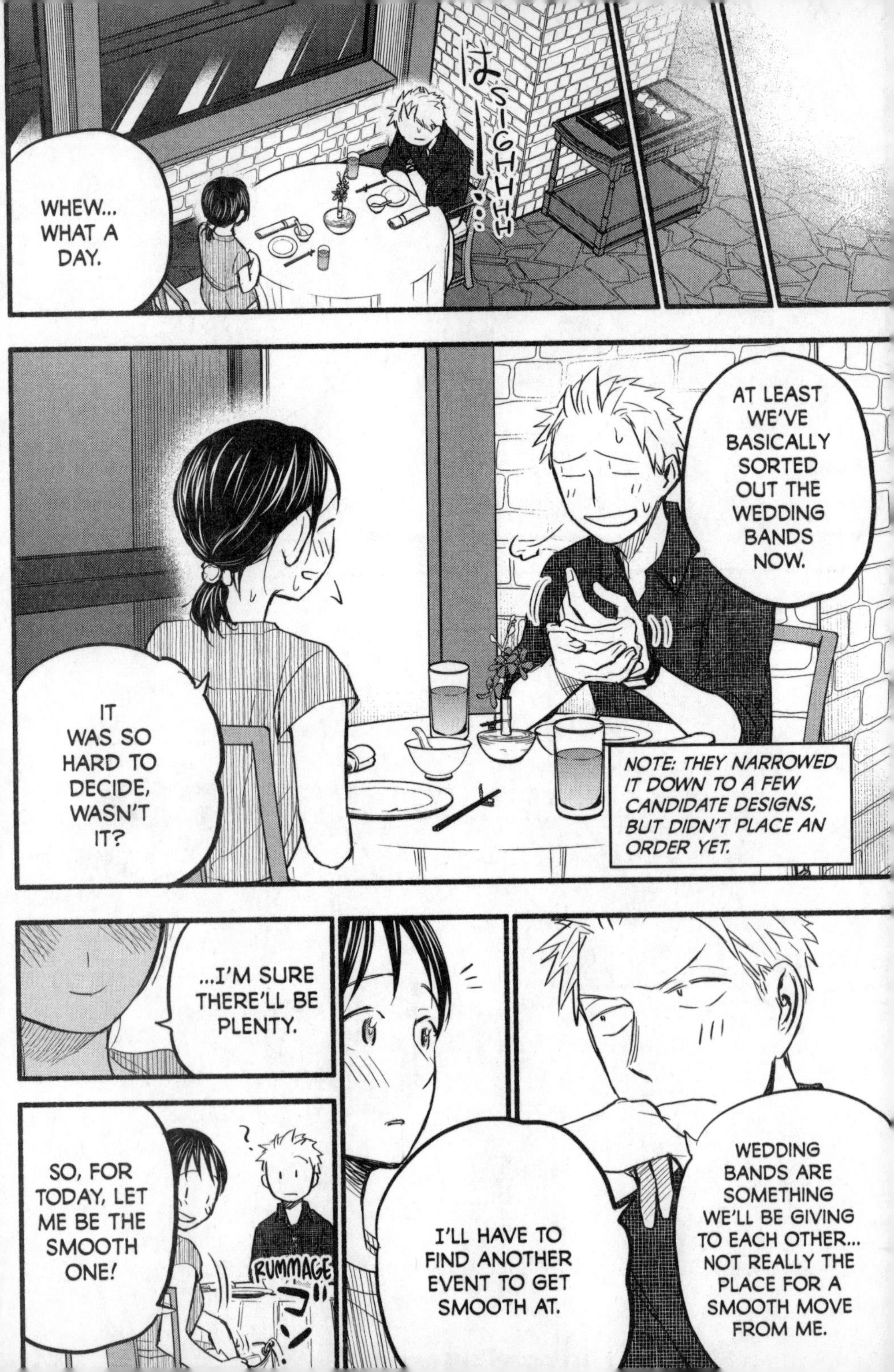
は
SIGHHHH...
WHEW... WHAT A DAY.
AT LEAST WE'VE BASICALLY SORTED OUT THE WEDDING BANDS NOW.
IT WAS SO HARD TO DECIDE, WASN'T IT?
NOTE: THEY NARROWED IT DOWN TO A FEW CANDIDATE DESIGNS, BUT DIDN'T PLACE AN ORDER YET.
WEDDING BANDS ARE SOMETHING WE'LL BE GIVING TO EACH OTHER... NOT REALLY THE PLACE FOR A SMOOTH MOVE FROM ME.
I'LL HAVE TO FIND ANOTHER EVENT TO GET SMOOTH AT.
...I'M SURE THERE'LL BE PLENTY.
SO, FOR TODAY, LET ME BE THE SMOOTH ONE!
?
RUMMAGE
ゴソ

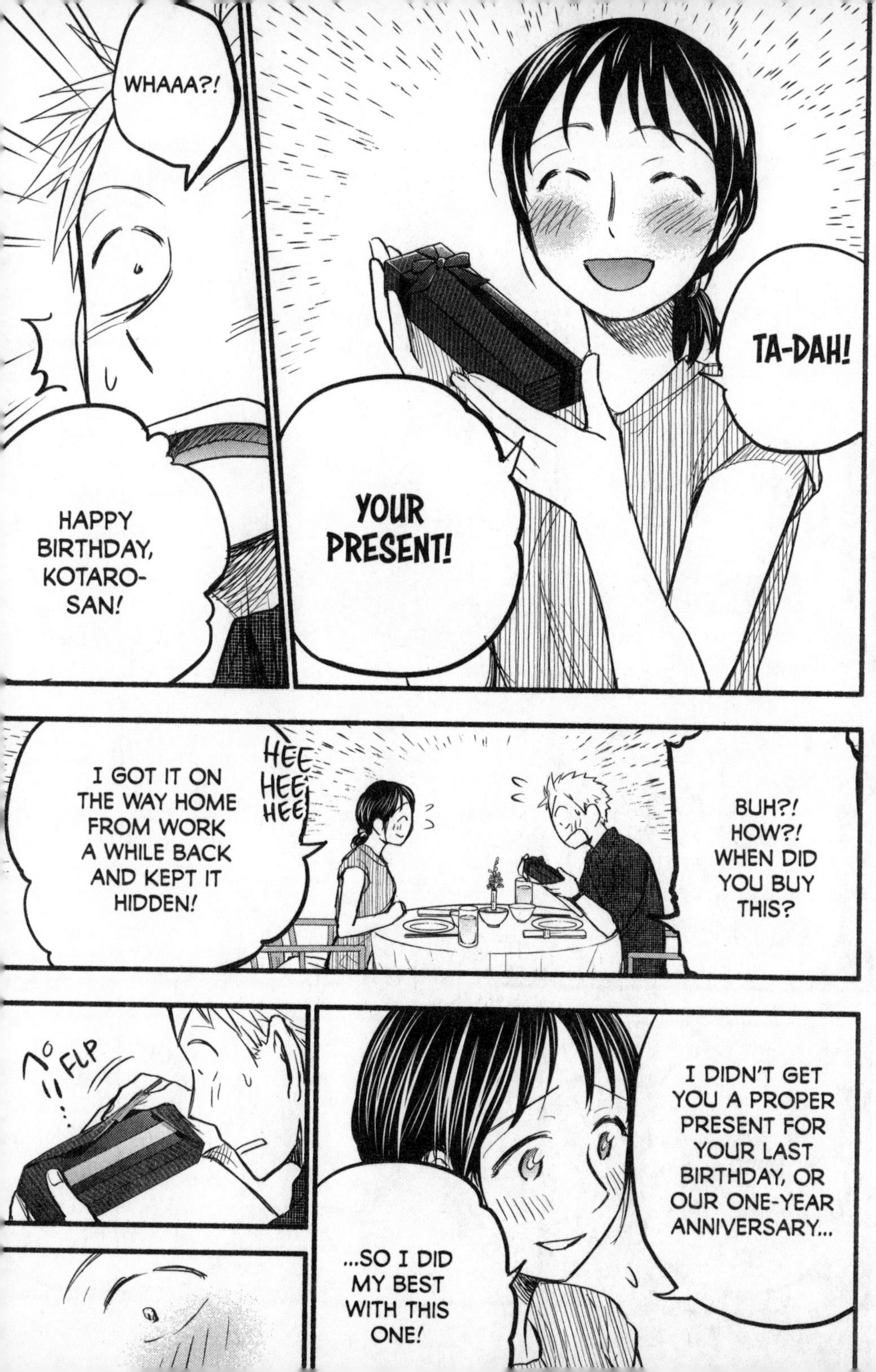
TA-DAH!
YOUR PRESENT!
WHAAA?!
HAPPY BIRTHDAY, KOTARO-SAN!
BUH?! HOW?! WHEN DID YOU BUY THIS?
HEE HEE HEE
I GOT IT ON THE WAY HOME FROM WORK A WHILE BACK AND KEPT IT HIDDEN!
I DIDN'T GET YOU A PROPER PRESENT FOR YOUR LAST BIRTHDAY, OR OUR ONE-YEAR ANNIVERSARY...
...SO I DID MY BEST WITH THIS ONE!
FLP

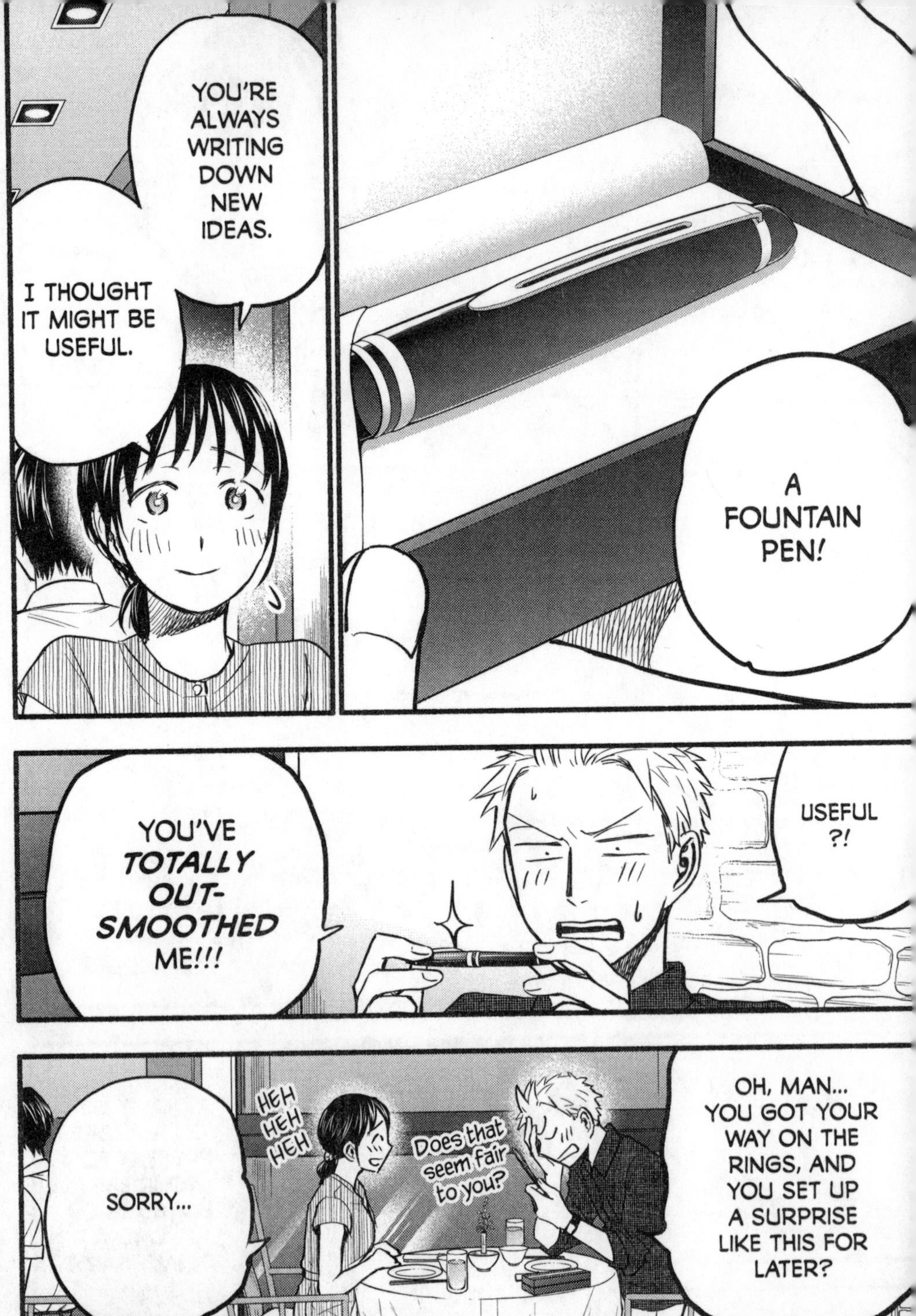
A FOUNTAIN PEN!
YOU'RE ALWAYS WRITING DOWN NEW IDEAS.
I THOUGHT IT MIGHT BE USEFUL.
USEFUL ?!
YOU'VE *TOTALLY OUT-SMOOTHED* ME!!!
OH, MAN... YOU GOT YOUR WAY ON THE RINGS, AND YOU SET UP A SURPRISE LIKE THIS FOR LATER?
Does that seem fair to you?
HEH HEH HEH
SORRY...

Chapter 84 / The End

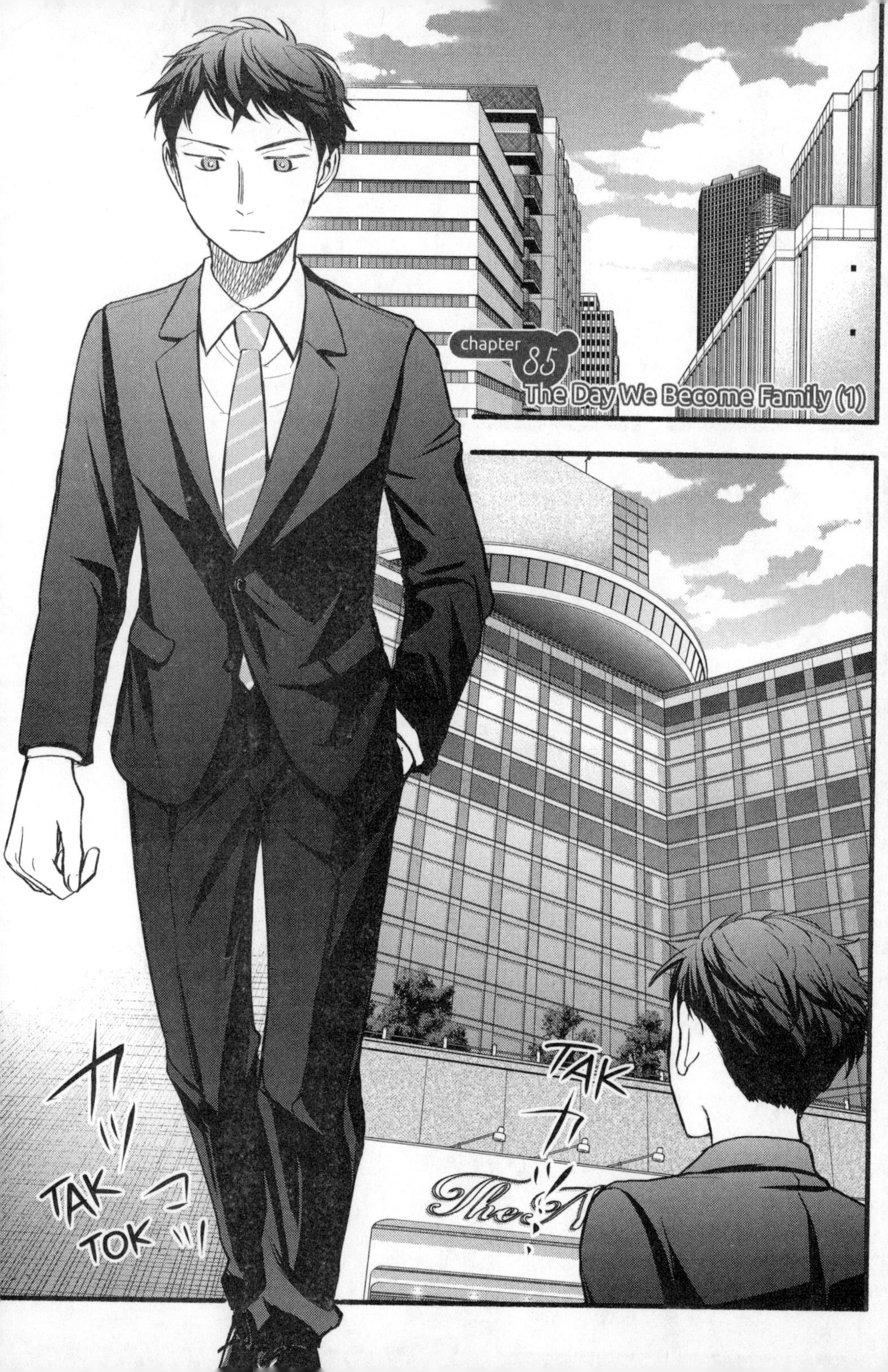
chapter 85
The Day We Become Family (1)
TAK
TAK
TOK

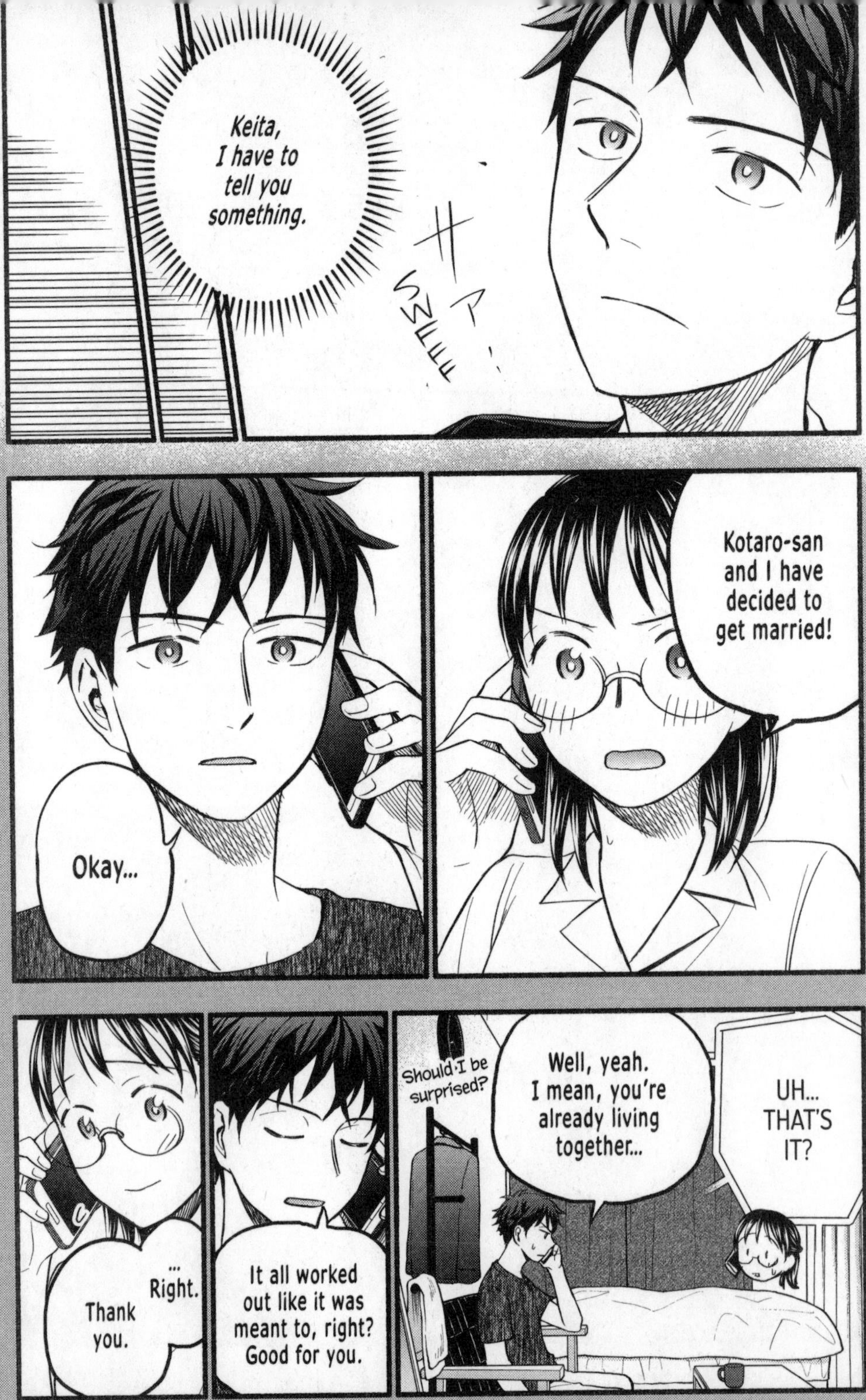
Keita, I have to tell you something.
SWEFF
Kotaro-san and I have decided to get married!
Okay...
UH... THAT'S IT?
Well, yeah. I mean, you're already living together...
Should I be surprised?
It all worked out like it was meant to, right? Good for you.
... Right.
Thank you.

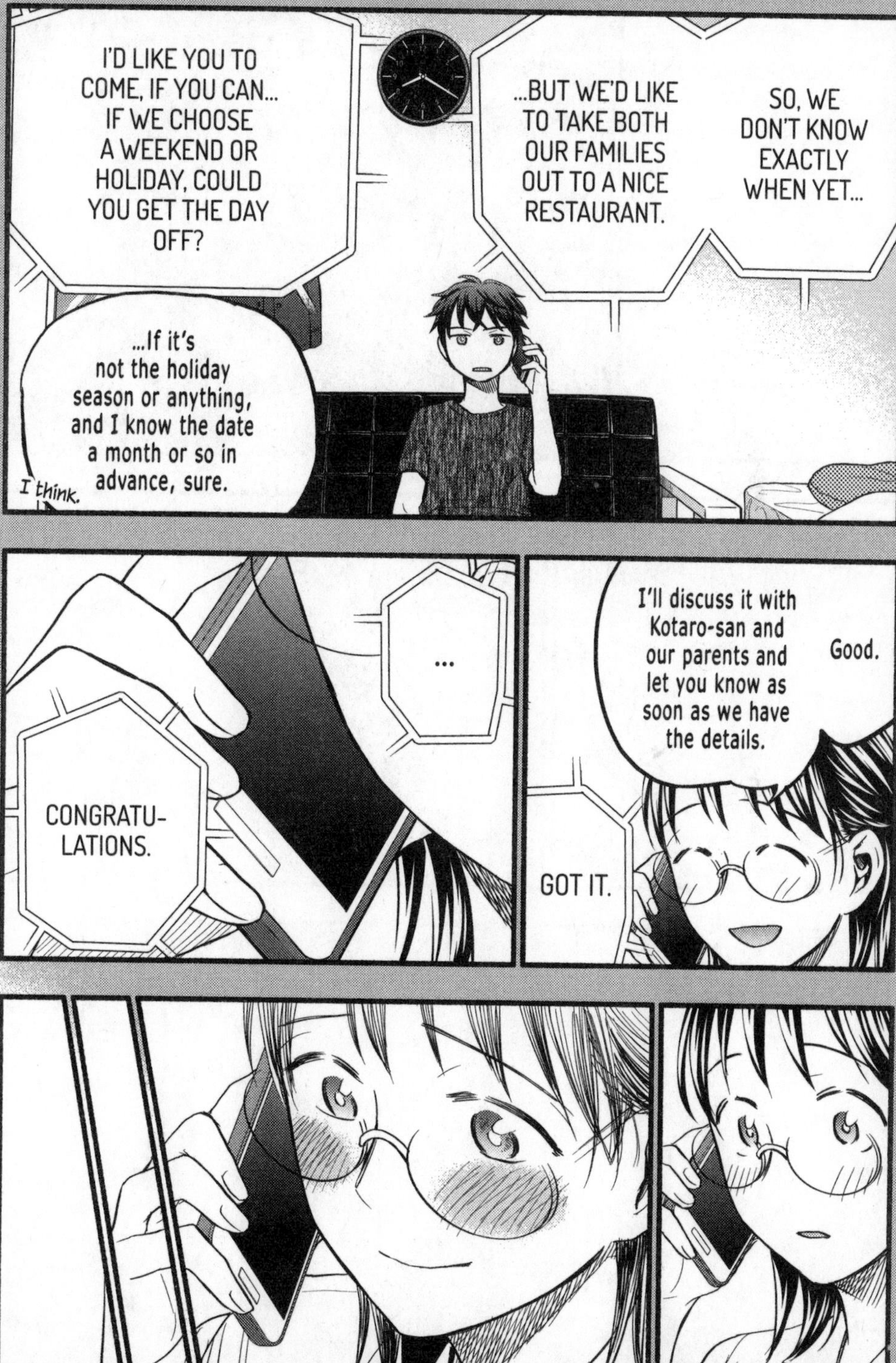
SO, WE DON'T KNOW EXACTLY WHEN YET...
...BUT WE'D LIKE TO TAKE BOTH OUR FAMILIES OUT TO A NICE RESTAURANT.
I'D LIKE YOU TO COME, IF YOU CAN... IF WE CHOOSE A WEEKEND OR HOLIDAY, COULD YOU GET THE DAY OFF?
...If it's not the holiday season or anything, and I know the date a month or so in advance, sure.
I think.
I'll discuss it with Kotaro-san and our parents and let you know as soon as we have the details.
Good.
GOT IT.
...
CONGRATU-LATIONS.

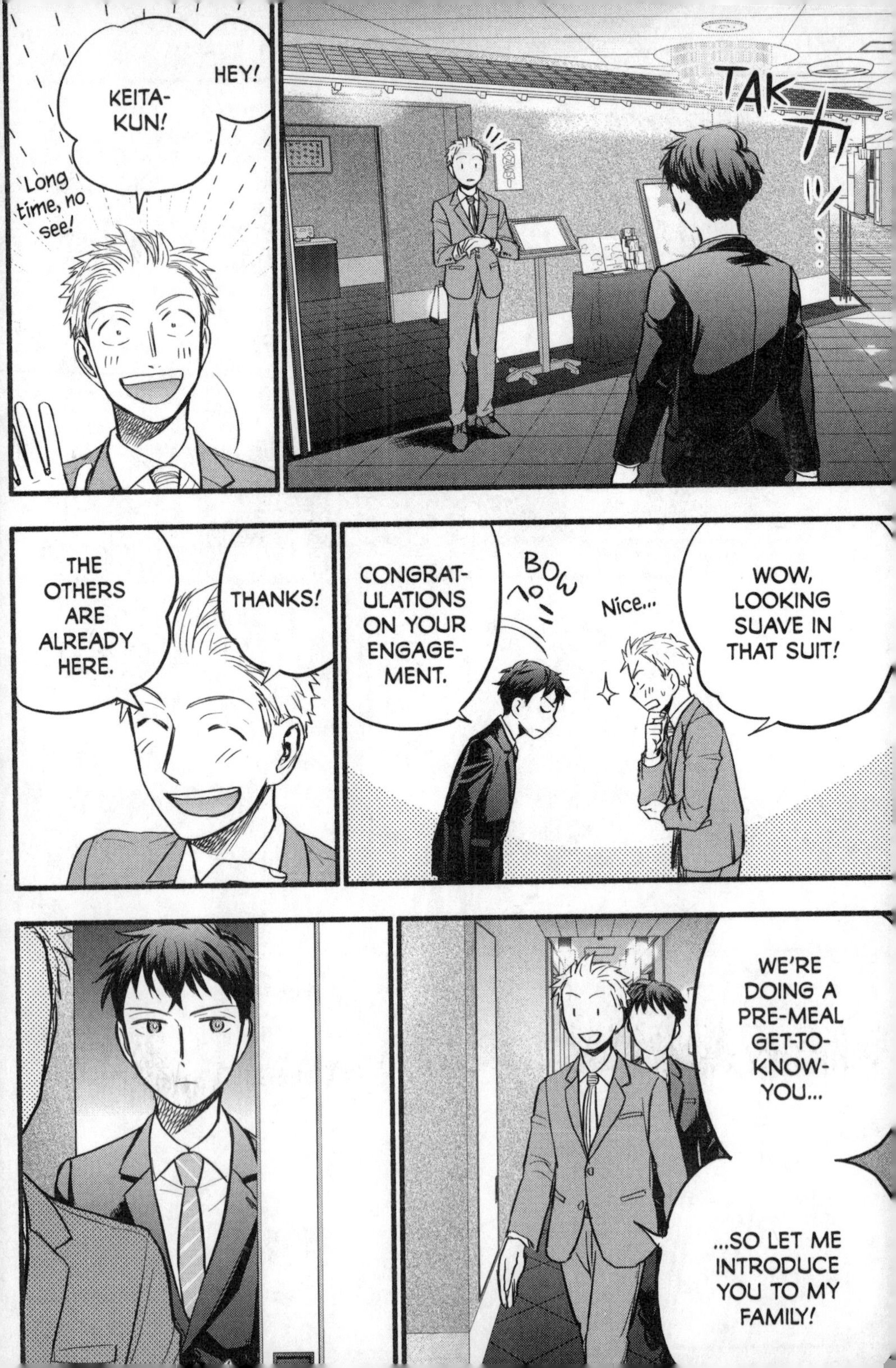
TAK
HEY! KEITA-KUN!
Long time, no see!
WOW, LOOKING SUAVE IN THAT SUIT!
Nice...
BOW
CONGRATULATIONS ON YOUR ENGAGEMENT.
THANKS!
THE OTHERS ARE ALREADY HERE.
WE'RE DOING A PRE-MEAL GET-TO-KNOW-YOU...
...SO LET ME INTRODUCE YOU TO MY FAMILY!

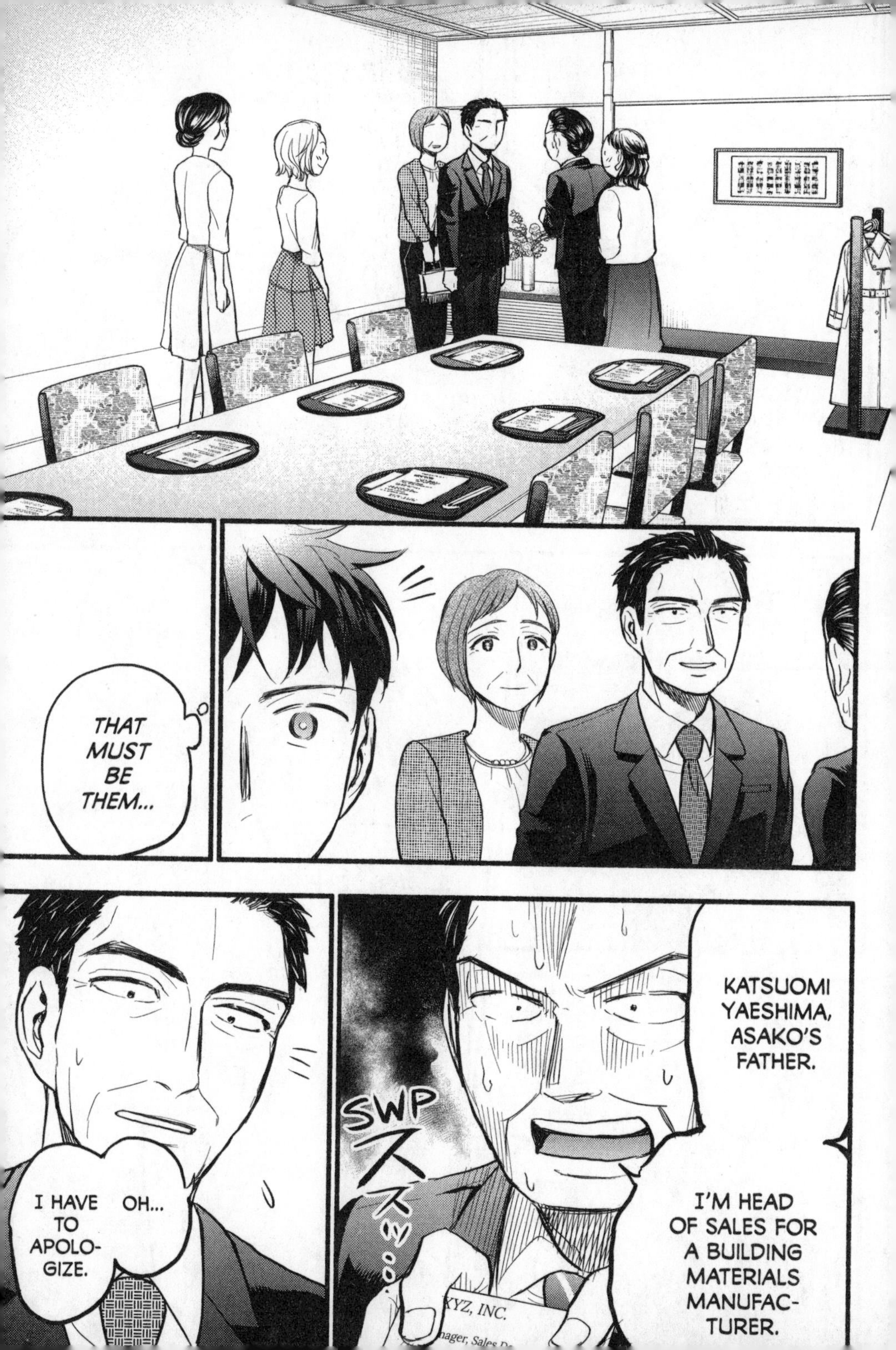
THAT MUST BE THEM...
KATSUOMI YAESHIMA, ASAKO'S FATHER.
I'M HEAD OF SALES FOR A BUILDING MATERIALS MANUFACTURER.
SWP
XYZ, INC.
OH...
I HAVE TO APOLOGIZE.

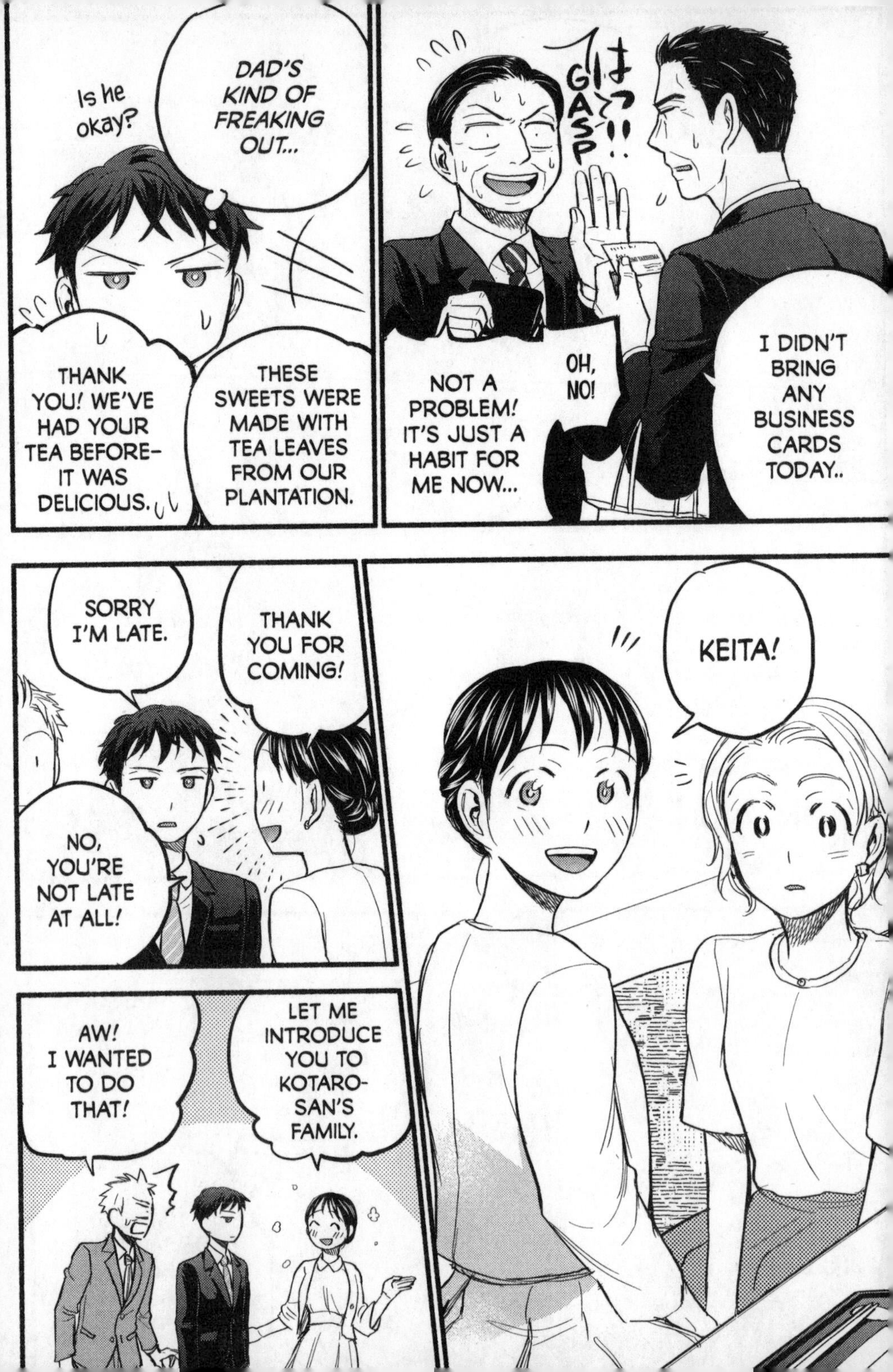

はっ!! GASP
I DIDN'T BRING ANY BUSINESS CARDS TODAY..
OH, NO!
NOT A PROBLEM! IT'S JUST A HABIT FOR ME NOW...
DAD'S KIND OF FREAKING OUT...
Is he okay?
THESE SWEETS WERE MADE WITH TEA LEAVES FROM OUR PLANTATION.
THANK YOU! WE'VE HAD YOUR TEA BEFORE– IT WAS DELICIOUS.
KEITA!
THANK YOU FOR COMING!
SORRY I'M LATE.
NO, YOU'RE NOT LATE AT ALL!
LET ME INTRODUCE YOU TO KOTARO-SAN'S FAMILY.
AW! I WANTED TO DO THAT!

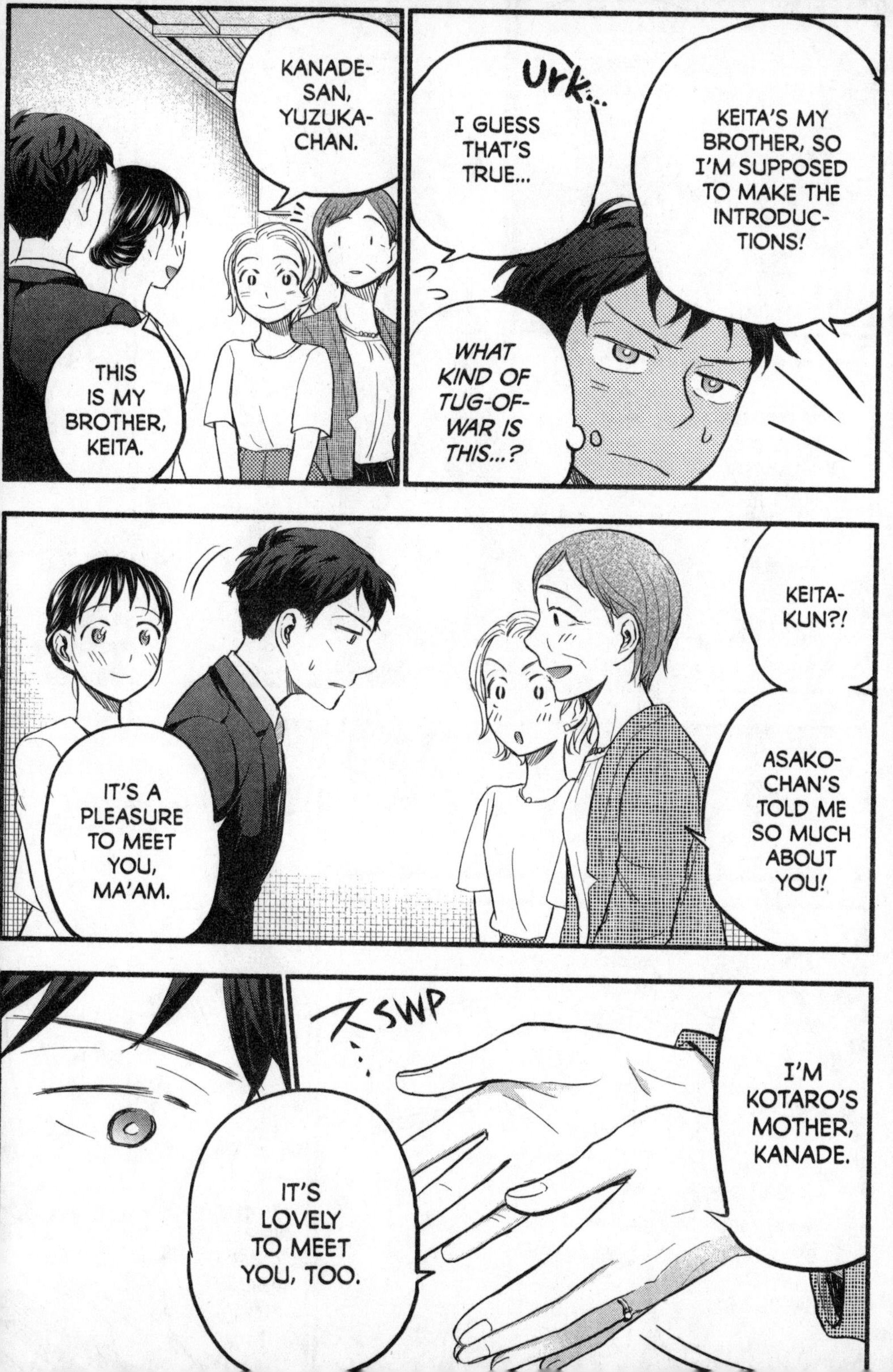
KEITA'S MY BROTHER, SO I'M SUPPOSED TO MAKE THE INTRODUCTIONS!
Urk...
I GUESS THAT'S TRUE...
WHAT KIND OF TUG-OF-WAR IS THIS...?
KANADE-SAN, YUZUKA-CHAN.
THIS IS MY BROTHER, KEITA.
KEITA-KUN?!
ASAKO-CHAN'S TOLD ME SO MUCH ABOUT YOU!
IT'S A PLEASURE TO MEET YOU, MA'AM.
I'M KOTARO'S MOTHER, KANADE.
SWP
IT'S LOVELY TO MEET YOU, TOO.

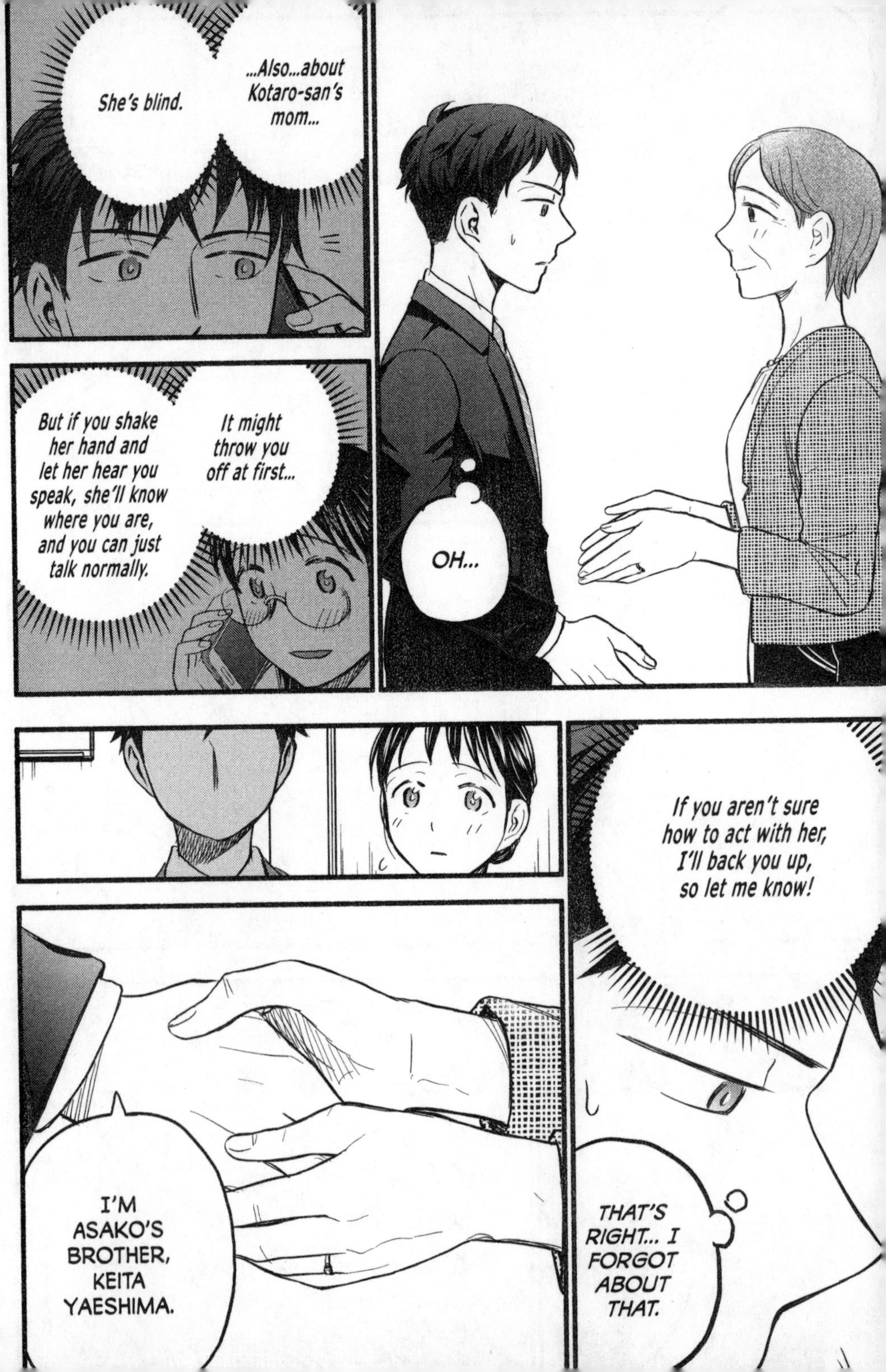
OH...
...Also...about Kotaro-san's mom...
She's blind.
It might throw you off at first...
But if you shake her hand and let her hear you speak, she'll know where you are, and you can just talk normally.
If you aren't sure how to act with her, I'll back you up, so let me know!
THAT'S RIGHT... I FORGOT ABOUT THAT.
I'M ASAKO'S BROTHER, KEITA YAESHIMA.

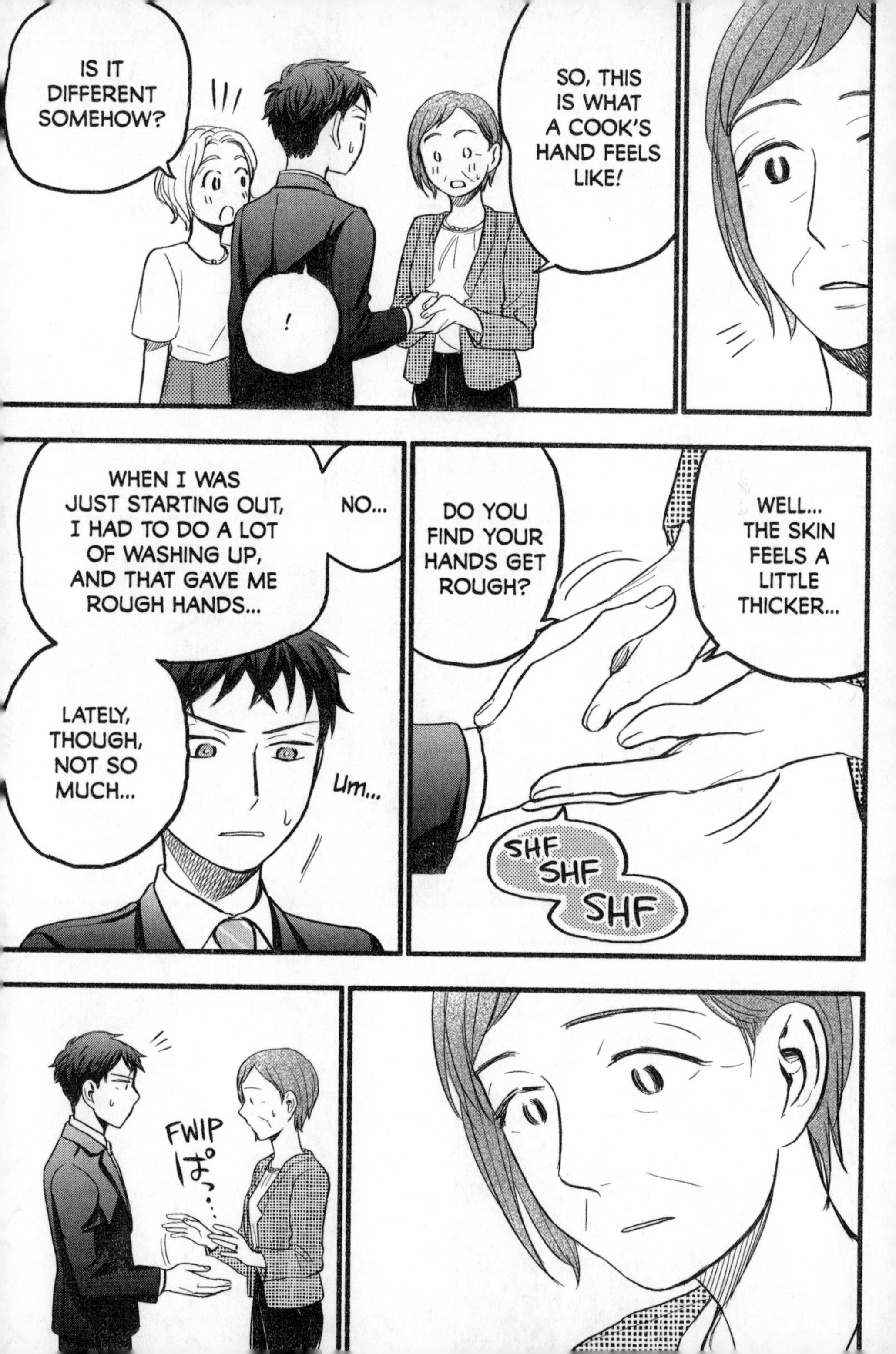
SO, THIS IS WHAT A COOK'S HAND FEELS LIKE!
IS IT DIFFERENT SOMEHOW?
!
WELL... THE SKIN FEELS A LITTLE THICKER...
DO YOU FIND YOUR HANDS GET ROUGH?
SHF SHF SHF
NO...
WHEN I WAS JUST STARTING OUT, I HAD TO DO A LOT OF WASHING UP, AND THAT GAVE ME ROUGH HANDS...
Um...
LATELY, THOUGH, NOT SO MUCH...
FWIP
ぱっ…

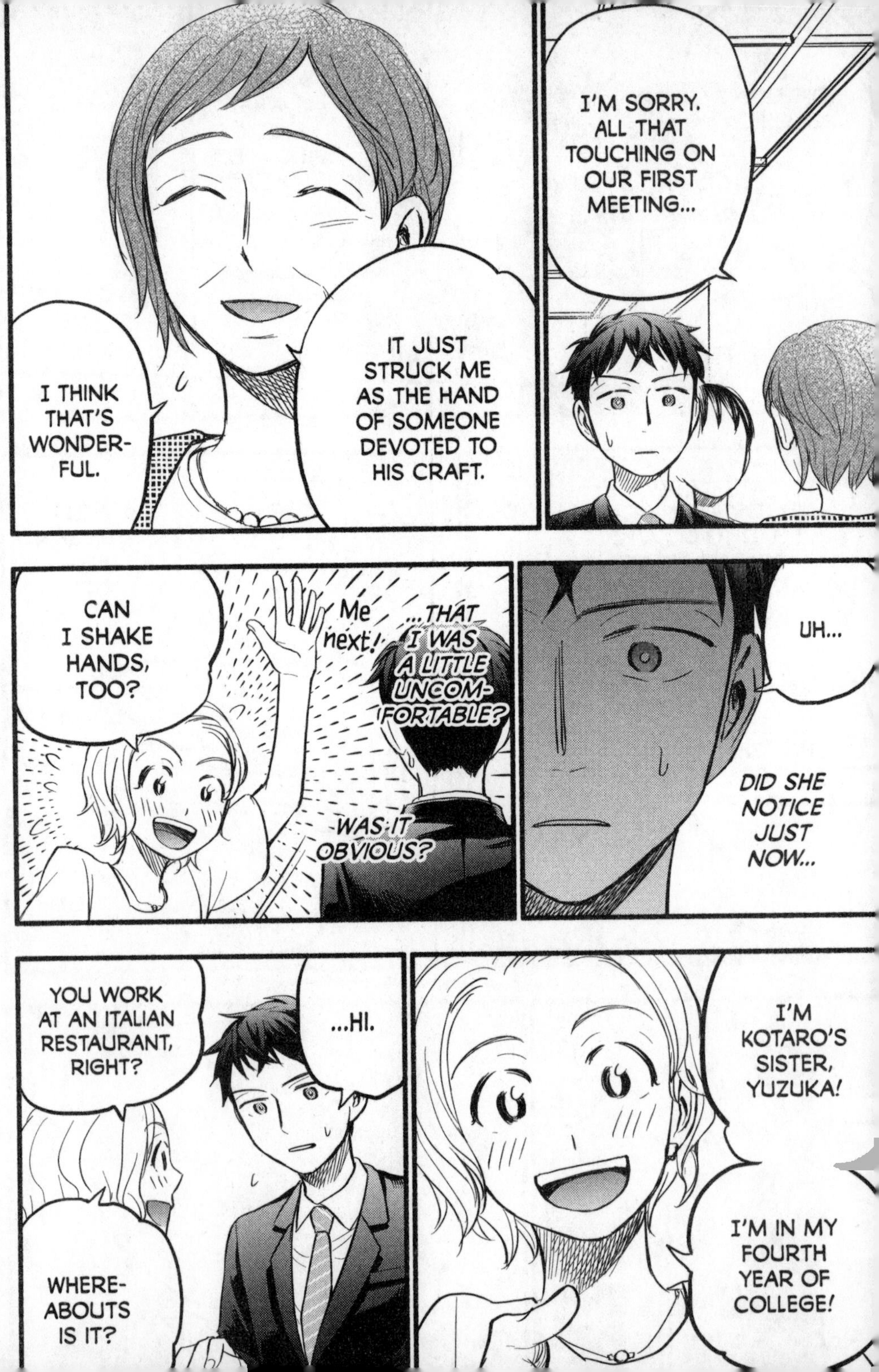
I'M SORRY. ALL THAT TOUCHING ON OUR FIRST MEETING...
IT JUST STRUCK ME AS THE HAND OF SOMEONE DEVOTED TO HIS CRAFT.
I THINK THAT'S WONDER-FUL.
UH...
DID SHE NOTICE JUST NOW...
...THAT I WAS A LITTLE UNCOM-FORTABLE?
WAS IT OBVIOUS?
Me next!
CAN I SHAKE HANDS, TOO?
I'M KOTARO'S SISTER, YUZUKA!
I'M IN MY FOURTH YEAR OF COLLEGE!
...HI.
YOU WORK AT AN ITALIAN RESTAURANT, RIGHT?
WHERE-ABOUTS IS IT?

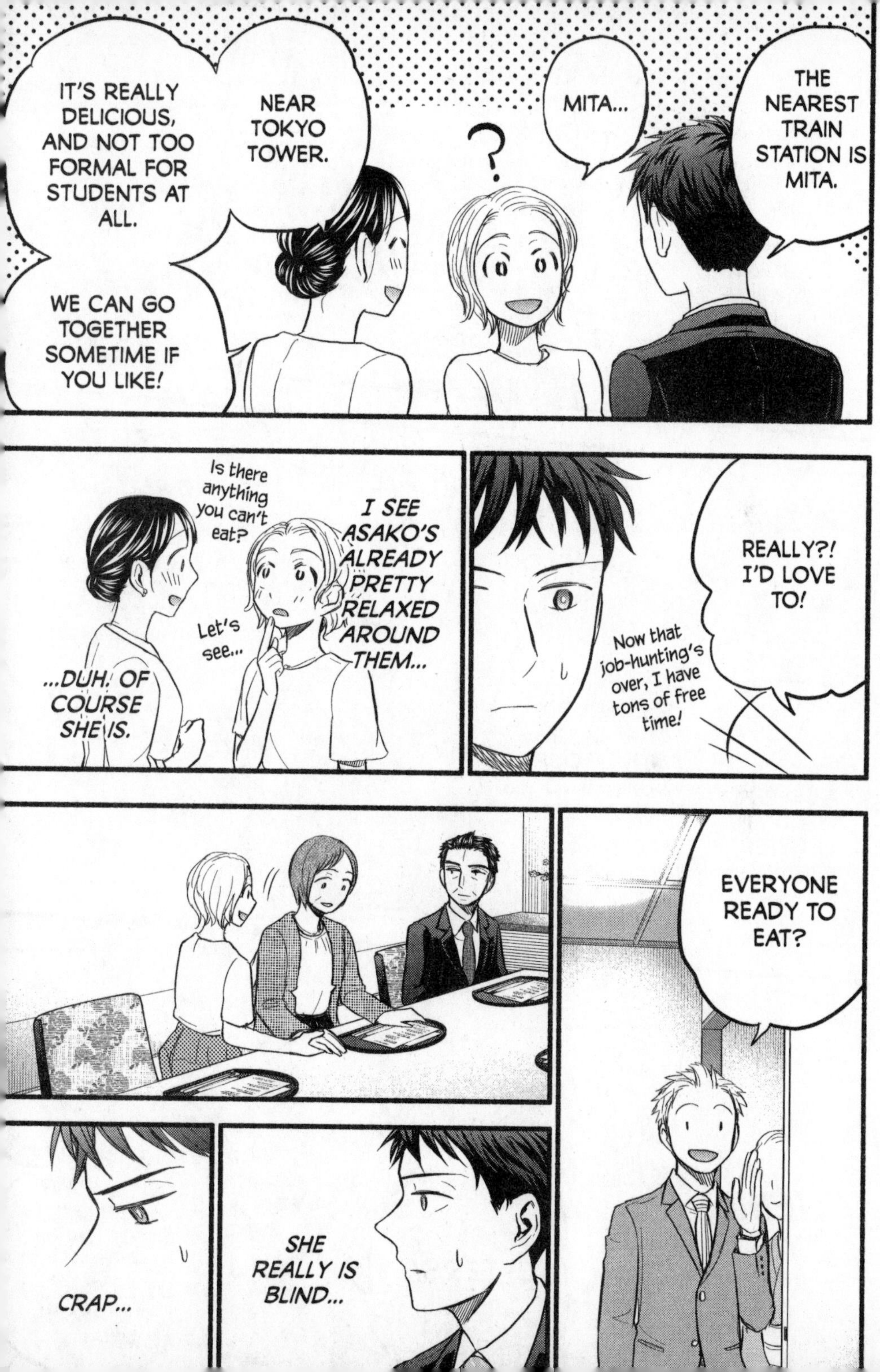
THE NEAREST TRAIN STATION IS MITA.
MITA...
?
NEAR TOKYO TOWER.
IT'S REALLY DELICIOUS, AND NOT TOO FORMAL FOR STUDENTS AT ALL.
WE CAN GO TOGETHER SOMETIME IF YOU LIKE!
REALLY?! I'D LOVE TO!
Now that job-hunting's over, I have tons of free time!
I SEE ASAKO'S ALREADY PRETTY RELAXED AROUND THEM...
Is there anything you can't eat?
Let's see...
...DUH. OF COURSE SHE IS.
EVERYONE READY TO EAT?
SHE REALLY IS BLIND...
CRAP...

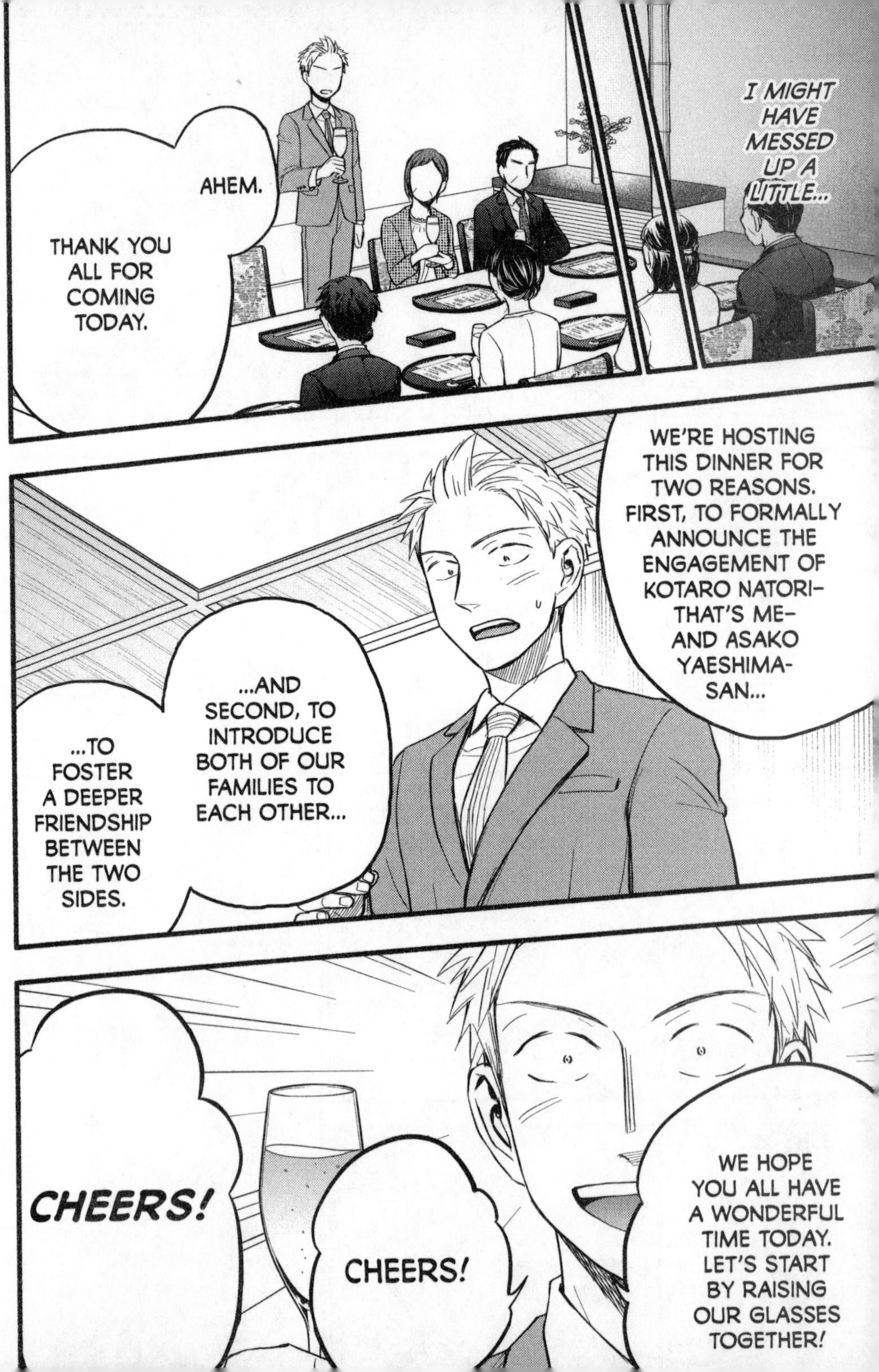
I MIGHT HAVE MESSED UP A LITTLE...
AHEM.
THANK YOU ALL FOR COMING TODAY.
WE'RE HOSTING THIS DINNER FOR TWO REASONS. FIRST, TO FORMALLY ANNOUNCE THE ENGAGEMENT OF KOTARO NATORI—THAT'S ME—AND ASAKO YAESHIMA-SAN...
...AND SECOND, TO INTRODUCE BOTH OF OUR FAMILIES TO EACH OTHER...
...TO FOSTER A DEEPER FRIENDSHIP BETWEEN THE TWO SIDES.
WE HOPE YOU ALL HAVE A WONDERFUL TIME TODAY. LET'S START BY RAISING OUR GLASSES TOGETHER!
CHEERS!
CHEERS!

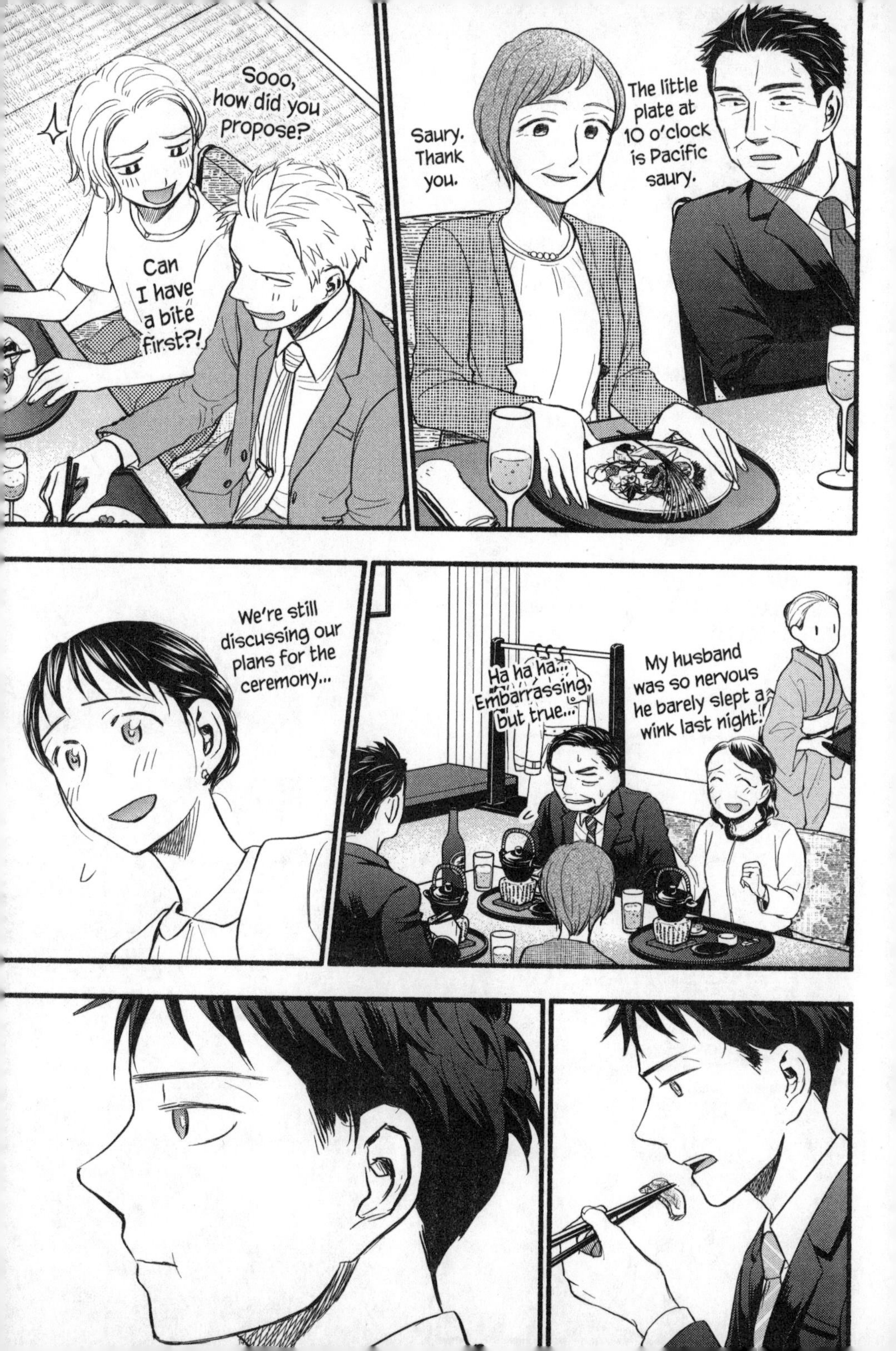
The little plate at 10 o'clock is Pacific saury.
Saury. Thank you.
Sooo, how did you propose?
Can I have a bite first?!
My husband was so nervous he barely slept a wink last night!
Ha ha ha... Embarrassing, but true...
We're still discussing our plans for the ceremony...

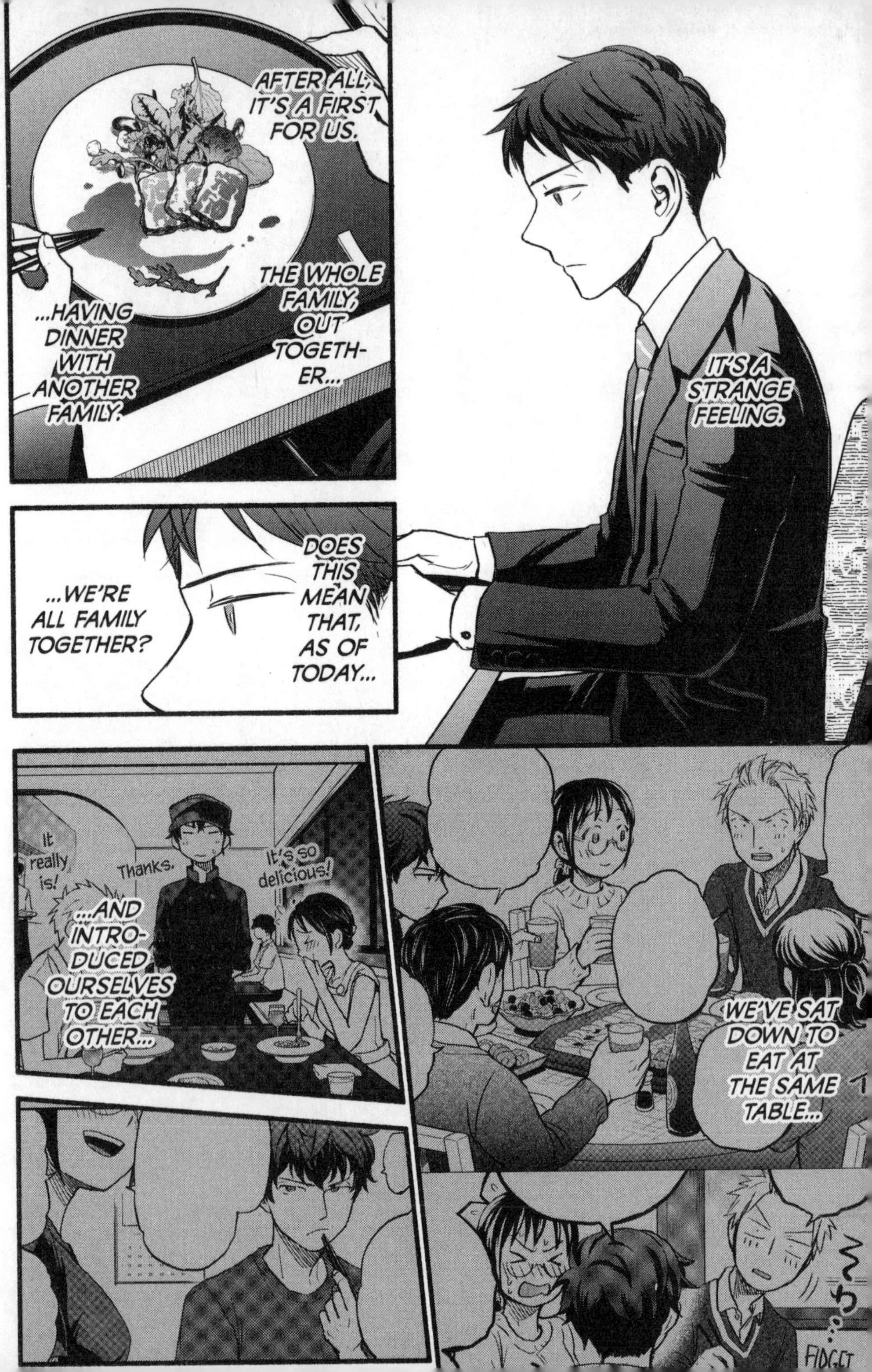
IT'S A STRANGE FEELING.
AFTER ALL, IT'S A FIRST FOR US.
THE WHOLE FAMILY, OUT TOGETH-ER...
...HAVING DINNER WITH ANOTHER FAMILY.
DOES THIS MEAN THAT, AS OF TODAY...
...WE'RE ALL FAMILY TOGETHER?
WE'VE SAT DOWN TO EAT AT THE SAME TABLE...
...AND INTRO-DUCED OURSELVES TO EACH OTHER...
It's so delicious!
Thanks.
It really is!
FIDGET

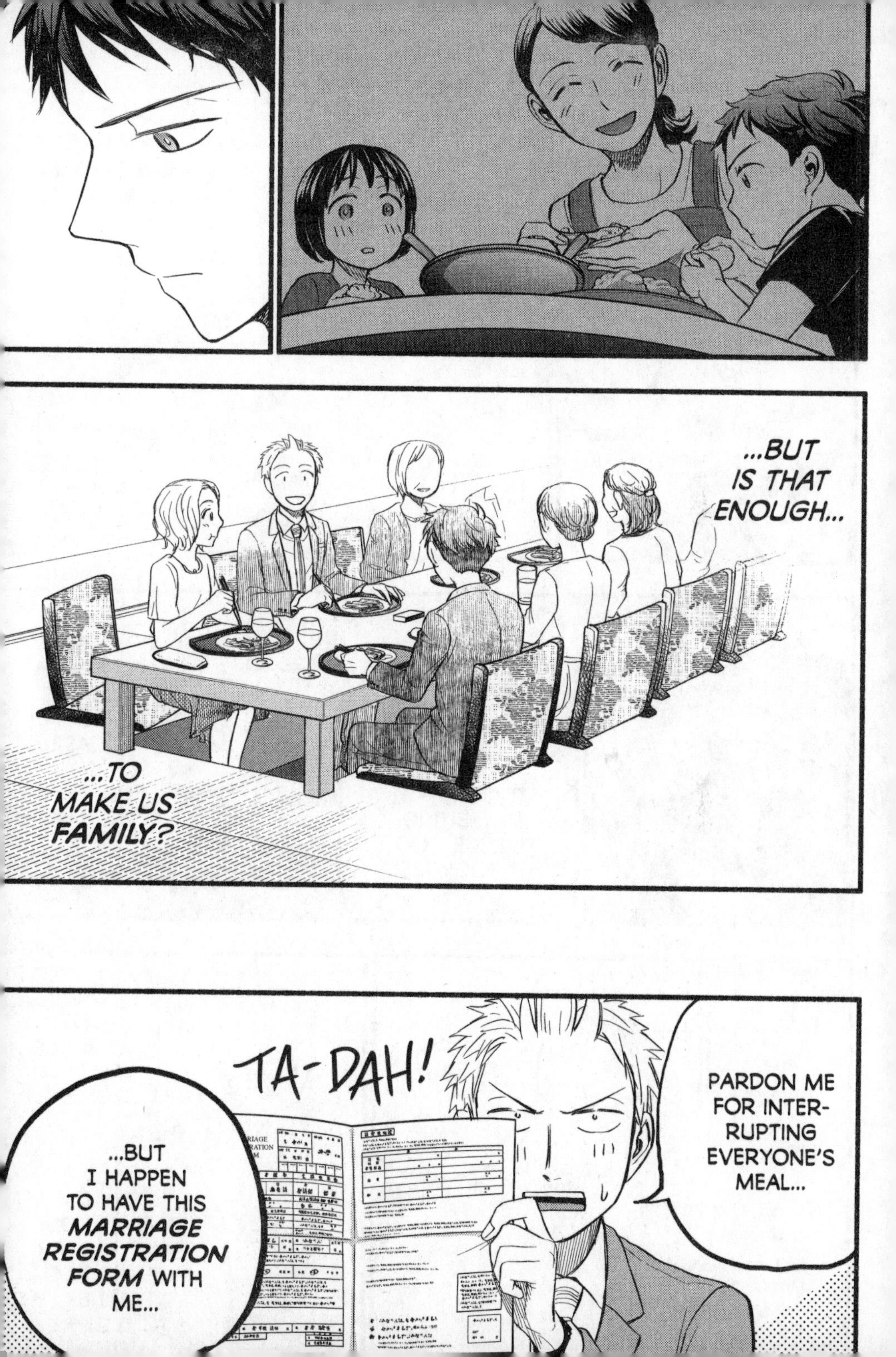
...BUT IS THAT ENOUGH...
...TO MAKE US FAMILY?
PARDON ME FOR INTER-RUPTING EVERYONE'S MEAL...
TA-DAH!
...BUT I HAPPEN TO HAVE THIS *MARRIAGE REGISTRATION FORM* WITH ME...

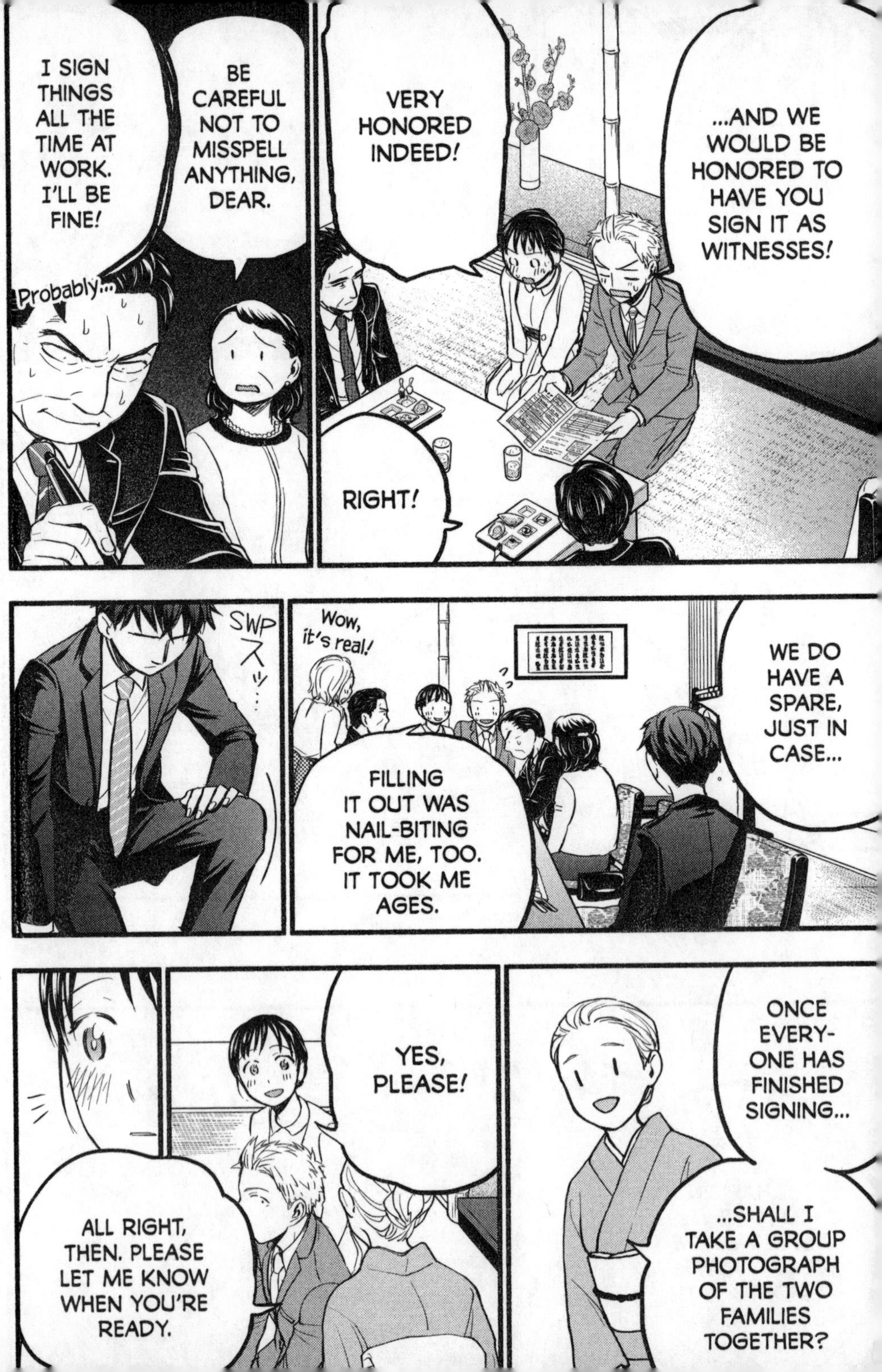
...AND WE WOULD BE HONORED TO HAVE YOU SIGN IT AS WITNESSES!
VERY HONORED INDEED!
RIGHT!
BE CAREFUL NOT TO MISSPELL ANYTHING, DEAR.
I SIGN THINGS ALL THE TIME AT WORK. I'LL BE FINE!
Probably...
WE DO HAVE A SPARE, JUST IN CASE...
Wow, it's real!
FILLING IT OUT WAS NAIL-BITING FOR ME, TOO. IT TOOK ME AGES.
SWP
スッ…
ONCE EVERY-ONE HAS FINISHED SIGNING...
...SHALL I TAKE A GROUP PHOTOGRAPH OF THE TWO FAMILIES TOGETHER?
YES, PLEASE!
ALL RIGHT, THEN. PLEASE LET ME KNOW WHEN YOU'RE READY.

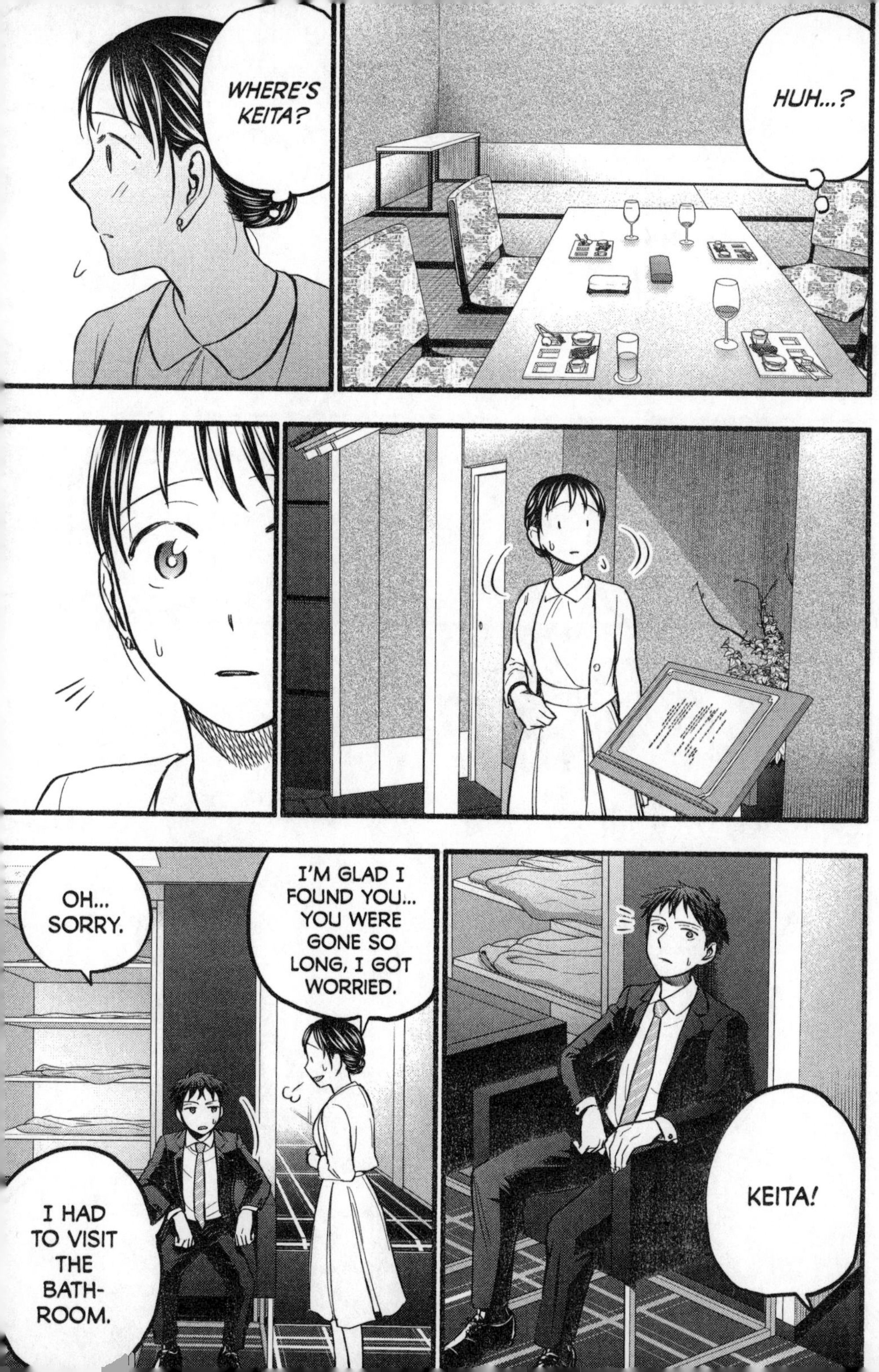
HUH...?
WHERE'S KEITA?
KEITA!
I'M GLAD I FOUND YOU... YOU WERE GONE SO LONG, I GOT WORRIED.
OH... SORRY.
I HAD TO VISIT THE BATH-ROOM.

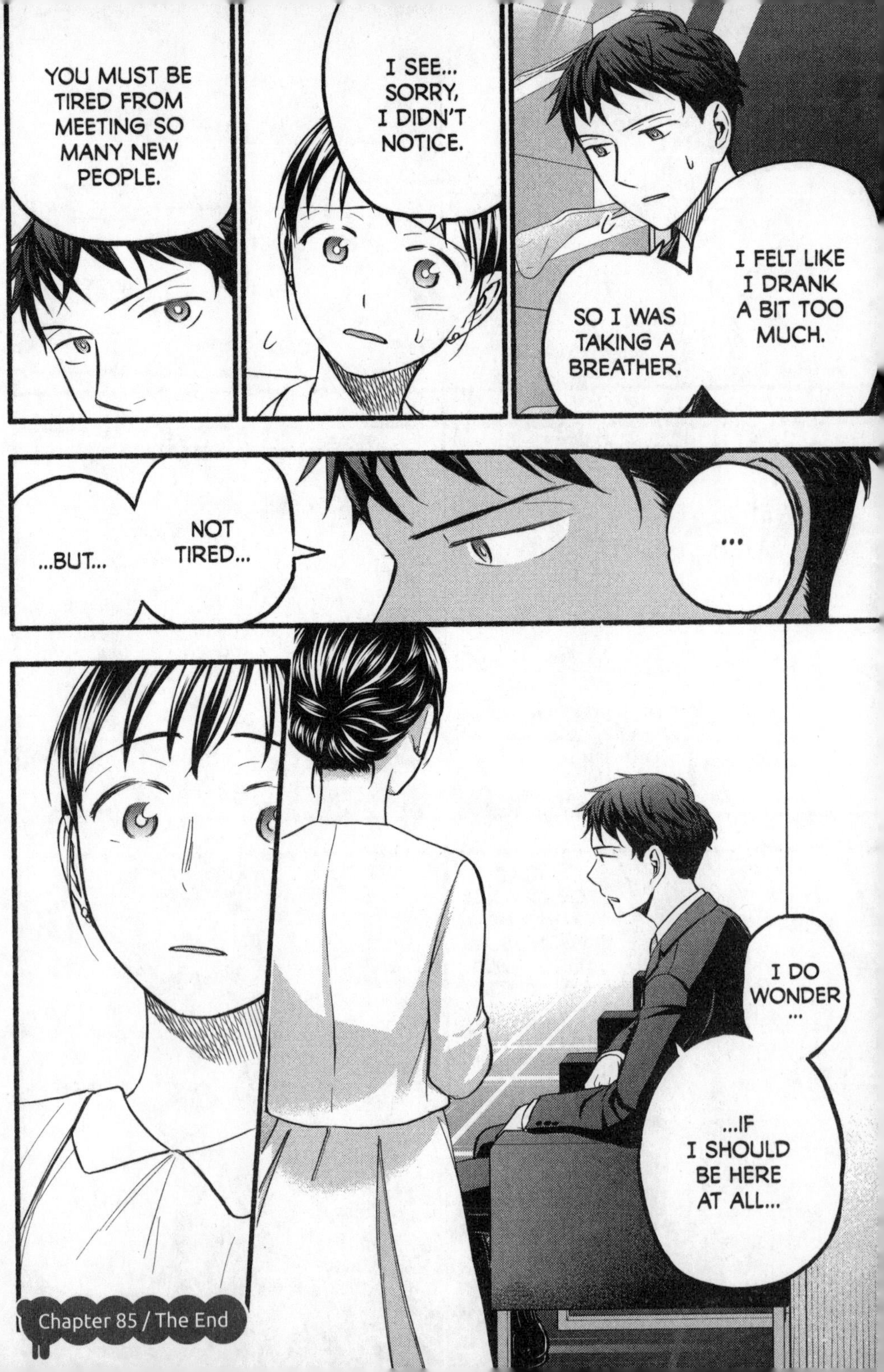
I FELT LIKE I DRANK A BIT TOO MUCH.
SO I WAS TAKING A BREATHER.
I SEE... SORRY, I DIDN'T NOTICE.
YOU MUST BE TIRED FROM MEETING SO MANY NEW PEOPLE.
...
NOT TIRED... ...BUT...
I DO WONDER ...
...IF I SHOULD BE HERE AT ALL...
Chapter 85 / The End

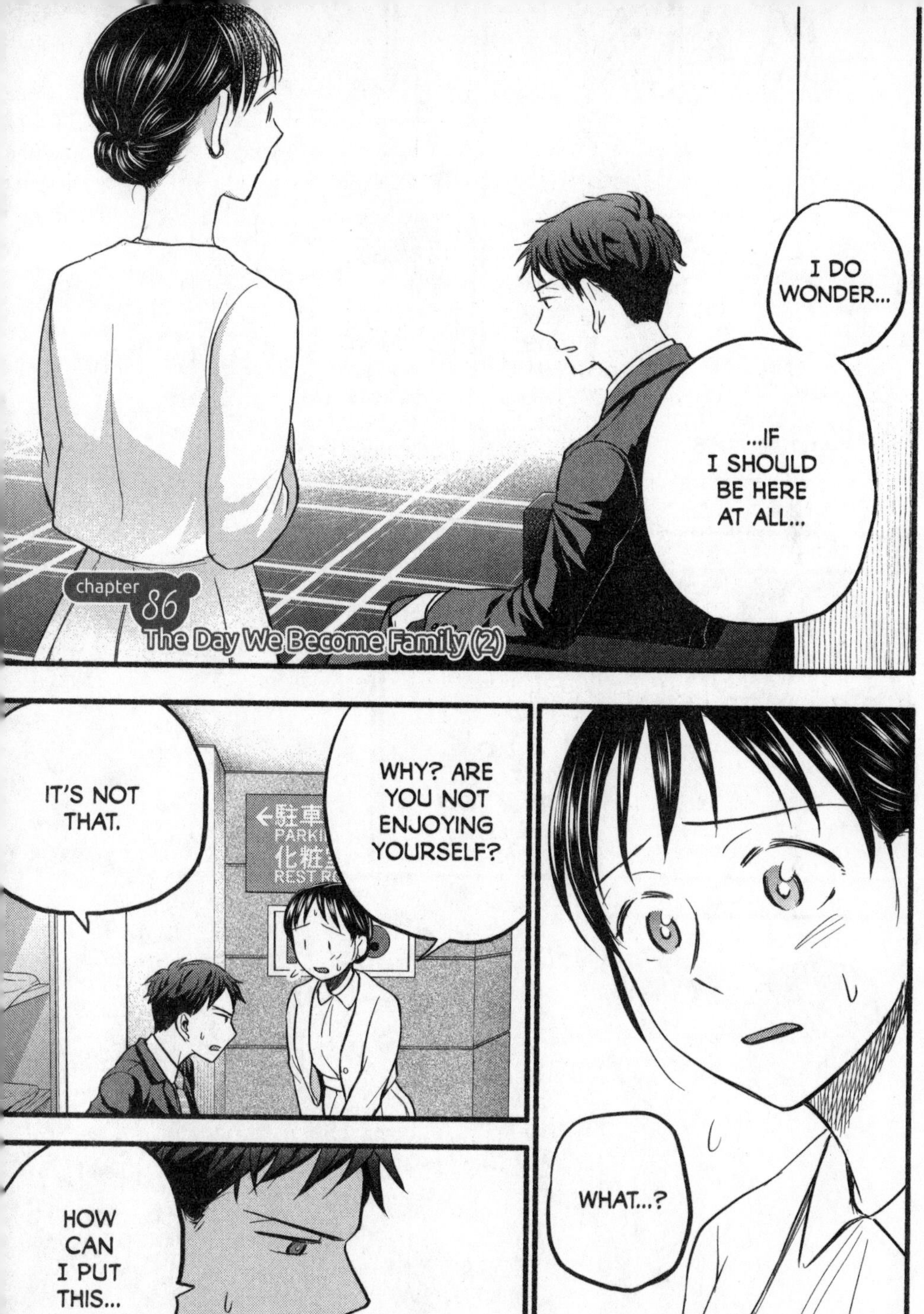
I DO WONDER...
...IF I SHOULD BE HERE AT ALL...
chapter 86
The Day We Become Family (2)
WHAT...?
WHY? ARE YOU NOT ENJOYING YOURSELF?
IT'S NOT THAT.
HOW CAN I PUT THIS...

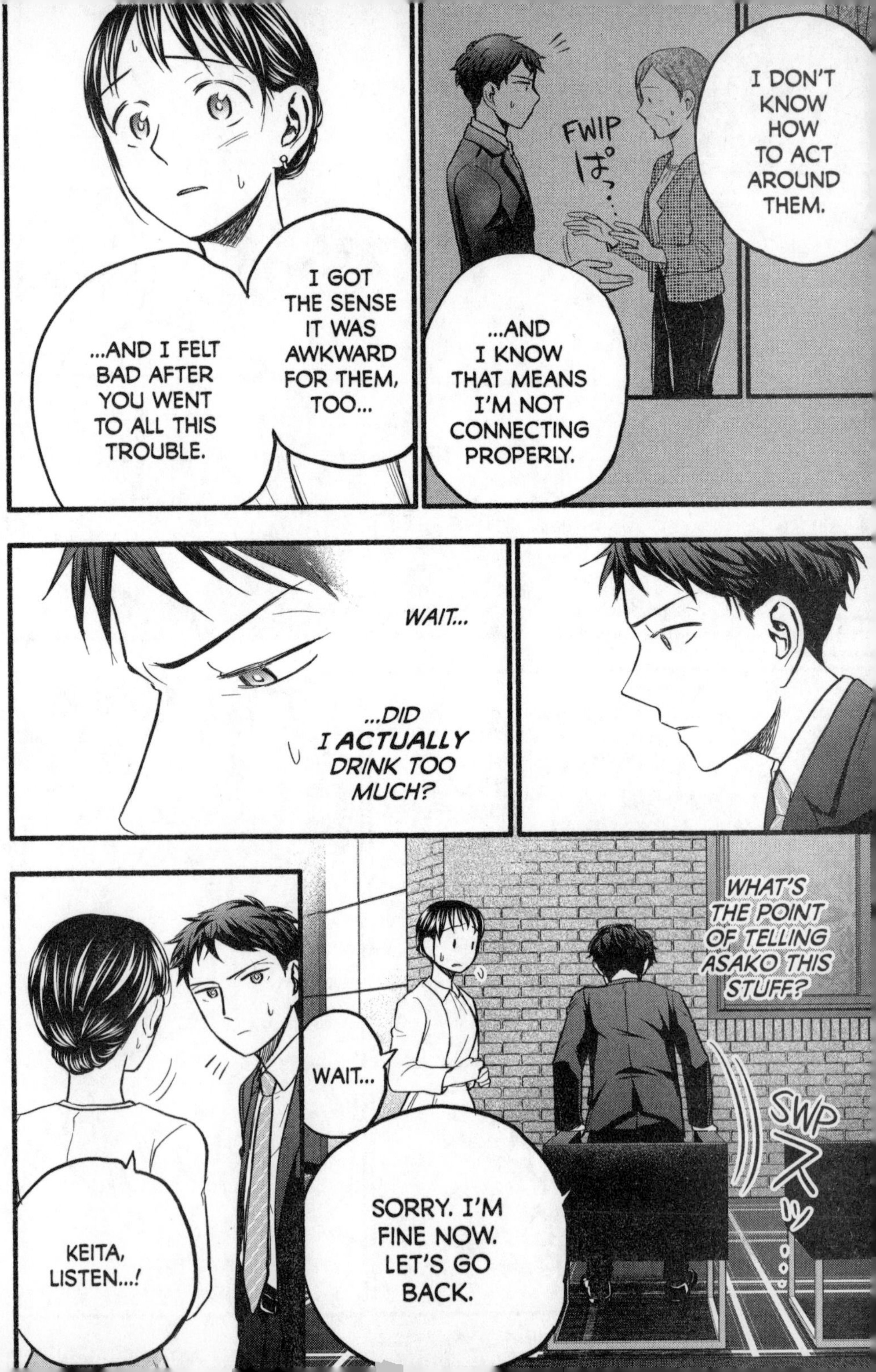
I DON'T KNOW HOW TO ACT AROUND THEM.
FWIP ぱっ…
...AND I KNOW THAT MEANS I'M NOT CONNECTING PROPERLY.
I GOT THE SENSE IT WAS AWKWARD FOR THEM, TOO...
...AND I FELT BAD AFTER YOU WENT TO ALL THIS TROUBLE.
WAIT...
...DID I ACTUALLY DRINK TOO MUCH?
WHAT'S THE POINT OF TELLING ASAKO THIS STUFF?
SWP スッ…
SORRY. I'M FINE NOW. LET'S GO BACK.
WAIT...
KEITA, LISTEN...!

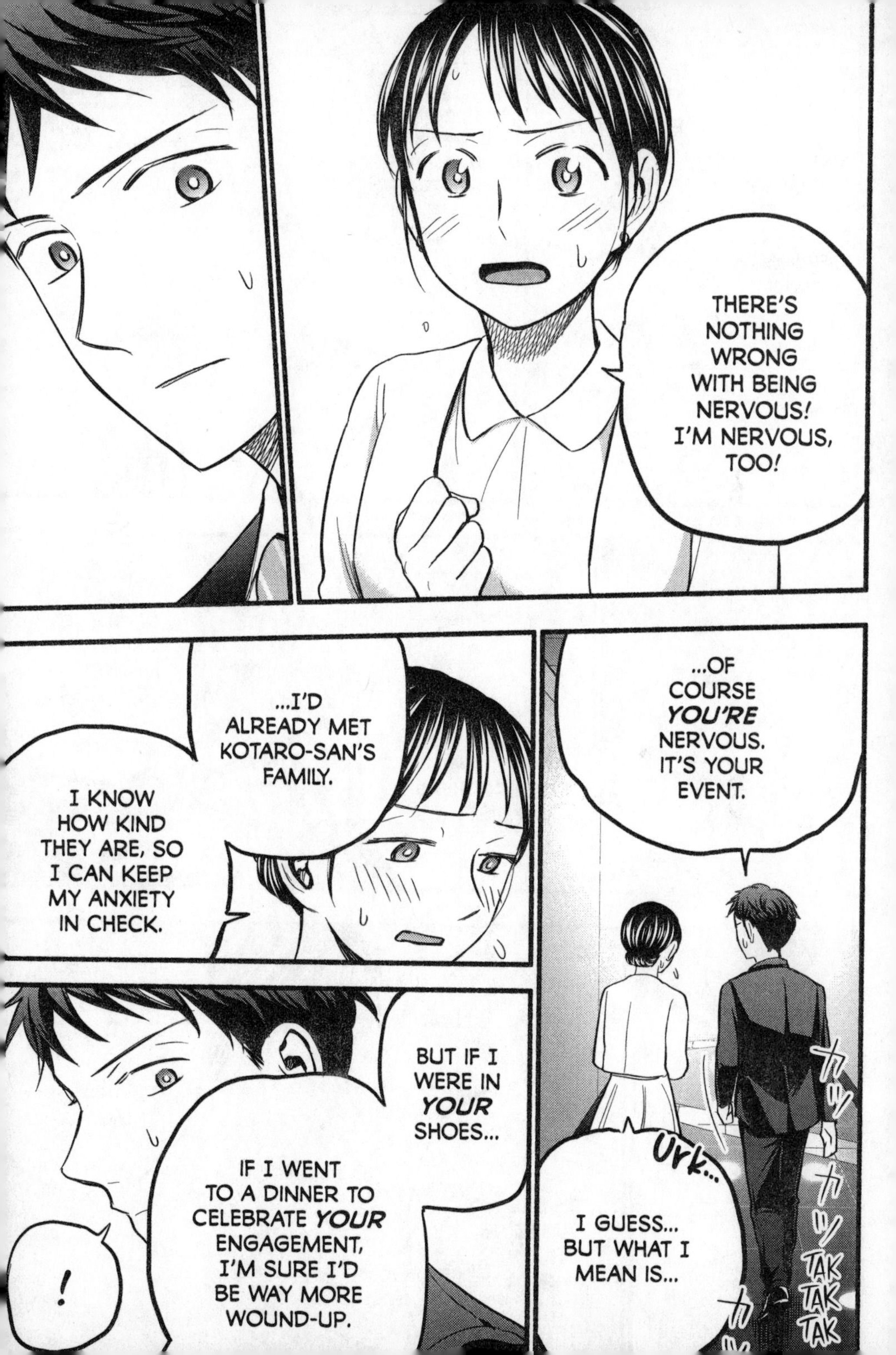
THERE'S NOTHING WRONG WITH BEING NERVOUS! I'M NERVOUS, TOO!
...OF COURSE *YOU'RE* NERVOUS. IT'S YOUR EVENT.
Urk...
I GUESS... BUT WHAT I MEAN IS...
TAK TAK TAK
...I'D ALREADY MET KOTARO-SAN'S FAMILY.
I KNOW HOW KIND THEY ARE, SO I CAN KEEP MY ANXIETY IN CHECK.
BUT IF I WERE IN *YOUR* SHOES...
IF I WENT TO A DINNER TO CELEBRATE *YOUR* ENGAGEMENT, I'M SURE I'D BE WAY MORE WOUND-UP.
!

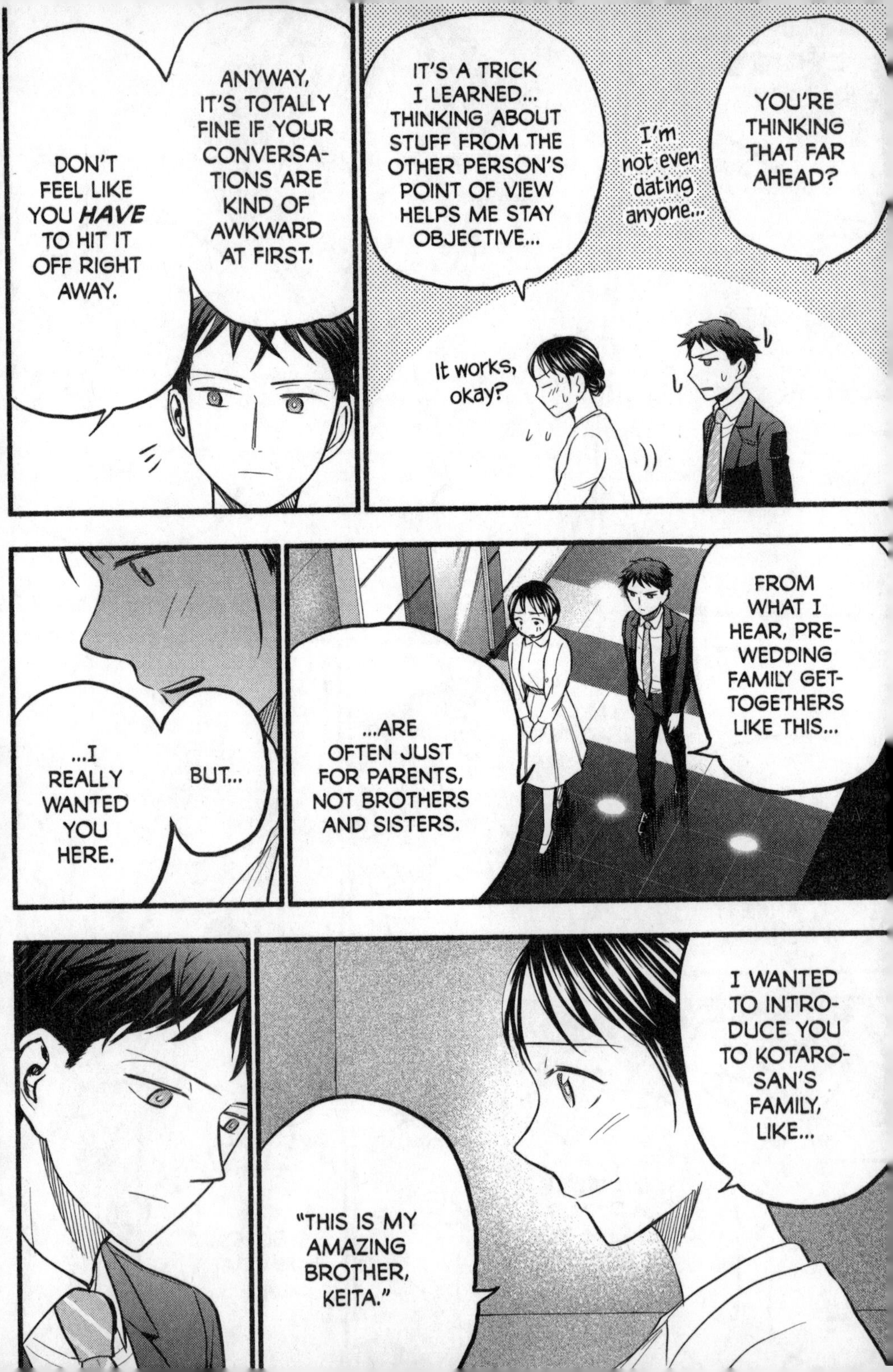

YOU'RE THINKING THAT FAR AHEAD?
I'm not even dating anyone...
IT'S A TRICK I LEARNED... THINKING ABOUT STUFF FROM THE OTHER PERSON'S POINT OF VIEW HELPS ME STAY OBJECTIVE...
It works, okay?
ANYWAY, IT'S TOTALLY FINE IF YOUR CONVERSATIONS ARE KIND OF AWKWARD AT FIRST.
DON'T FEEL LIKE YOU *HAVE* TO HIT IT OFF RIGHT AWAY.
FROM WHAT I HEAR, PRE-WEDDING FAMILY GET-TOGETHERS LIKE THIS...
...ARE OFTEN JUST FOR PARENTS, NOT BROTHERS AND SISTERS.
BUT...
...I REALLY WANTED YOU HERE.
I WANTED TO INTRODUCE YOU TO KOTARO-SAN'S FAMILY, LIKE...
"THIS IS MY AMAZING BROTHER, KEITA."

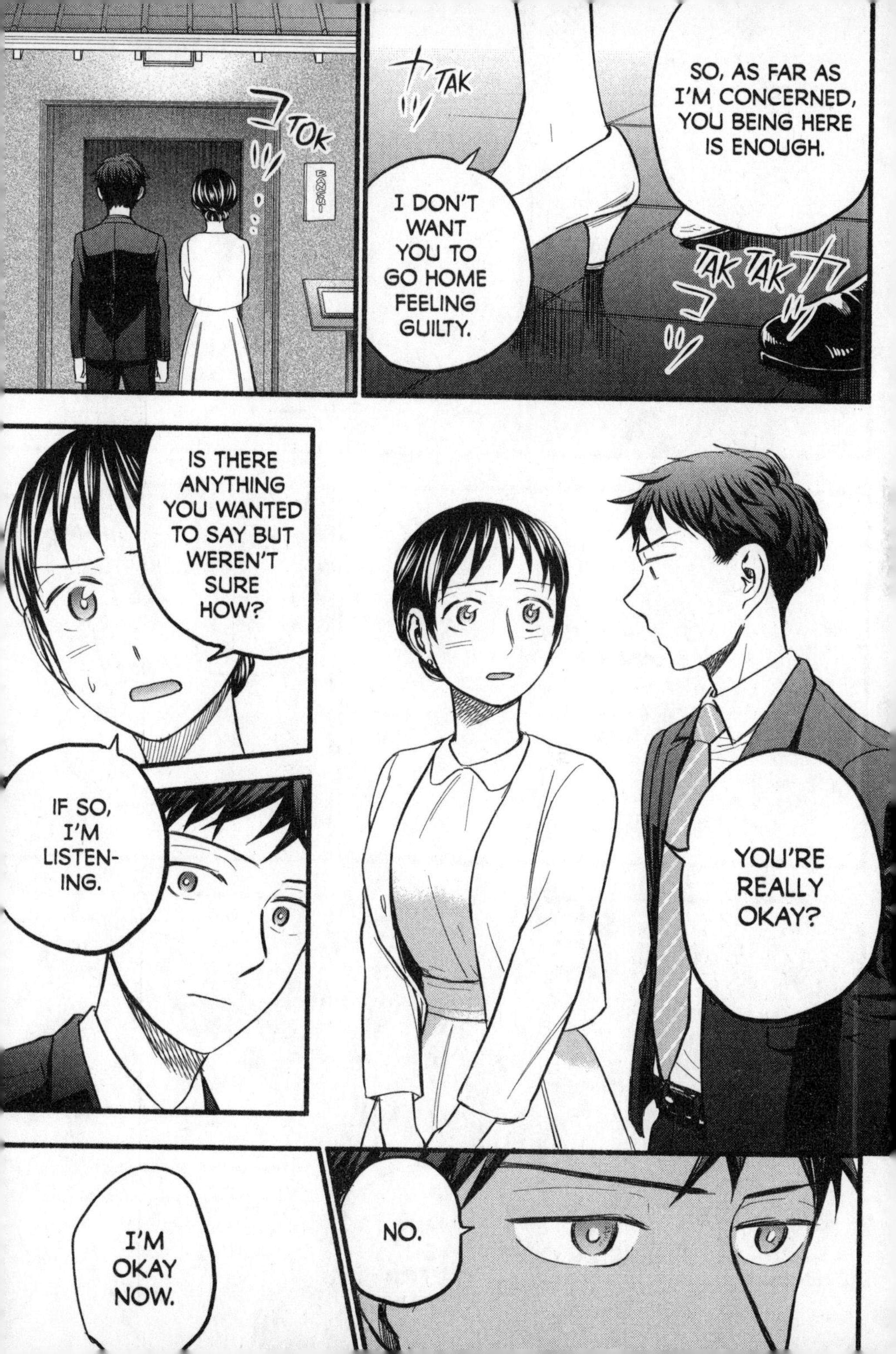
SO, AS FAR AS I'M CONCERNED, YOU BEING HERE IS ENOUGH.
TAK
I DON'T WANT YOU TO GO HOME FEELING GUILTY.
TAK TAK
TOK
RANSUI
YOU'RE REALLY OKAY?
IS THERE ANYTHING YOU WANTED TO SAY BUT WEREN'T SURE HOW?
IF SO, I'M LISTEN-ING.
NO.
I'M OKAY NOW.

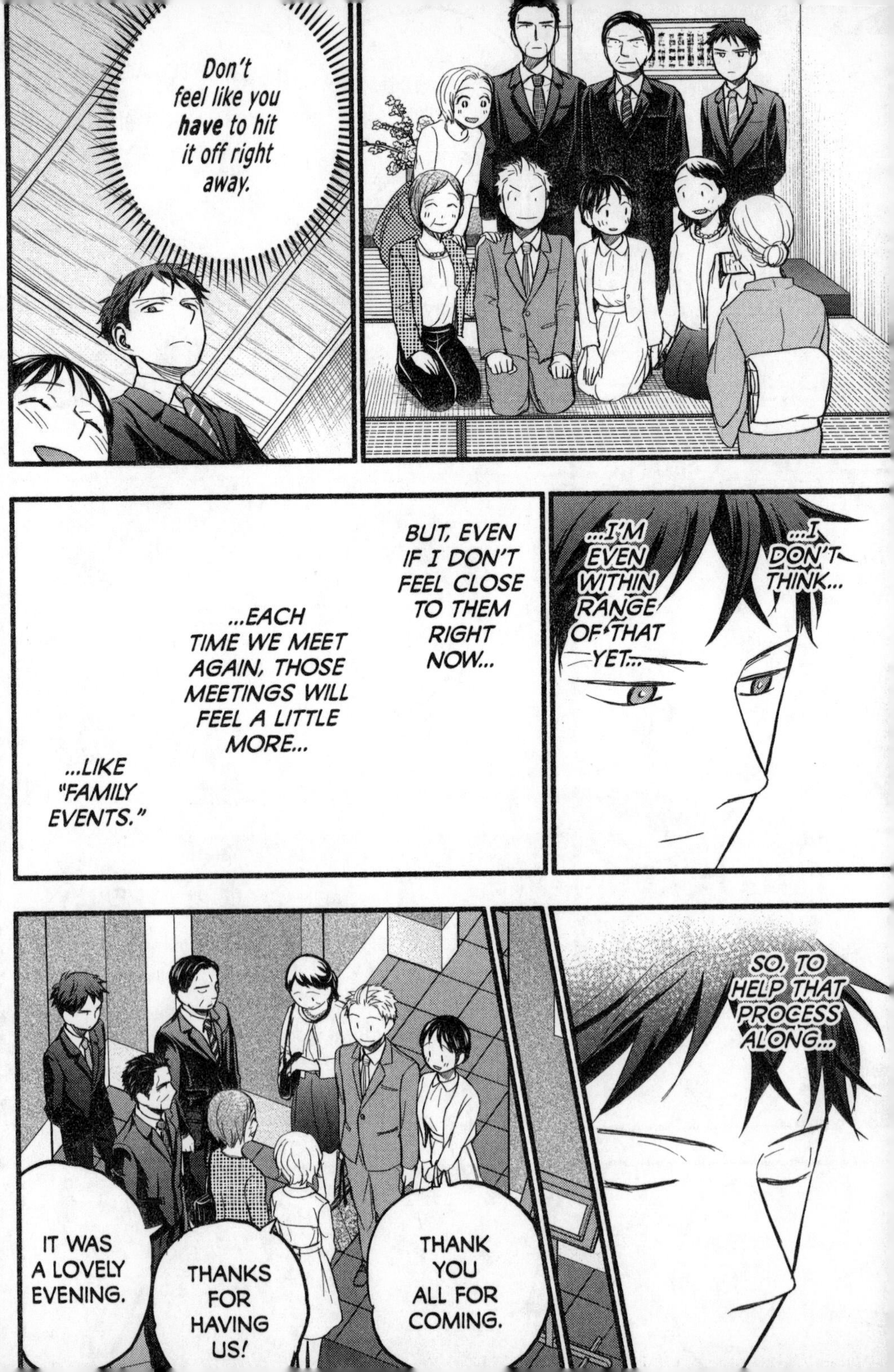
Don't feel like you **have** to hit it off right away.
...I DON'T THINK...
...I'M EVEN WITHIN RANGE OF THAT YET...
BUT, EVEN IF I DON'T FEEL CLOSE TO THEM RIGHT NOW...
...EACH TIME WE MEET AGAIN, THOSE MEETINGS WILL FEEL A LITTLE MORE...
...LIKE "FAMILY EVENTS."
SO, TO HELP THAT PROCESS ALONG...
THANK YOU ALL FOR COMING.
THANKS FOR HAVING US!
IT WAS A LOVELY EVENING.

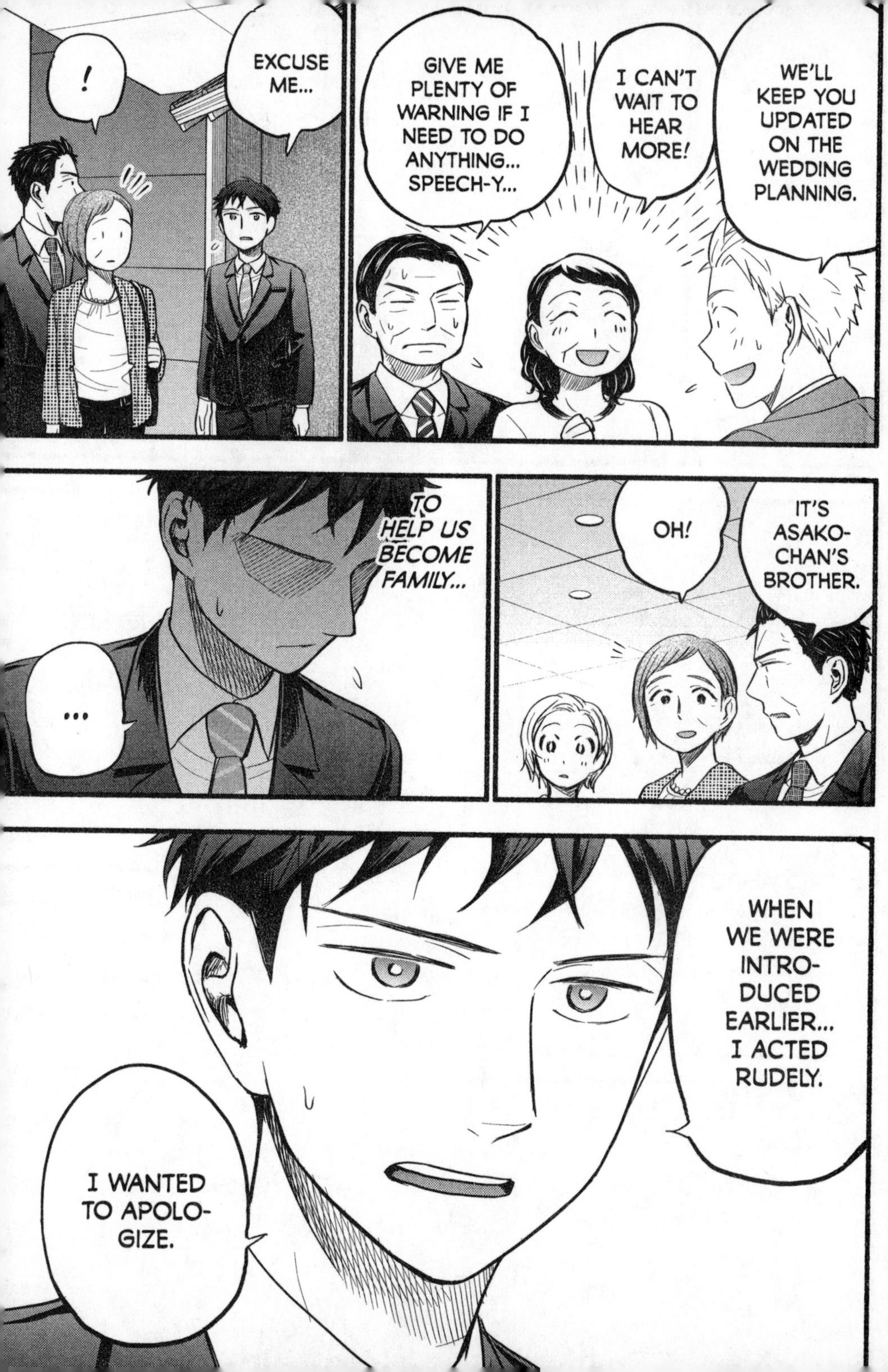
WE'LL KEEP YOU UPDATED ON THE WEDDING PLANNING.
I CAN'T WAIT TO HEAR MORE!
GIVE ME PLENTY OF WARNING IF I NEED TO DO ANYTHING... SPEECH-Y...
EXCUSE ME...
!
IT'S ASAKO-CHAN'S BROTHER.
OH!
TO HELP US BECOME FAMILY...
...
WHEN WE WERE INTRODUCED EARLIER... I ACTED RUDELY.
I WANTED TO APOLOGIZE.

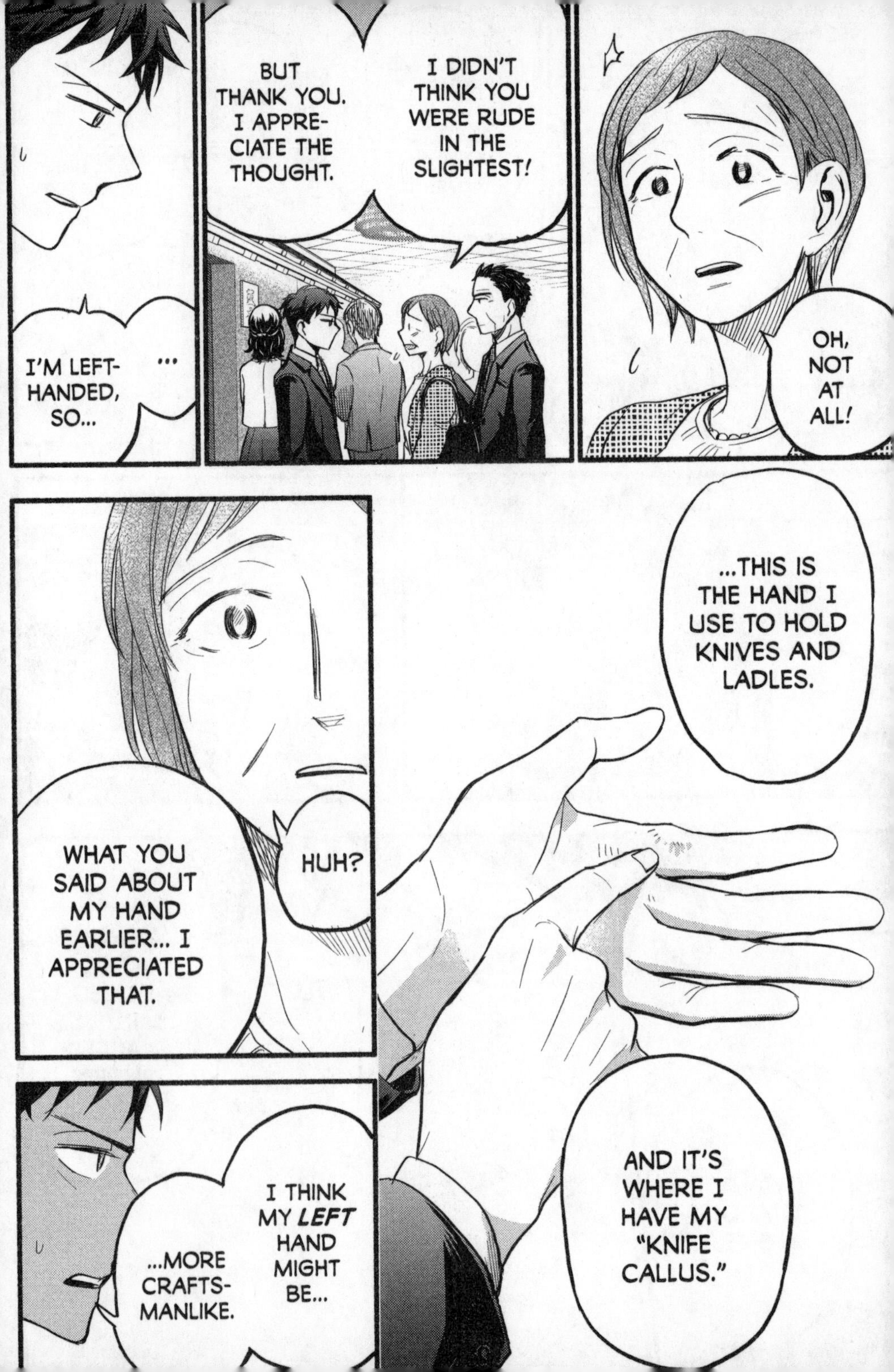
OH, NOT AT ALL!
I DIDN'T THINK YOU WERE RUDE IN THE SLIGHTEST!
BUT THANK YOU. I APPRECIATE THE THOUGHT.
...
I'M LEFT-HANDED, SO...
...THIS IS THE HAND I USE TO HOLD KNIVES AND LADLES.
AND IT'S WHERE I HAVE MY "KNIFE CALLUS."
HUH?
WHAT YOU SAID ABOUT MY HAND EARLIER... I APPRECIATED THAT.
I THINK MY *LEFT* HAND MIGHT BE...
...MORE CRAFTSMANLIKE.

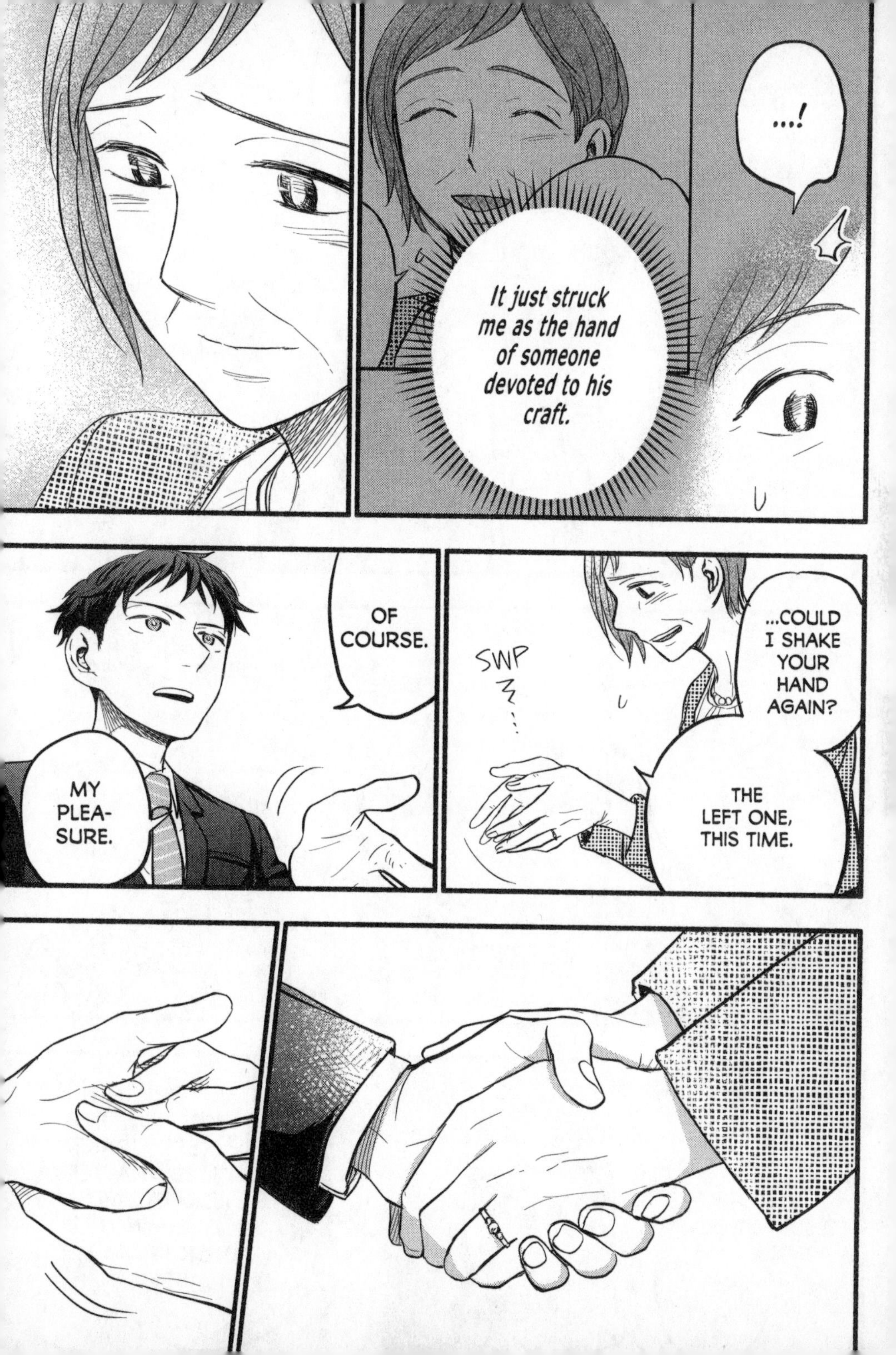

...!
It just struck me as the hand of someone devoted to his craft.
...COULD I SHAKE YOUR HAND AGAIN?
THE LEFT ONE, THIS TIME.
SWP
OF COURSE.
MY PLEA-SURE.

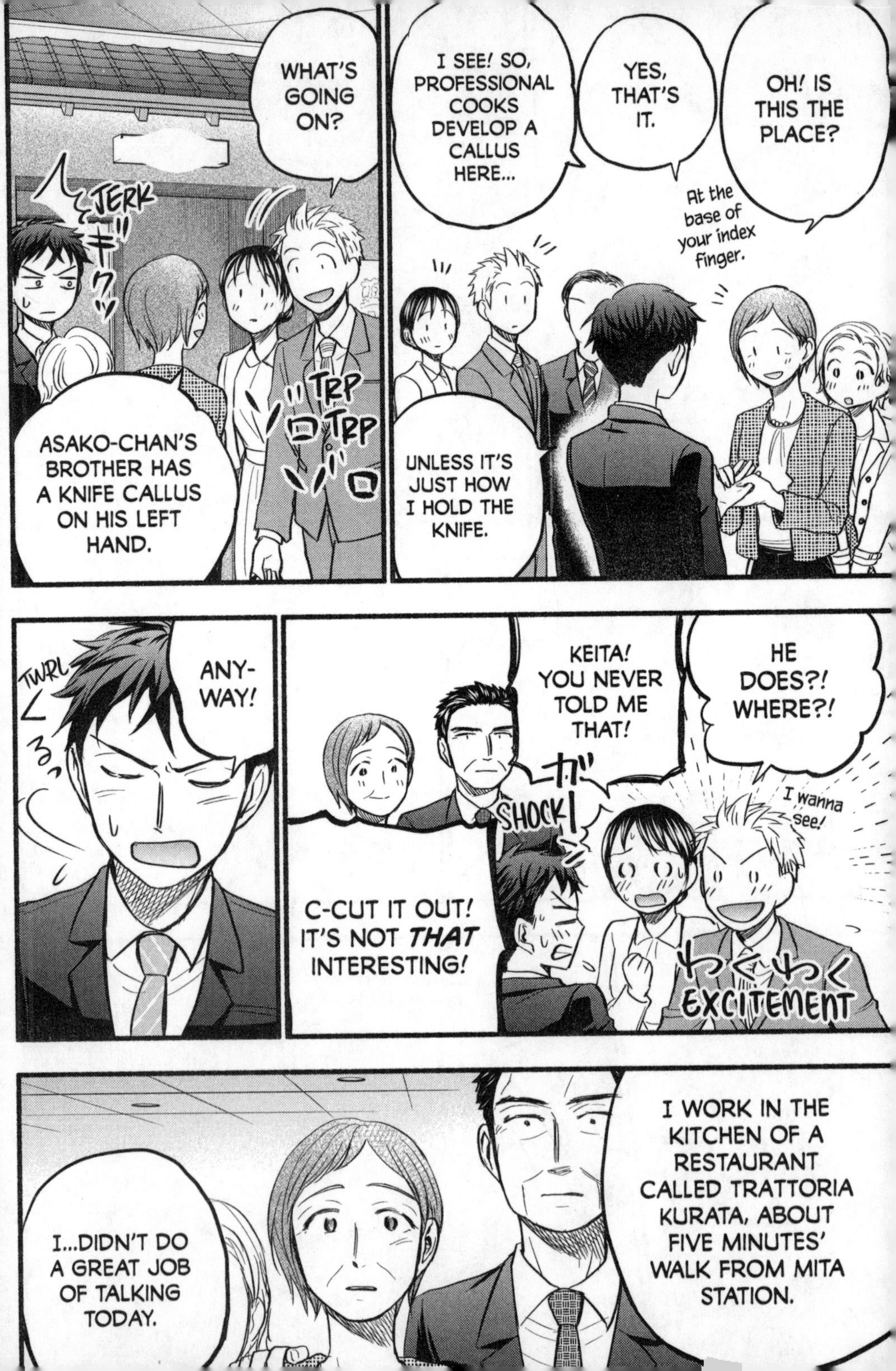

OH! IS THIS THE PLACE?
YES, THAT'S IT.
I SEE! SO, PROFESSIONAL COOKS DEVELOP A CALLUS HERE...
At the base of your index finger.
UNLESS IT'S JUST HOW I HOLD THE KNIFE.
WHAT'S GOING ON?
JERK
TRP TRP
ASAKO-CHAN'S BROTHER HAS A KNIFE CALLUS ON HIS LEFT HAND.
HE DOES?! WHERE?!
KEITA! YOU NEVER TOLD ME THAT!
I wanna see!
SHOCK
C-CUT IT OUT! IT'S NOT *THAT* INTERESTING!
わくわく
EXCITEMENT
ANY-WAY!
TWRL
I WORK IN THE KITCHEN OF A RESTAURANT CALLED TRATTORIA KURATA, ABOUT FIVE MINUTES' WALK FROM MITA STATION.
I...DIDN'T DO A GREAT JOB OF TALKING TODAY.

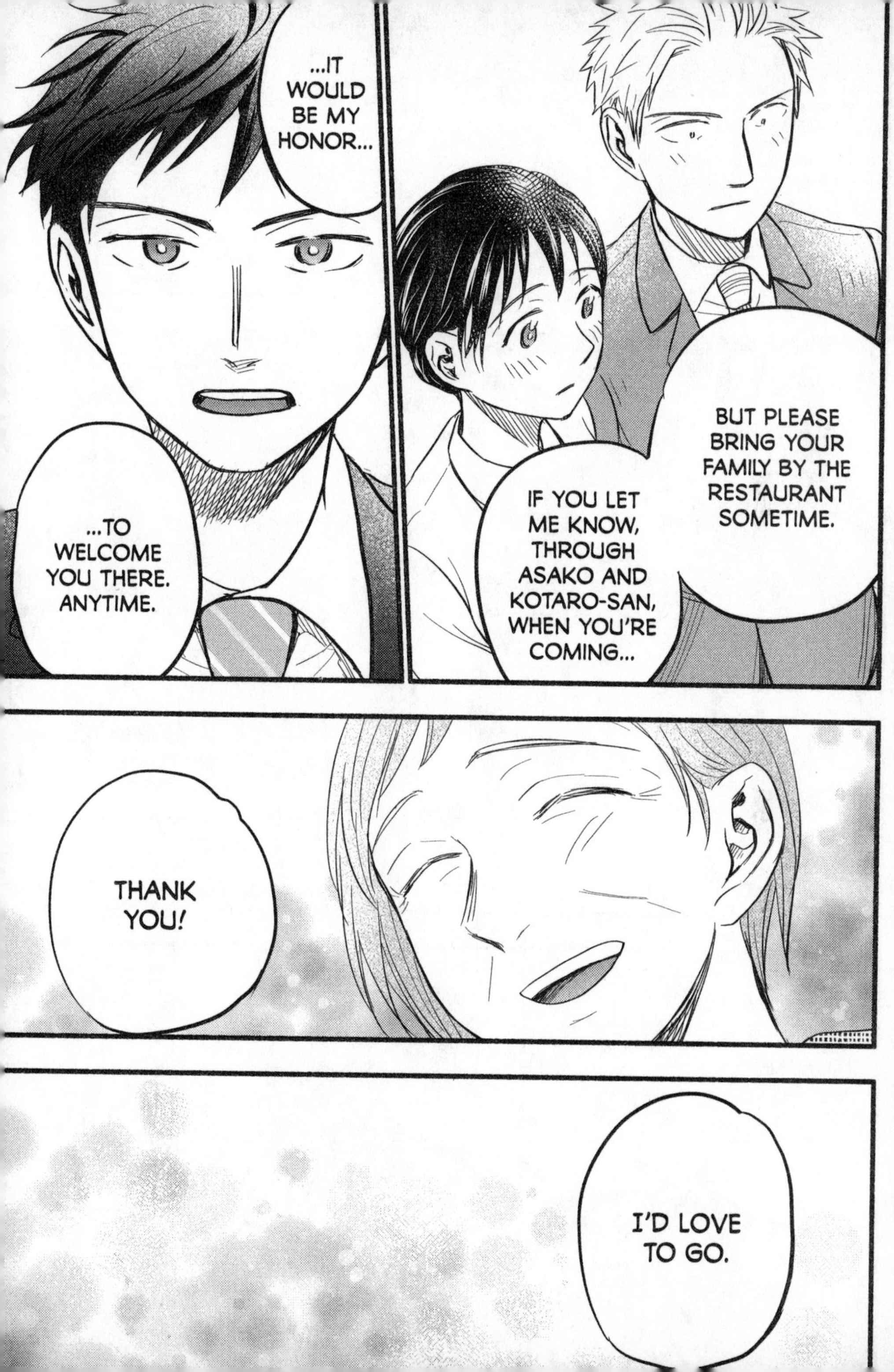
BUT PLEASE BRING YOUR FAMILY BY THE RESTAURANT SOMETIME.
IF YOU LET ME KNOW, THROUGH ASAKO AND KOTARO-SAN, WHEN YOU'RE COMING...
...IT WOULD BE MY HONOR...
...TO WELCOME YOU THERE. ANYTIME.
THANK YOU!
I'D LOVE TO GO.

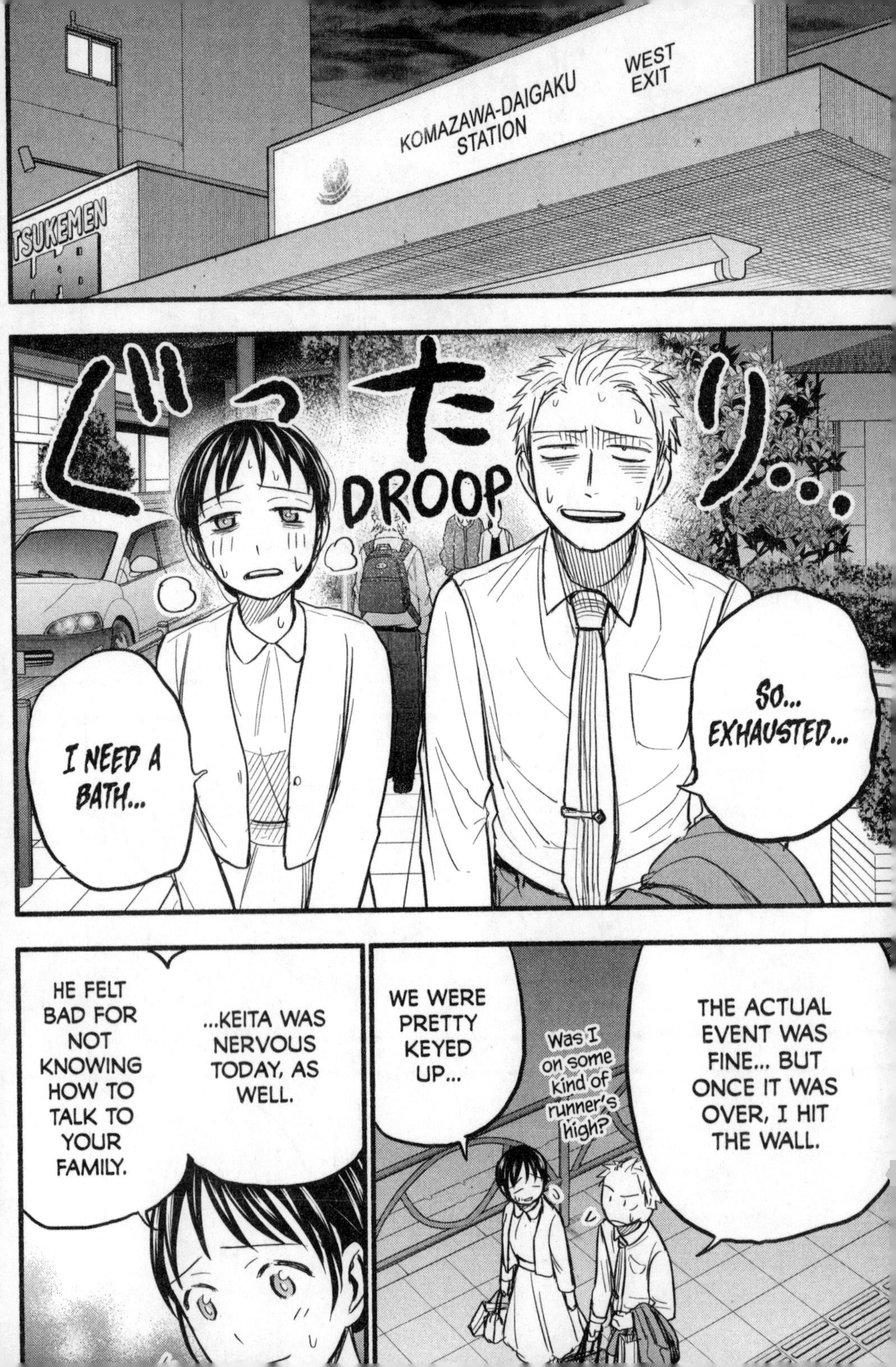
WEST EXIT
KOMAZAWA-DAIGAKU STATION
TSUKEMEN
ぐったり…
DROOP
SO... EXHAUSTED...
I NEED A BATH...
THE ACTUAL EVENT WAS FINE... BUT ONCE IT WAS OVER, I HIT THE WALL.
Was I on some kind of runner's high?
WE WERE PRETTY KEYED UP...
...KEITA WAS NERVOUS TODAY, AS WELL.
HE FELT BAD FOR NOT KNOWING HOW TO TALK TO YOUR FAMILY.

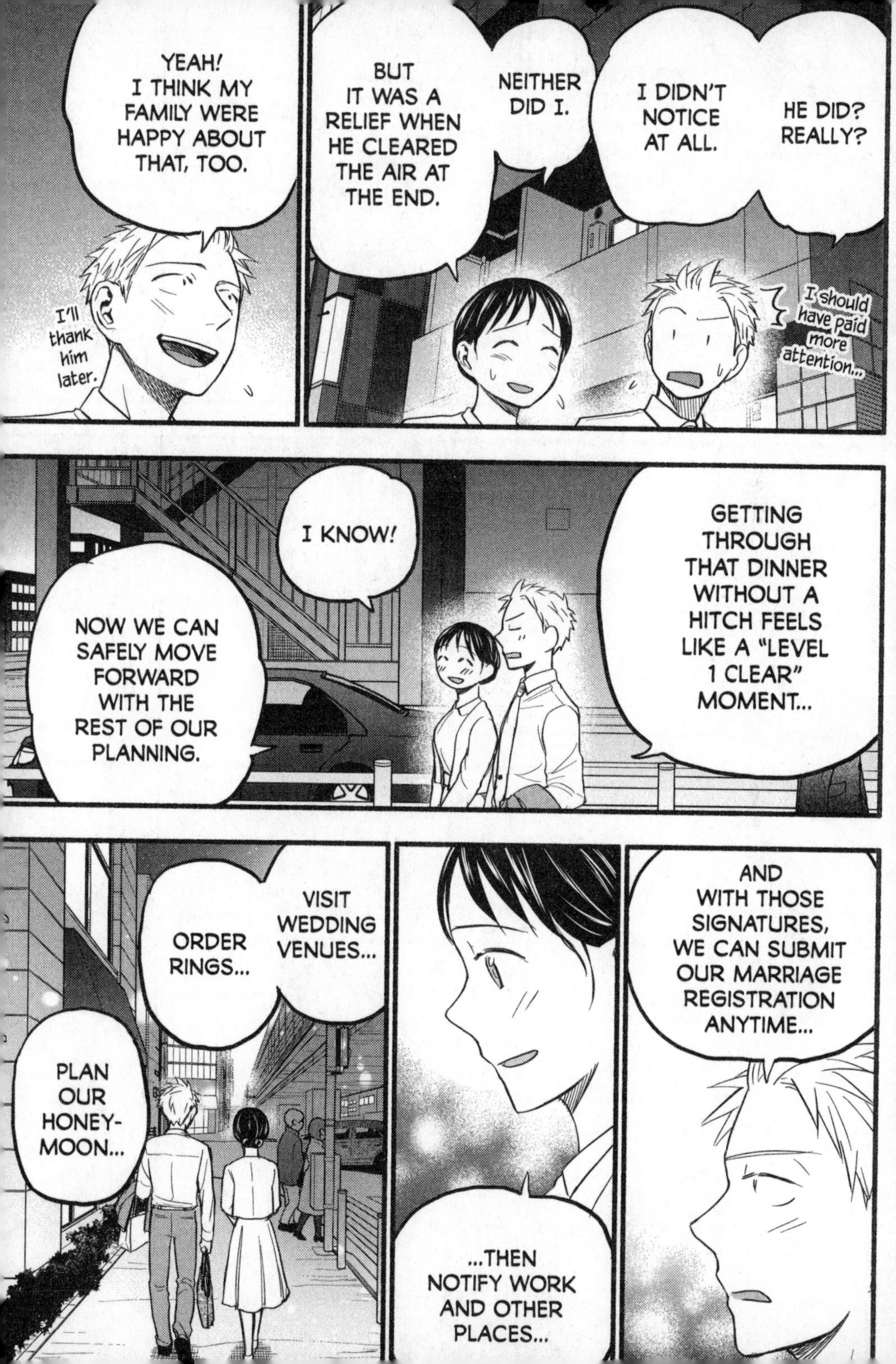
HE DID? REALLY?
I DIDN'T NOTICE AT ALL.
NEITHER DID I.
BUT IT WAS A RELIEF WHEN HE CLEARED THE AIR AT THE END.
I should have paid more attention...
YEAH! I THINK MY FAMILY WERE HAPPY ABOUT THAT, TOO.
I'll thank him later.
GETTING THROUGH THAT DINNER WITHOUT A HITCH FEELS LIKE A "LEVEL 1 CLEAR" MOMENT...
I KNOW!
NOW WE CAN SAFELY MOVE FORWARD WITH THE REST OF OUR PLANNING.
AND WITH THOSE SIGNATURES, WE CAN SUBMIT OUR MARRIAGE REGISTRATION ANYTIME...
...THEN NOTIFY WORK AND OTHER PLACES...
VISIT WEDDING VENUES...
ORDER RINGS...
PLAN OUR HONEYMOON...

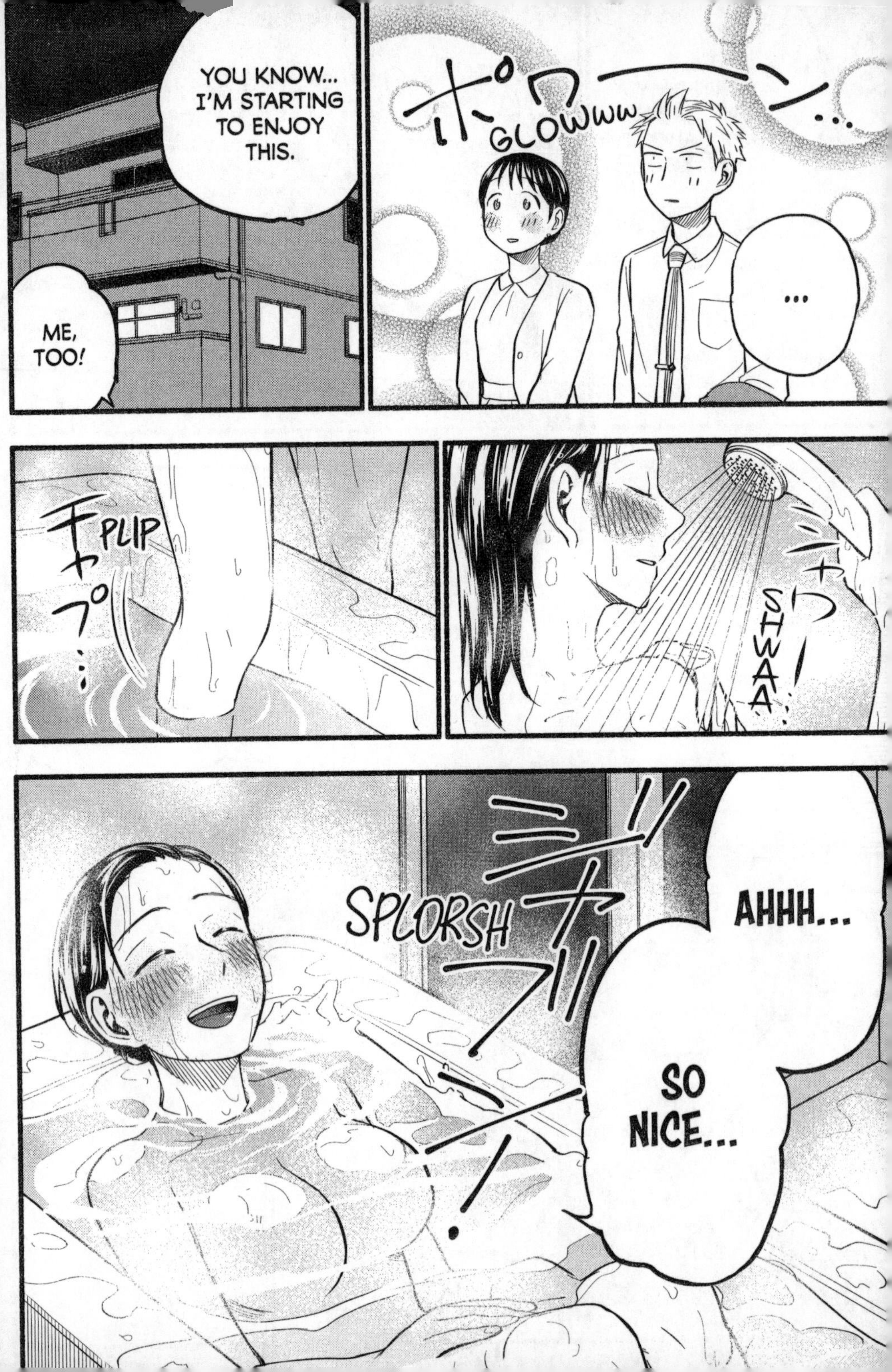
GLOWWW
...
YOU KNOW... I'M STARTING TO ENJOY THIS.
ME, TOO!
SHWAA
PLIP
SPLORSH
AHHH...
SO NICE...

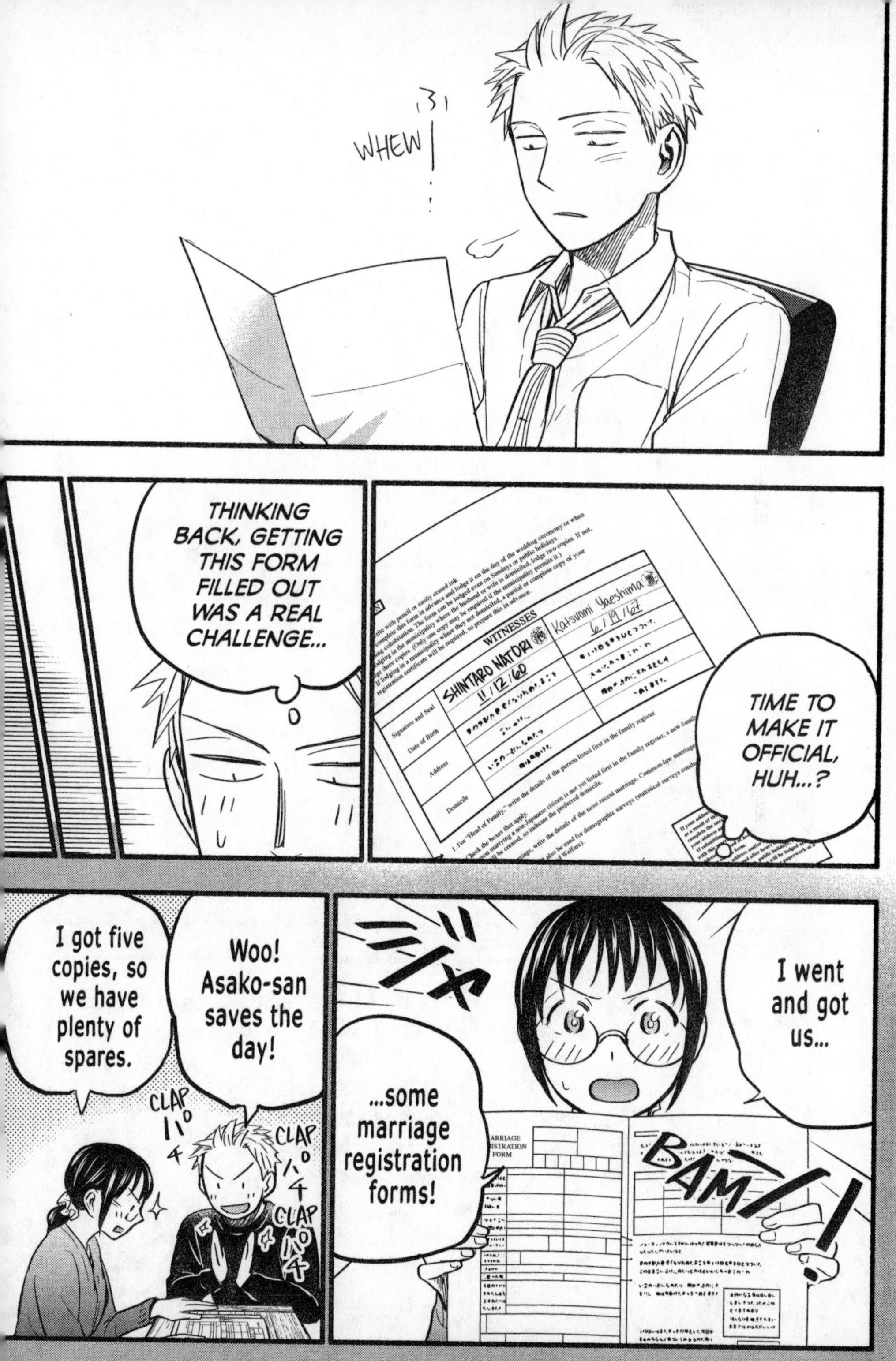

WHEW
TIME TO MAKE IT OFFICIAL, HUH...?
WITNESSES
Signature and Seal
Date of Birth
Address
Domicile
SHINTARO NATORI
11/12/60
Katsuomi Yaeshima
6/19/67
THINKING BACK, GETTING THIS FORM FILLED OUT WAS A REAL CHALLENGE...
I went and got us...
...some marriage registration forms!
BAM!!
Woo! Asako-san saves the day!
I got five copies, so we have plenty of spares.
CLAP
CLAP
CLAP

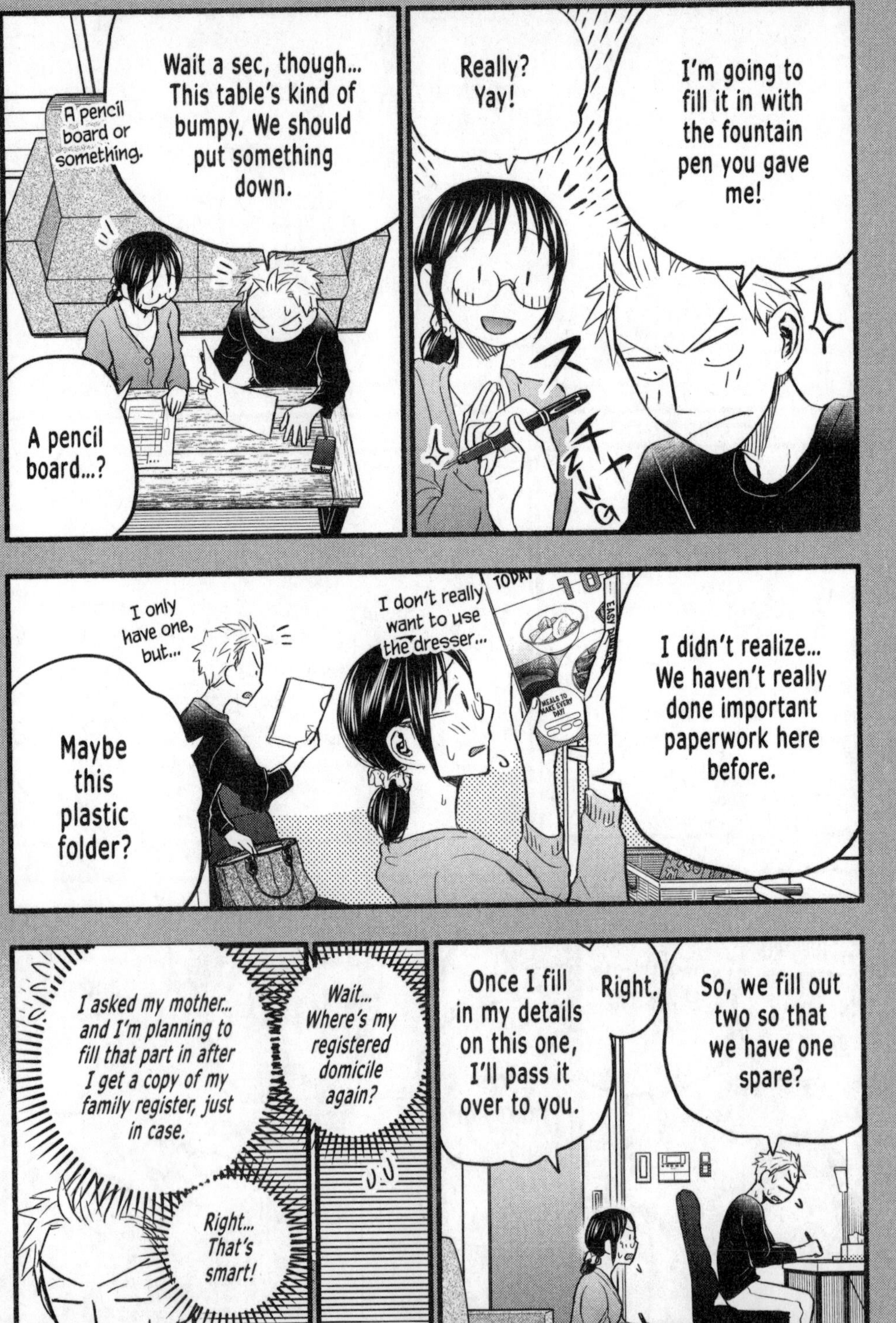
I'm going to fill it in with the fountain pen you gave me!
Really? Yay!
ZING
Wait a sec, though... This table's kind of bumpy. We should put something down.
A pencil board or something.
A pencil board...?
I didn't realize... We haven't really done important paperwork here before.
I don't really want to use the dresser...
I only have one, but...
Maybe this plastic folder?
So, we fill out two so that we have one spare?
Right.
Once I fill in my details on this one, I'll pass it over to you.
Wait... Where's my registered domicile again?
I asked my mother... and I'm planning to fill that part in after I get a copy of my family register, just in case.
Right... That's smart!

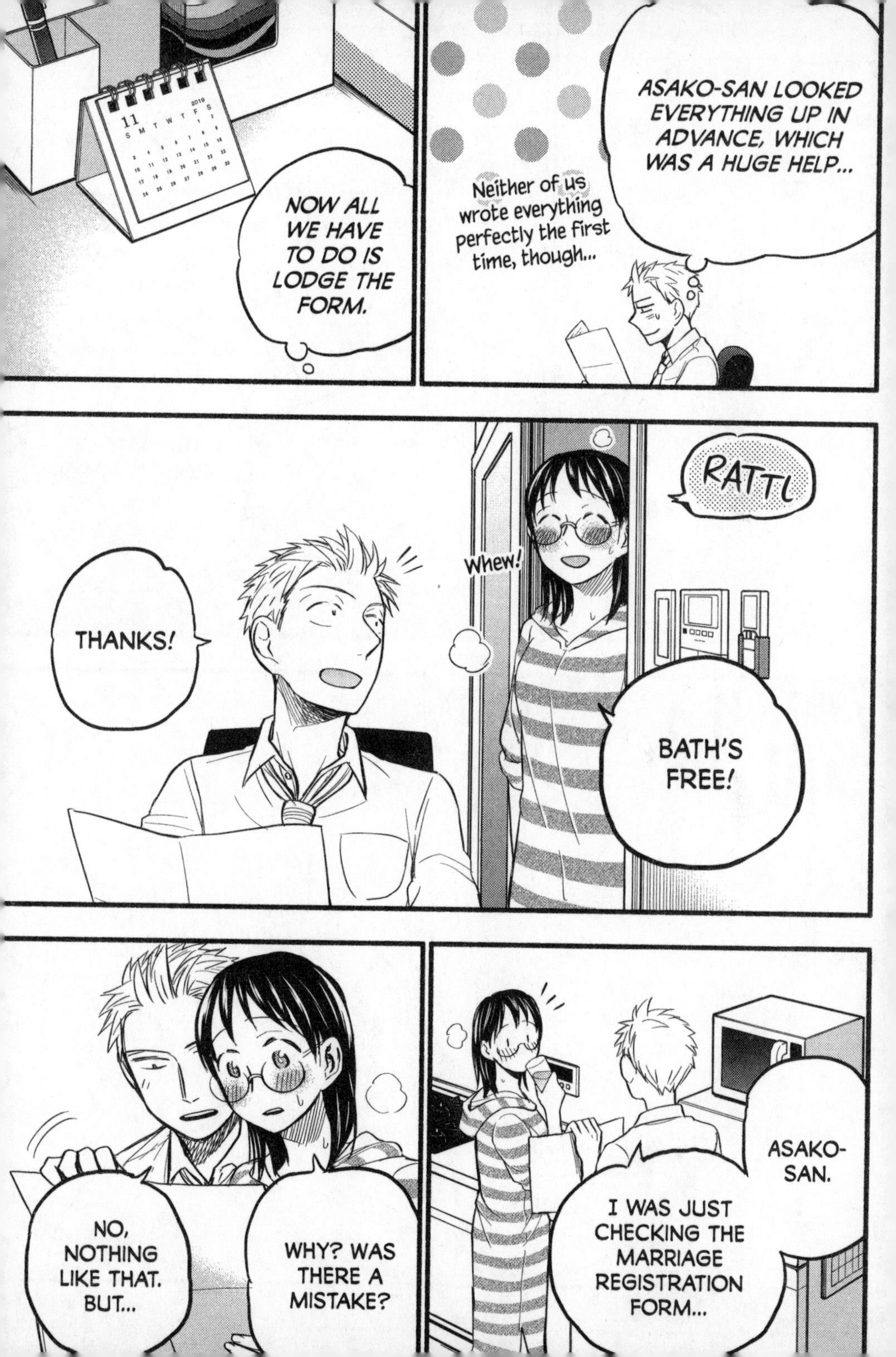

ASAKO-SAN LOOKED EVERYTHING UP IN ADVANCE, WHICH WAS A HUGE HELP...
Neither of us wrote everything perfectly the first time, though...
NOW ALL WE HAVE TO DO IS LODGE THE FORM.
RATTL
BATH'S FREE!
Whew!
THANKS!
ASAKO-SAN.
I WAS JUST CHECKING THE MARRIAGE REGISTRATION FORM...
WHY? WAS THERE A MISTAKE?
NO, NOTHING LIKE THAT. BUT...

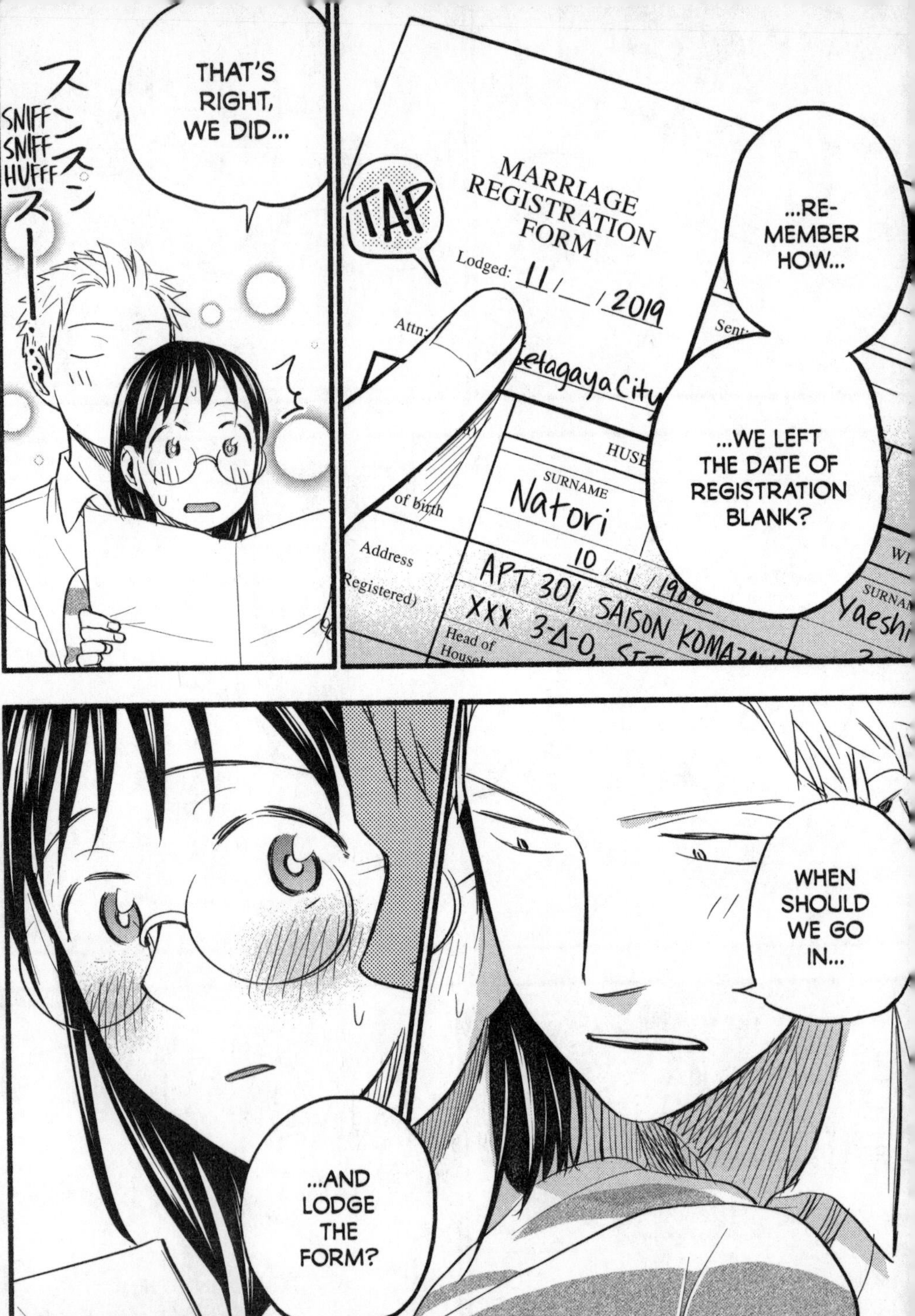
TAP
MARRIAGE REGISTRATION FORM
Lodged: 11 / / 2019
Attn:
Setagaya City
SURNAME
Natori
of birth
10 / 1 / 198
Address
(Registered)
APT 301, SAISON KOMAZA
XXX 3-Δ-0,
Head of
Sent
SURNAME
Yaeshi
...RE-MEMBER HOW...
...WE LEFT THE DATE OF REGISTRATION BLANK?
THAT'S RIGHT, WE DID...
スンスン
SNIFF SNIFF
スー
HUFFF
WHEN SHOULD WE GO IN...
...AND LODGE THE FORM?

Chapter 86 / The End

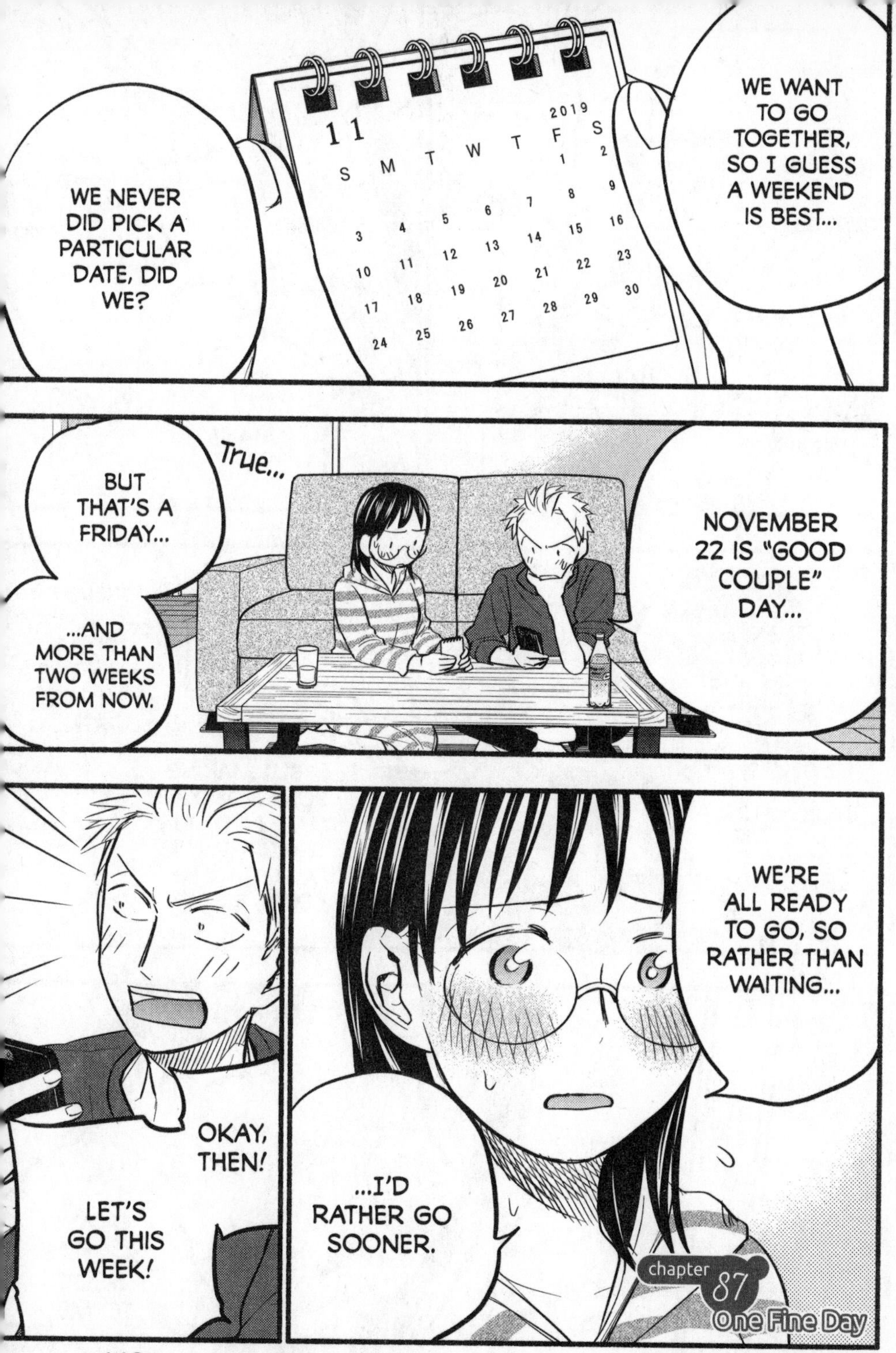
WE WANT TO GO TOGETHER, SO I GUESS A WEEKEND IS BEST...
11 2019
S M T W T F S
WE NEVER DID PICK A PARTICULAR DATE, DID WE?
NOVEMBER 22 IS "GOOD COUPLE" DAY...
True...
BUT THAT'S A FRIDAY...
...AND MORE THAN TWO WEEKS FROM NOW.
WE'RE ALL READY TO GO, SO RATHER THAN WAITING...
...I'D RATHER GO SOONER.
chapter 87
One Fine Day
OKAY, THEN!
LET'S GO THIS WEEK!

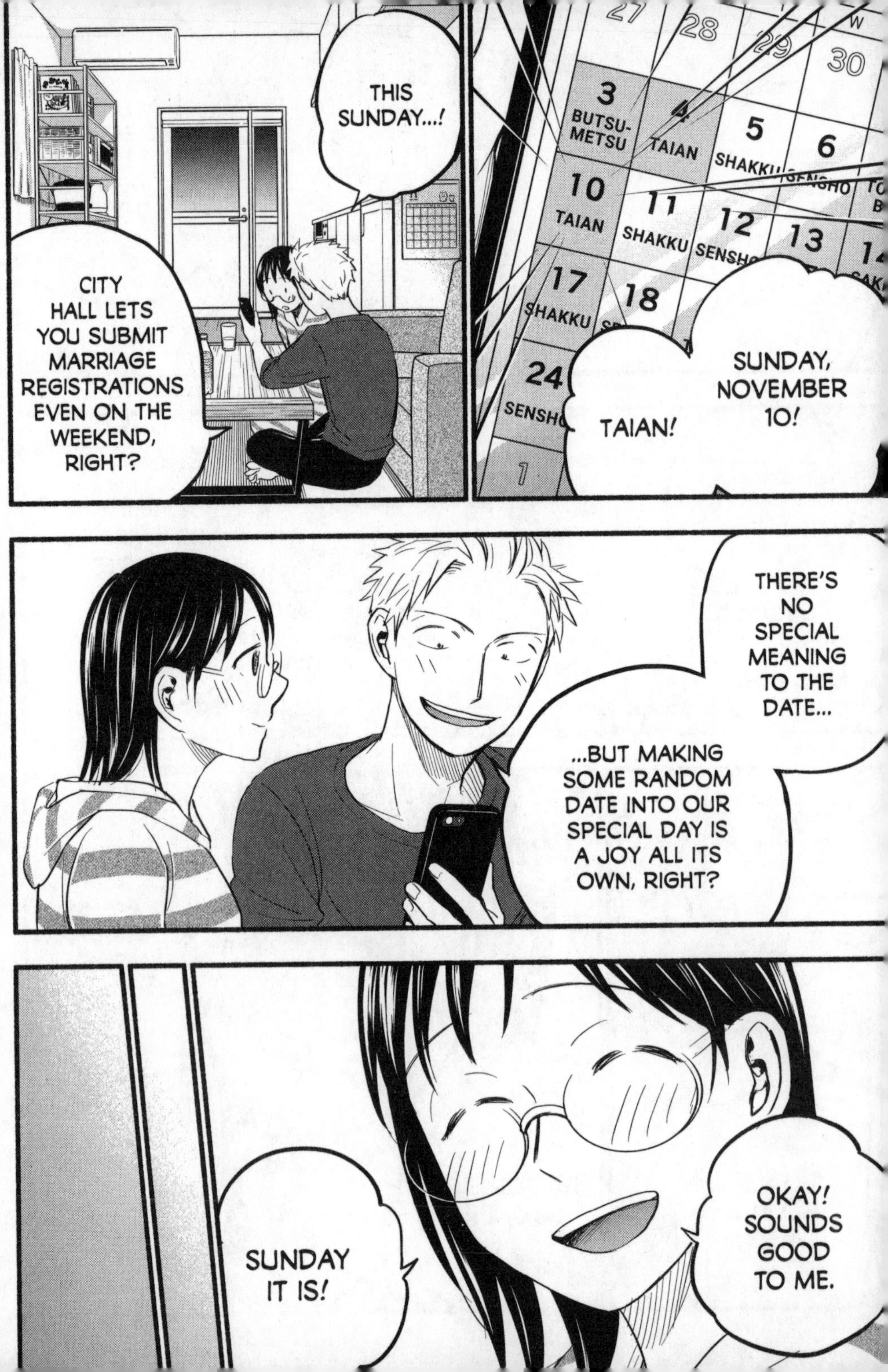
27 28 29 30
3 BUTSUMETSU
4 TAIAN
5 SHAKKU
6
10 TAIAN
11 SHAKKU
12 SENSHO
13
17 SHAKKU
18
24 SENSHO
SUNDAY, NOVEMBER 10!
TAIAN!
THIS SUNDAY...!
CITY HALL LETS YOU SUBMIT MARRIAGE REGISTRATIONS EVEN ON THE WEEKEND, RIGHT?
THERE'S NO SPECIAL MEANING TO THE DATE...
...BUT MAKING SOME RANDOM DATE INTO OUR SPECIAL DAY IS A JOY ALL ITS OWN, RIGHT?
OKAY! SOUNDS GOOD TO ME.
SUNDAY IT IS!

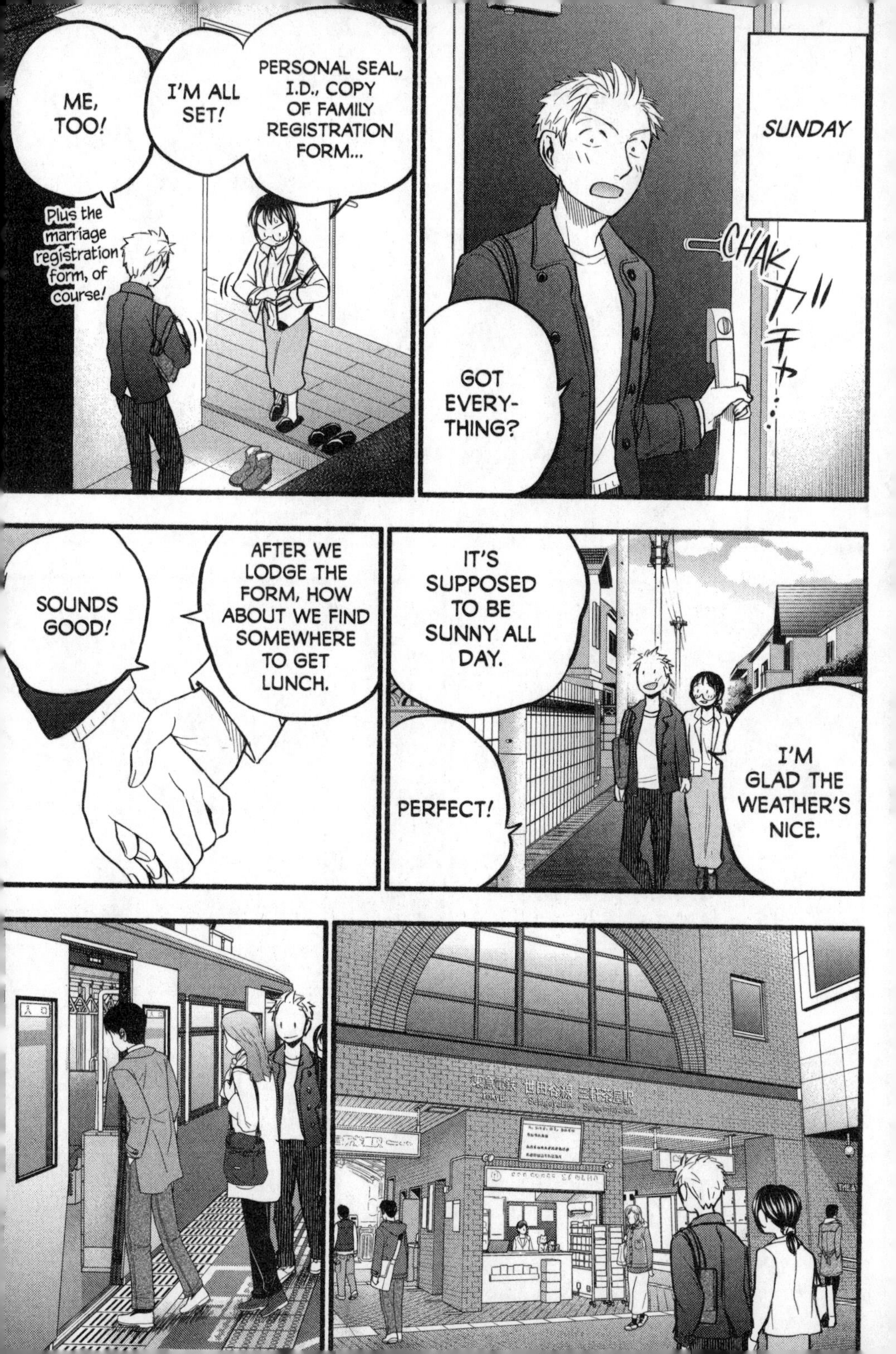
SUNDAY
CHAK
ガチャ
GOT EVERY-THING?
PERSONAL SEAL, I.D., COPY OF FAMILY REGISTRATION FORM...
I'M ALL SET!
ME, TOO!
Plus the marriage registration form, of course!
IT'S SUPPOSED TO BE SUNNY ALL DAY.
I'M GLAD THE WEATHER'S NICE.
PERFECT!
AFTER WE LODGE THE FORM, HOW ABOUT WE FIND SOMEWHERE TO GET LUNCH.
SOUNDS GOOD!

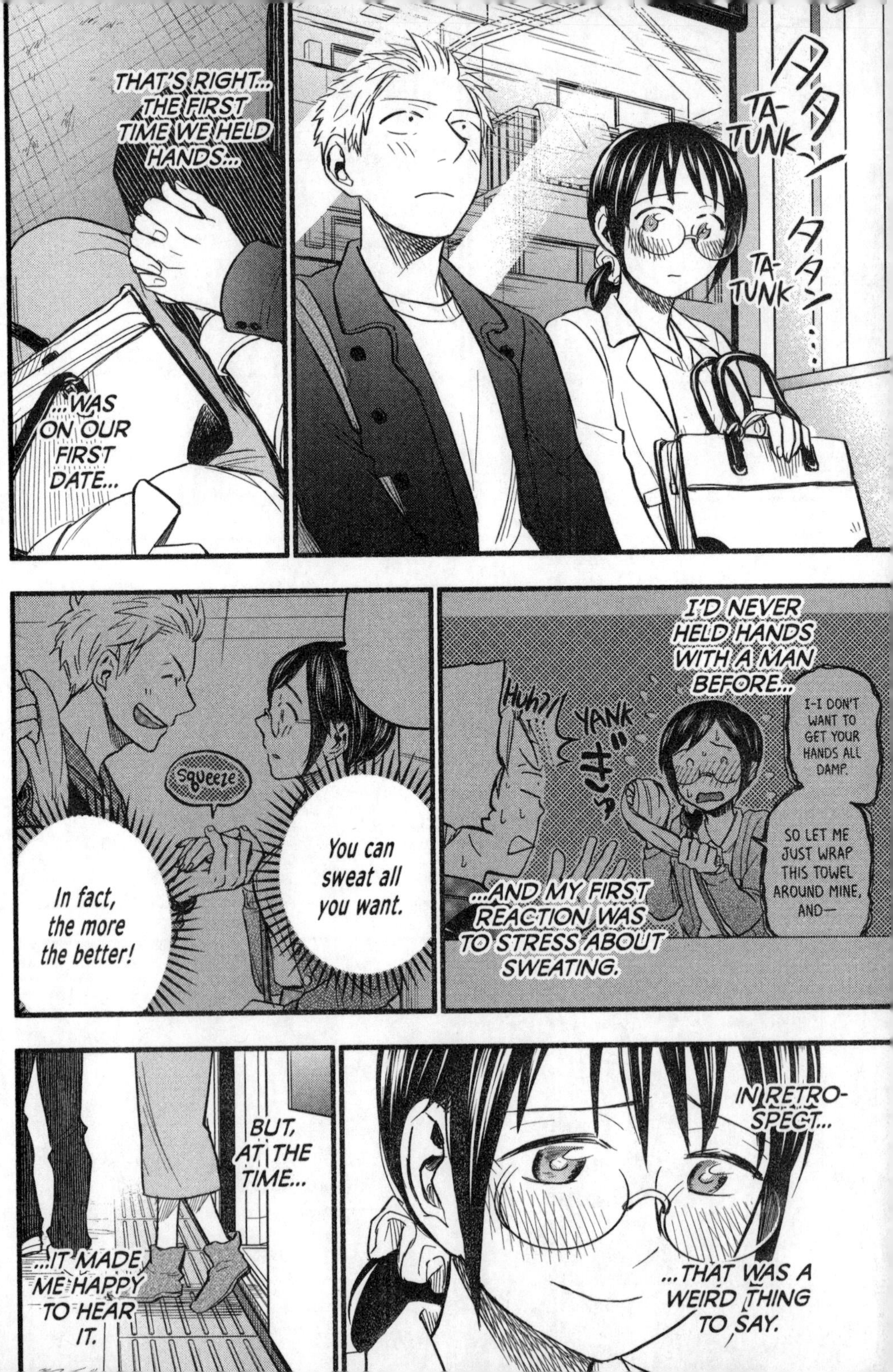
TA-TUNK
TA-TUNK
THAT'S RIGHT... THE FIRST TIME WE HELD HANDS...
...WAS ON OUR FIRST DATE...
I'D NEVER HELD HANDS WITH A MAN BEFORE...
Huh?!
YANK
I-I DON'T WANT TO GET YOUR HANDS ALL DAMP.
SO LET ME JUST WRAP THIS TOWEL AROUND MINE, AND—
...AND MY FIRST REACTION WAS TO STRESS ABOUT SWEATING.
Squeeze
You can sweat all you want.
In fact, the more the better!
IN RETRO-SPECT...
...THAT WAS A WEIRD THING TO SAY.
BUT, AT THE TIME...
...IT MADE ME HAPPY TO HEAR IT.

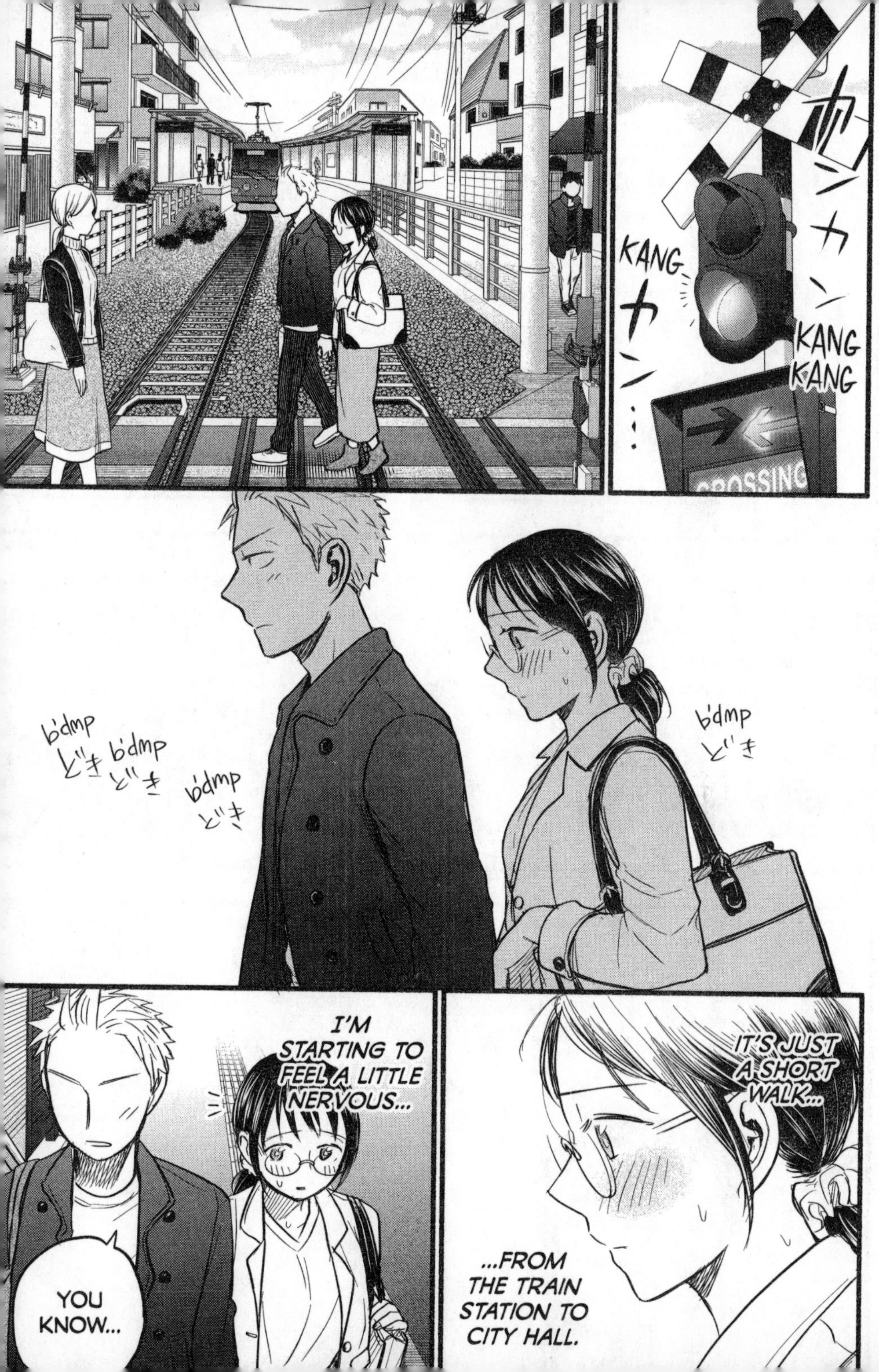
カンカン
KANG KANG
KANG
カン…
CROSSING
b'dmp
どき
b'dmp
どき
b'dmp
どき
b'dmp
どき
IT'S JUST A SHORT WALK...
...FROM THE TRAIN STATION TO CITY HALL.
I'M STARTING TO FEEL A LITTLE NERVOUS...
YOU KNOW...

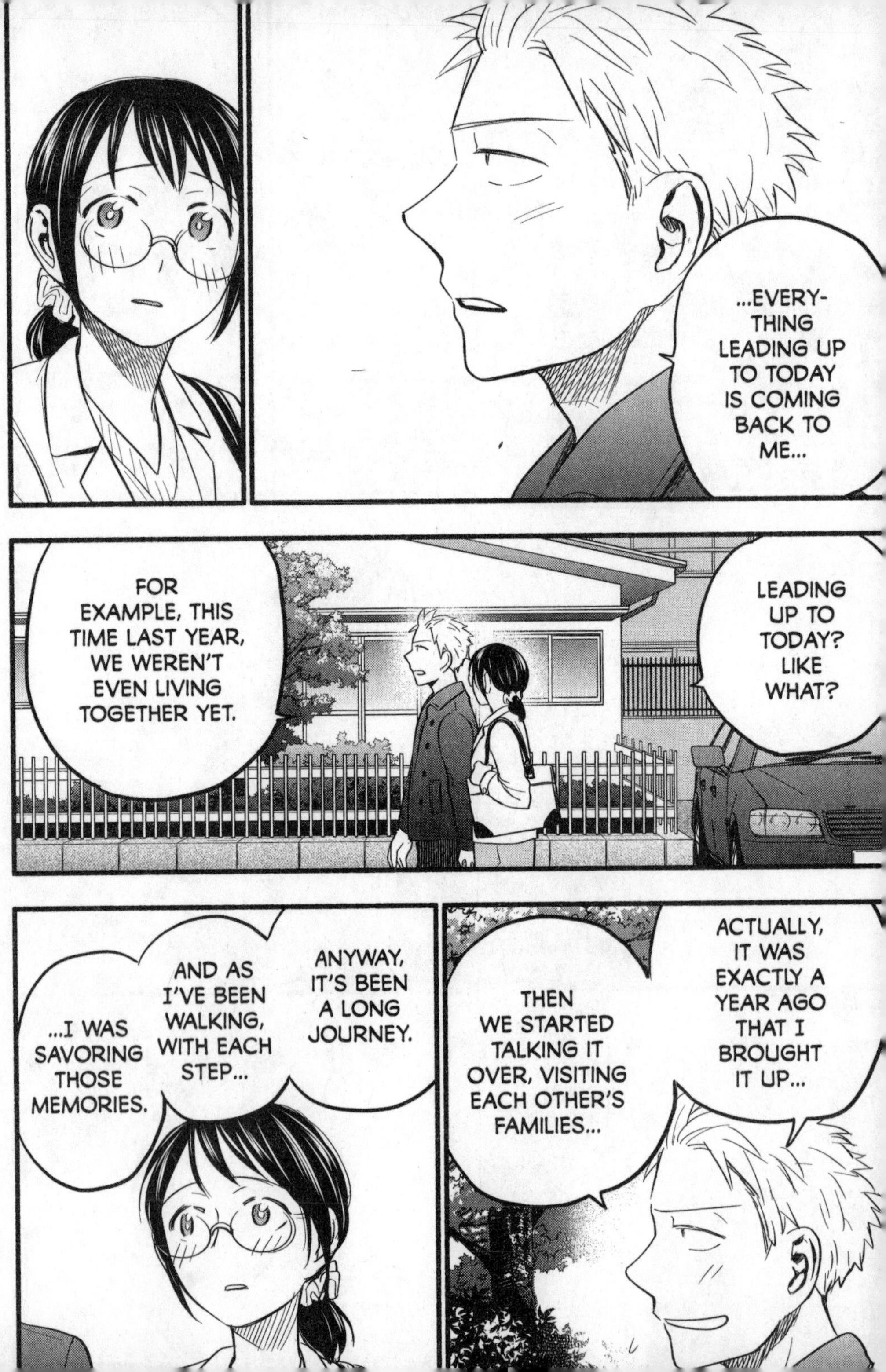
...EVERY-THING LEADING UP TO TODAY IS COMING BACK TO ME...
LEADING UP TO TODAY? LIKE WHAT?
FOR EXAMPLE, THIS TIME LAST YEAR, WE WEREN'T EVEN LIVING TOGETHER YET.
ACTUALLY, IT WAS EXACTLY A YEAR AGO THAT I BROUGHT IT UP...
THEN WE STARTED TALKING IT OVER, VISITING EACH OTHER'S FAMILIES...
ANYWAY, IT'S BEEN A LONG JOURNEY.
AND AS I'VE BEEN WALKING, WITH EACH STEP...
...I WAS SAVORING THOSE MEMORIES.

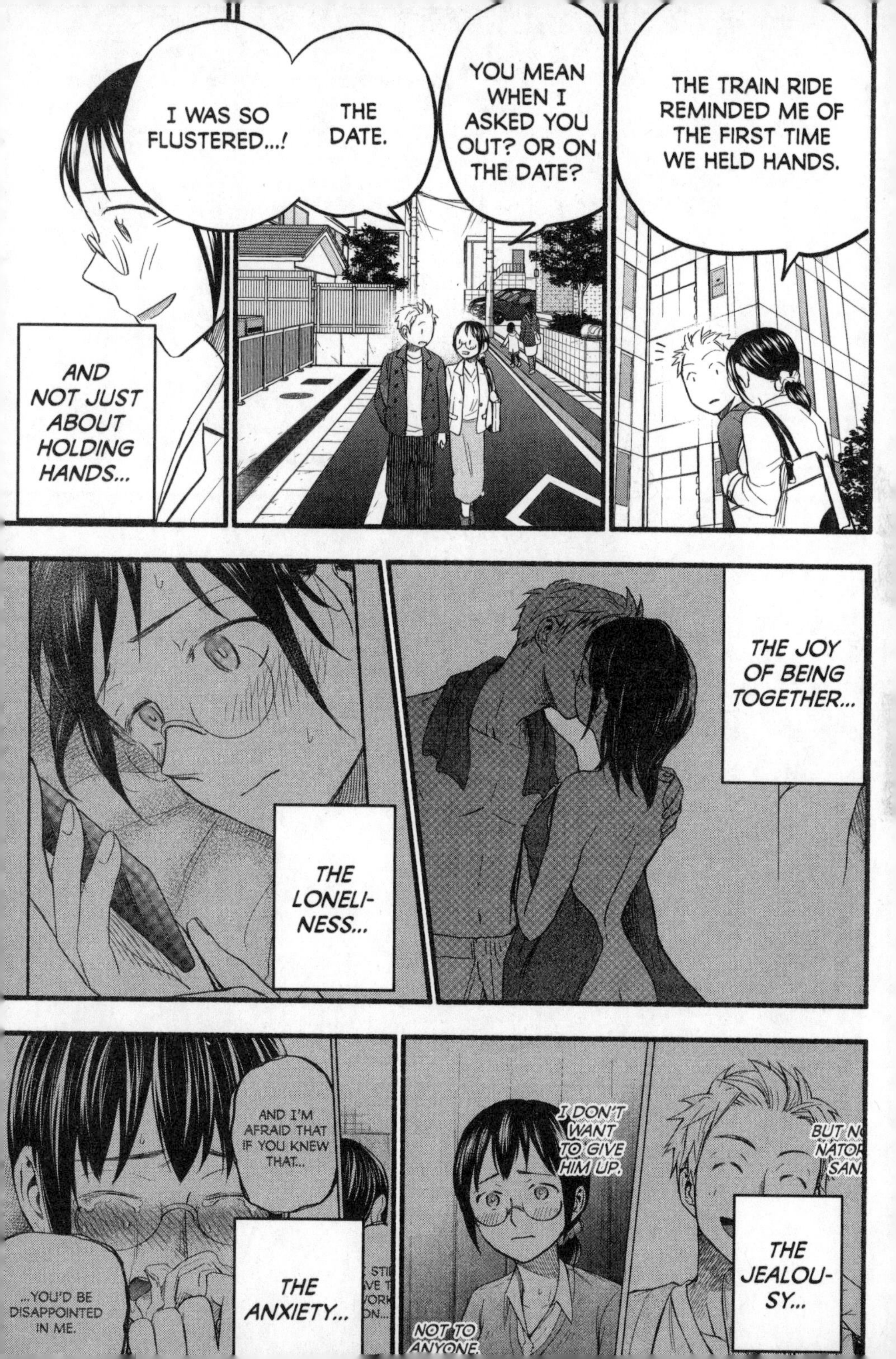
THE TRAIN RIDE REMINDED ME OF THE FIRST TIME WE HELD HANDS.
YOU MEAN WHEN I ASKED YOU OUT? OR ON THE DATE?
THE DATE.
I WAS SO FLUSTERED...!
AND NOT JUST ABOUT HOLDING HANDS...
THE JOY OF BEING TOGETHER...
THE LONELI-NESS...
I DON'T WANT TO GIVE HIM UP.
THE JEALOU-SY...
NOT TO ANYONE.
AND I'M AFRAID THAT IF YOU KNEW THAT...
...YOU'D BE DISAPPOINTED IN ME.
THE ANXIETY...

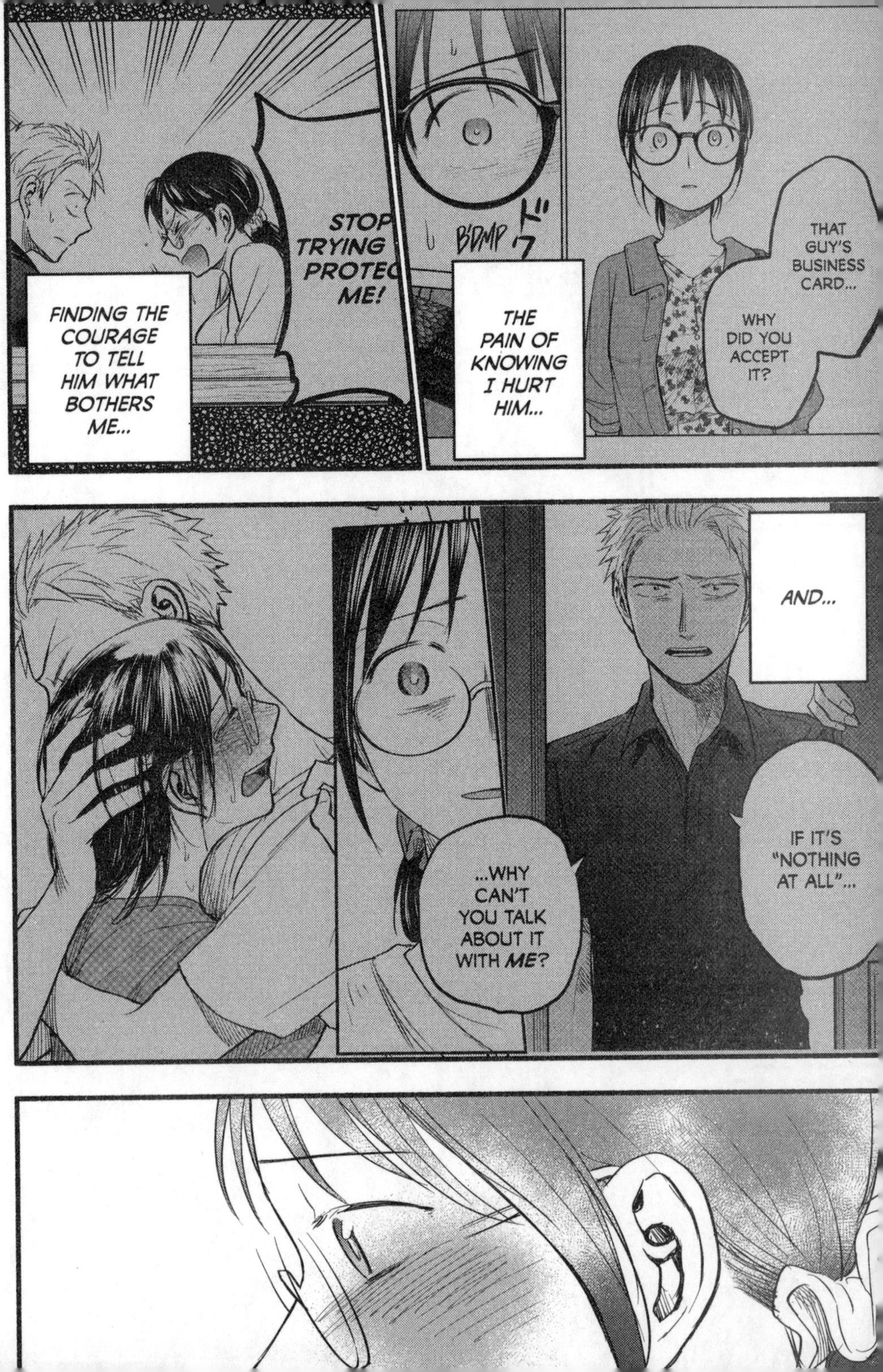
THAT GUY'S BUSINESS CARD...
WHY DID YOU ACCEPT IT?
THE PAIN OF KNOWING I HURT HIM...
B'DMP
ドク
STOP TRYING PROTEC ME!
FINDING THE COURAGE TO TELL HIM WHAT BOTHERS ME...
AND...
IF IT'S "NOTHING AT ALL"...
...WHY CAN'T YOU TALK ABOUT IT WITH *ME*?

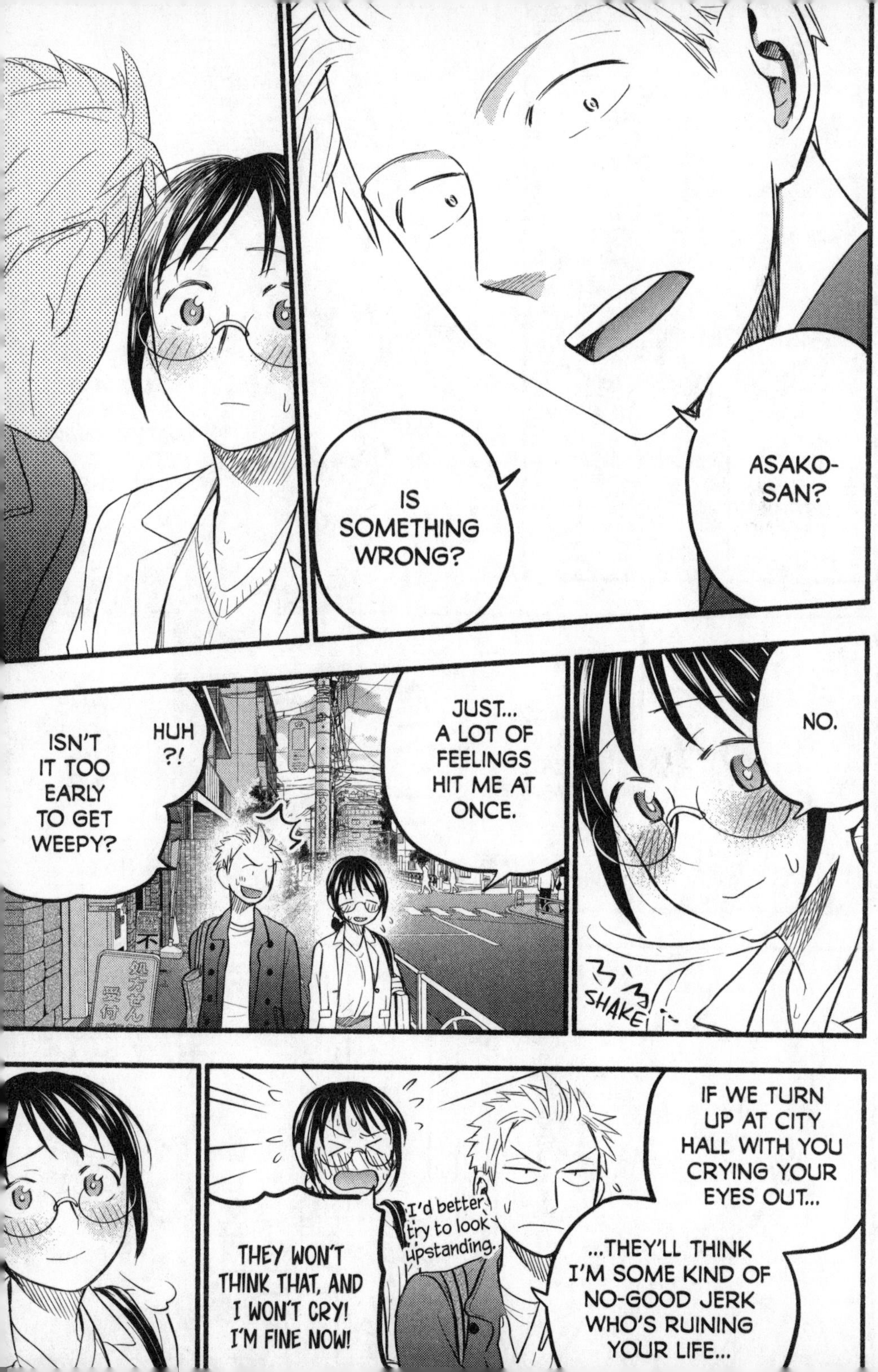
ASAKO-SAN?
IS SOMETHING WRONG?
NO.
SHAKE
JUST... A LOT OF FEELINGS HIT ME AT ONCE.
HUH ?!
ISN'T IT TOO EARLY TO GET WEEPY?
処方せん 受付
IF WE TURN UP AT CITY HALL WITH YOU CRYING YOUR EYES OUT...
...THEY'LL THINK I'M SOME KIND OF NO-GOOD JERK WHO'S RUINING YOUR LIFE...
I'd better try to look upstanding.
THEY WON'T THINK THAT, AND I WON'T CRY! I'M FINE NOW!

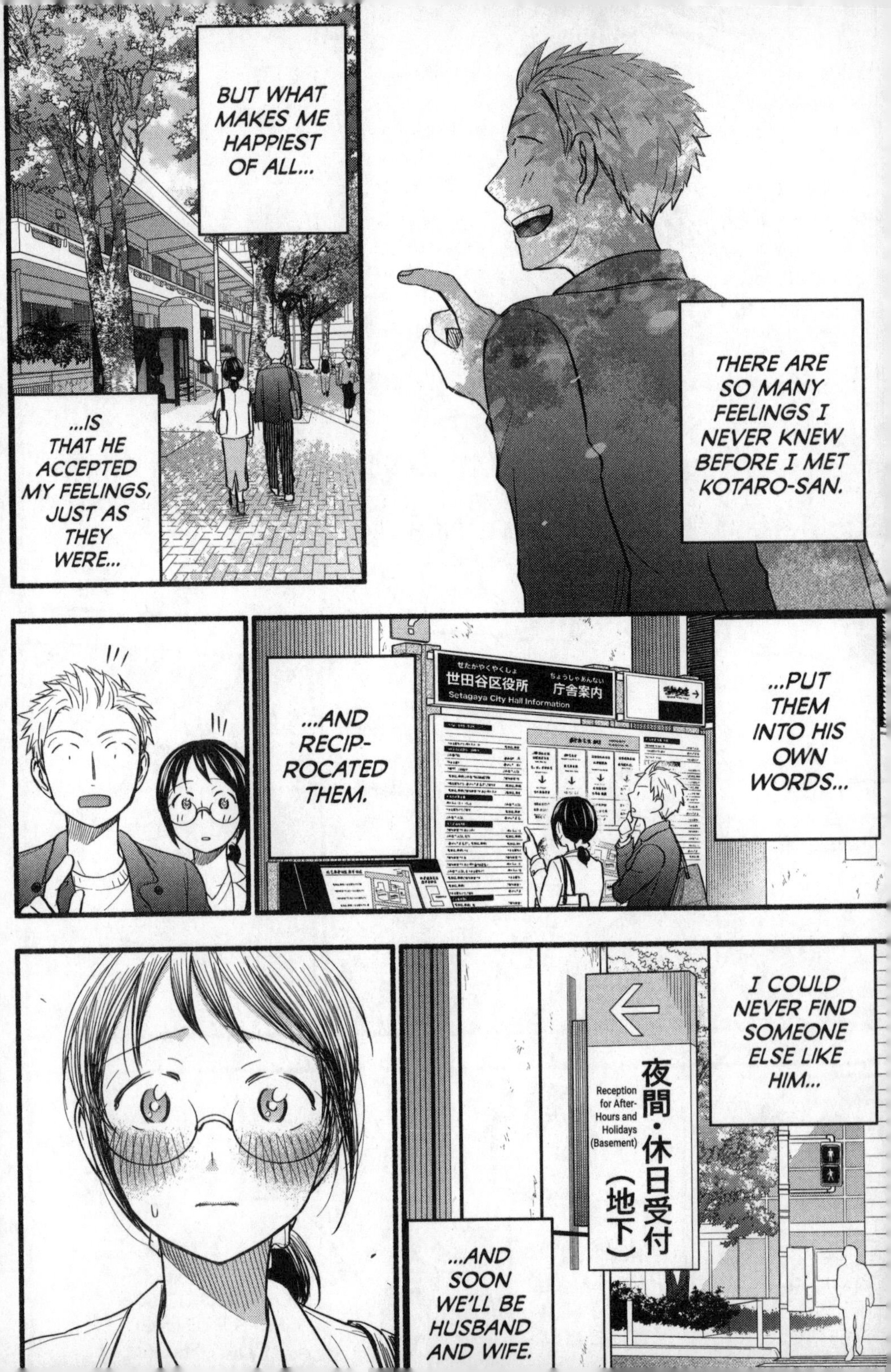
THERE ARE SO MANY FEELINGS I NEVER KNEW BEFORE I MET KOTARO-SAN.
BUT WHAT MAKES ME HAPPIEST OF ALL...
...IS THAT HE ACCEPTED MY FEELINGS, JUST AS THEY WERE...
...PUT THEM INTO HIS OWN WORDS...
世田谷区役所 庁舎案内
Setagaya City Hall Information
...AND RECIP-ROCATED THEM.
I COULD NEVER FIND SOMEONE ELSE LIKE HIM...
夜間・休日受付（地下）
Reception for After-Hours and Holidays (Basement)
...AND SOON WE'LL BE HUSBAND AND WIFE.

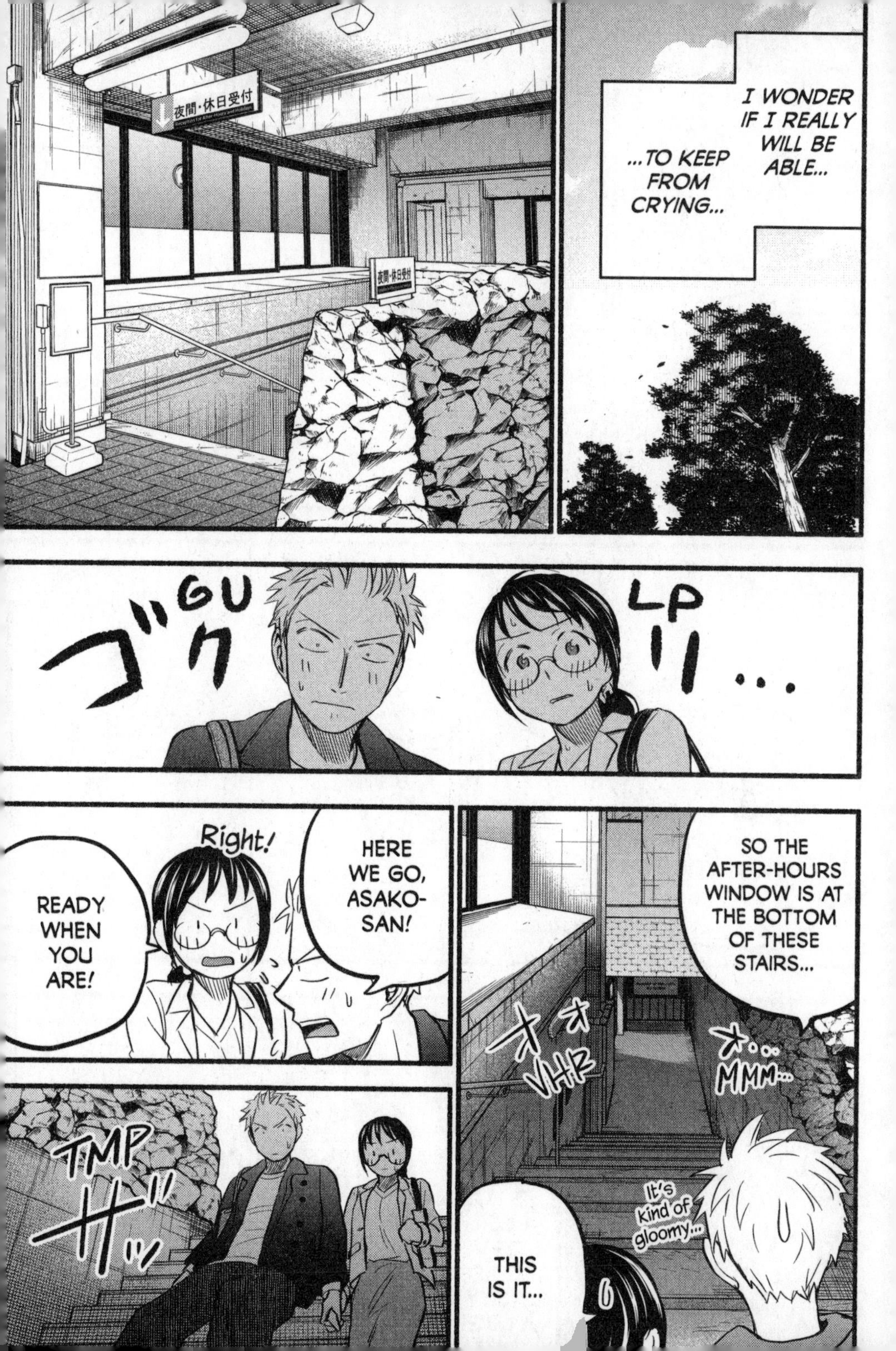
I WONDER IF I REALLY WILL BE ABLE...
...TO KEEP FROM CRYING...
夜間・休日受付
夜間・休日受付
LP
リ...
GU
ゴク
SO THE AFTER-HOURS WINDOW IS AT THE BOTTOM OF THESE STAIRS...
オ... MMM...
オ VHR
HERE WE GO, ASAKO-SAN!
Right!
READY WHEN YOU ARE!
It's kind of gloomy...
THIS IS IT...
TMP
ザッ

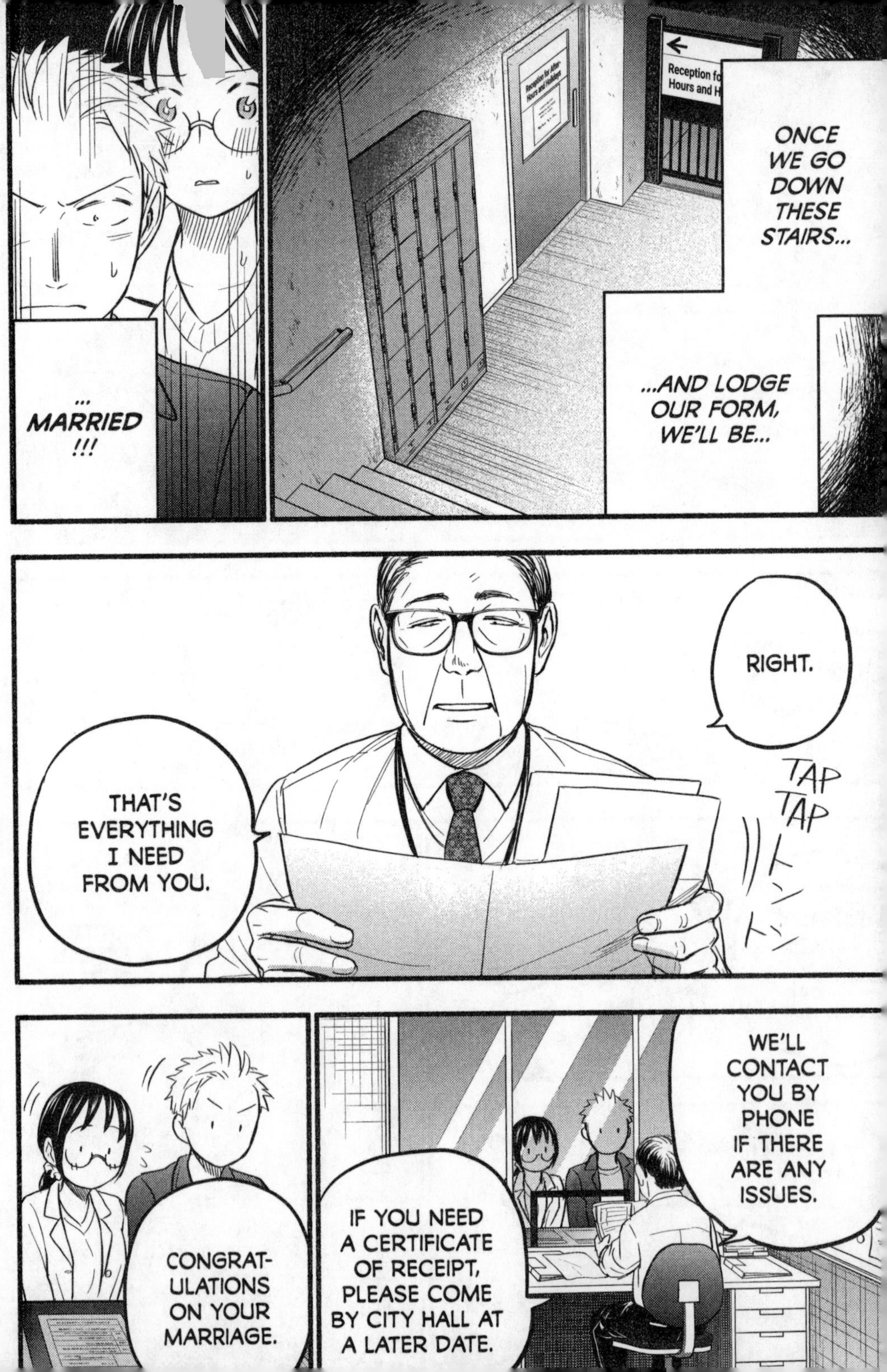
Reception for After-Hours and Holidays
ONCE WE GO DOWN THESE STAIRS...
...AND LODGE OUR FORM, WE'LL BE...
... MARRIED !!!
RIGHT.
TAP TAP
THAT'S EVERYTHING I NEED FROM YOU.
WE'LL CONTACT YOU BY PHONE IF THERE ARE ANY ISSUES.
IF YOU NEED A CERTIFICATE OF RECEIPT, PLEASE COME BY CITY HALL AT A LATER DATE.
CONGRAT-ULATIONS ON YOUR MARRIAGE.

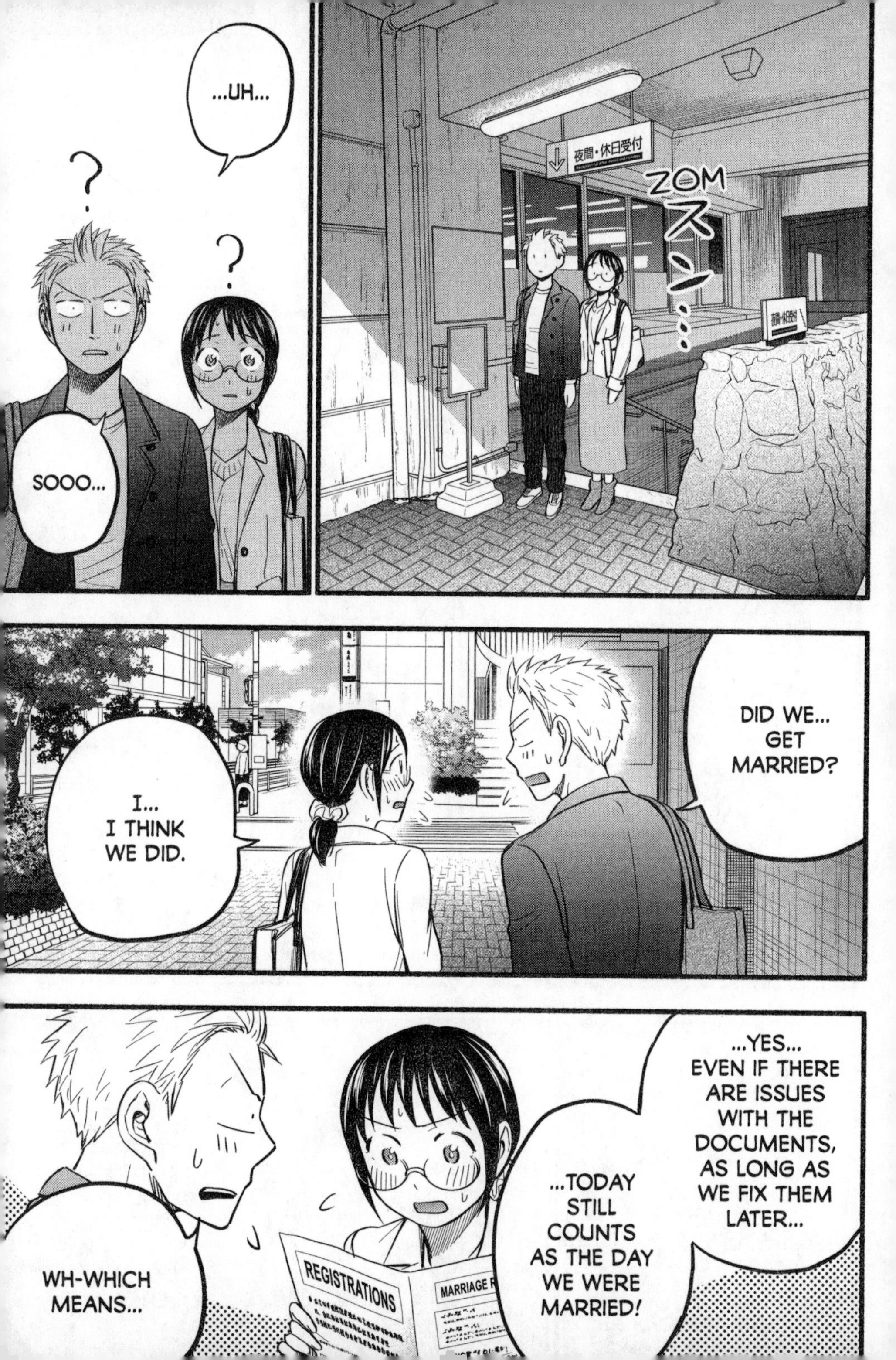
夜間・休日受付
ZOM
ズン…
...UH...
SOOO...
DID WE... GET MARRIED?
I... I THINK WE DID.
...YES... EVEN IF THERE ARE ISSUES WITH THE DOCUMENTS, AS LONG AS WE FIX THEM LATER...
...TODAY STILL COUNTS AS THE DAY WE WERE MARRIED!
WH-WHICH MEANS...
REGISTRATIONS

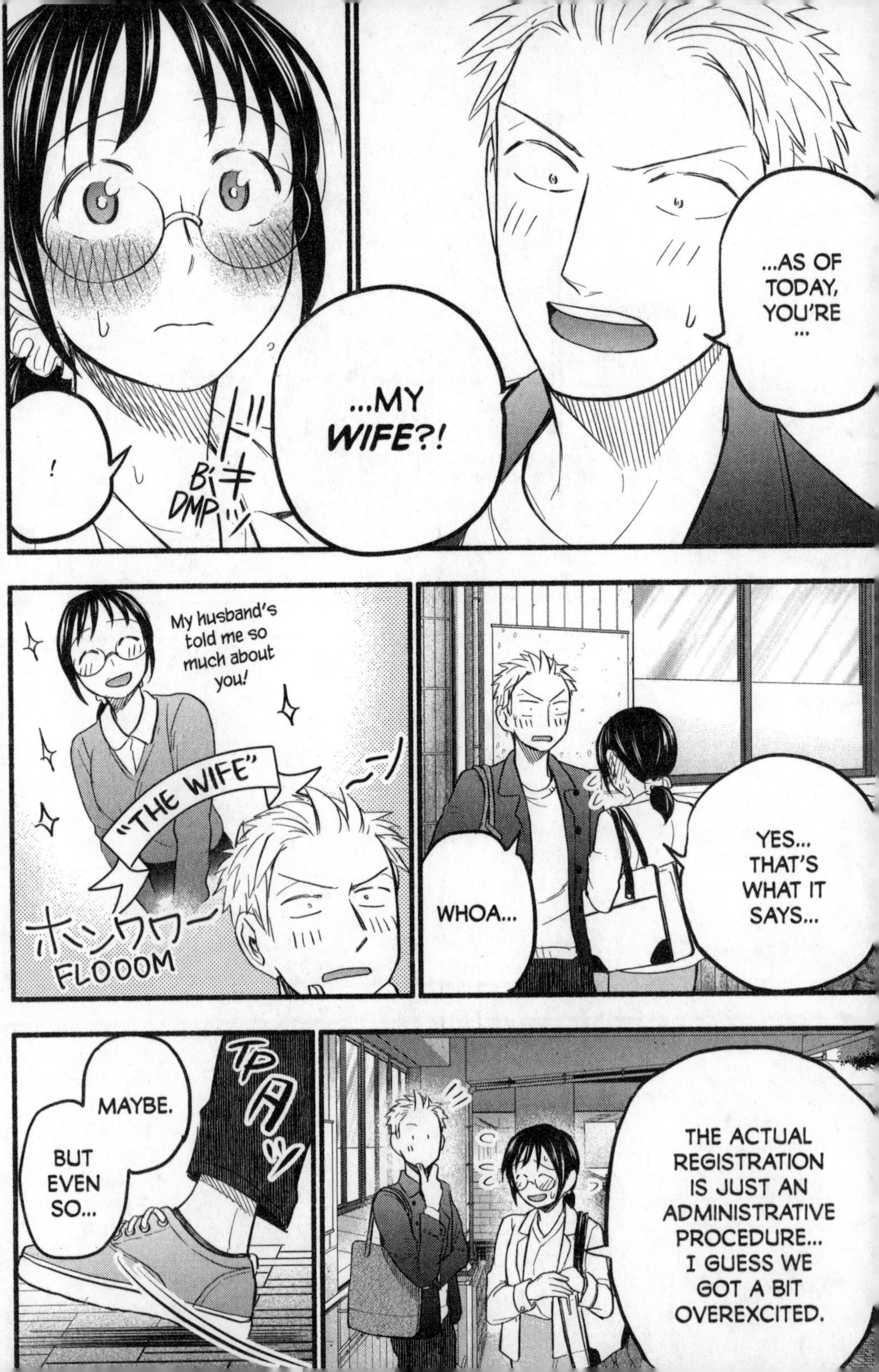
...AS OF TODAY, YOU'RE ...
...MY WIFE?!
!
BI DMP
YES... THAT'S WHAT IT SAYS...
WHOA...
My husband's told me so much about you!
"THE WIFE"
FLOOOM
THE ACTUAL REGISTRATION IS JUST AN ADMINISTRATIVE PROCEDURE... I GUESS WE GOT A BIT OVEREXCITED.
MAYBE.
BUT EVEN SO...

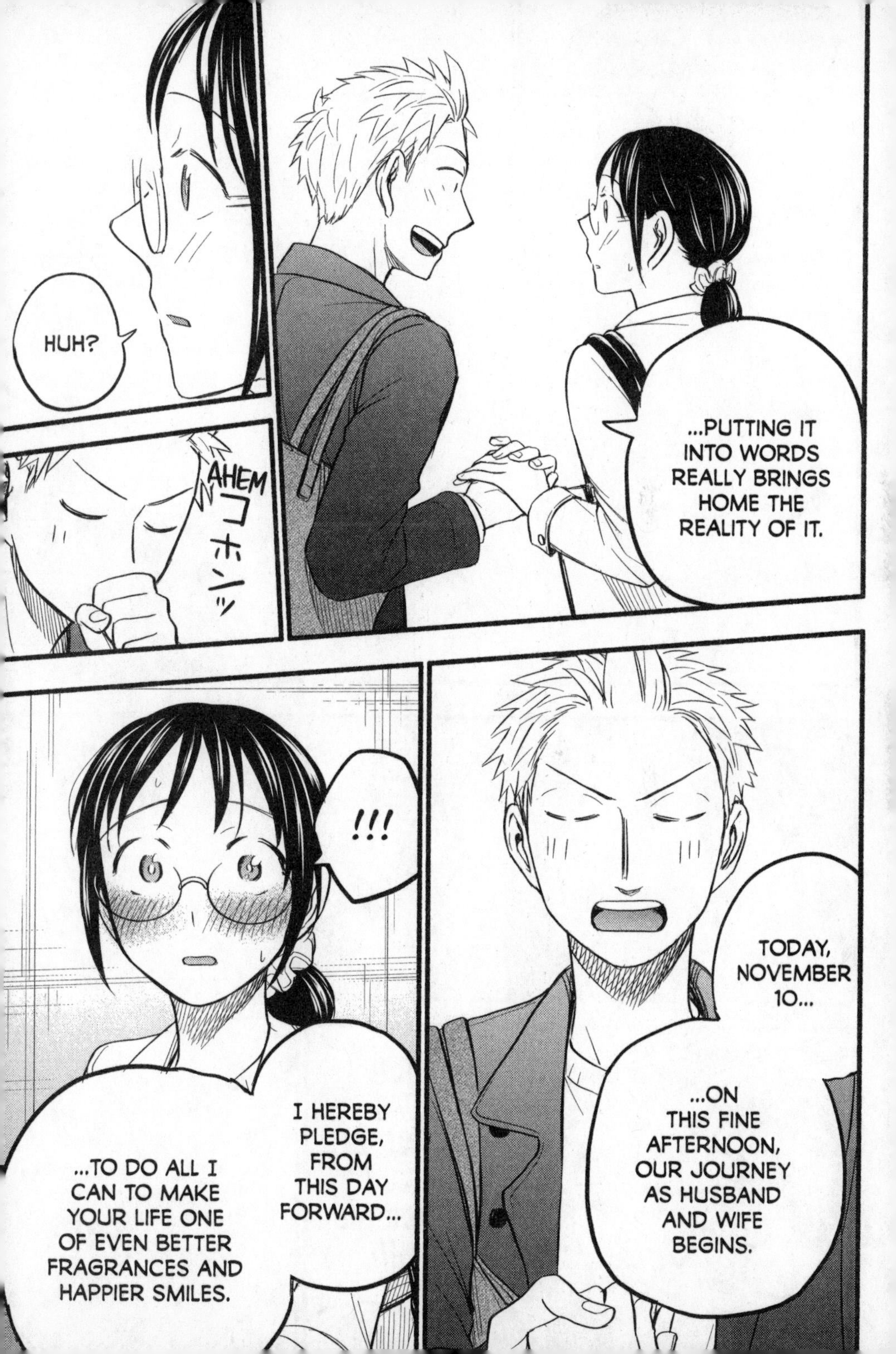
...PUTTING IT INTO WORDS REALLY BRINGS HOME THE REALITY OF IT.
HUH?
AHEM
コホンッ
TODAY, NOVEMBER 10...
...ON THIS FINE AFTERNOON, OUR JOURNEY AS HUSBAND AND WIFE BEGINS.
!!!
I HEREBY PLEDGE, FROM THIS DAY FORWARD...
...TO DO ALL I CAN TO MAKE YOUR LIFE ONE OF EVEN BETTER FRAGRANCES AND HAPPIER SMILES.

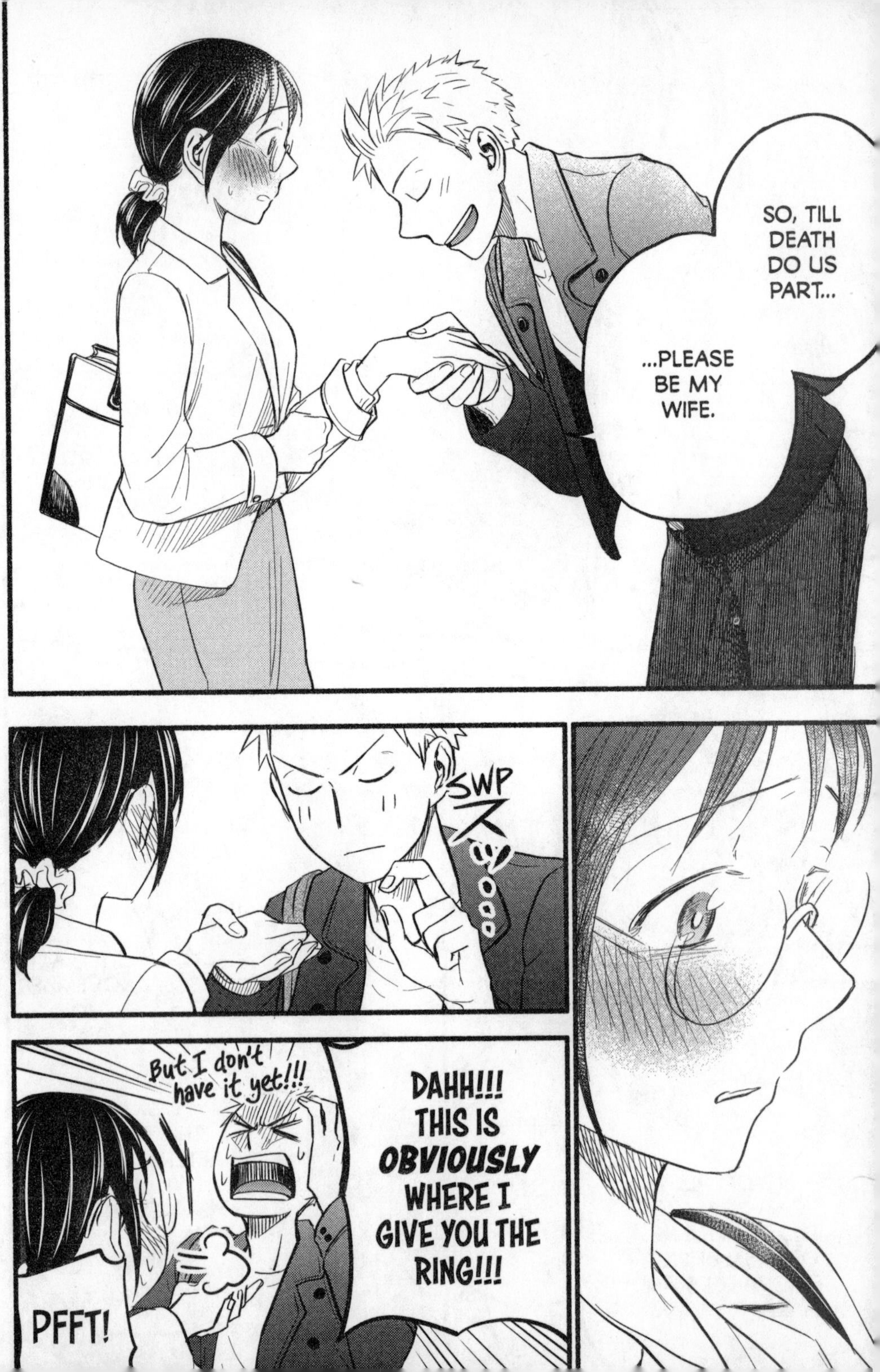
SO, TILL DEATH DO US PART...
...PLEASE BE MY WIFE.
SWP
DAHH!!! THIS IS OBVIOUSLY WHERE I GIVE YOU THE RING!!!
But I don't have it yet!!!
PFFT!

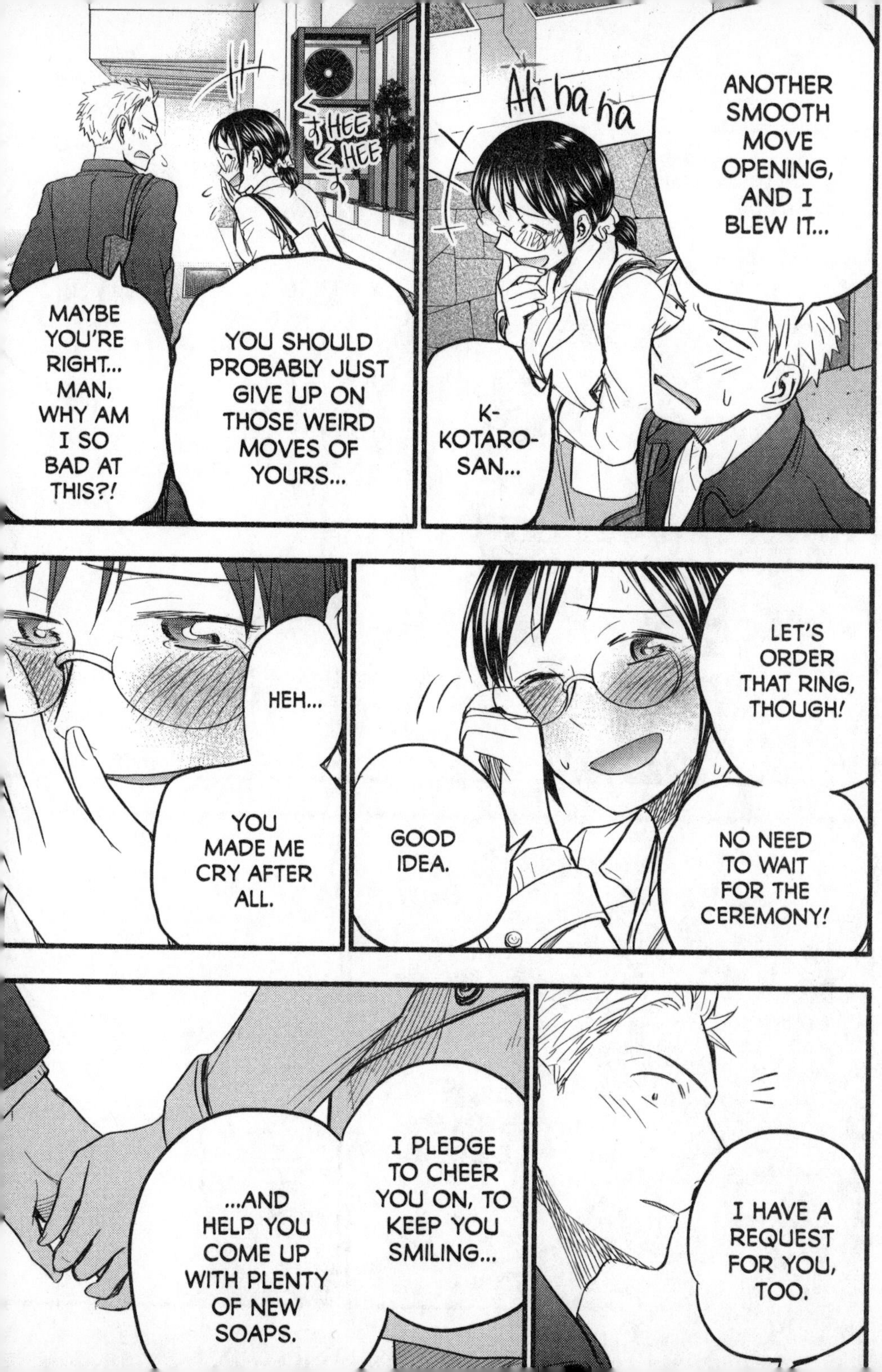
Ah ha ha
ANOTHER SMOOTH MOVE OPENING, AND I BLEW IT...
K-KOTARO-SAN...
HEE HEE
YOU SHOULD PROBABLY JUST GIVE UP ON THOSE WEIRD MOVES OF YOURS...
MAYBE YOU'RE RIGHT... MAN, WHY AM I SO BAD AT THIS?!
LET'S ORDER THAT RING, THOUGH!
NO NEED TO WAIT FOR THE CEREMONY!
GOOD IDEA.
HEH...
YOU MADE ME CRY AFTER ALL.
I HAVE A REQUEST FOR YOU, TOO.
I PLEDGE TO CHEER YOU ON, TO KEEP YOU SMILING...
...AND HELP YOU COME UP WITH PLENTY OF NEW SOAPS.

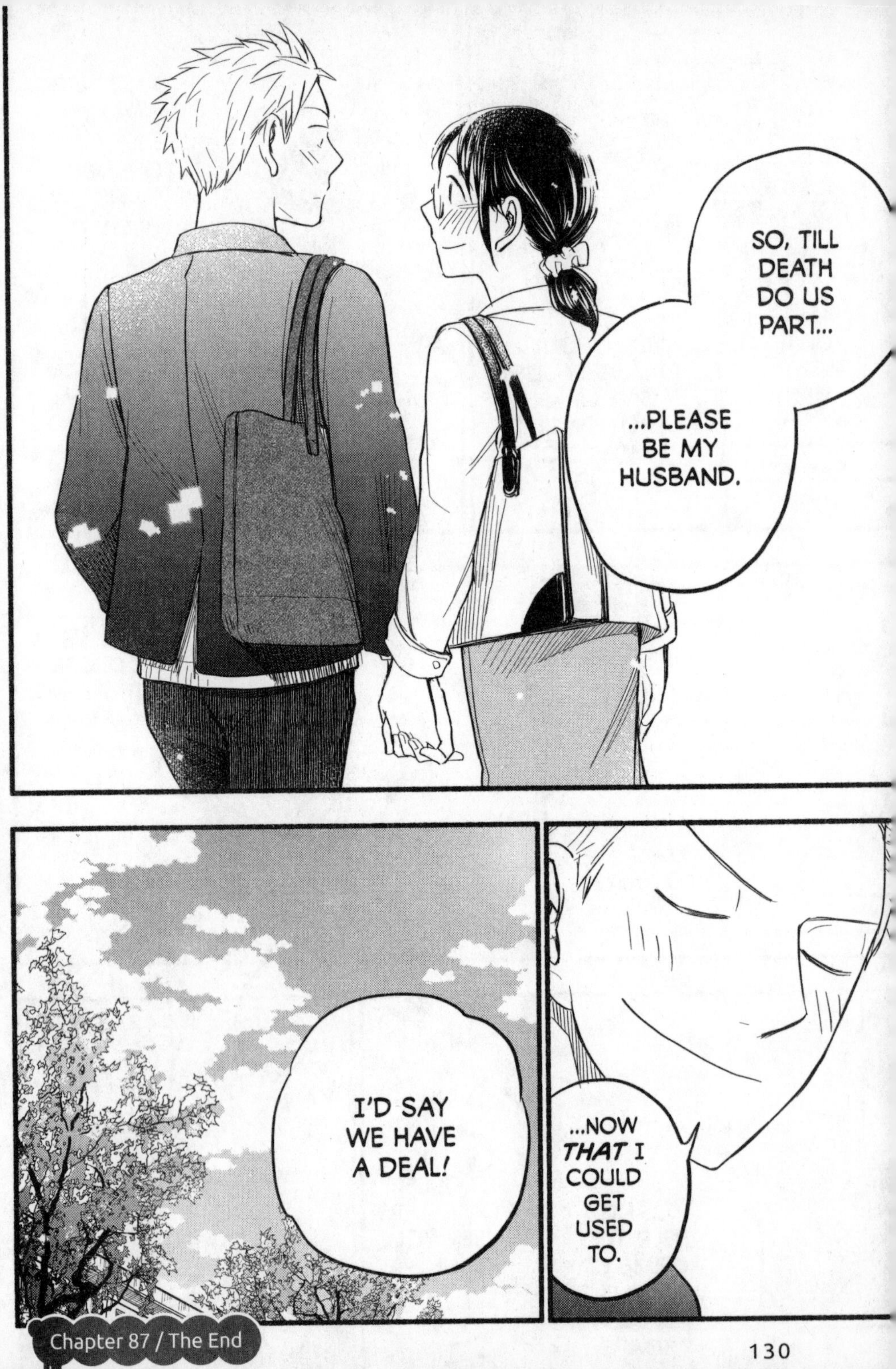
SO, TILL DEATH DO US PART...
...PLEASE BE MY HUSBAND.
...NOW *THAT* I COULD GET USED TO.
I'D SAY WE HAVE A DEAL!

Chapter 87 / The End

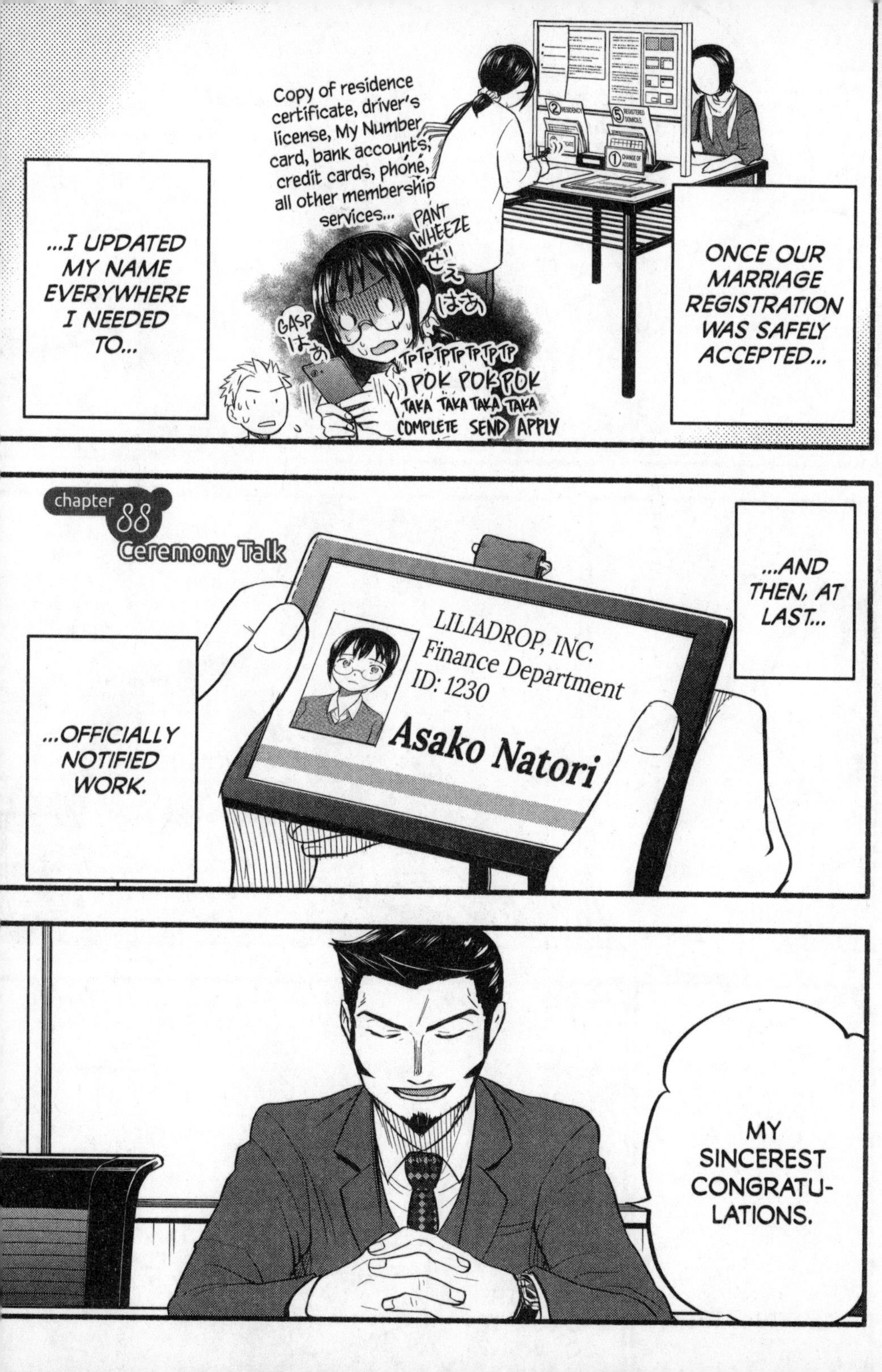
ONCE OUR MARRIAGE REGISTRATION WAS SAFELY ACCEPTED...
2 RESIDENCY
5 REGISTERED DOMICILE
1 CHANGE OF ADDRESS
Copy of residence certificate, driver's license, My Number card, bank accounts, credit cards, phone, all other membership services...
PANT WHEEZE ぜぇ はぁ
GASP はぁ
TPTPTPTPTPTPTP
POK POK POK
TAKA TAKA TAKA TAKA
COMPLETE SEND APPLY
...I UPDATED MY NAME EVERYWHERE I NEEDED TO...
...AND THEN, AT LAST...
chapter 88
Ceremony Talk
LILIADROP, INC.
Finance Department
ID: 1230
Asako Natori
...OFFICIALLY NOTIFIED WORK.
MY SINCEREST CONGRATULATIONS.

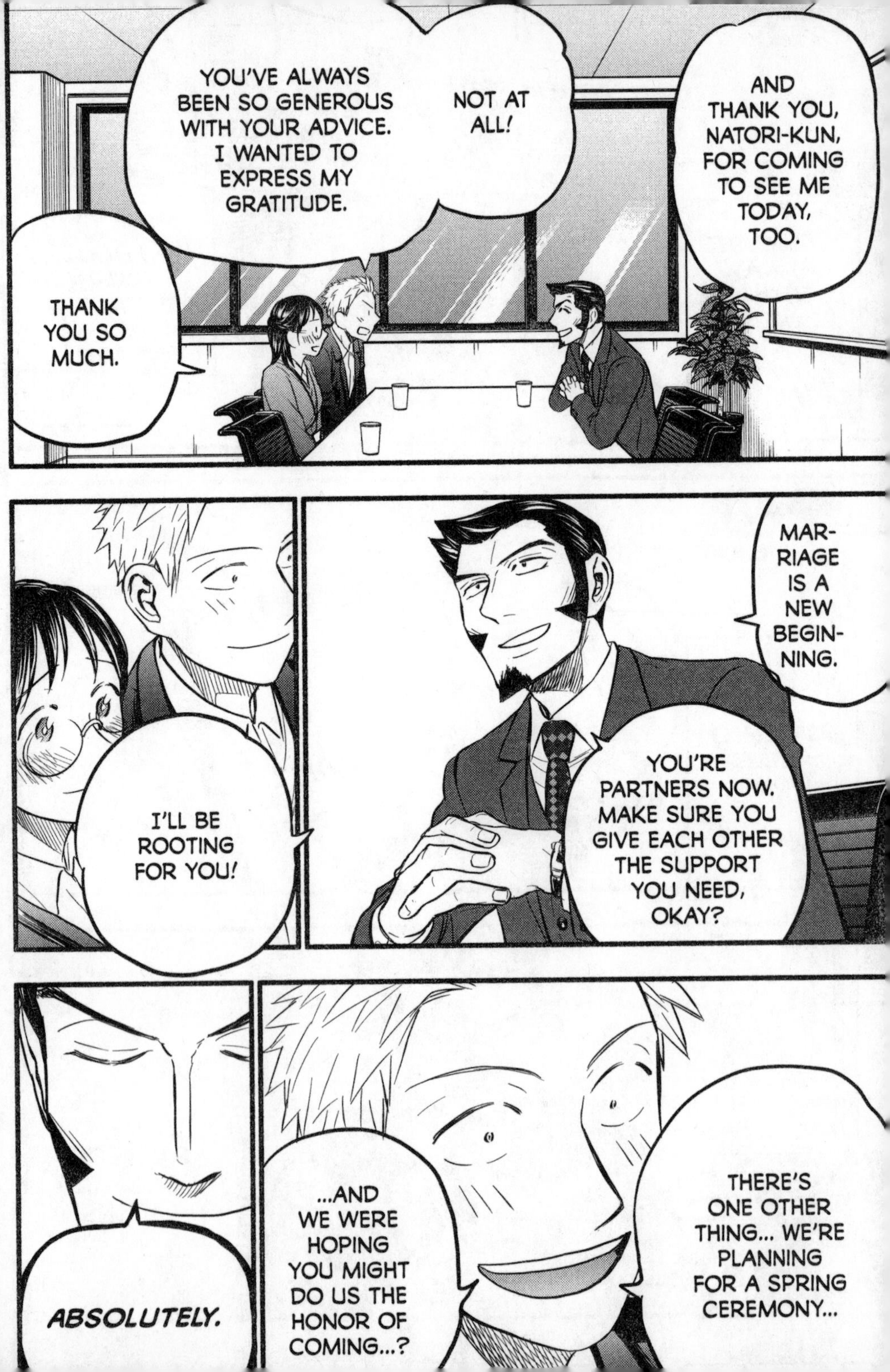
AND THANK YOU, NATORI-KUN, FOR COMING TO SEE ME TODAY, TOO.
NOT AT ALL!
YOU'VE ALWAYS BEEN SO GENEROUS WITH YOUR ADVICE. I WANTED TO EXPRESS MY GRATITUDE.
THANK YOU SO MUCH.
MAR-RIAGE IS A NEW BEGIN-NING.
YOU'RE PARTNERS NOW. MAKE SURE YOU GIVE EACH OTHER THE SUPPORT YOU NEED, OKAY?
I'LL BE ROOTING FOR YOU!
THERE'S ONE OTHER THING... WE'RE PLANNING FOR A SPRING CEREMONY...
...AND WE WERE HOPING YOU MIGHT DO US THE HONOR OF COMING...?
ABSOLUTELY.

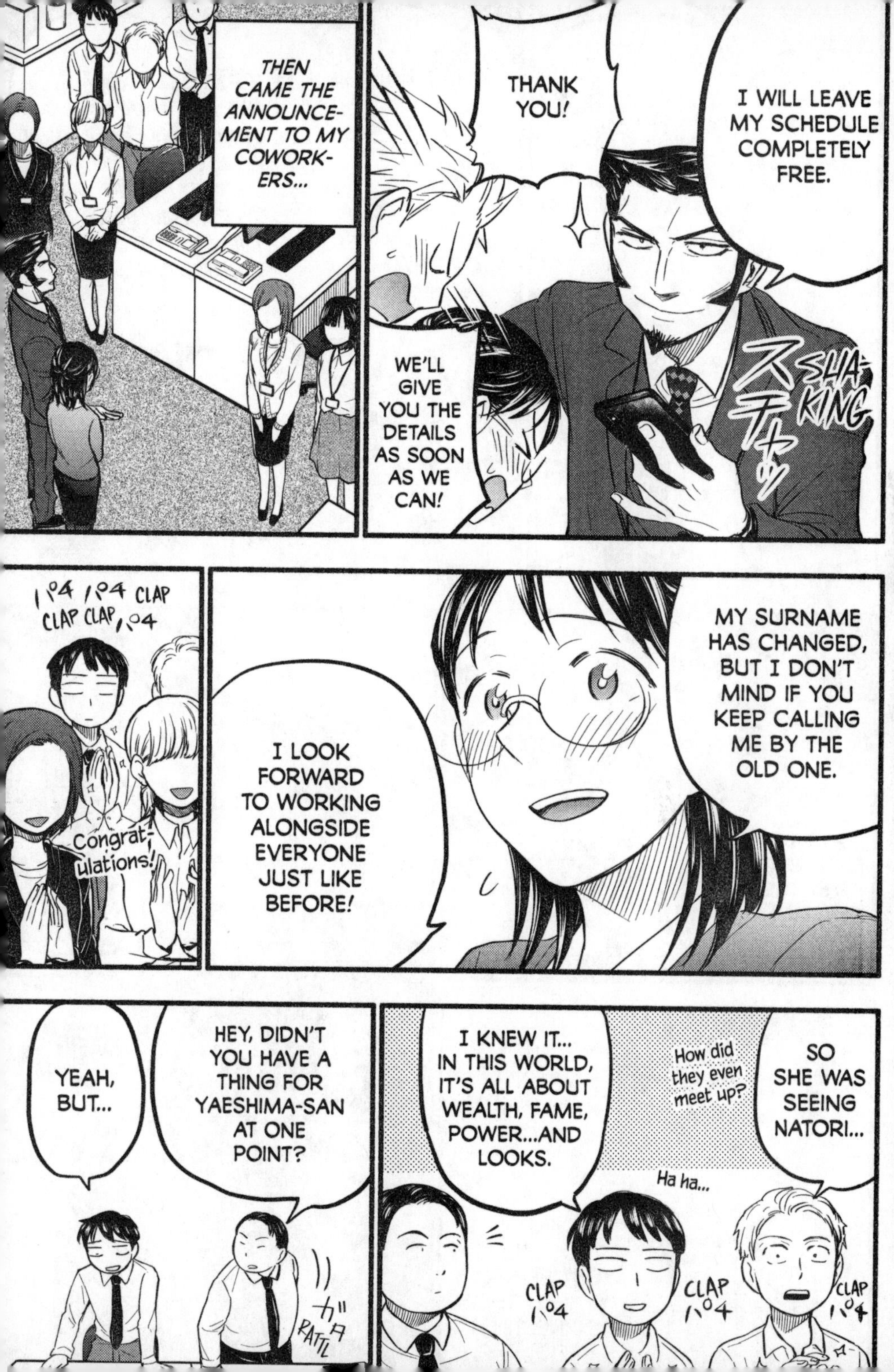
I WILL LEAVE MY SCHEDULE COMPLETELY FREE.
THANK YOU!
WE'LL GIVE YOU THE DETAILS AS SOON AS WE CAN!
スチャッ SHAKING
THEN CAME THE ANNOUNCEMENT TO MY COWORKERS...
MY SURNAME HAS CHANGED, BUT I DON'T MIND IF YOU KEEP CALLING ME BY THE OLD ONE.
I LOOK FORWARD TO WORKING ALONGSIDE EVERYONE JUST LIKE BEFORE!
パチ パチ CLAP CLAP CLAP パチ
Congratulations!
SO SHE WAS SEEING NATORI...
How did they even meet up?
I KNEW IT... IN THIS WORLD, IT'S ALL ABOUT WEALTH, FAME, POWER...AND LOOKS.
Ha ha...
CLAP パチ
CLAP パチ
CLAP パチ
HEY, DIDN'T YOU HAVE A THING FOR YAESHIMA-SAN AT ONE POINT?
YEAH, BUT...
ガタ RATTL

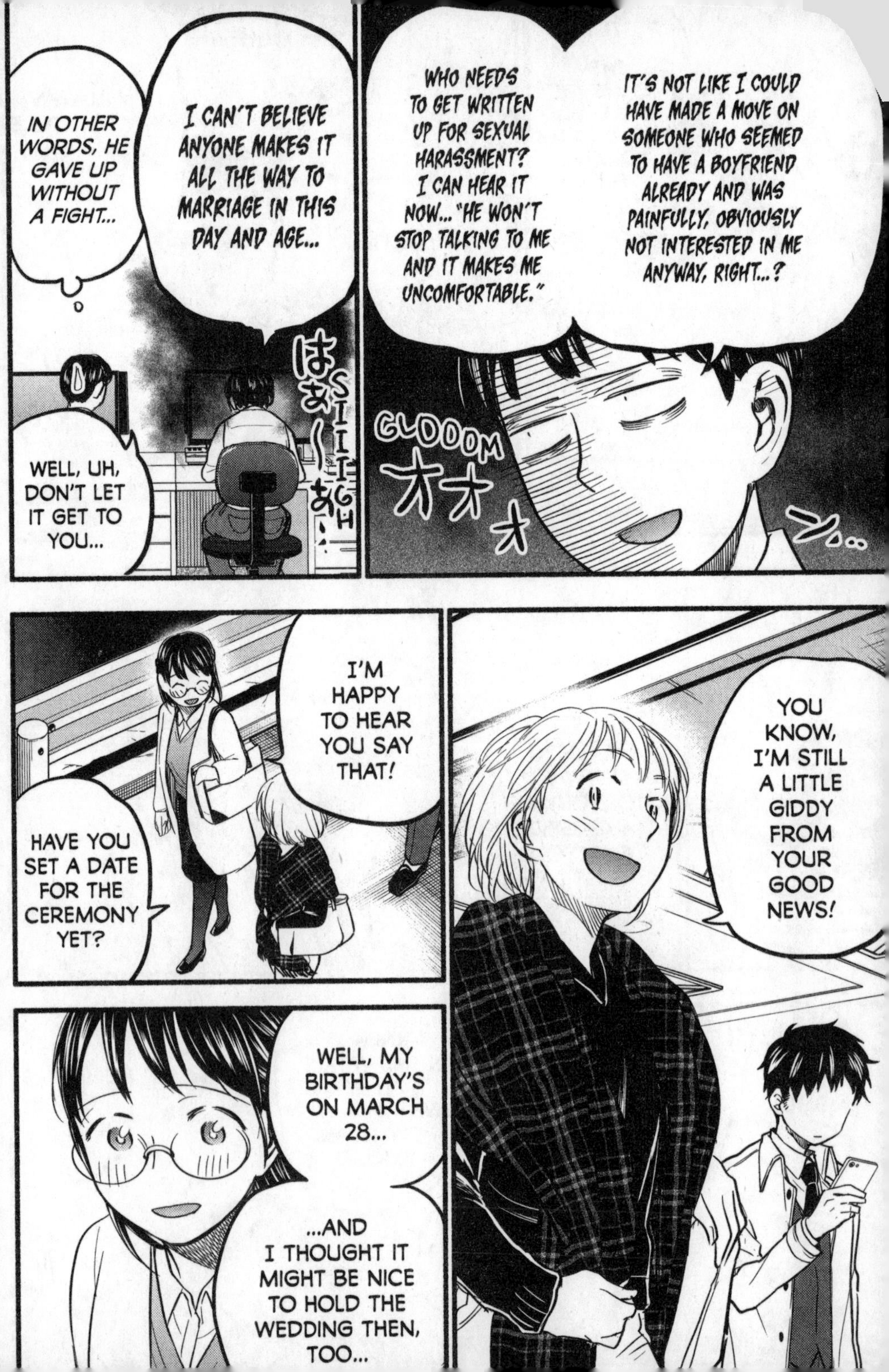
IT'S NOT LIKE I COULD HAVE MADE A MOVE ON SOMEONE WHO SEEMED TO HAVE A BOYFRIEND ALREADY AND WAS PAINFULLY, OBVIOUSLY NOT INTERESTED IN ME ANYWAY, RIGHT...?
WHO NEEDS TO GET WRITTEN UP FOR SEXUAL HARASSMENT? I CAN HEAR IT NOW... "HE WON'T STOP TALKING TO ME AND IT MAKES ME UNCOMFORTABLE."
GLOOOM
I CAN'T BELIEVE ANYONE MAKES IT ALL THE WAY TO MARRIAGE IN THIS DAY AND AGE...
IN OTHER WORDS, HE GAVE UP WITHOUT A FIGHT...
SIIIGH
WELL, UH, DON'T LET IT GET TO YOU...
YOU KNOW, I'M STILL A LITTLE GIDDY FROM YOUR GOOD NEWS!
I'M HAPPY TO HEAR YOU SAY THAT!
HAVE YOU SET A DATE FOR THE CEREMONY YET?
WELL, MY BIRTHDAY'S ON MARCH 28...
...AND I THOUGHT IT MIGHT BE NICE TO HOLD THE WEDDING THEN, TOO...

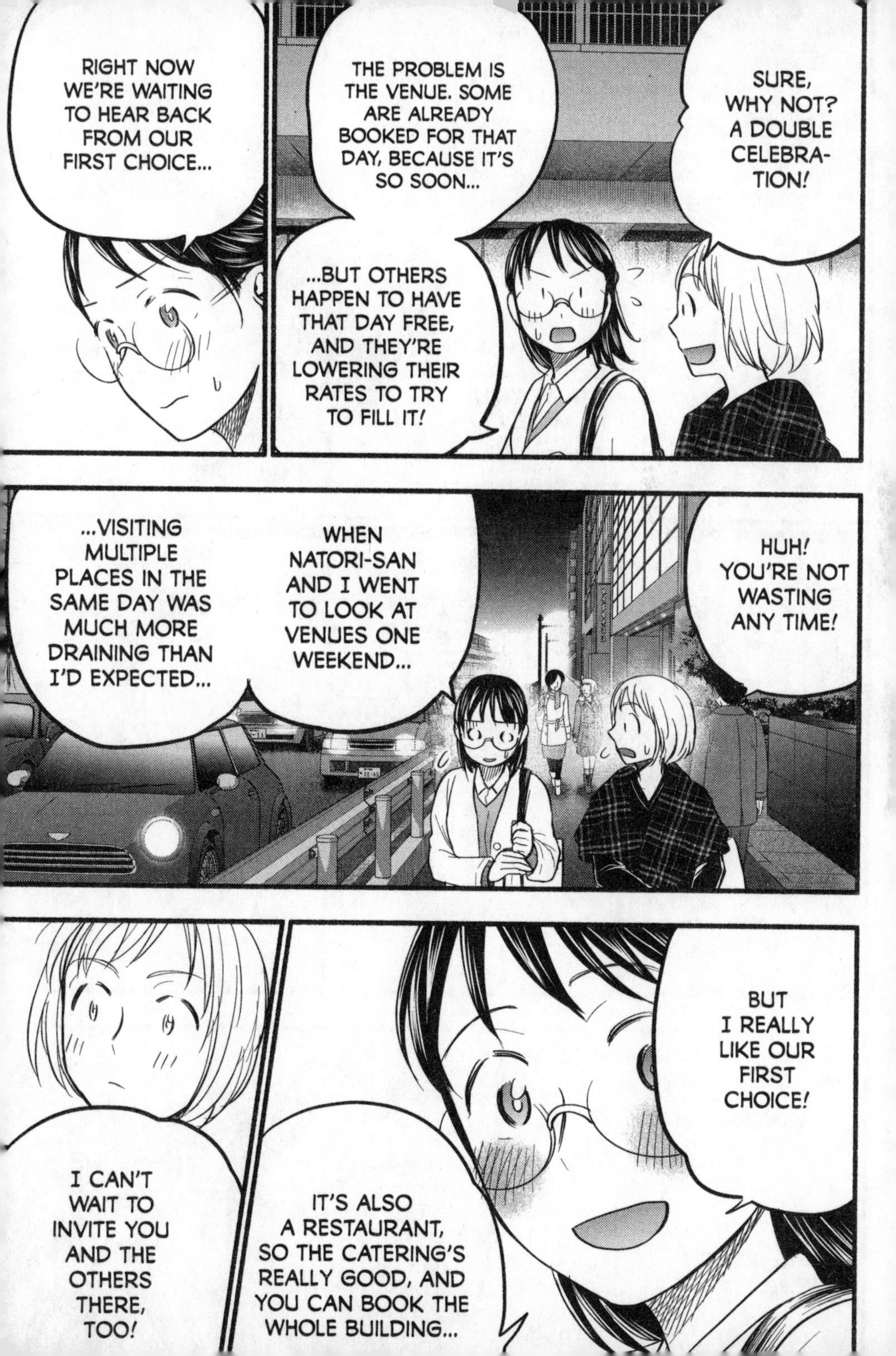
SURE, WHY NOT? A DOUBLE CELEBRATION!
THE PROBLEM IS THE VENUE. SOME ARE ALREADY BOOKED FOR THAT DAY, BECAUSE IT'S SO SOON...
...BUT OTHERS HAPPEN TO HAVE THAT DAY FREE, AND THEY'RE LOWERING THEIR RATES TO TRY TO FILL IT!
RIGHT NOW WE'RE WAITING TO HEAR BACK FROM OUR FIRST CHOICE...
HUH! YOU'RE NOT WASTING ANY TIME!
WHEN NATORI-SAN AND I WENT TO LOOK AT VENUES ONE WEEKEND...
...VISITING MULTIPLE PLACES IN THE SAME DAY WAS MUCH MORE DRAINING THAN I'D EXPECTED...
BUT I REALLY LIKE OUR FIRST CHOICE!
IT'S ALSO A RESTAURANT, SO THE CATERING'S REALLY GOOD, AND YOU CAN BOOK THE WHOLE BUILDING...
I CAN'T WAIT TO INVITE YOU AND THE OTHERS THERE, TOO!

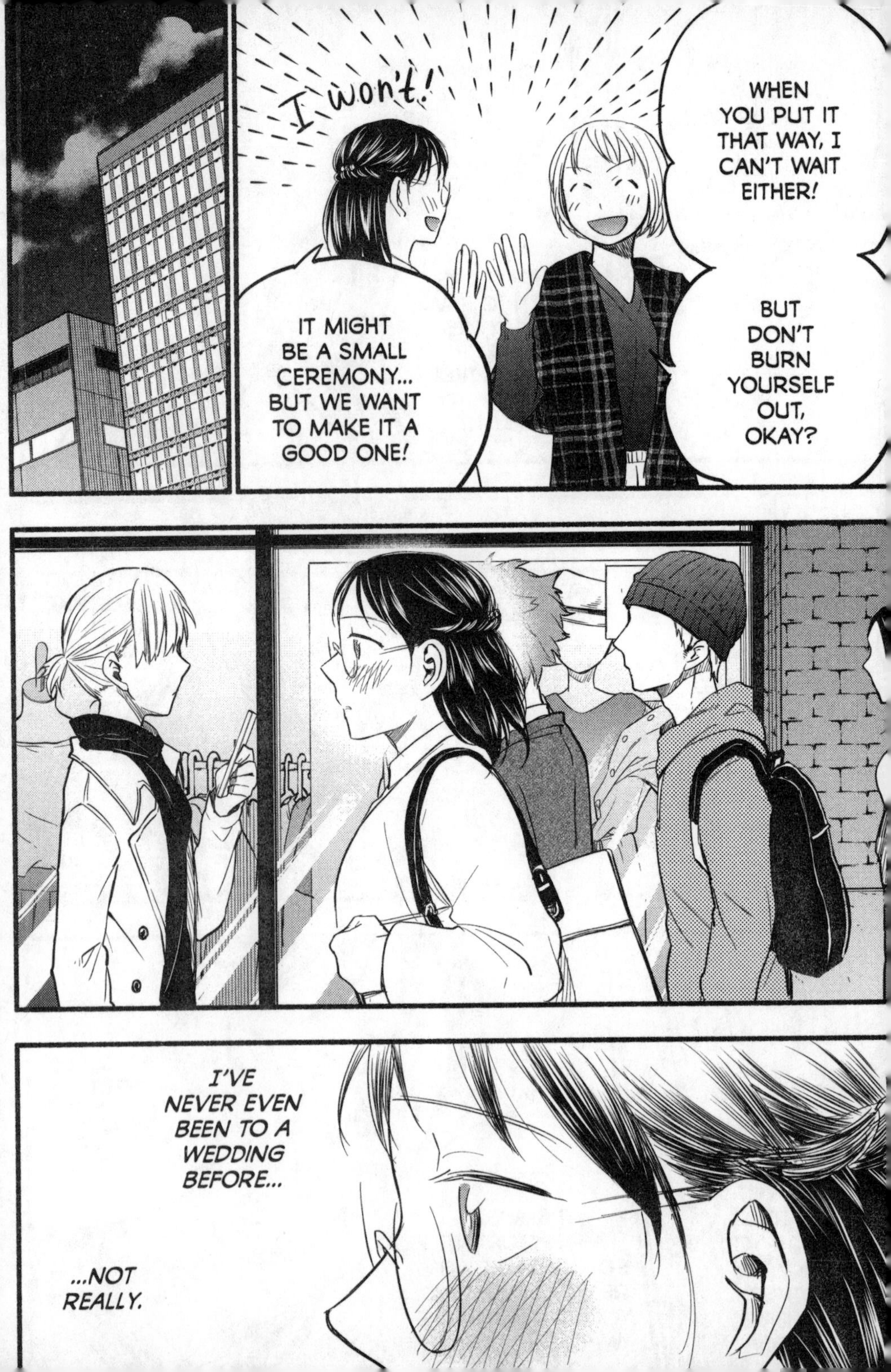
WHEN YOU PUT IT THAT WAY, I CAN'T WAIT EITHER!
BUT DON'T BURN YOURSELF OUT, OKAY?
I won't!
IT MIGHT BE A SMALL CEREMONY... BUT WE WANT TO MAKE IT A GOOD ONE!
I'VE NEVER EVEN BEEN TO A WEDDING BEFORE...
...NOT REALLY.

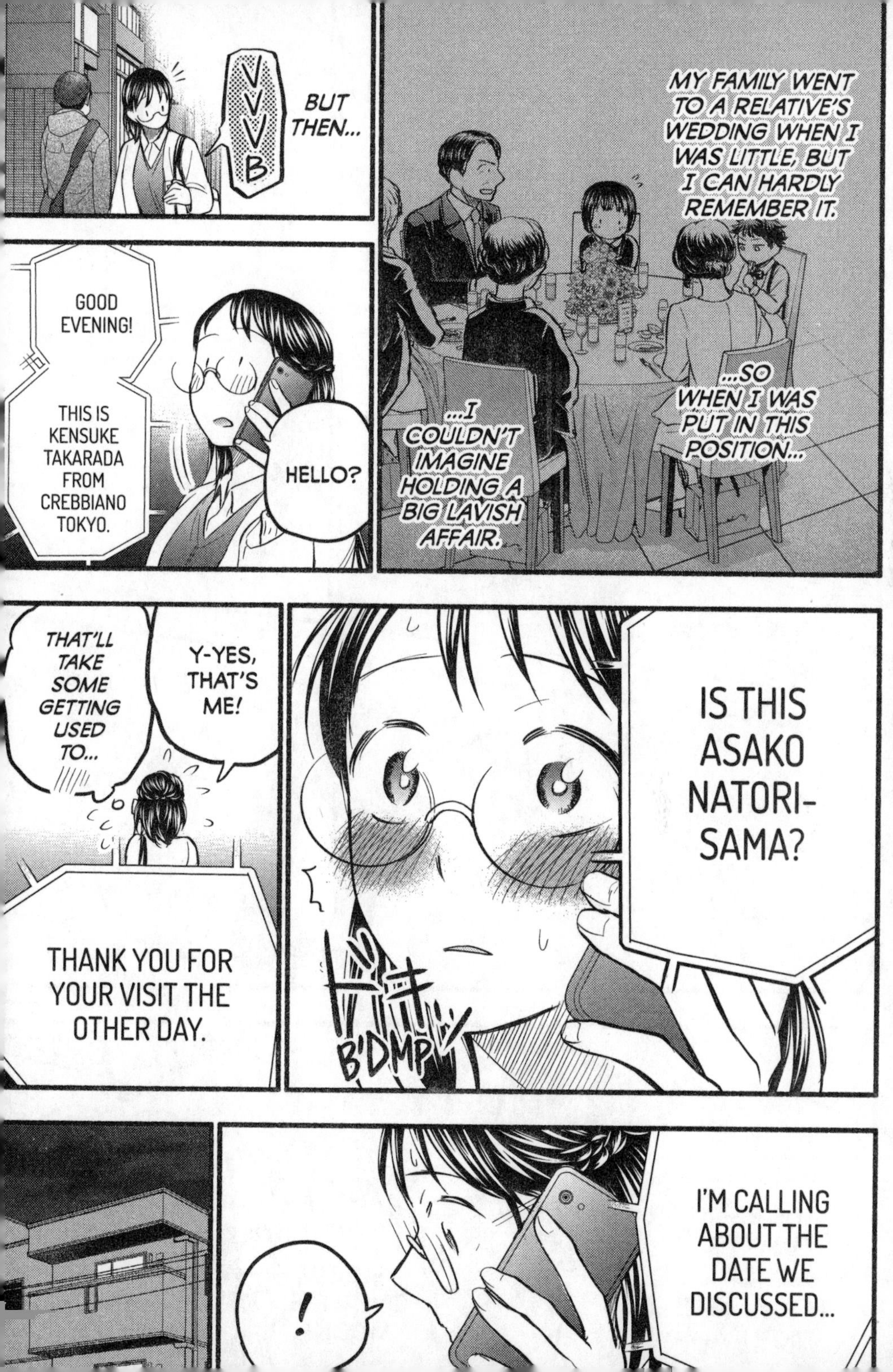
MY FAMILY WENT TO A RELATIVE'S WEDDING WHEN I WAS LITTLE, BUT I CAN HARDLY REMEMBER IT.
...SO WHEN I WAS PUT IN THIS POSITION...
...I COULDN'T IMAGINE HOLDING A BIG LAVISH AFFAIR.
BUT THEN...
VVVB
HELLO?
GOOD EVENING!
THIS IS KENSUKE TAKARADA FROM CREBBIANO TOKYO.
IS THIS ASAKO NATORI-SAMA?
B'DMP
Y-YES, THAT'S ME!
THAT'LL TAKE SOME GETTING USED TO...
THANK YOU FOR YOUR VISIT THE OTHER DAY.
I'M CALLING ABOUT THE DATE WE DISCUSSED...
!

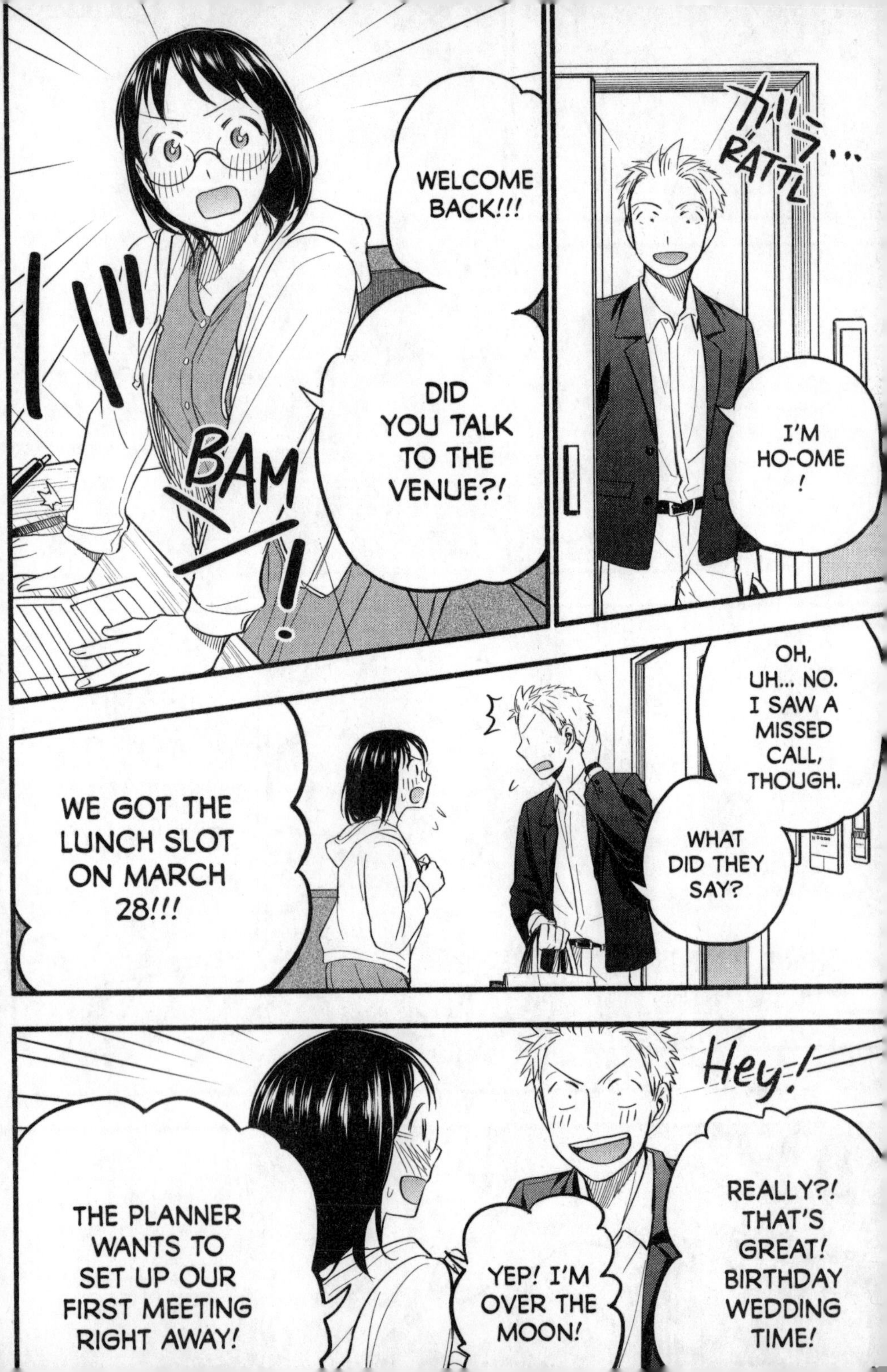
RATTL
I'M HO-OME!
WELCOME BACK!!!
DID YOU TALK TO THE VENUE?!
BAM
OH, UH... NO. I SAW A MISSED CALL, THOUGH.
WHAT DID THEY SAY?
WE GOT THE LUNCH SLOT ON MARCH 28!!!
Hey!
REALLY?! THAT'S GREAT! BIRTHDAY WEDDING TIME!
YEP! I'M OVER THE MOON!
THE PLANNER WANTS TO SET UP OUR FIRST MEETING RIGHT AWAY!

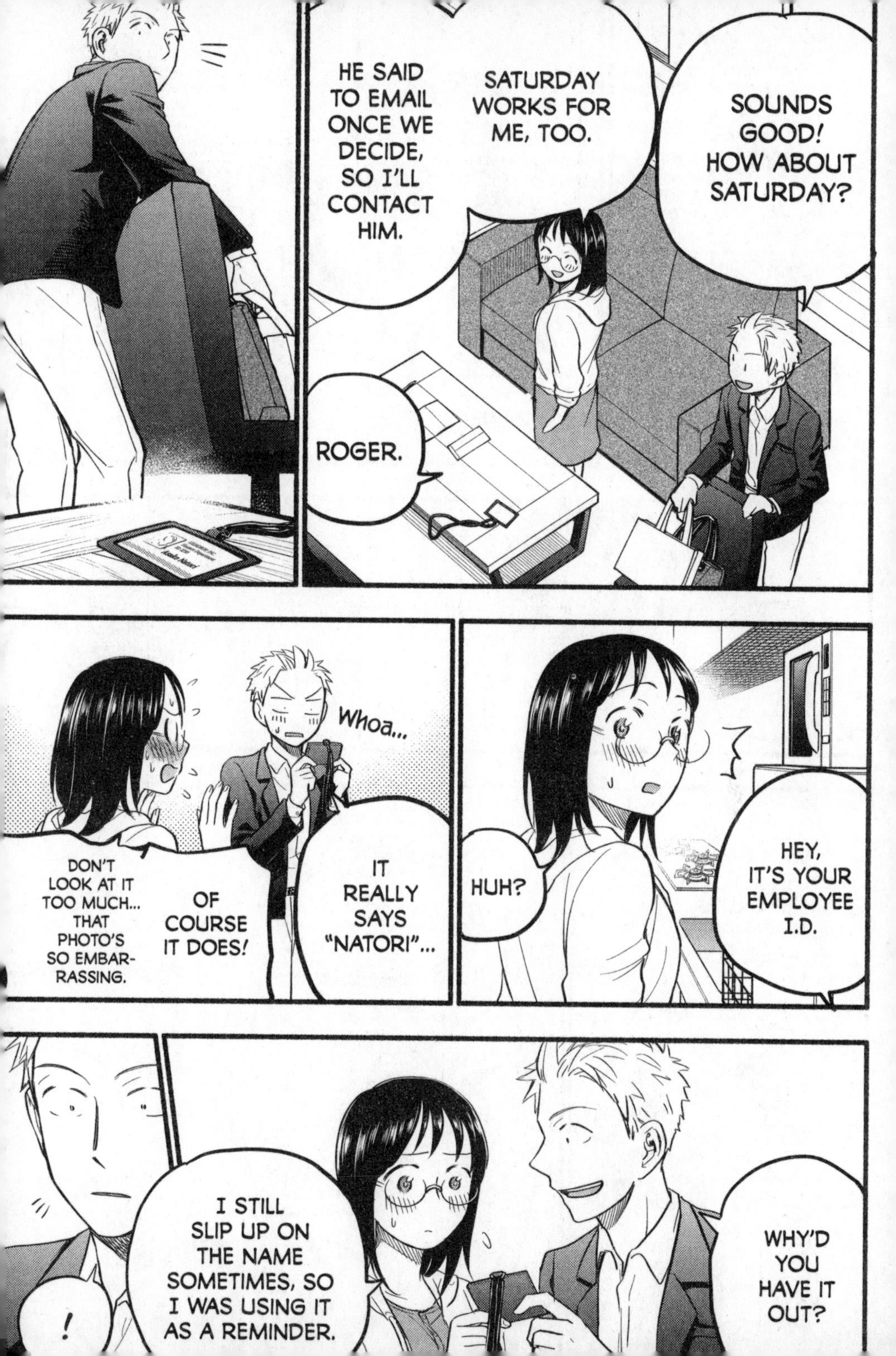
SOUNDS GOOD! HOW ABOUT SATURDAY?
SATURDAY WORKS FOR ME, TOO.
HE SAID TO EMAIL ONCE WE DECIDE, SO I'LL CONTACT HIM.
ROGER.
HEY, IT'S YOUR EMPLOYEE I.D.
HUH?
Whoa...
IT REALLY SAYS "NATORI"...
OF COURSE IT DOES!
DON'T LOOK AT IT TOO MUCH... THAT PHOTO'S SO EMBARRASSING.
WHY'D YOU HAVE IT OUT?
I STILL SLIP UP ON THE NAME SOMETIMES, SO I WAS USING IT AS A REMINDER.
!

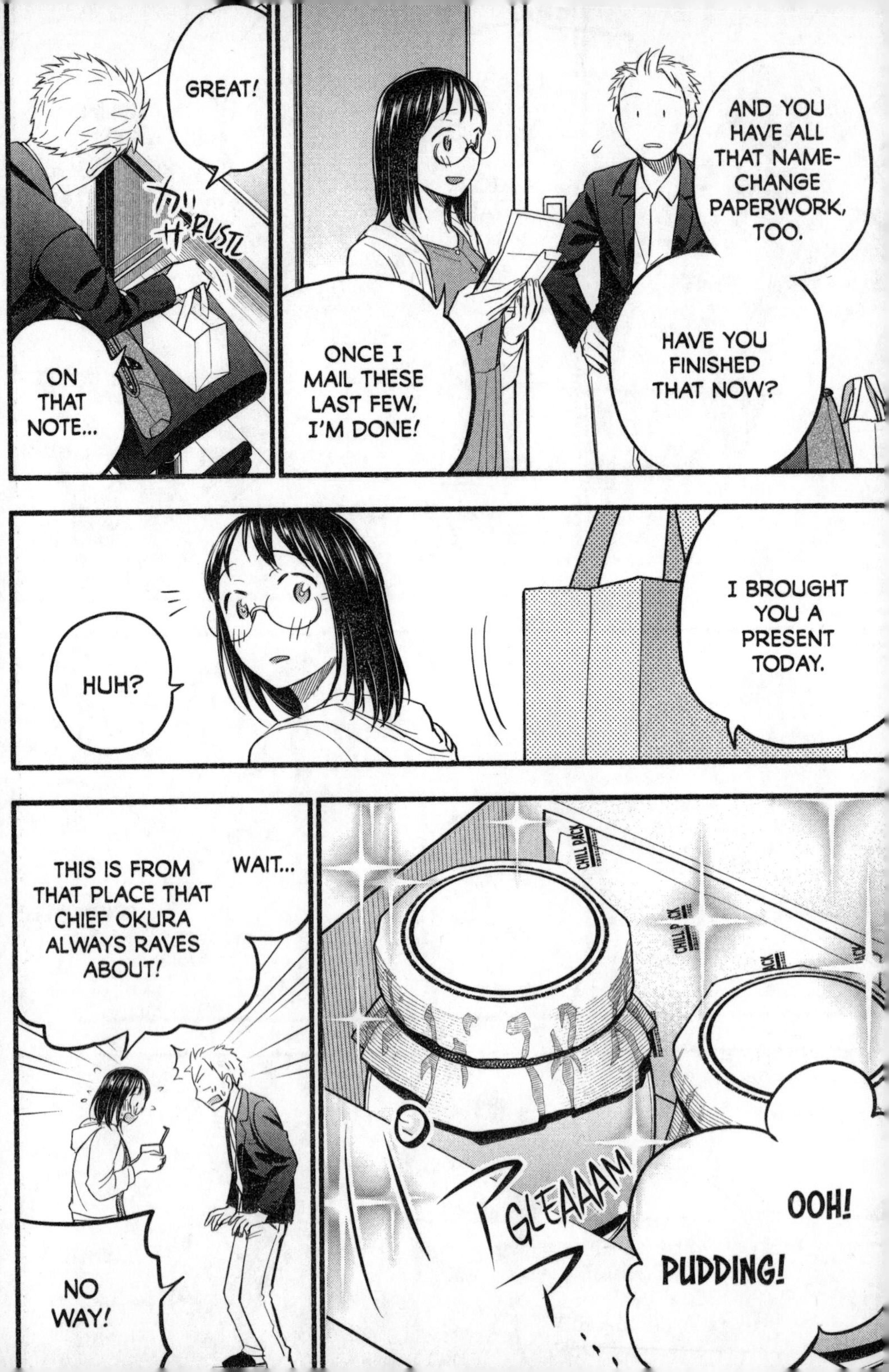
AND YOU HAVE ALL THAT NAME-CHANGE PAPERWORK, TOO.
HAVE YOU FINISHED THAT NOW?
ONCE I MAIL THESE LAST FEW, I'M DONE!
GREAT!
RUSTL
ON THAT NOTE...
I BROUGHT YOU A PRESENT TODAY.
HUH?
GLEAAAM
OOH!
PUDDING!
WAIT...
THIS IS FROM THAT PLACE THAT CHIEF OKURA ALWAYS RAVES ABOUT!
NO WAY!

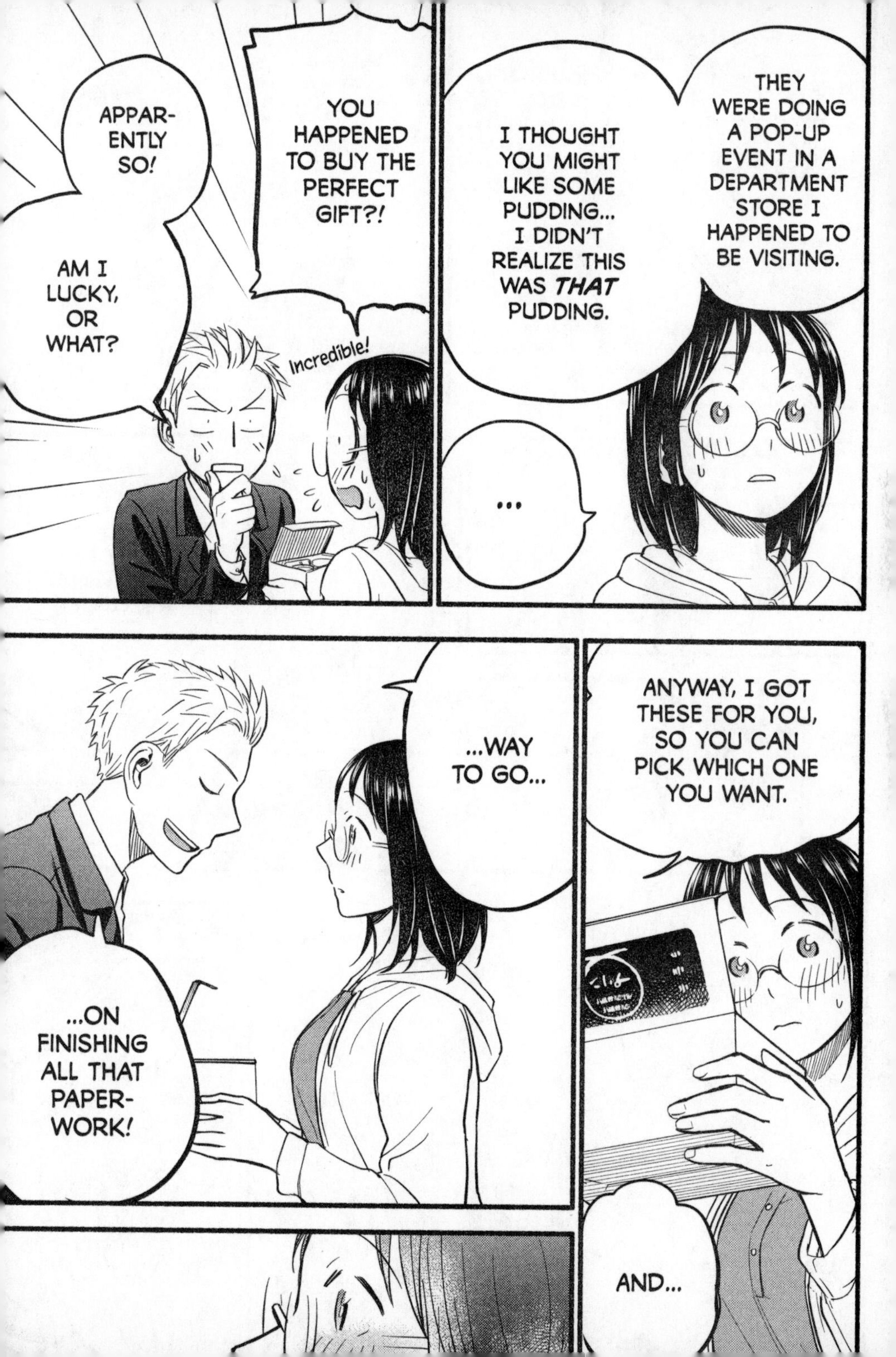
THEY WERE DOING A POP-UP EVENT IN A DEPARTMENT STORE I HAPPENED TO BE VISITING.
I THOUGHT YOU MIGHT LIKE SOME PUDDING... I DIDN'T REALIZE THIS WAS *THAT* PUDDING.
...
YOU HAPPENED TO BUY THE PERFECT GIFT?!
Incredible!
APPAR-ENTLY SO!
AM I LUCKY, OR WHAT?
ANYWAY, I GOT THESE FOR YOU, SO YOU CAN PICK WHICH ONE YOU WANT.
AND...
...WAY TO GO...
...ON FINISHING ALL THAT PAPER-WORK!

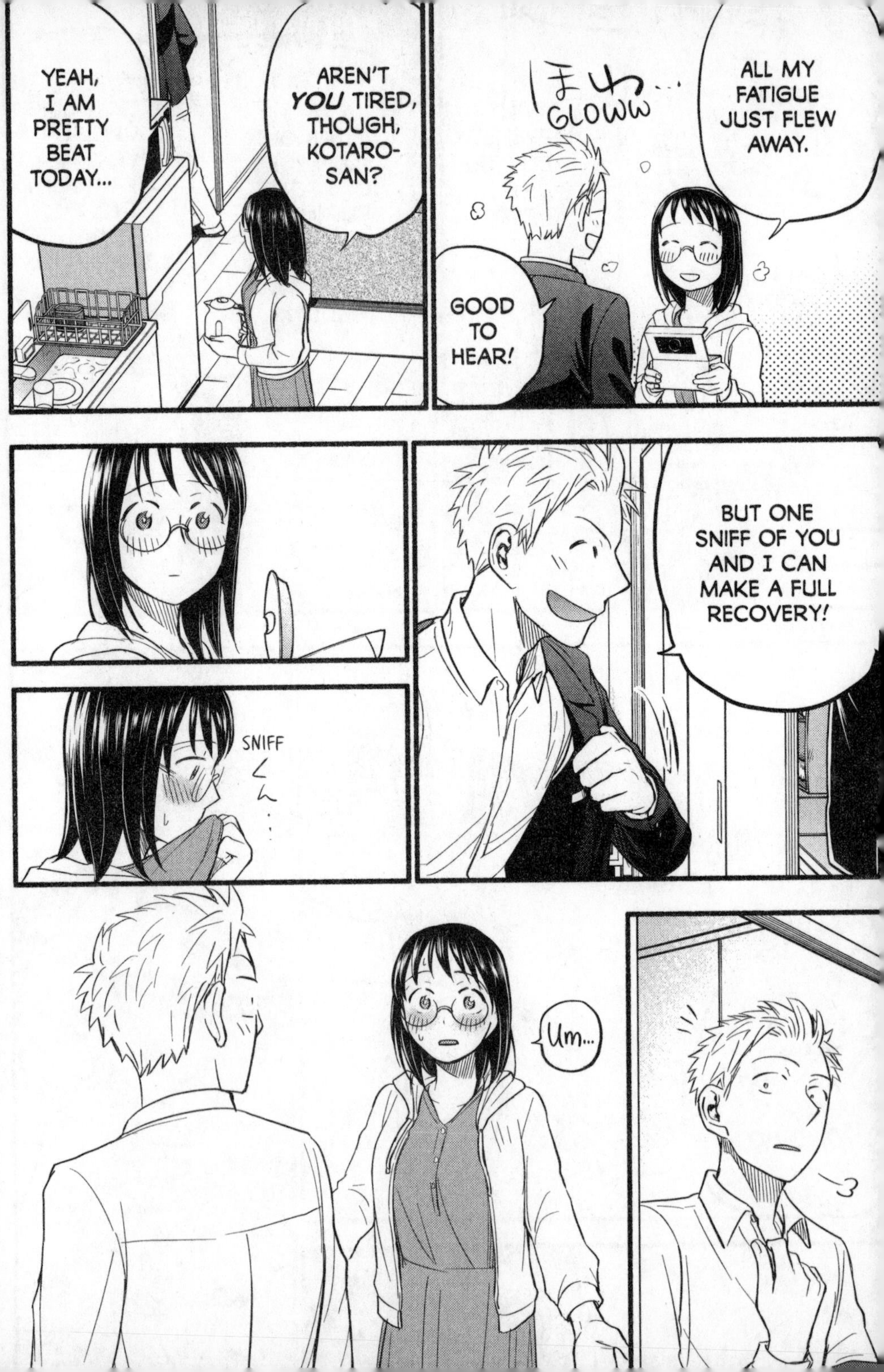
ALL MY FATIGUE JUST FLEW AWAY.
ほわ… GLOWW
GOOD TO HEAR!
AREN'T *YOU* TIRED, THOUGH, KOTARO-SAN?
YEAH, I AM PRETTY BEAT TODAY...
BUT ONE SNIFF OF YOU AND I CAN MAKE A FULL RECOVERY!
SNIFF くん…
Um...

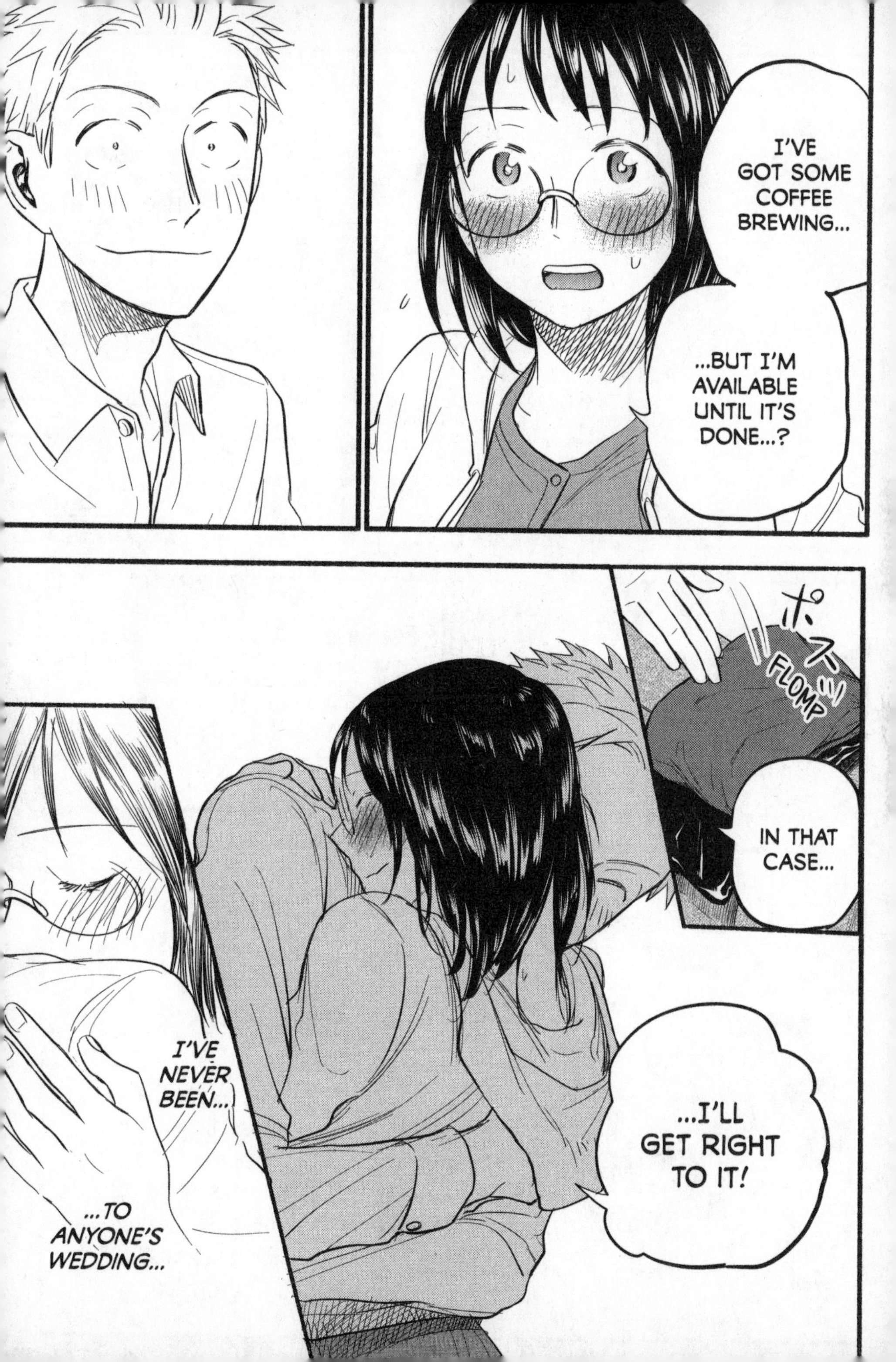
I'VE GOT SOME COFFEE BREWING...
...BUT I'M AVAILABLE UNTIL IT'S DONE...?
ポスッ
FLOMP
IN THAT CASE...
...I'LL GET RIGHT TO IT!
I'VE NEVER BEEN...
...TO ANYONE'S WEDDING...

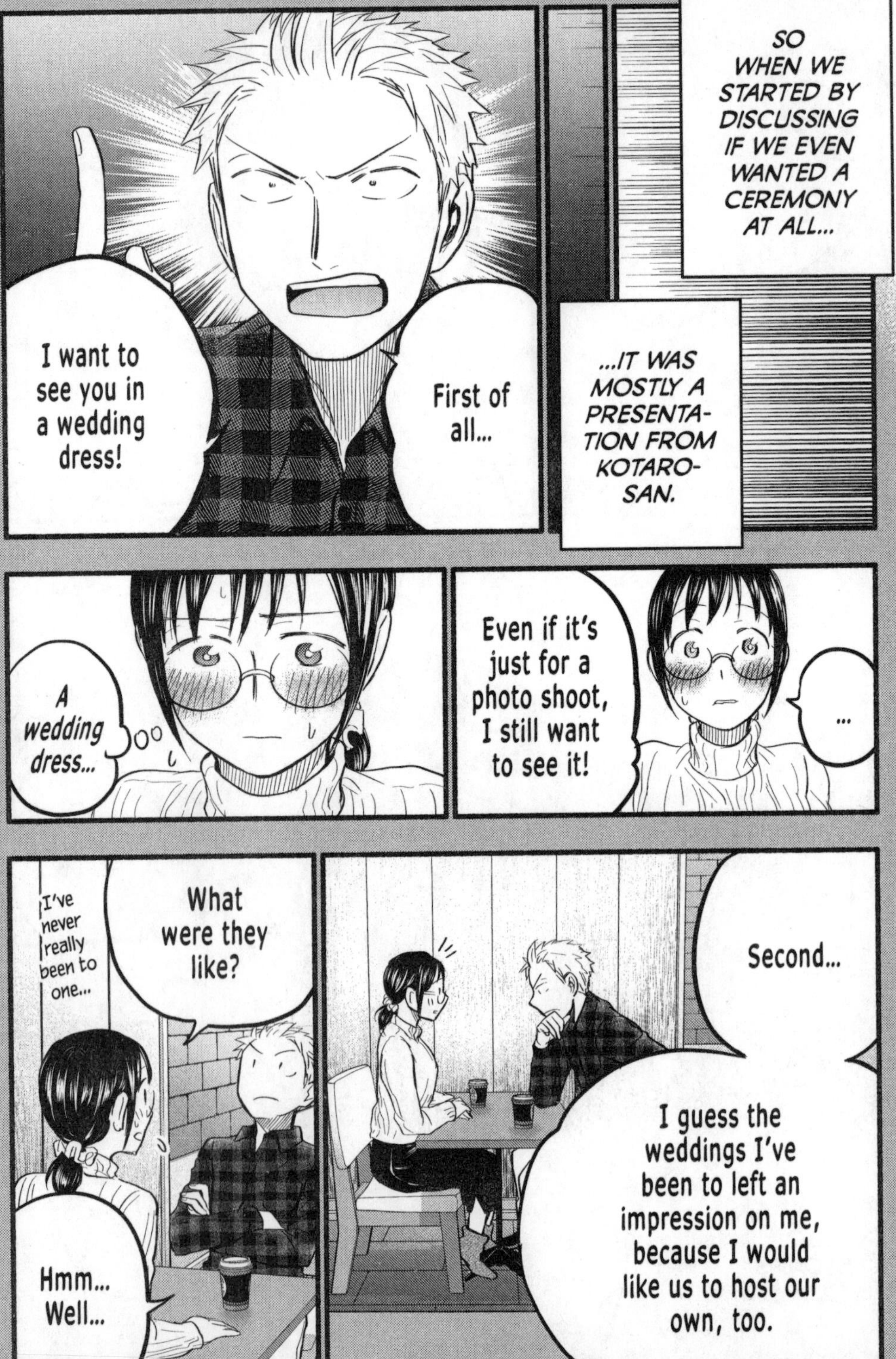

SO WHEN WE STARTED BY DISCUSSING IF WE EVEN WANTED A CEREMONY AT ALL...
...IT WAS MOSTLY A PRESENTATION FROM KOTARO-SAN.
First of all...
I want to see you in a wedding dress!
Even if it's just for a photo shoot, I still want to see it!
...
A wedding dress...
Second...
I guess the weddings I've been to left an impression on me, because I would like us to host our own, too.
What were they like?
I've never really been to one...
Hmm... Well...

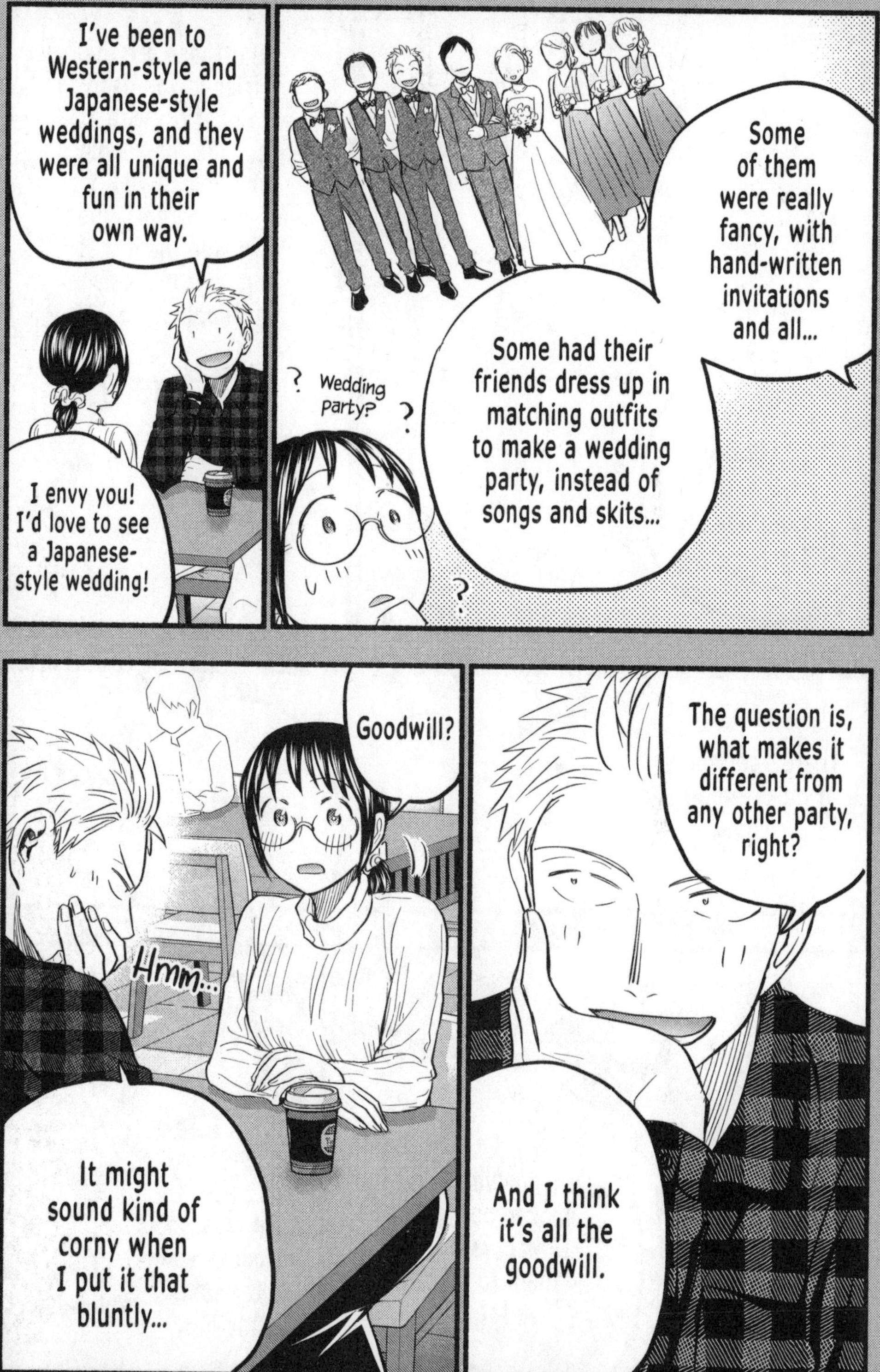
Some of them were really fancy, with hand-written invitations and all...
Some had their friends dress up in matching outfits to make a wedding party, instead of songs and skits...
Wedding party?
I've been to Western-style and Japanese-style weddings, and they were all unique and fun in their own way.
I envy you! I'd love to see a Japanese-style wedding!
The question is, what makes it different from any other party, right?
And I think it's all the goodwill.
Goodwill?
Hmm...
It might sound kind of corny when I put it that bluntly...

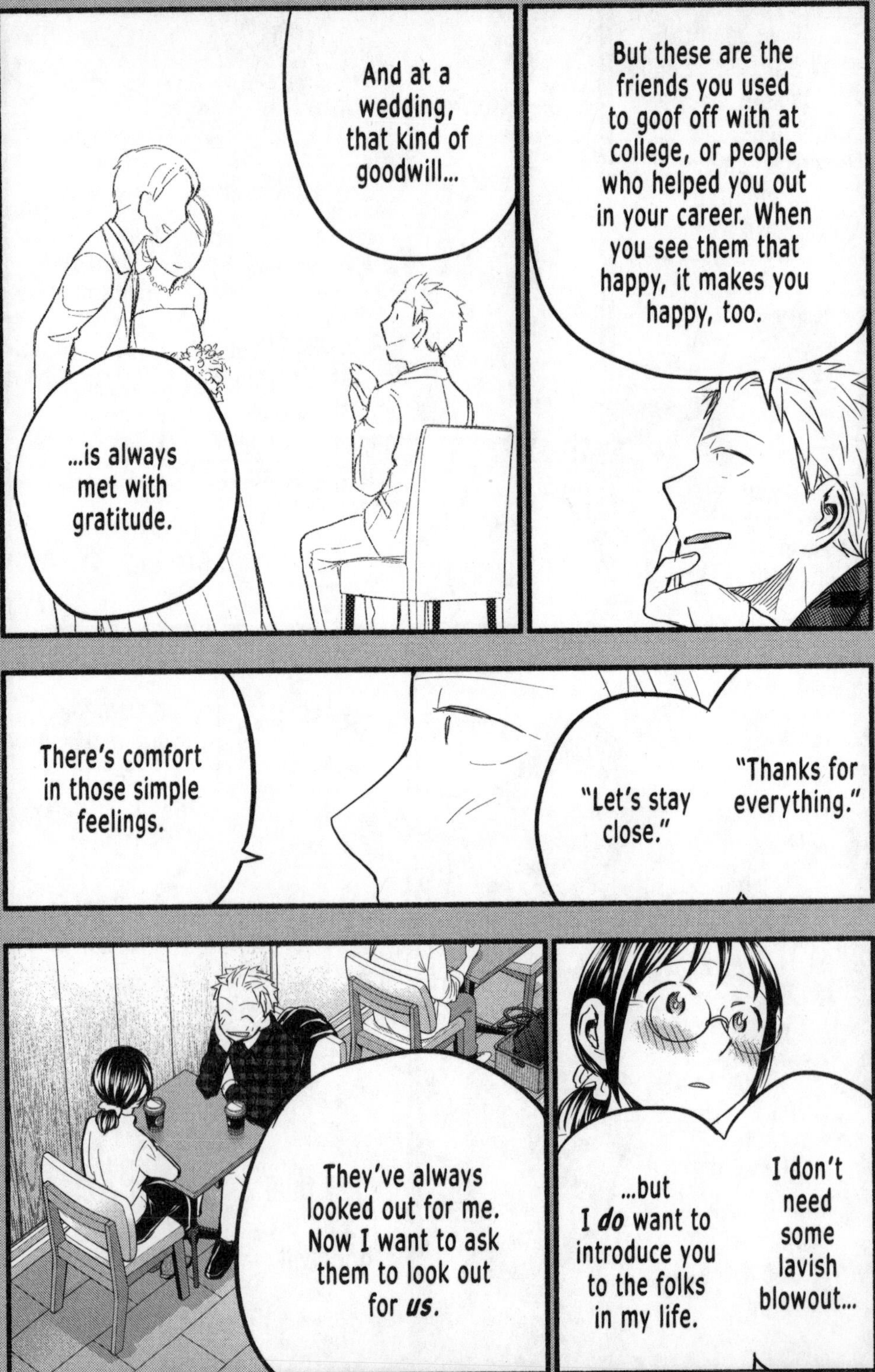
But these are the friends you used to goof off with at college, or people who helped you out in your career. When you see them that happy, it makes you happy, too.
And at a wedding, that kind of goodwill...
...is always met with gratitude.
"Thanks for everything."
"Let's stay close."
There's comfort in those simple feelings.
I don't need some lavish blowout...
...but I *do* want to introduce you to the folks in my life.
They've always looked out for me. Now I want to ask them to look out for *us*.

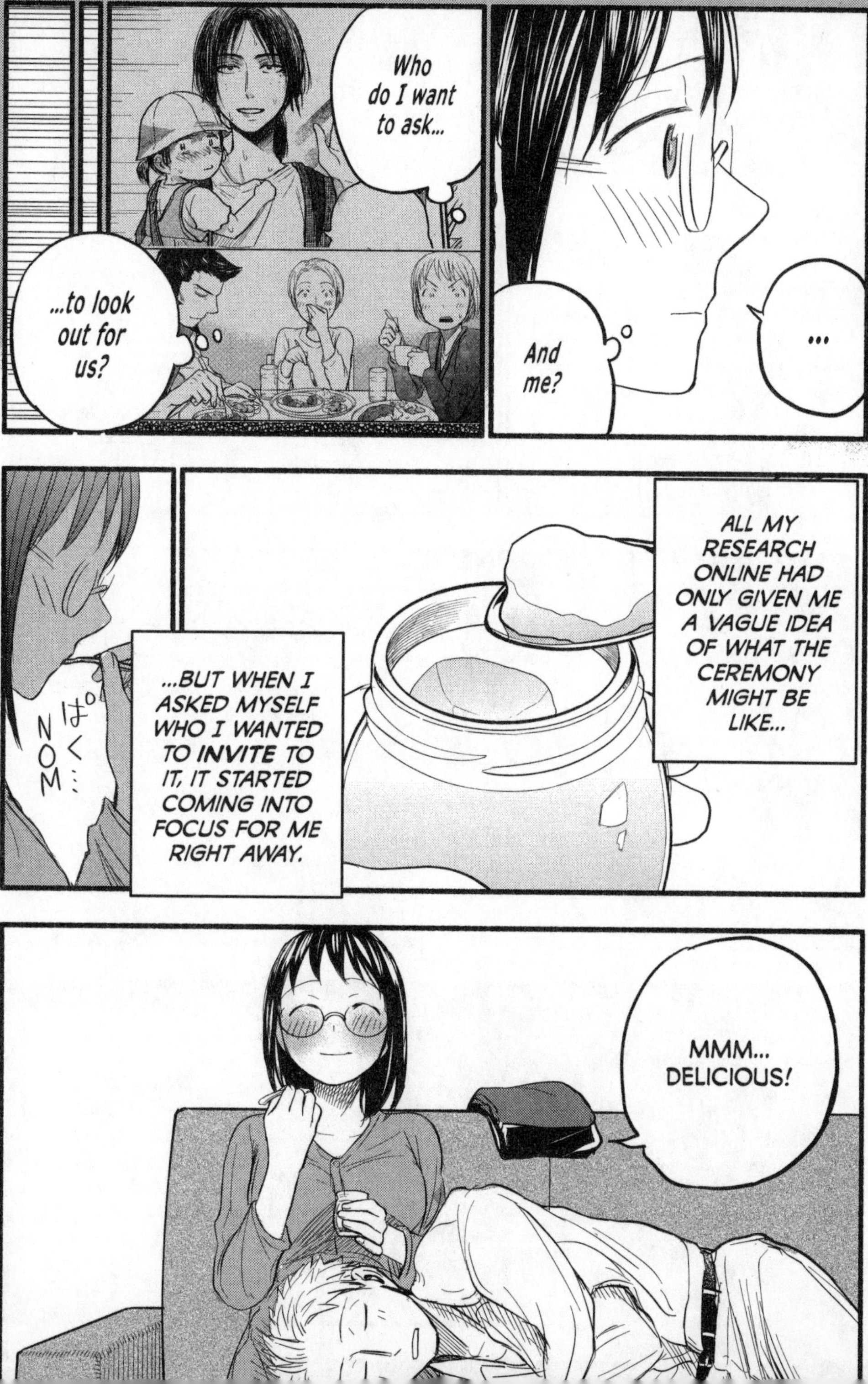
...
And me?
Who do I want to ask...
...to look out for us?
ALL MY RESEARCH ONLINE HAD ONLY GIVEN ME A VAGUE IDEA OF WHAT THE CEREMONY MIGHT BE LIKE...
...BUT WHEN I ASKED MYSELF WHO I WANTED TO **INVITE** TO IT, IT STARTED COMING INTO FOCUS FOR ME RIGHT AWAY.
ぱく
NOM...
MMM... DELICIOUS!

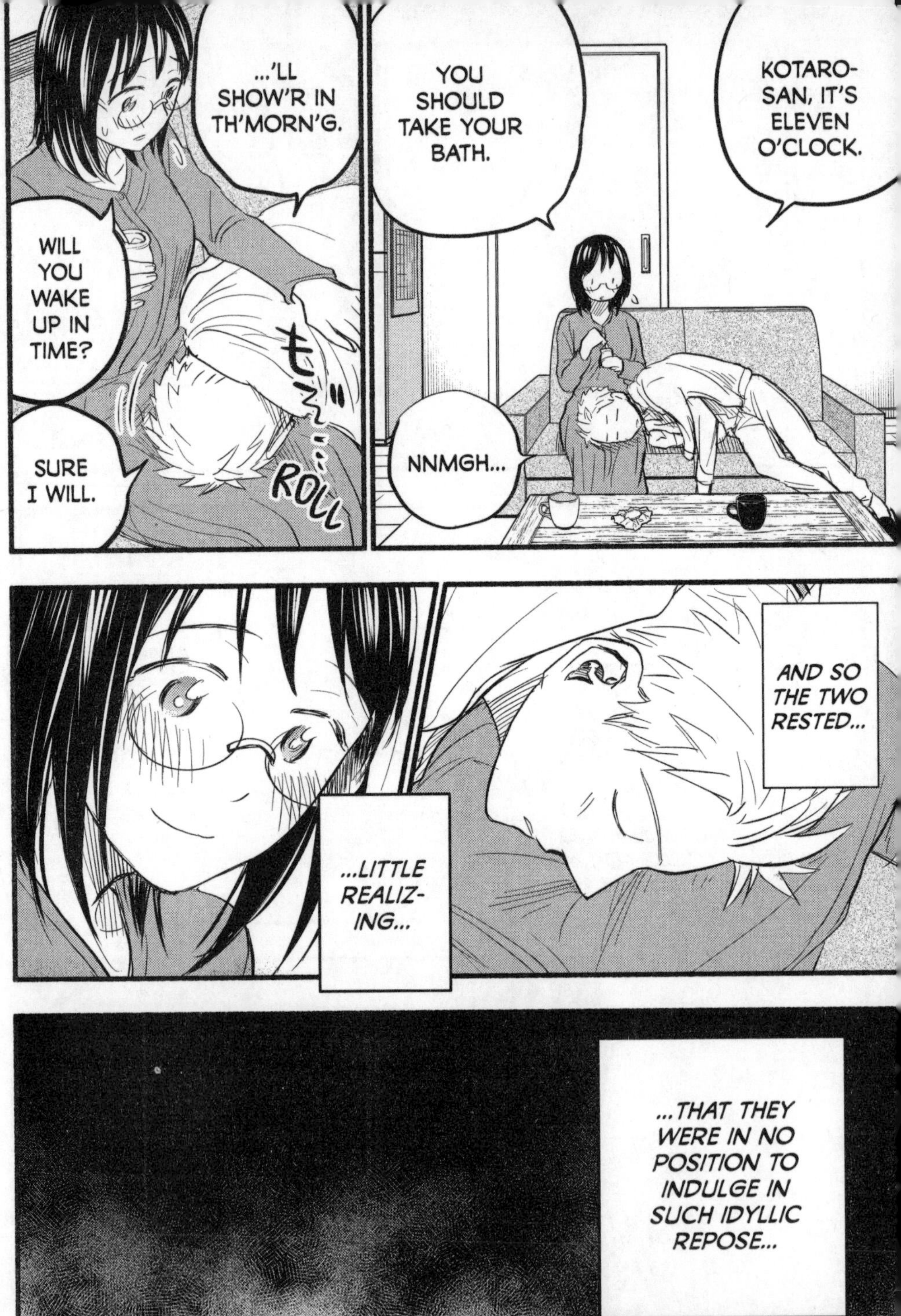
KOTARO-SAN, IT'S ELEVEN O'CLOCK.
YOU SHOULD TAKE YOUR BATH.
NNMGH...
...'LL SHOW'R IN TH'MORN'G.
WILL YOU WAKE UP IN TIME?
ROLL
SURE I WILL.
AND SO THE TWO RESTED...
...LITTLE REALIZING...
...THAT THEY WERE IN NO POSITION TO INDULGE IN SUCH IDYLLIC REPOSE...

Chapter 88 / The End

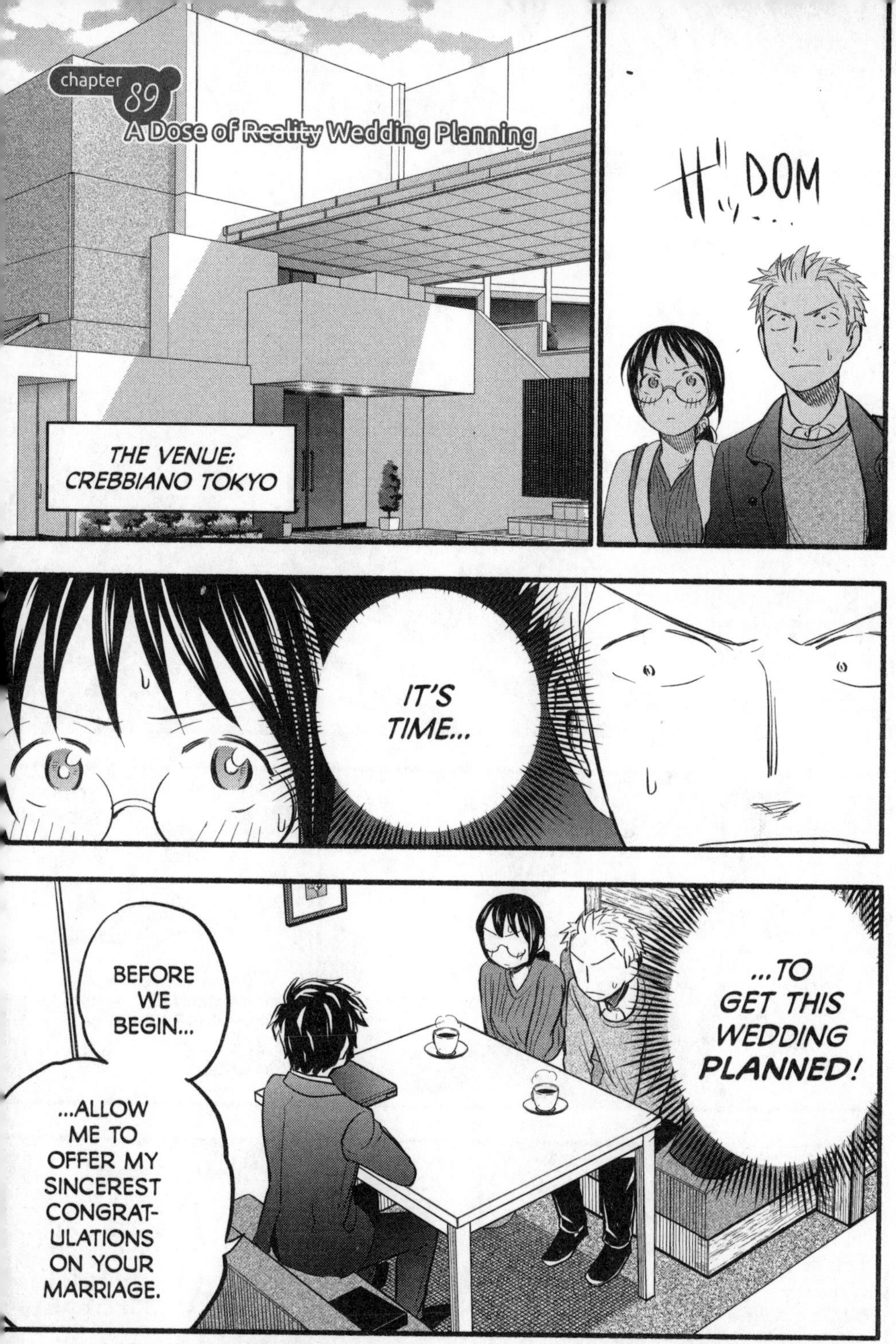
DOM
chapter 89
A Dose of Reality Wedding Planning
THE VENUE: CREBBIANO TOKYO
IT'S TIME...
...TO GET THIS WEDDING PLANNED!
BEFORE WE BEGIN...
...ALLOW ME TO OFFER MY SINCEREST CONGRAT-ULATIONS ON YOUR MARRIAGE.

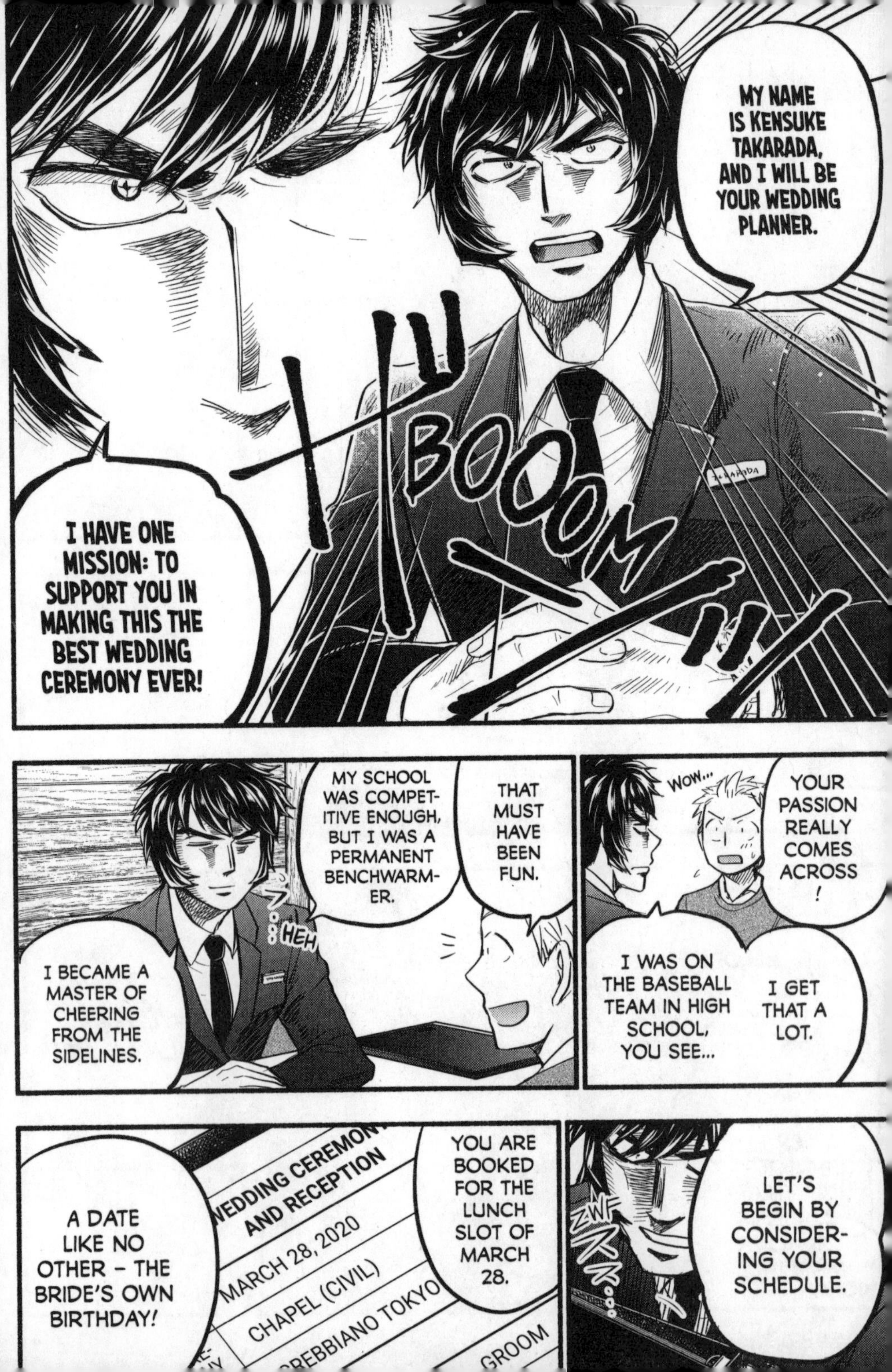

MY NAME IS KENSUKE TAKARADA, AND I WILL BE YOUR WEDDING PLANNER.
TAKARADA
BOOOOM
I HAVE ONE MISSION: TO SUPPORT YOU IN MAKING THIS THE BEST WEDDING CEREMONY EVER!
YOUR PASSION REALLY COMES ACROSS!
WOW...
I GET THAT A LOT.
I WAS ON THE BASEBALL TEAM IN HIGH SCHOOL, YOU SEE...
THAT MUST HAVE BEEN FUN.
MY SCHOOL WAS COMPETITIVE ENOUGH, BUT I WAS A PERMANENT BENCHWARMER.
HEH
I BECAME A MASTER OF CHEERING FROM THE SIDELINES.
ZWF
LET'S BEGIN BY CONSIDERING YOUR SCHEDULE.
YOU ARE BOOKED FOR THE LUNCH SLOT OF MARCH 28.
WEDDING CEREMON AND RECEPTION
MARCH 28, 2020
CHAPEL (CIVIL)
REBBIANO TOKYO
GROOM
A DATE LIKE NO OTHER – THE BRIDE'S OWN BIRTHDAY!

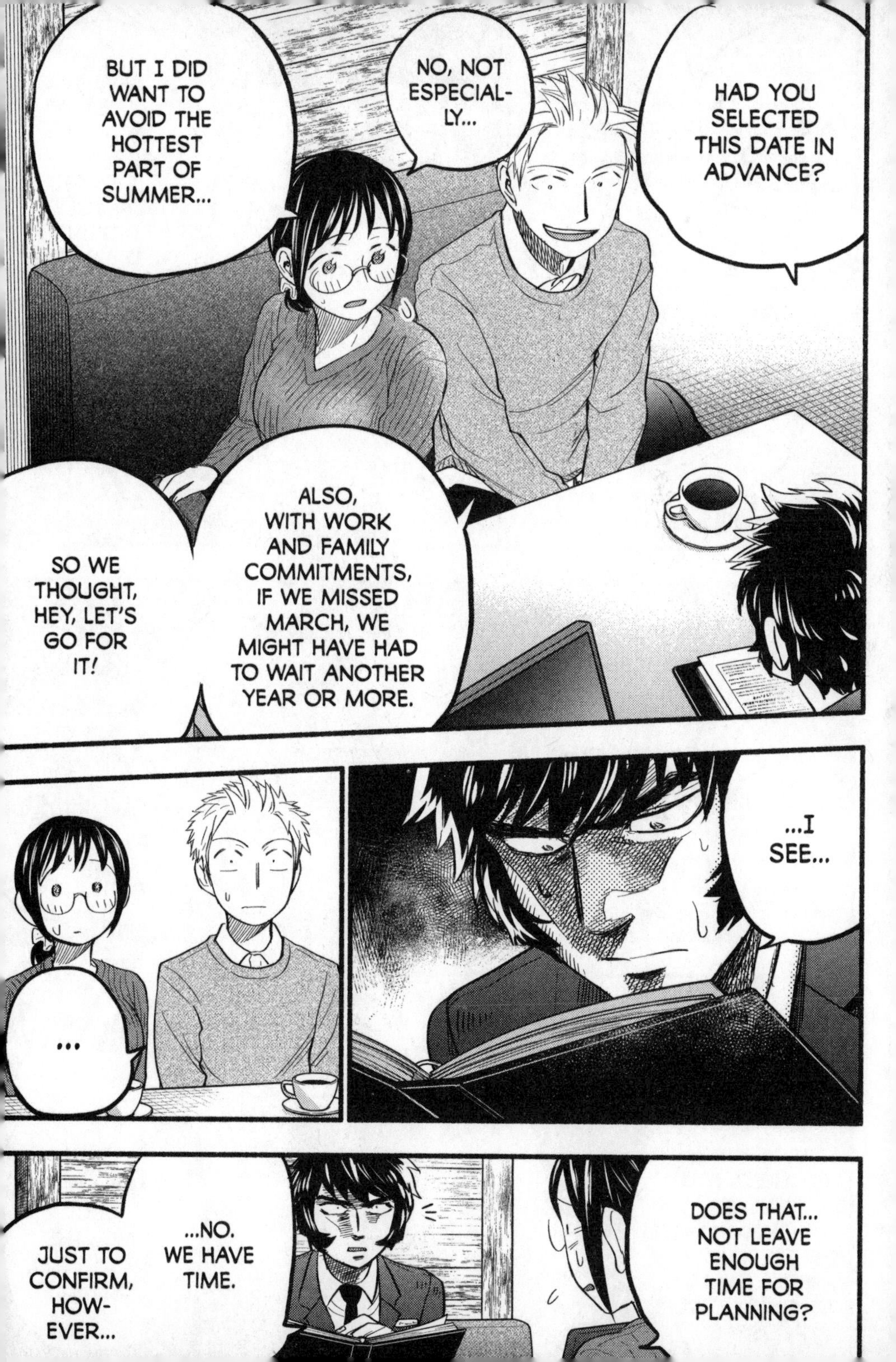
HAD YOU SELECTED THIS DATE IN ADVANCE?
NO, NOT ESPECIAL-LY...
BUT I DID WANT TO AVOID THE HOTTEST PART OF SUMMER...
ALSO, WITH WORK AND FAMILY COMMITMENTS, IF WE MISSED MARCH, WE MIGHT HAVE HAD TO WAIT ANOTHER YEAR OR MORE.
SO WE THOUGHT, HEY, LET'S GO FOR IT!
...I SEE...
...
DOES THAT... NOT LEAVE ENOUGH TIME FOR PLANNING?
...NO. WE HAVE TIME.
JUST TO CONFIRM, HOW-EVER...

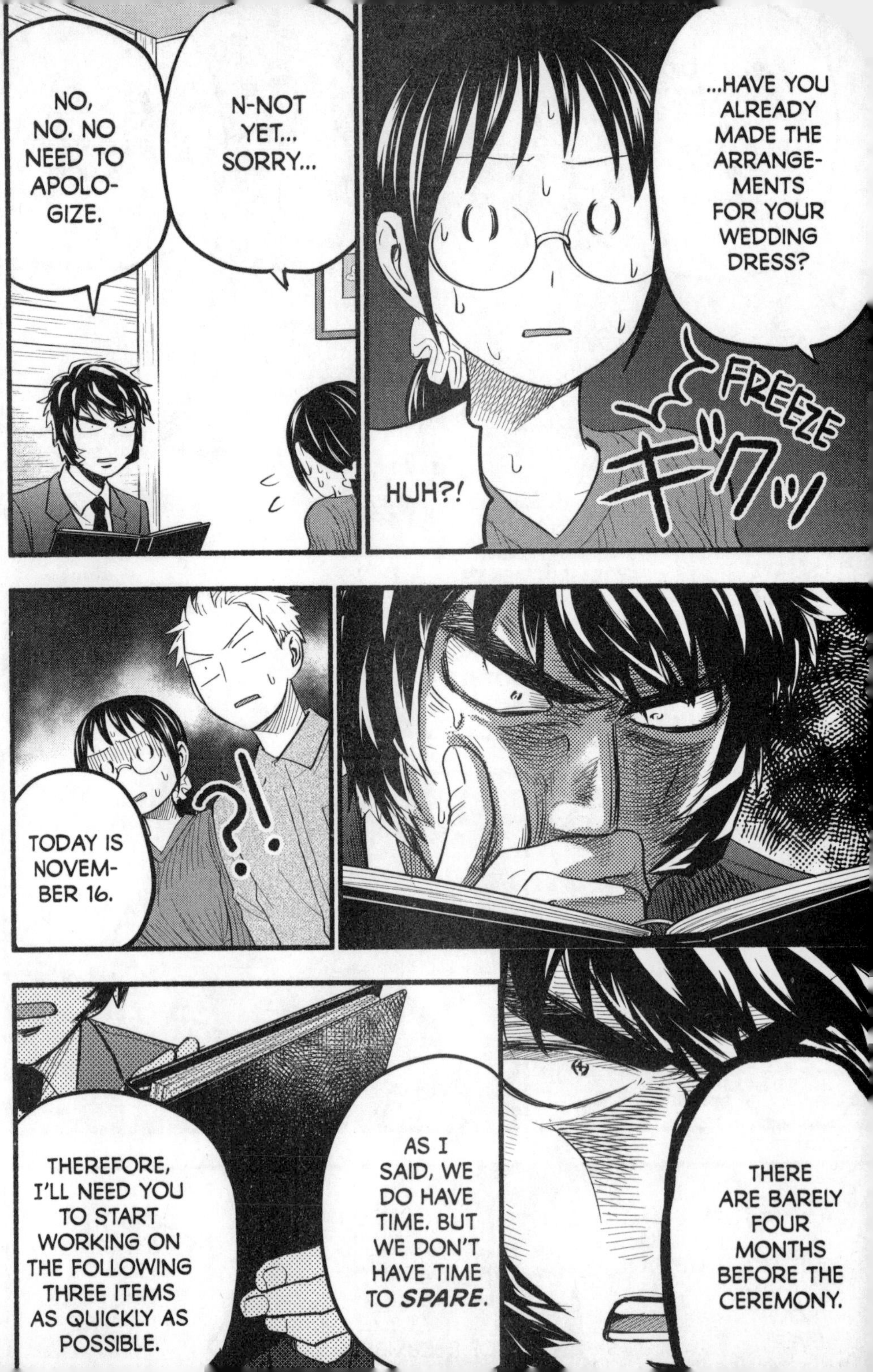
...HAVE YOU ALREADY MADE THE ARRANGEMENTS FOR YOUR WEDDING DRESS?
FREEZE
ギクッ
HUH?!
N-NOT YET... SORRY...
NO, NO. NO NEED TO APOLOGIZE.
TODAY IS NOVEMBER 16.
?!
THERE ARE BARELY FOUR MONTHS BEFORE THE CEREMONY.
AS I SAID, WE DO HAVE TIME. BUT WE DON'T HAVE TIME TO SPARE.
THEREFORE, I'LL NEED YOU TO START WORKING ON THE FOLLOWING THREE ITEMS AS QUICKLY AS POSSIBLE.

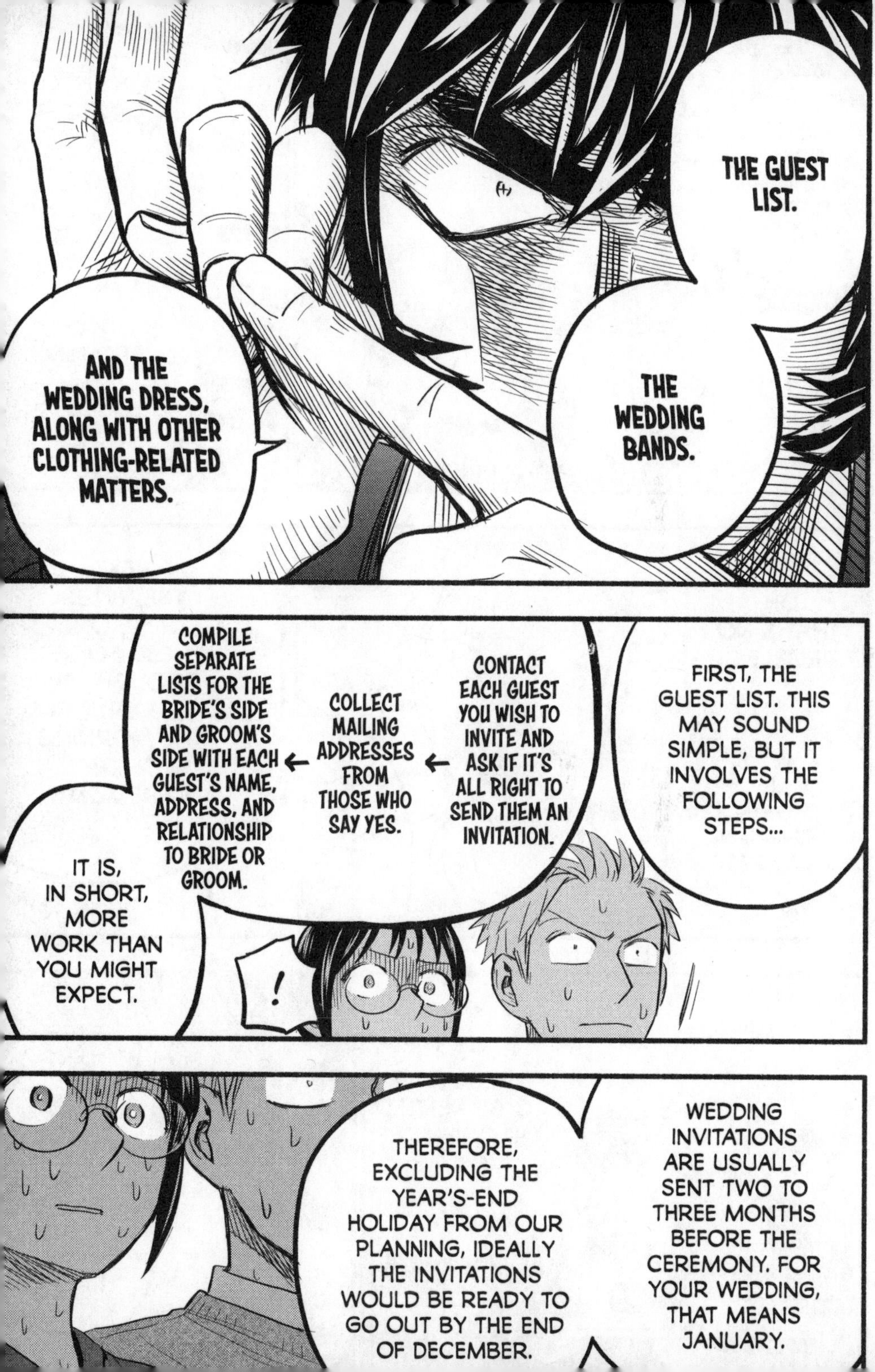
THE GUEST LIST.
THE WEDDING BANDS.
AND THE WEDDING DRESS, ALONG WITH OTHER CLOTHING-RELATED MATTERS.
FIRST, THE GUEST LIST. THIS MAY SOUND SIMPLE, BUT IT INVOLVES THE FOLLOWING STEPS...
CONTACT EACH GUEST YOU WISH TO INVITE AND ASK IF IT'S ALL RIGHT TO SEND THEM AN INVITATION.
← COLLECT MAILING ADDRESSES FROM THOSE WHO SAY YES.
← COMPILE SEPARATE LISTS FOR THE BRIDE'S SIDE AND GROOM'S SIDE WITH EACH GUEST'S NAME, ADDRESS, AND RELATIONSHIP TO BRIDE OR GROOM.
!
IT IS, IN SHORT, MORE WORK THAN YOU MIGHT EXPECT.
WEDDING INVITATIONS ARE USUALLY SENT TWO TO THREE MONTHS BEFORE THE CEREMONY. FOR YOUR WEDDING, THAT MEANS JANUARY.
THEREFORE, EXCLUDING THE YEAR'S-END HOLIDAY FROM OUR PLANNING, IDEALLY THE INVITATIONS WOULD BE READY TO GO OUT BY THE END OF DECEMBER.

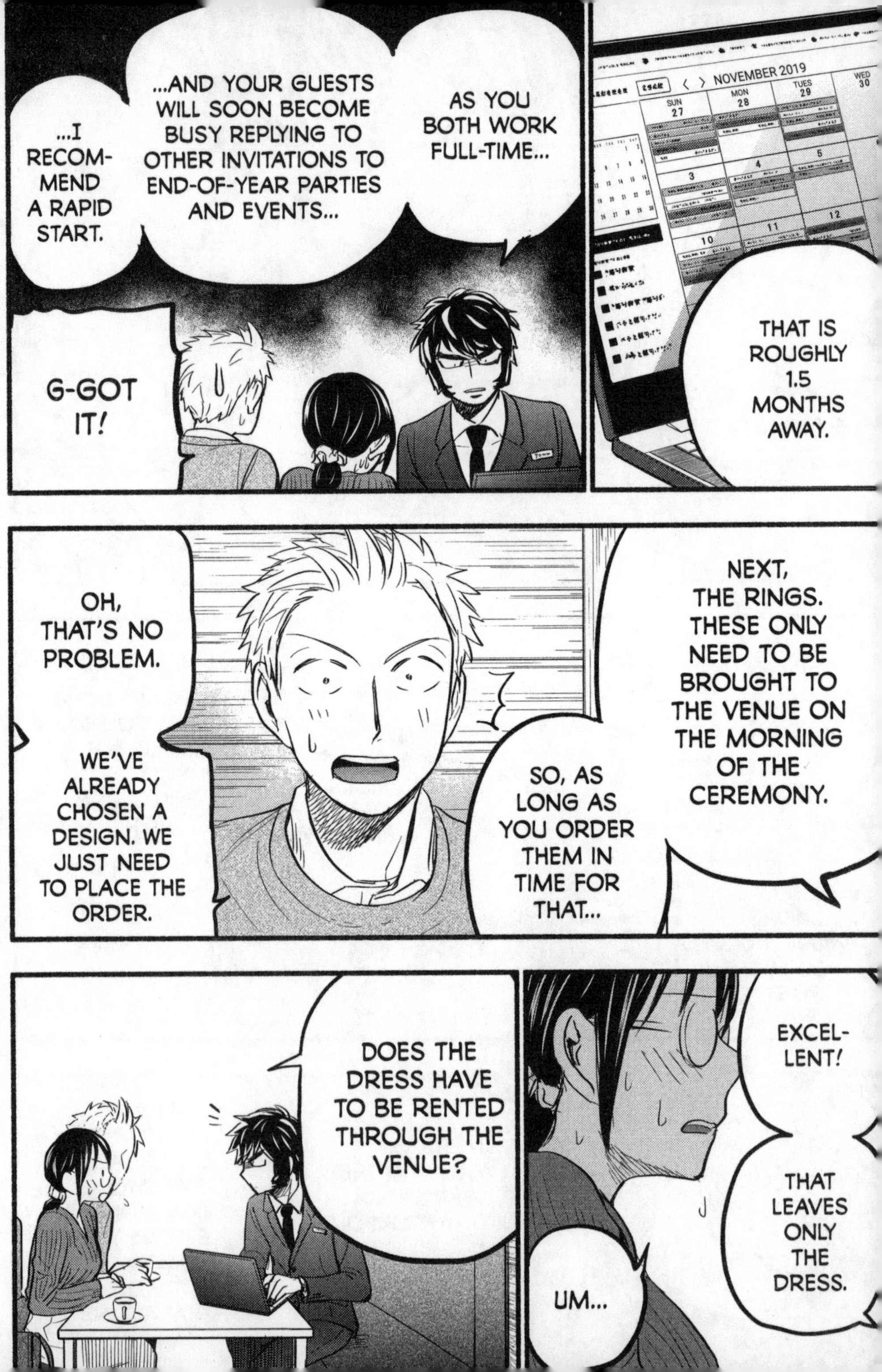
NOVEMBER 2019
THAT IS ROUGHLY 1.5 MONTHS AWAY.
AS YOU BOTH WORK FULL-TIME...
...AND YOUR GUESTS WILL SOON BECOME BUSY REPLYING TO OTHER INVITATIONS TO END-OF-YEAR PARTIES AND EVENTS...
...I RECOM-MEND A RAPID START.
G-GOT IT!
NEXT, THE RINGS. THESE ONLY NEED TO BE BROUGHT TO THE VENUE ON THE MORNING OF THE CEREMONY.
SO, AS LONG AS YOU ORDER THEM IN TIME FOR THAT...
OH, THAT'S NO PROBLEM.
WE'VE ALREADY CHOSEN A DESIGN. WE JUST NEED TO PLACE THE ORDER.
EXCEL-LENT!
THAT LEAVES ONLY THE DRESS.
UM...
DOES THE DRESS HAVE TO BE RENTED THROUGH THE VENUE?

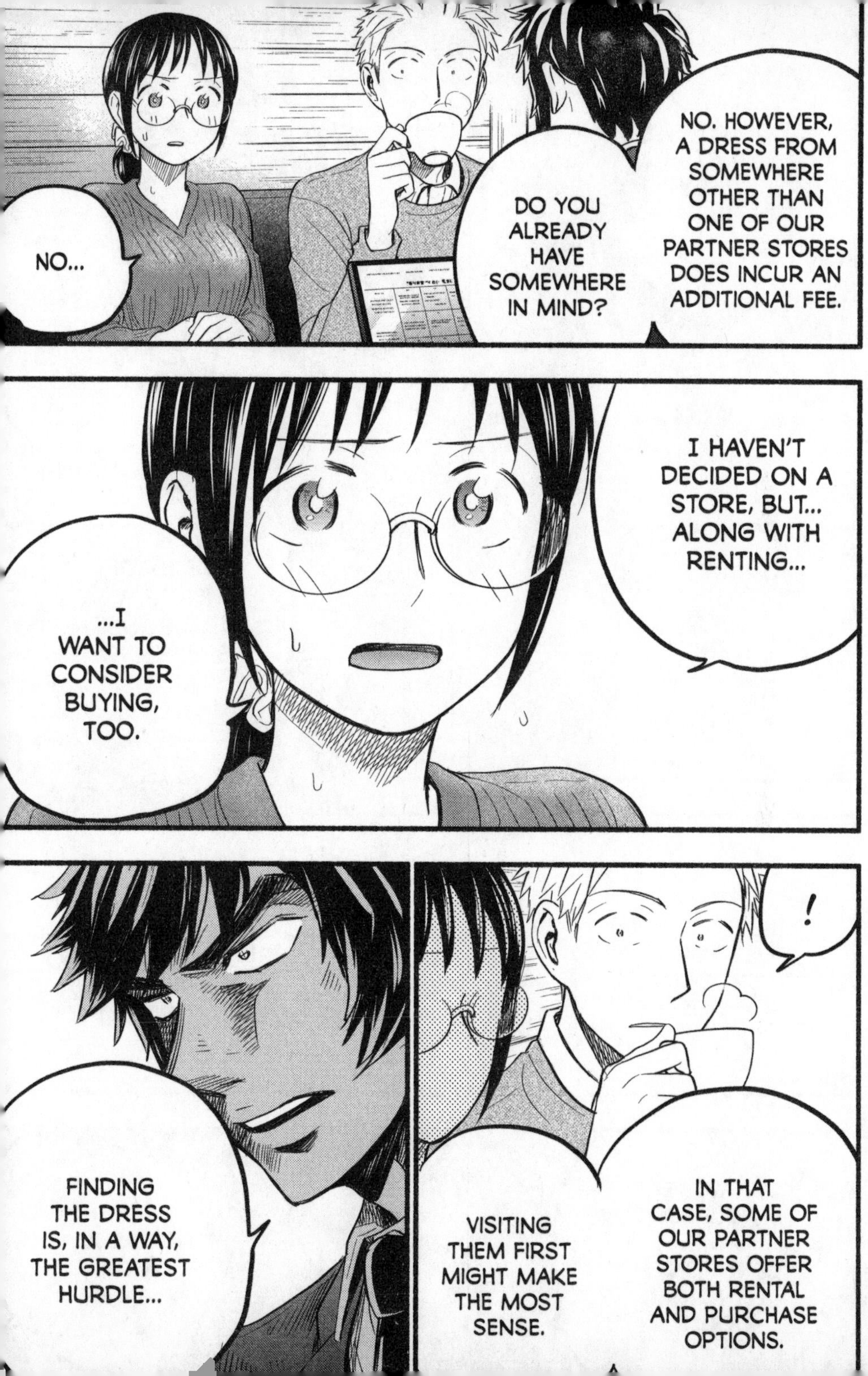
NO. HOWEVER, A DRESS FROM SOMEWHERE OTHER THAN ONE OF OUR PARTNER STORES DOES INCUR AN ADDITIONAL FEE.
DO YOU ALREADY HAVE SOMEWHERE IN MIND?
NO...
I HAVEN'T DECIDED ON A STORE, BUT... ALONG WITH RENTING...
...I WANT TO CONSIDER BUYING, TOO.
!
IN THAT CASE, SOME OF OUR PARTNER STORES OFFER BOTH RENTAL AND PURCHASE OPTIONS.
VISITING THEM FIRST MIGHT MAKE THE MOST SENSE.
FINDING THE DRESS IS, IN A WAY, THE GREATEST HURDLE...

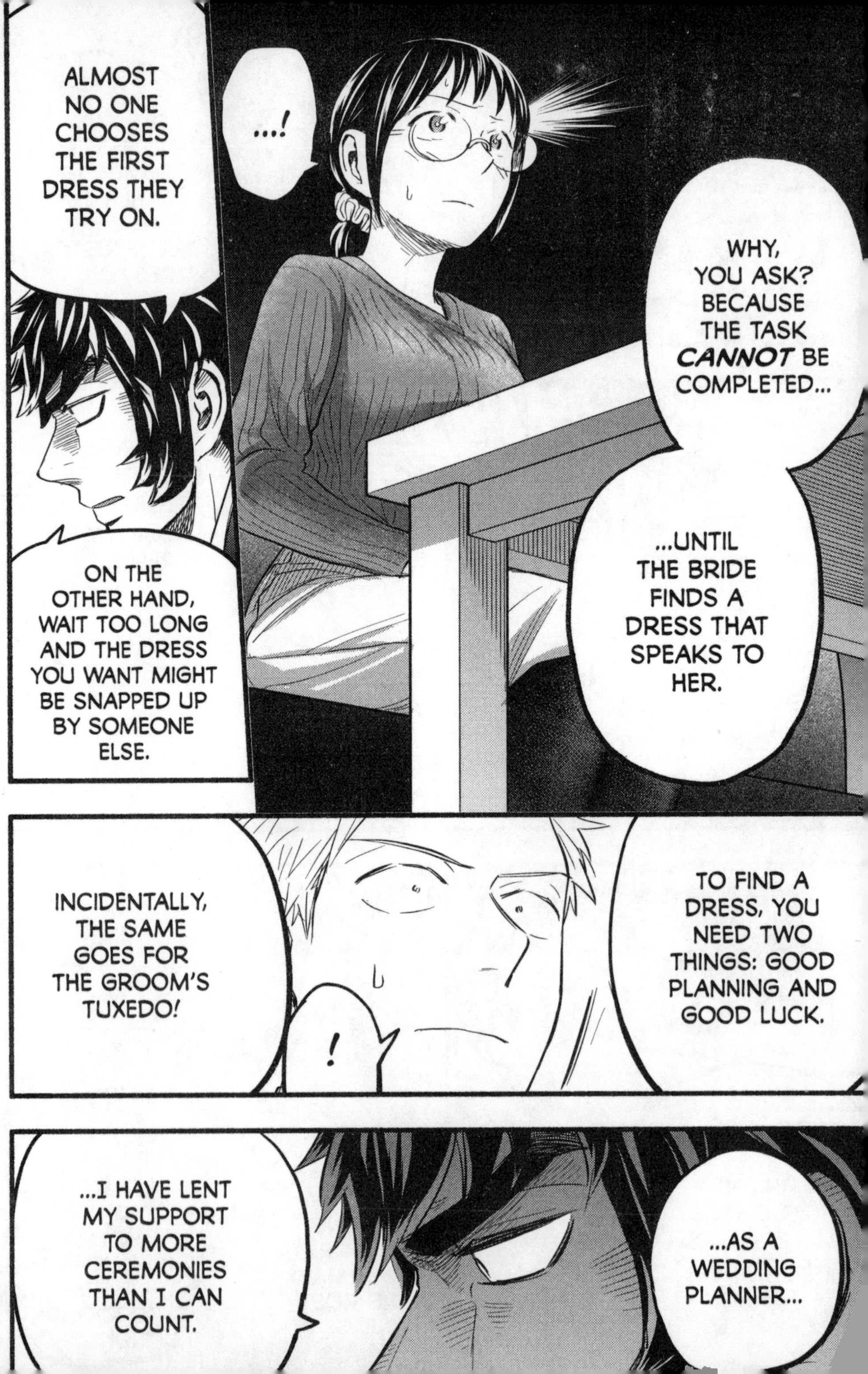
WHY, YOU ASK? BECAUSE THE TASK *CANNOT* BE COMPLETED...
...UNTIL THE BRIDE FINDS A DRESS THAT SPEAKS TO HER.
...!
ALMOST NO ONE CHOOSES THE FIRST DRESS THEY TRY ON.
ON THE OTHER HAND, WAIT TOO LONG AND THE DRESS YOU WANT MIGHT BE SNAPPED UP BY SOMEONE ELSE.
TO FIND A DRESS, YOU NEED TWO THINGS: GOOD PLANNING AND GOOD LUCK.
!
INCIDENTALLY, THE SAME GOES FOR THE GROOM'S TUXEDO!
...AS A WEDDING PLANNER...
...I HAVE LENT MY SUPPORT TO MORE CEREMONIES THAN I CAN COUNT.

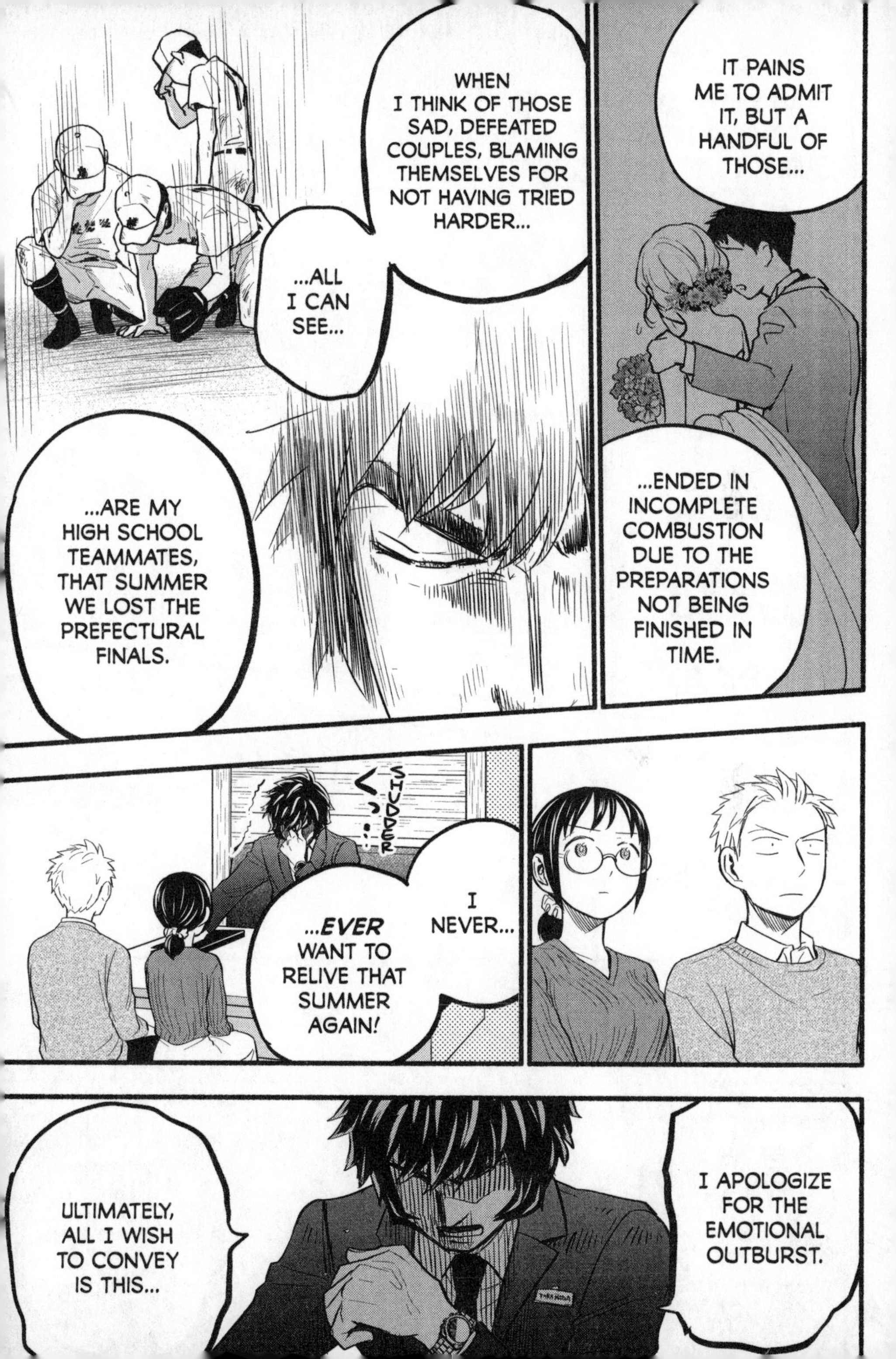
IT PAINS ME TO ADMIT IT, BUT A HANDFUL OF THOSE...
...ENDED IN INCOMPLETE COMBUSTION DUE TO THE PREPARATIONS NOT BEING FINISHED IN TIME.
WHEN I THINK OF THOSE SAD, DEFEATED COUPLES, BLAMING THEMSELVES FOR NOT HAVING TRIED HARDER...
...ALL I CAN SEE...
...ARE MY HIGH SCHOOL TEAMMATES, THAT SUMMER WE LOST THE PREFECTURAL FINALS.
SHUDDER
I NEVER...
...*EVER* WANT TO RELIVE THAT SUMMER AGAIN!
I APOLOGIZE FOR THE EMOTIONAL OUTBURST.
ULTIMATELY, ALL I WISH TO CONVEY IS THIS...

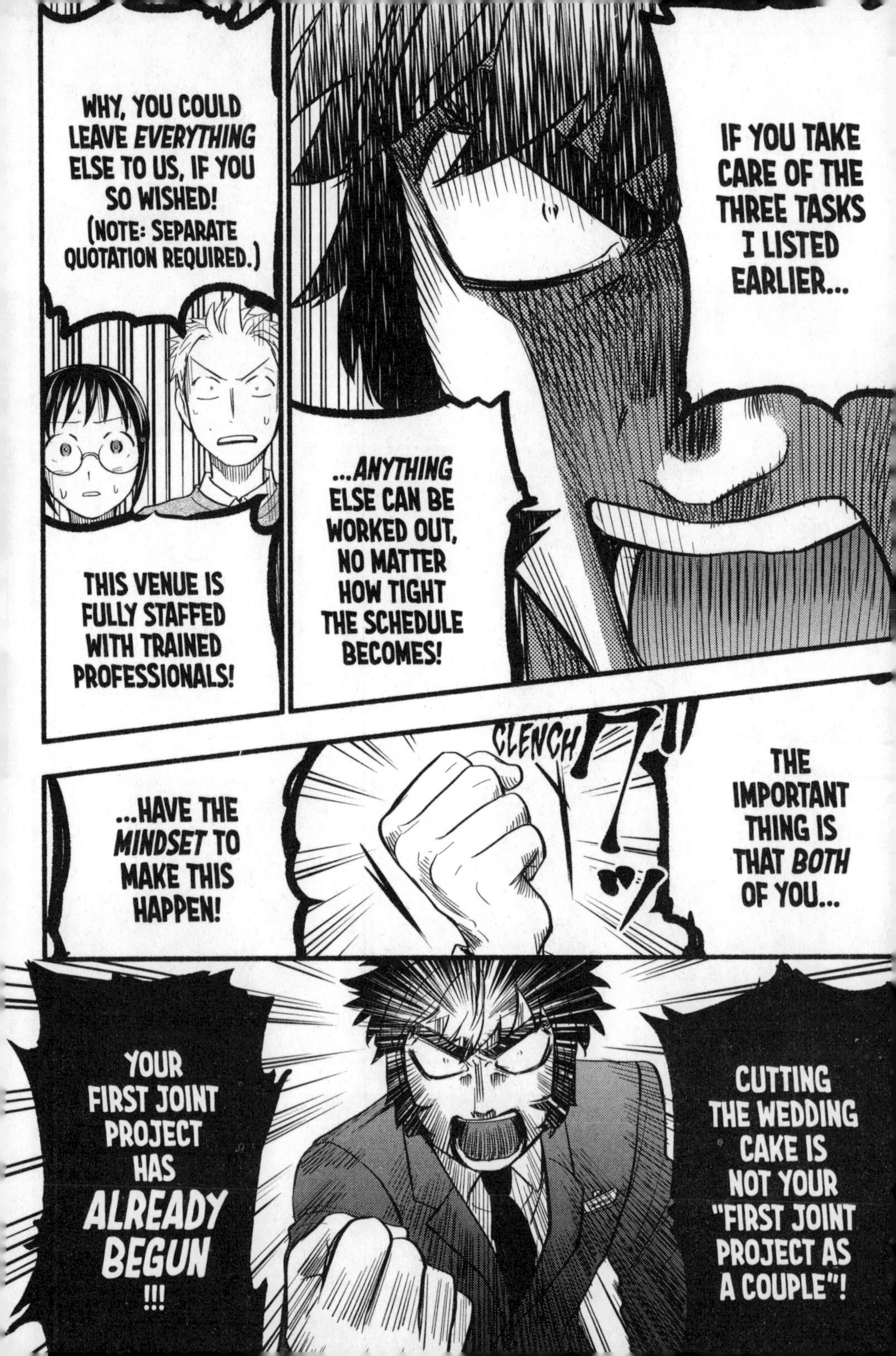
IF YOU TAKE CARE OF THE THREE TASKS I LISTED EARLIER...
...ANYTHING ELSE CAN BE WORKED OUT, NO MATTER HOW TIGHT THE SCHEDULE BECOMES!
WHY, YOU COULD LEAVE EVERYTHING ELSE TO US, IF YOU SO WISHED! (NOTE: SEPARATE QUOTATION REQUIRED.)
THIS VENUE IS FULLY STAFFED WITH TRAINED PROFESSIONALS!
THE IMPORTANT THING IS THAT BOTH OF YOU...
CLENCH
...HAVE THE MINDSET TO MAKE THIS HAPPEN!
CUTTING THE WEDDING CAKE IS NOT YOUR "FIRST JOINT PROJECT AS A COUPLE"!
YOUR FIRST JOINT PROJECT HAS ALREADY BEGUN!!!

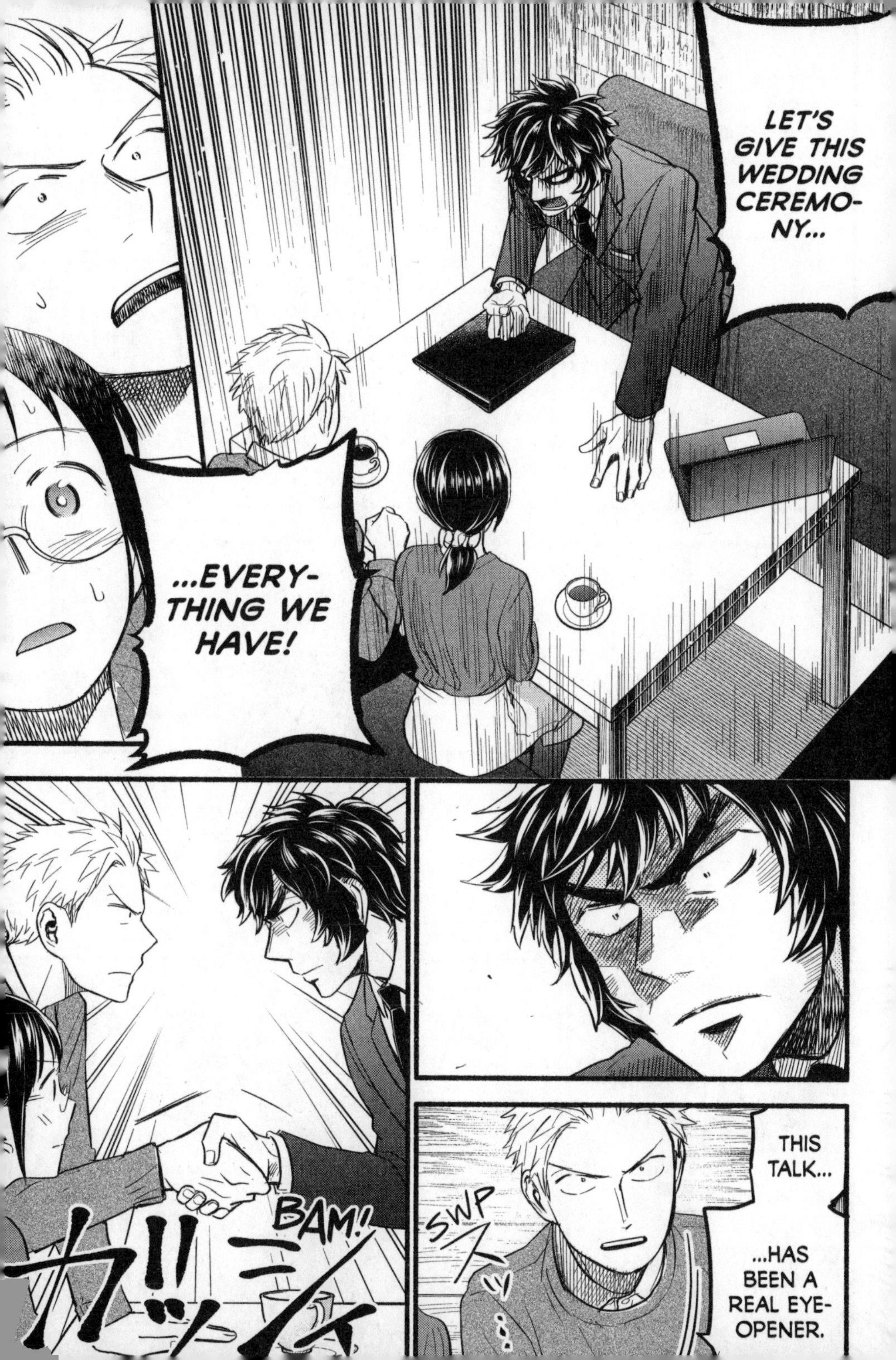
LET'S GIVE THIS WEDDING CEREMONY...
...EVERYTHING WE HAVE!
THIS TALK...
...HAS BEEN A REAL EYE-OPENER.
SWP
BAM!

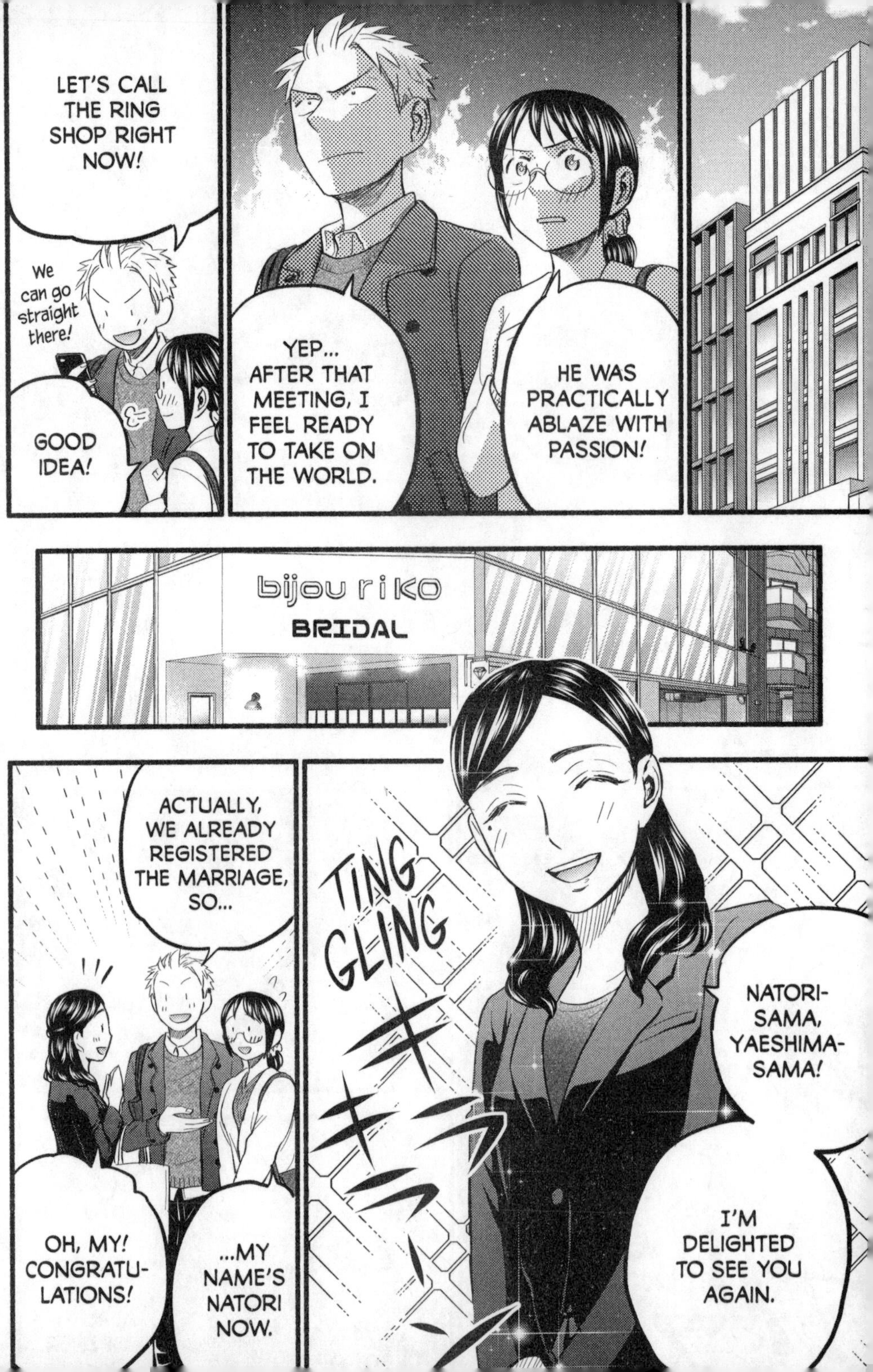
HE WAS PRACTICALLY ABLAZE WITH PASSION!
YEP... AFTER THAT MEETING, I FEEL READY TO TAKE ON THE WORLD.
LET'S CALL THE RING SHOP RIGHT NOW!
We can go straight there!
GOOD IDEA!
bijou riKO
BRIDAL
TING GLING
NATORI-SAMA, YAESHIMA-SAMA!
I'M DELIGHTED TO SEE YOU AGAIN.
ACTUALLY, WE ALREADY REGISTERED THE MARRIAGE, SO...
...MY NAME'S NATORI NOW.
OH, MY! CONGRATULATIONS!

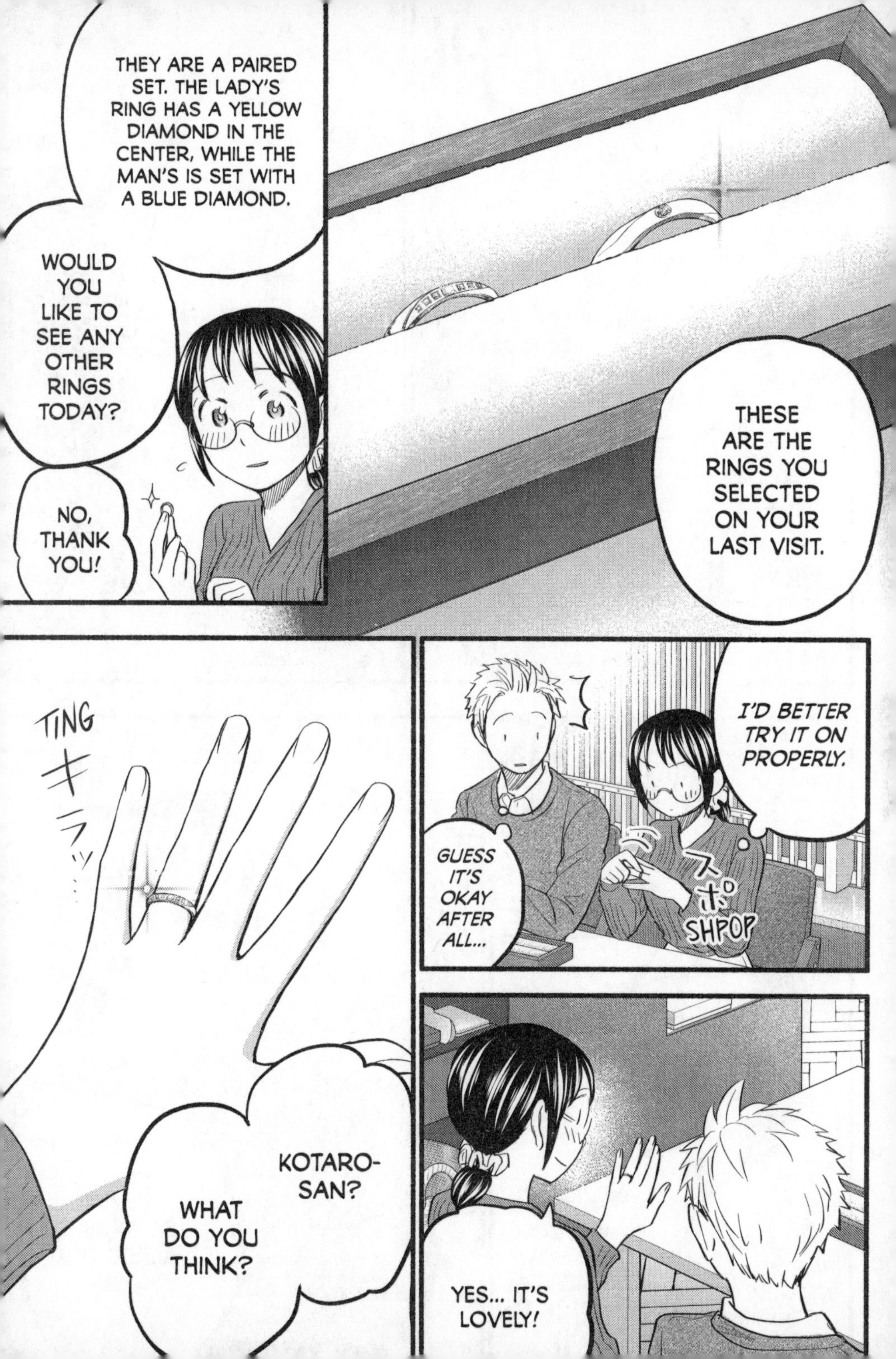
THESE ARE THE RINGS YOU SELECTED ON YOUR LAST VISIT.
THEY ARE A PAIRED SET. THE LADY'S RING HAS A YELLOW DIAMOND IN THE CENTER, WHILE THE MAN'S IS SET WITH A BLUE DIAMOND.
WOULD YOU LIKE TO SEE ANY OTHER RINGS TODAY?
NO, THANK YOU!
I'D BETTER TRY IT ON PROPERLY.
スポ SHPOP
GUESS IT'S OKAY AFTER ALL...
YES... IT'S LOVELY!
TING キラッ
KOTARO-SAN?
WHAT DO YOU THINK?

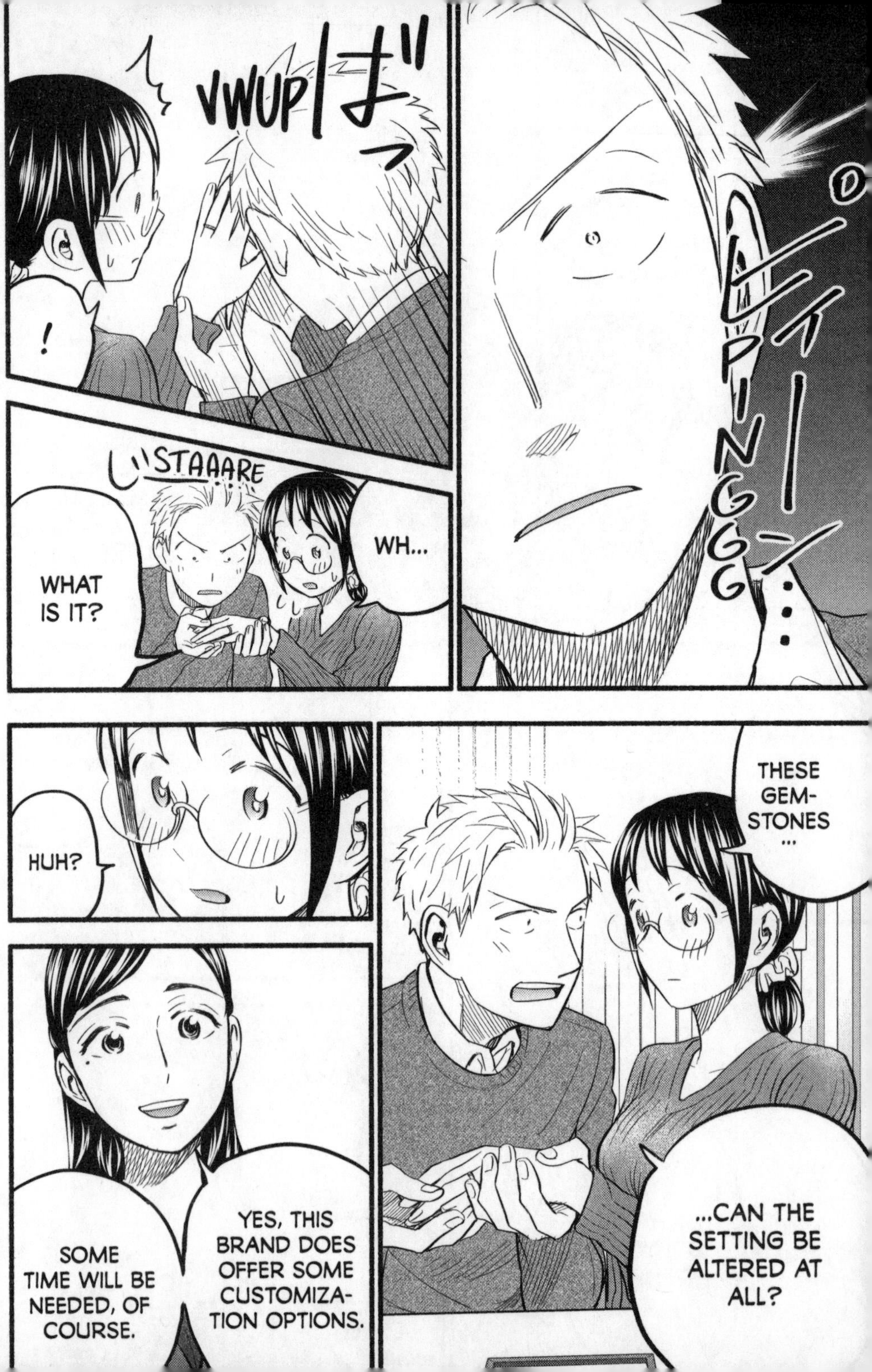
DPINGGG...
VWUP
!
STAAARE
WH...
WHAT IS IT?
THESE GEM-STONES...
...CAN THE SETTING BE ALTERED AT ALL?
HUH?
YES, THIS BRAND DOES OFFER SOME CUSTOMIZA-TION OPTIONS.
SOME TIME WILL BE NEEDED, OF COURSE.

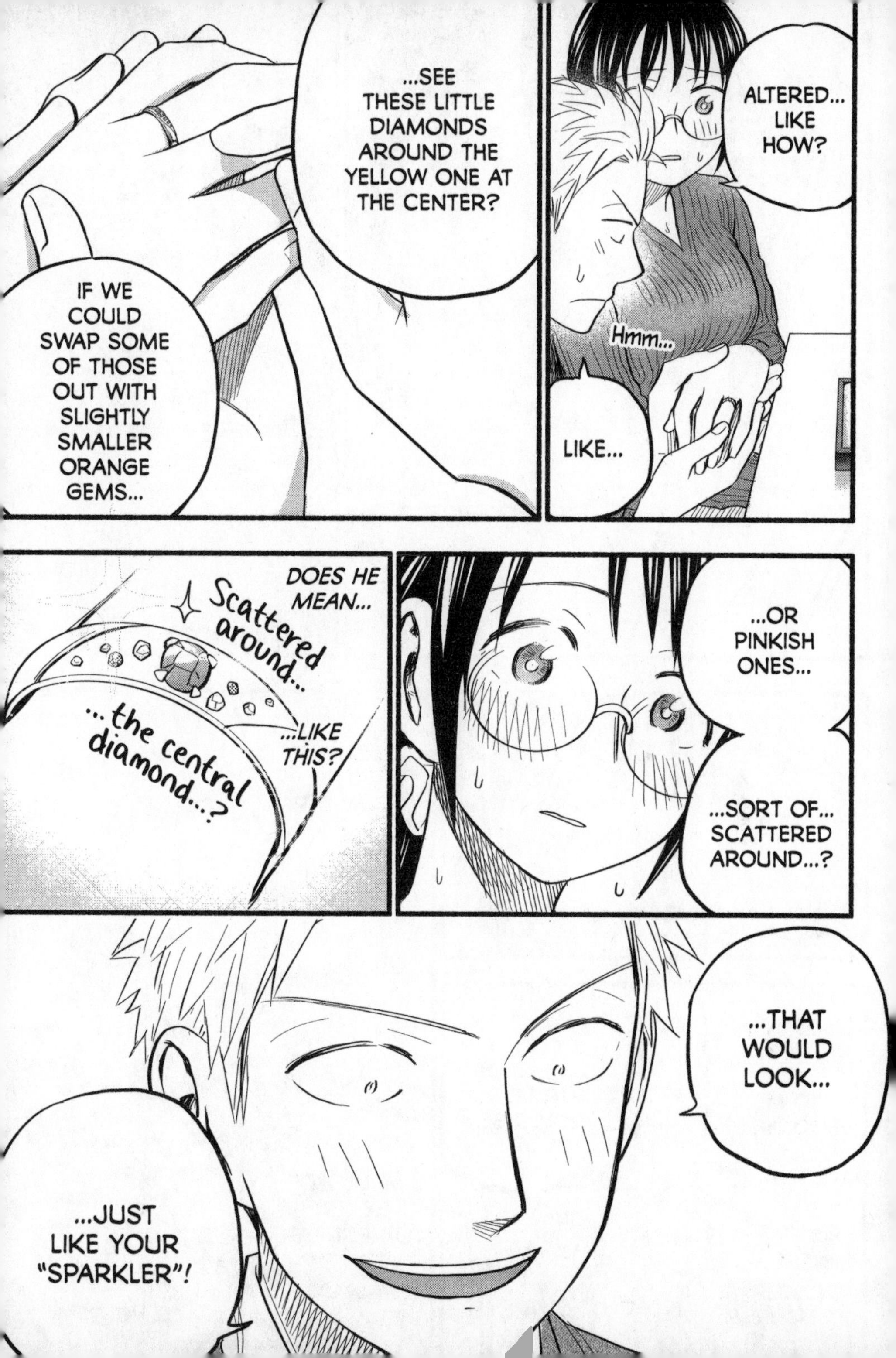
ALTERED... LIKE HOW?
Hmm...
LIKE...
...SEE THESE LITTLE DIAMONDS AROUND THE YELLOW ONE AT THE CENTER?
IF WE COULD SWAP SOME OF THOSE OUT WITH SLIGHTLY SMALLER ORANGE GEMS...
...OR PINKISH ONES...
...SORT OF... SCATTERED AROUND...?
DOES HE MEAN...
Scattered around...
...the central diamond...?
...LIKE THIS?
...THAT WOULD LOOK...
...JUST LIKE YOUR "SPARKLER"!

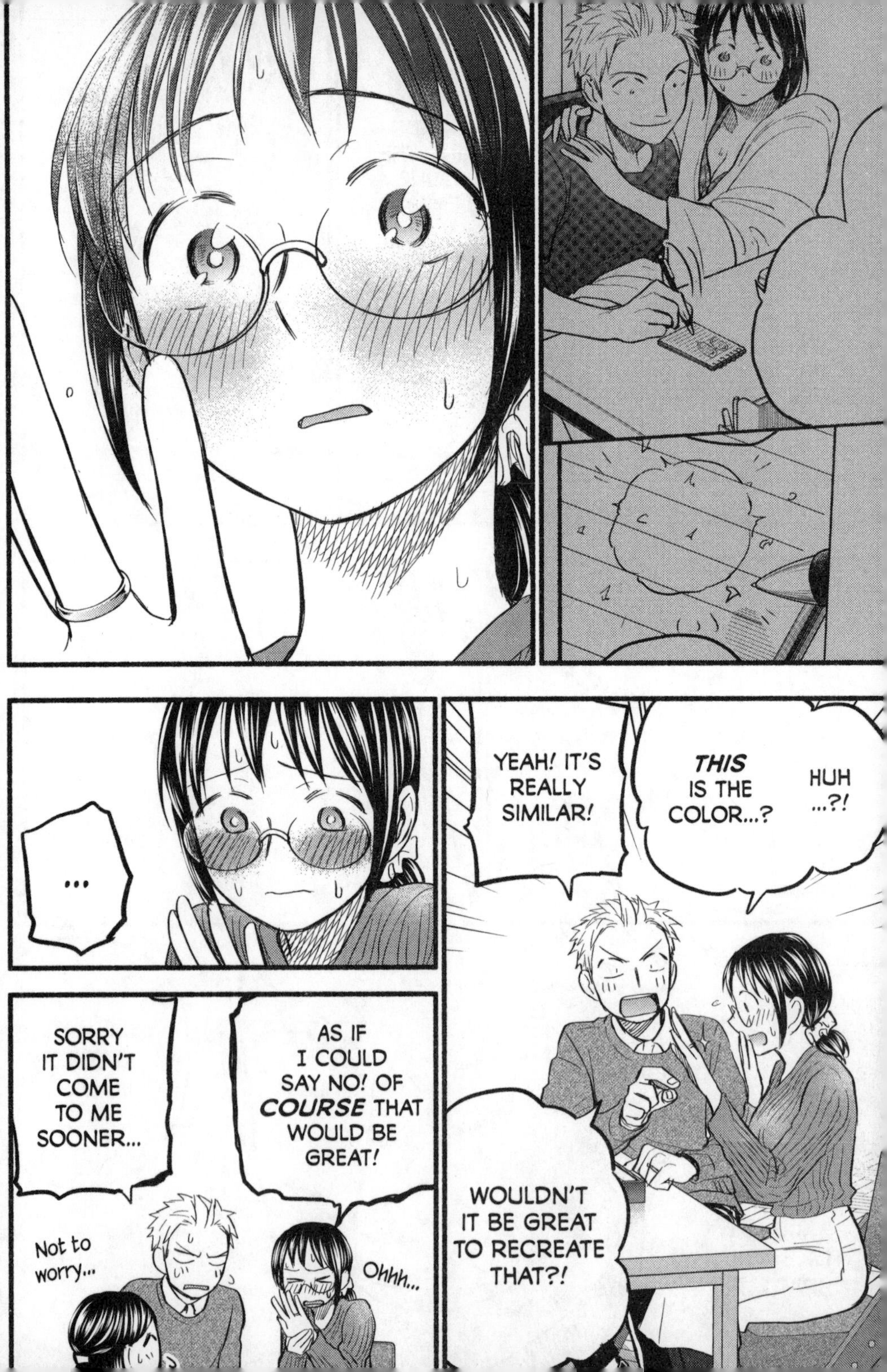
HUH ...?!
THIS IS THE COLOR...?
YEAH! IT'S REALLY SIMILAR!
WOULDN'T IT BE GREAT TO RECREATE THAT?!
...
AS IF I COULD SAY NO! OF COURSE THAT WOULD BE GREAT!
SORRY IT DIDN'T COME TO ME SOONER...
Ohhh...
Not to worry...

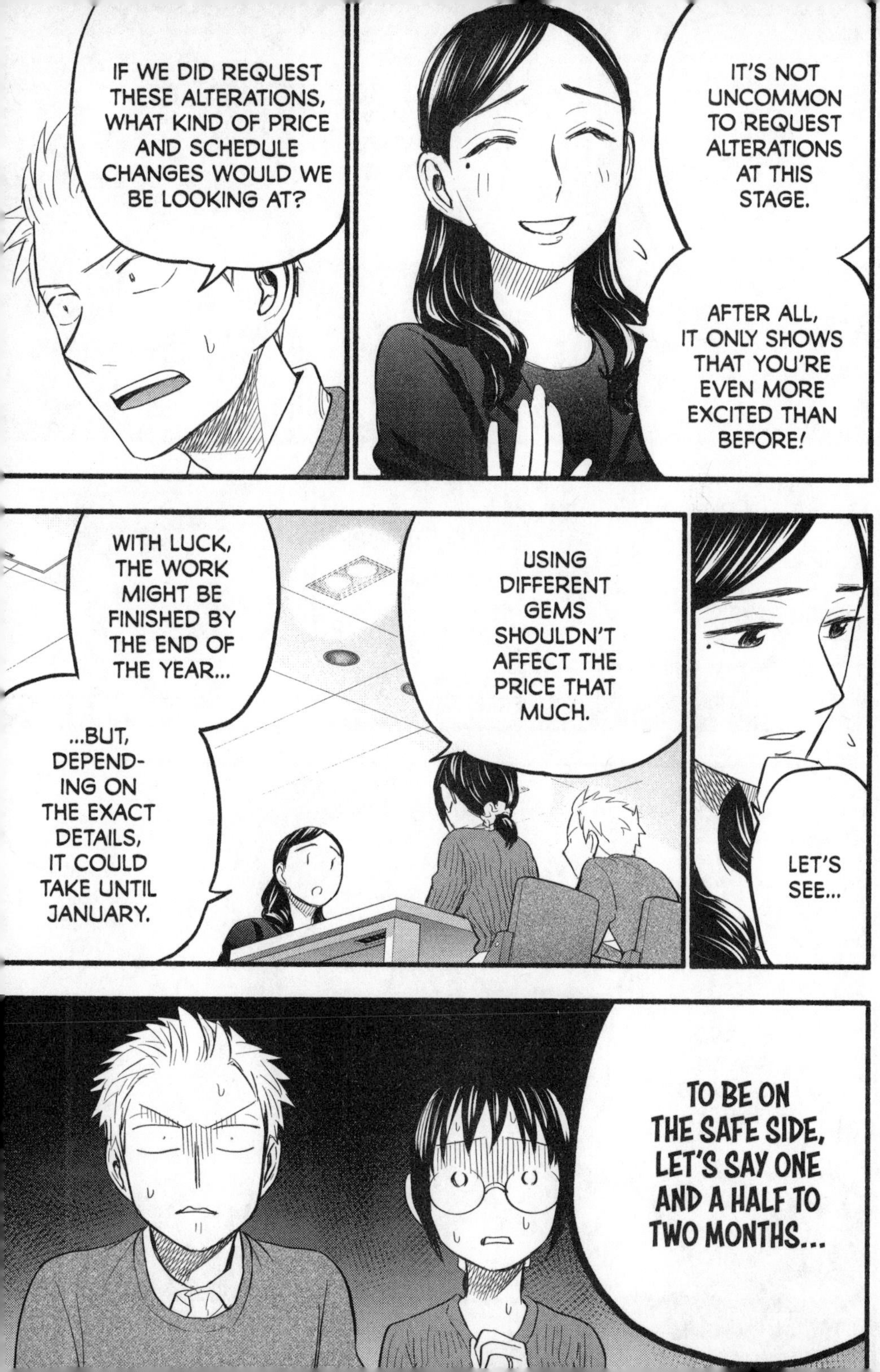
IT'S NOT UNCOMMON TO REQUEST ALTERATIONS AT THIS STAGE.
AFTER ALL, IT ONLY SHOWS THAT YOU'RE EVEN MORE EXCITED THAN BEFORE!
IF WE DID REQUEST THESE ALTERATIONS, WHAT KIND OF PRICE AND SCHEDULE CHANGES WOULD WE BE LOOKING AT?
LET'S SEE...
USING DIFFERENT GEMS SHOULDN'T AFFECT THE PRICE THAT MUCH.
WITH LUCK, THE WORK MIGHT BE FINISHED BY THE END OF THE YEAR...
...BUT, DEPEND-ING ON THE EXACT DETAILS, IT COULD TAKE UNTIL JANUARY.
TO BE ON THE SAFE SIDE, LET'S SAY ONE AND A HALF TO TWO MONTHS...

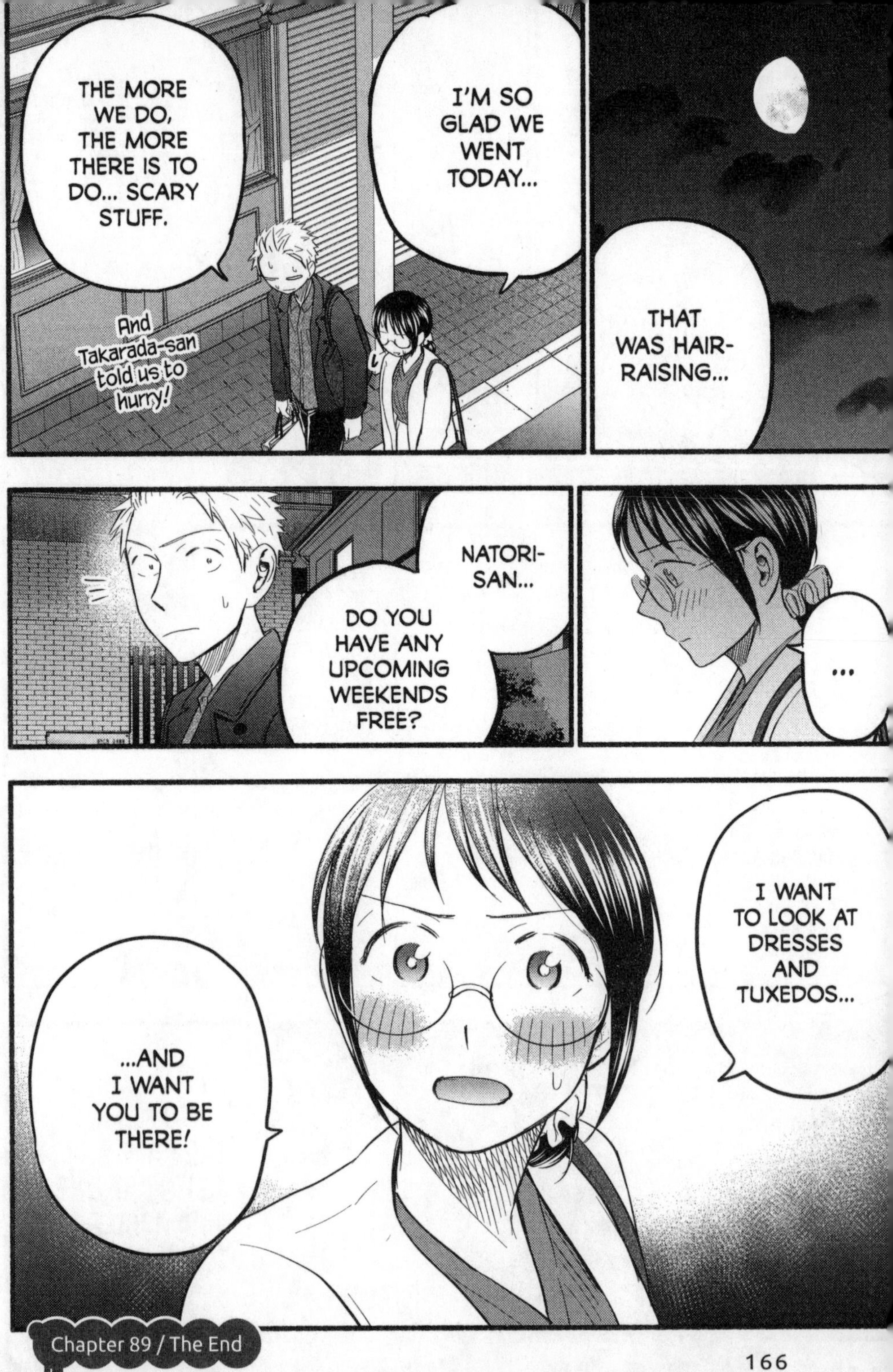
THAT WAS HAIR-RAISING...
I'M SO GLAD WE WENT TODAY...
THE MORE WE DO, THE MORE THERE IS TO DO... SCARY STUFF.
And Takarada-san told us to hurry!
...
NATORI-SAN...
DO YOU HAVE ANY UPCOMING WEEKENDS FREE?
I WANT TO LOOK AT DRESSES AND TUXEDOS...
...AND I WANT YOU TO BE THERE!

Chapter 89 / The End

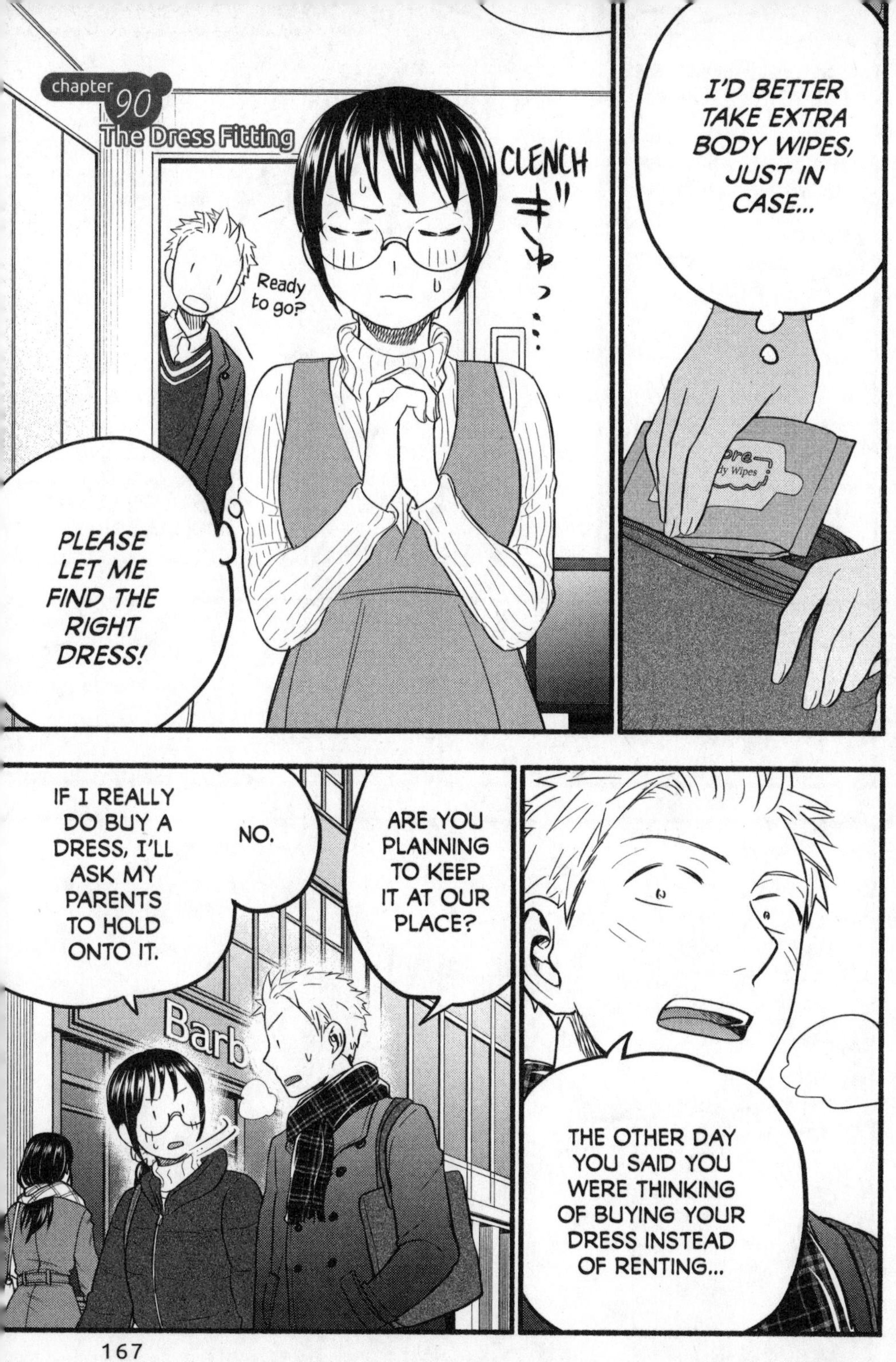
I'D BETTER TAKE EXTRA BODY WIPES, JUST IN CASE...
chapter 90
The Dress Fitting
CLENCH
ぎゅっ…
Ready to go?
PLEASE LET ME FIND THE RIGHT DRESS!
THE OTHER DAY YOU SAID YOU WERE THINKING OF BUYING YOUR DRESS INSTEAD OF RENTING...
ARE YOU PLANNING TO KEEP IT AT OUR PLACE?
NO.
IF I REALLY DO BUY A DRESS, I'LL ASK MY PARENTS TO HOLD ONTO IT.
Barb

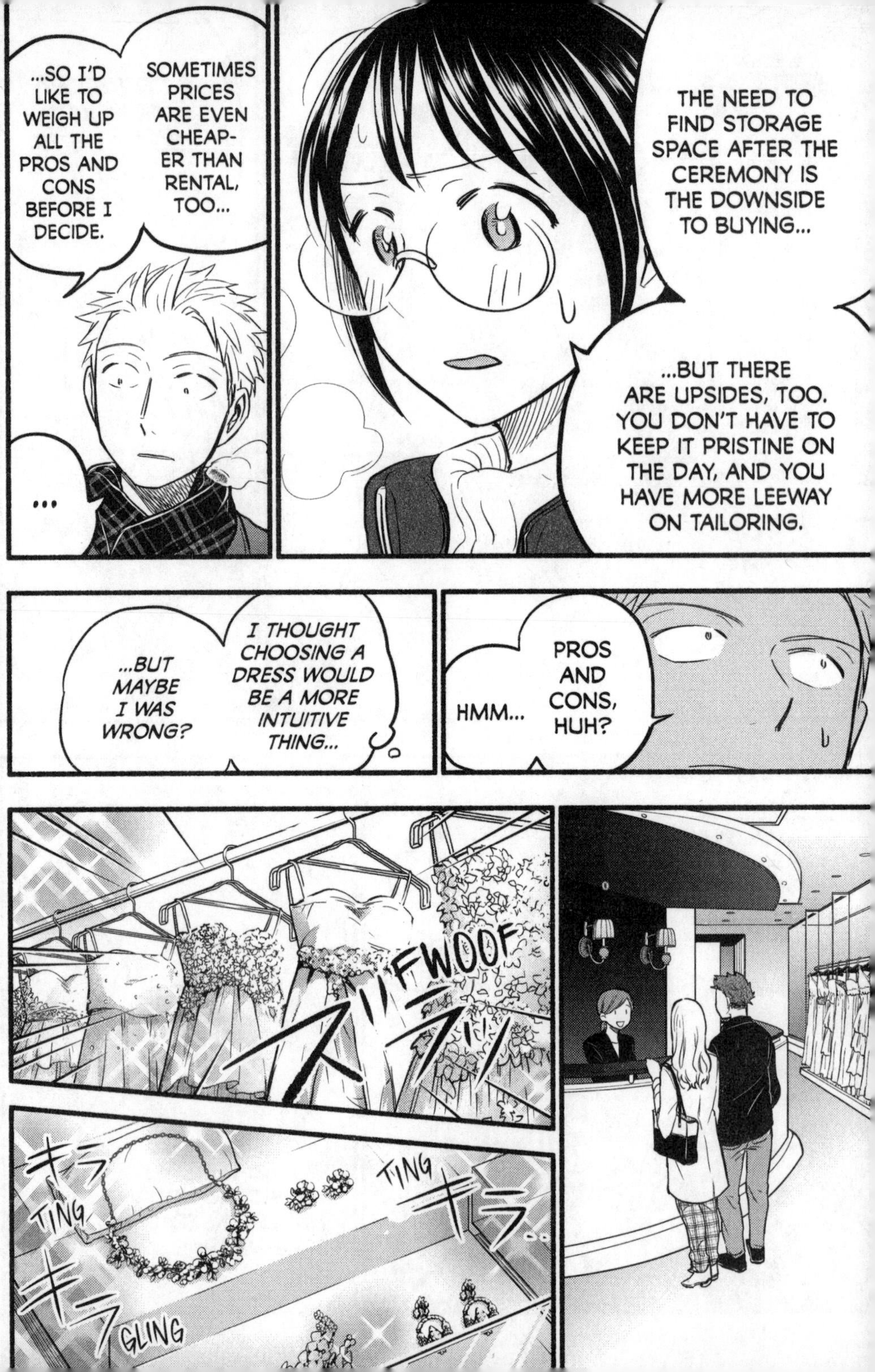
THE NEED TO FIND STORAGE SPACE AFTER THE CEREMONY IS THE DOWNSIDE TO BUYING...
...BUT THERE ARE UPSIDES, TOO. YOU DON'T HAVE TO KEEP IT PRISTINE ON THE DAY, AND YOU HAVE MORE LEEWAY ON TAILORING.
SOMETIMES PRICES ARE EVEN CHEAP-ER THAN RENTAL, TOO...
...SO I'D LIKE TO WEIGH UP ALL THE PROS AND CONS BEFORE I DECIDE.
...
PROS AND CONS, HUH?
HMM...
I THOUGHT CHOOSING A DRESS WOULD BE A MORE INTUITIVE THING...
...BUT MAYBE I WAS WRONG?
FWOOF
TING
TING
GLING

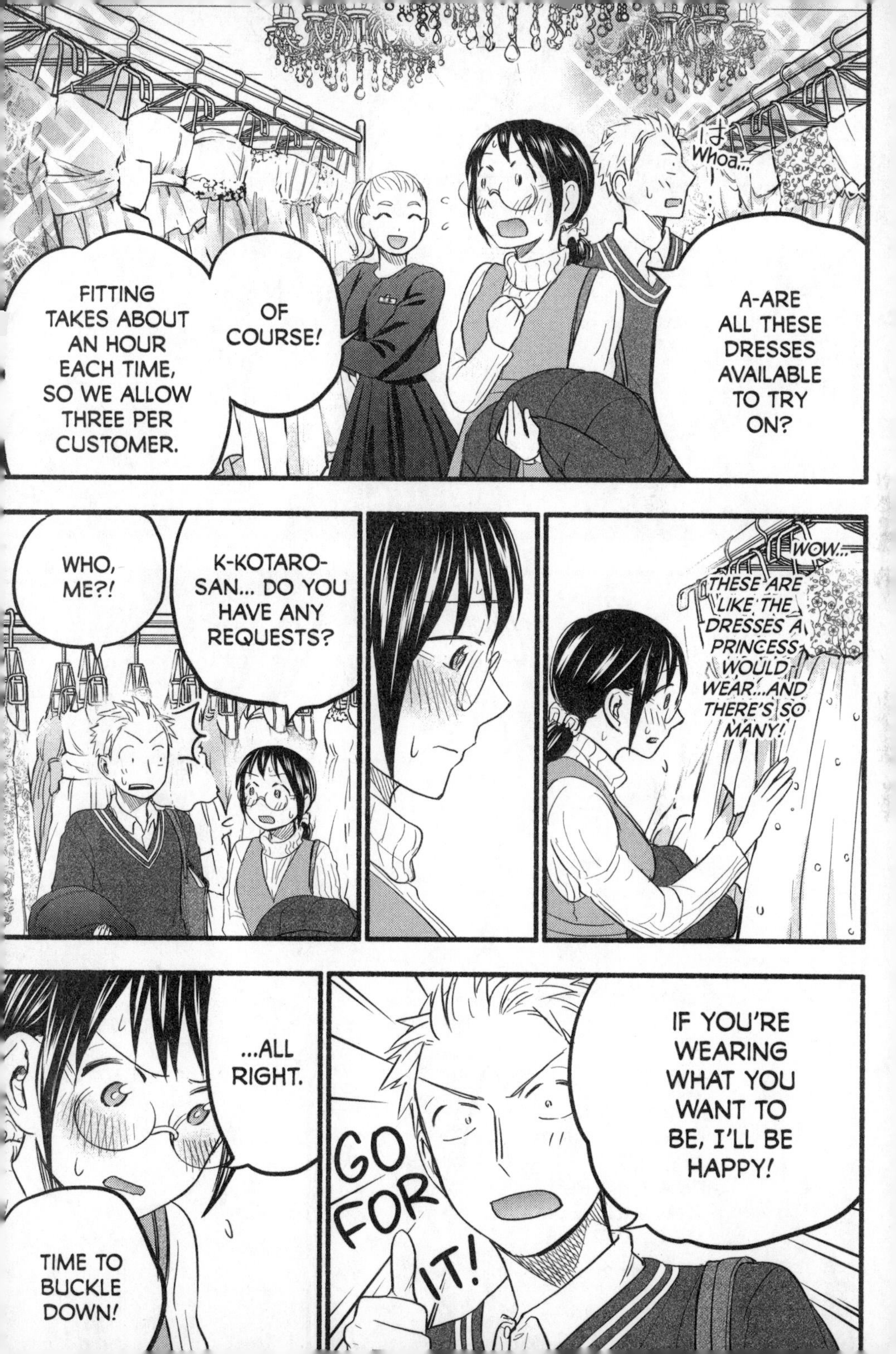
は
Whoa...
A-ARE ALL THESE DRESSES AVAILABLE TO TRY ON?
OF COURSE!
FITTING TAKES ABOUT AN HOUR EACH TIME, SO WE ALLOW THREE PER CUSTOMER.
WOW...
THESE ARE LIKE THE DRESSES A PRINCESS WOULD WEAR...AND THERE'S SO MANY!
K-KOTARO-SAN... DO YOU HAVE ANY REQUESTS?
WHO, ME?!
IF YOU'RE WEARING WHAT YOU WANT TO BE, I'LL BE HAPPY!
GO FOR IT!
...ALL RIGHT.
TIME TO BUCKLE DOWN!

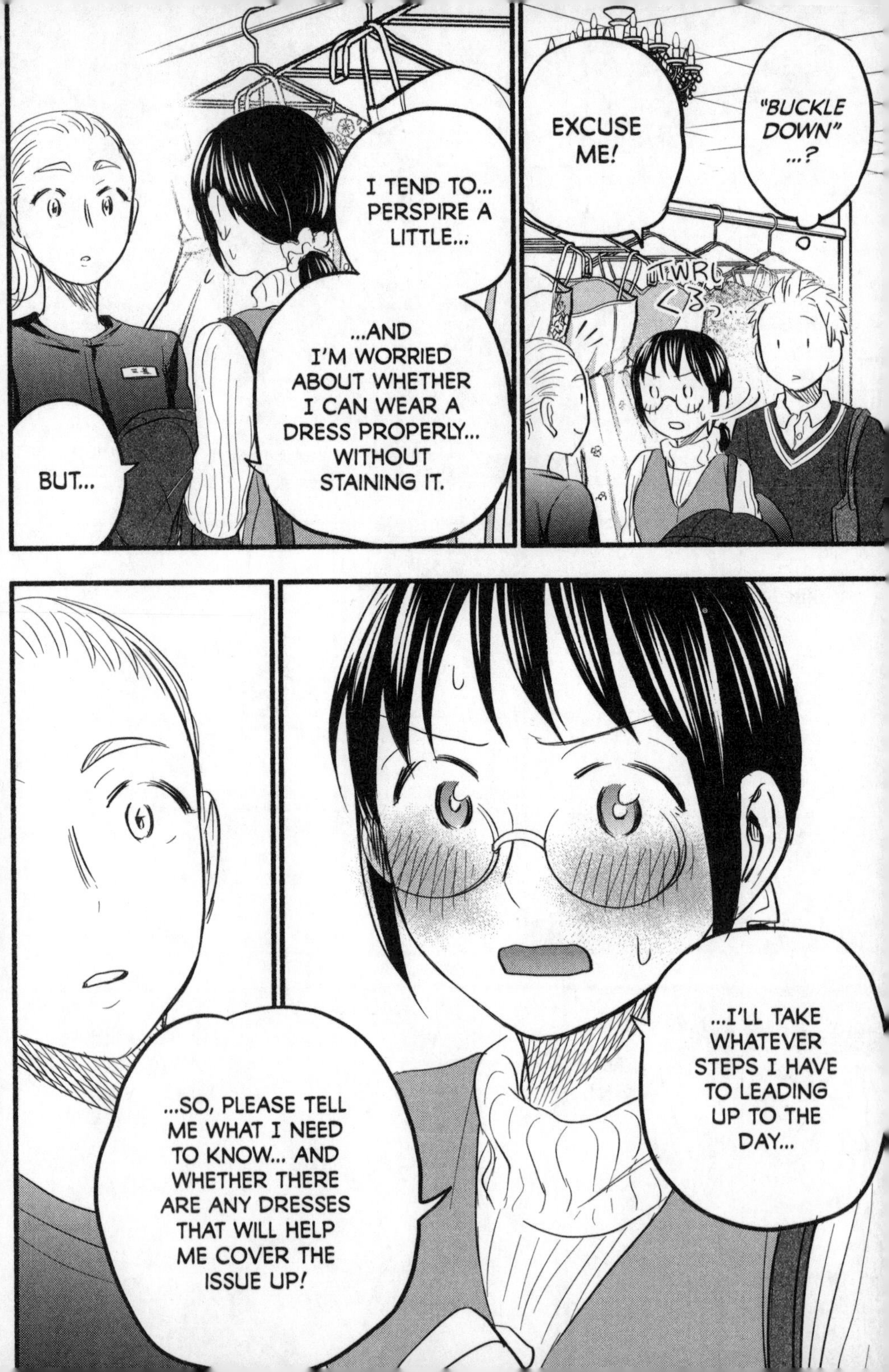
"BUCKLE DOWN" ...?
EXCUSE ME!
TWRL
くるっ
I TEND TO... PERSPIRE A LITTLE...
...AND I'M WORRIED ABOUT WHETHER I CAN WEAR A DRESS PROPERLY... WITHOUT STAINING IT.
BUT...
...I'LL TAKE WHATEVER STEPS I HAVE TO LEADING UP TO THE DAY...
...SO, PLEASE TELL ME WHAT I NEED TO KNOW... AND WHETHER THERE ARE ANY DRESSES THAT WILL HELP ME COVER THE ISSUE UP!

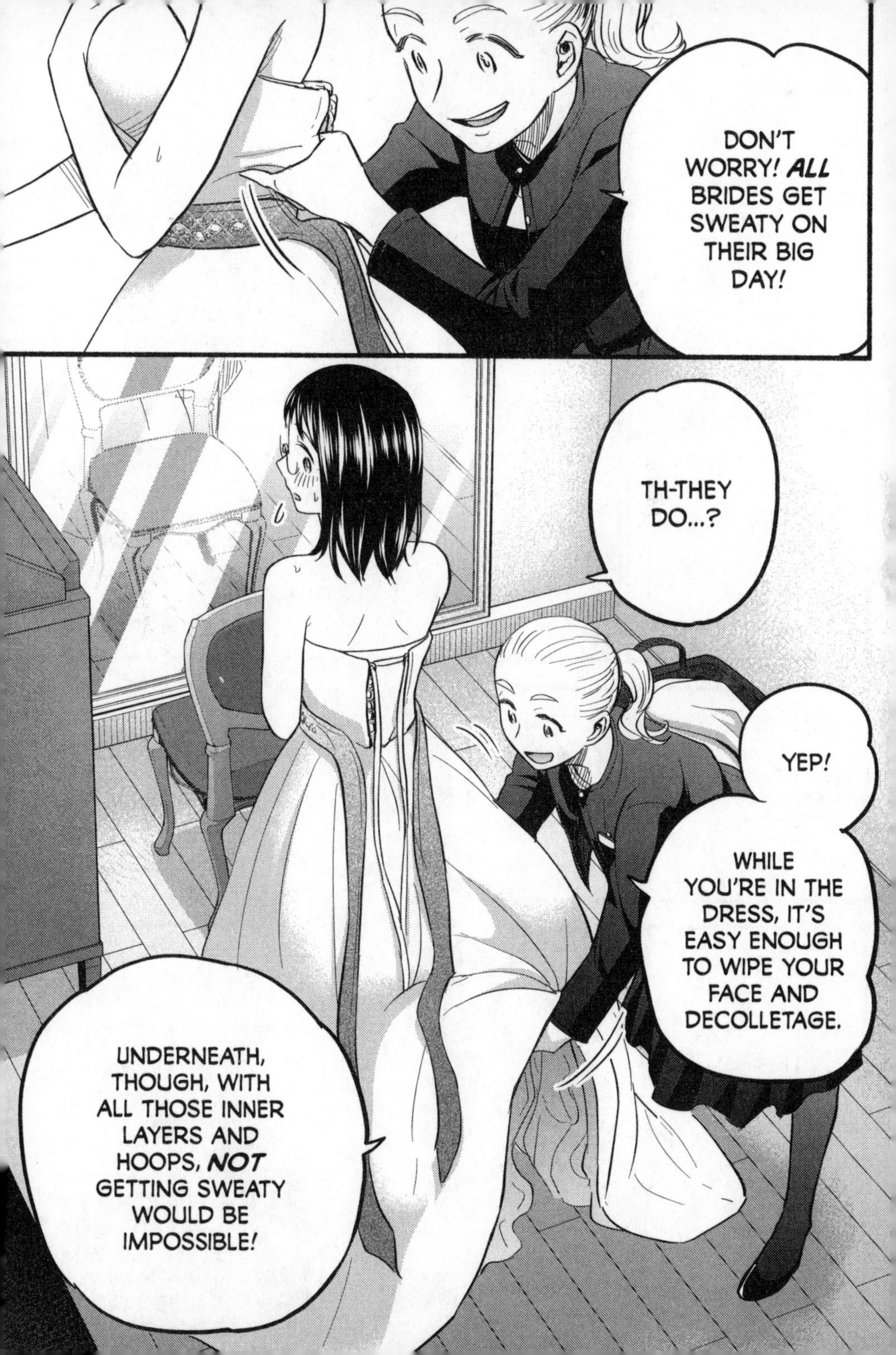
DON'T WORRY! ALL BRIDES GET SWEATY ON THEIR BIG DAY!
TH-THEY DO...?
YEP!
WHILE YOU'RE IN THE DRESS, IT'S EASY ENOUGH TO WIPE YOUR FACE AND DECOLLETAGE.
UNDERNEATH, THOUGH, WITH ALL THOSE INNER LAYERS AND HOOPS, NOT GETTING SWEATY WOULD BE IMPOSSIBLE!

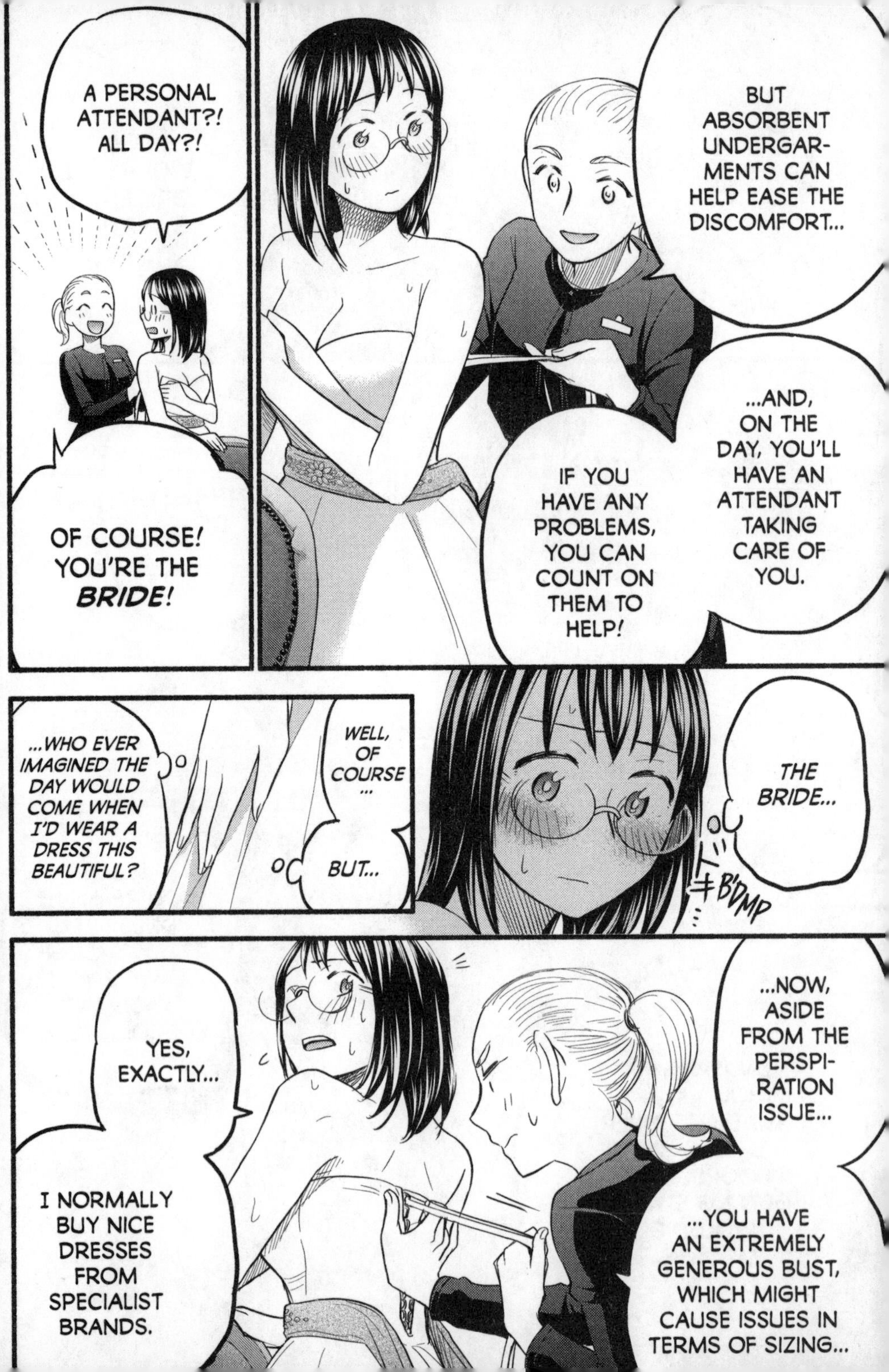
BUT ABSORBENT UNDERGARMENTS CAN HELP EASE THE DISCOMFORT...
...AND, ON THE DAY, YOU'LL HAVE AN ATTENDANT TAKING CARE OF YOU.
IF YOU HAVE ANY PROBLEMS, YOU CAN COUNT ON THEM TO HELP!
A PERSONAL ATTENDANT?! ALL DAY?!
OF COURSE! YOU'RE THE *BRIDE*!
THE BRIDE...
B'DMP
WELL, OF COURSE...
BUT...
...WHO EVER IMAGINED THE DAY WOULD COME WHEN I'D WEAR A DRESS THIS BEAUTIFUL?
...NOW, ASIDE FROM THE PERSPIRATION ISSUE...
...YOU HAVE AN EXTREMELY GENEROUS BUST, WHICH MIGHT CAUSE ISSUES IN TERMS OF SIZING...
YES, EXACTLY...
I NORMALLY BUY NICE DRESSES FROM SPECIALIST BRANDS.

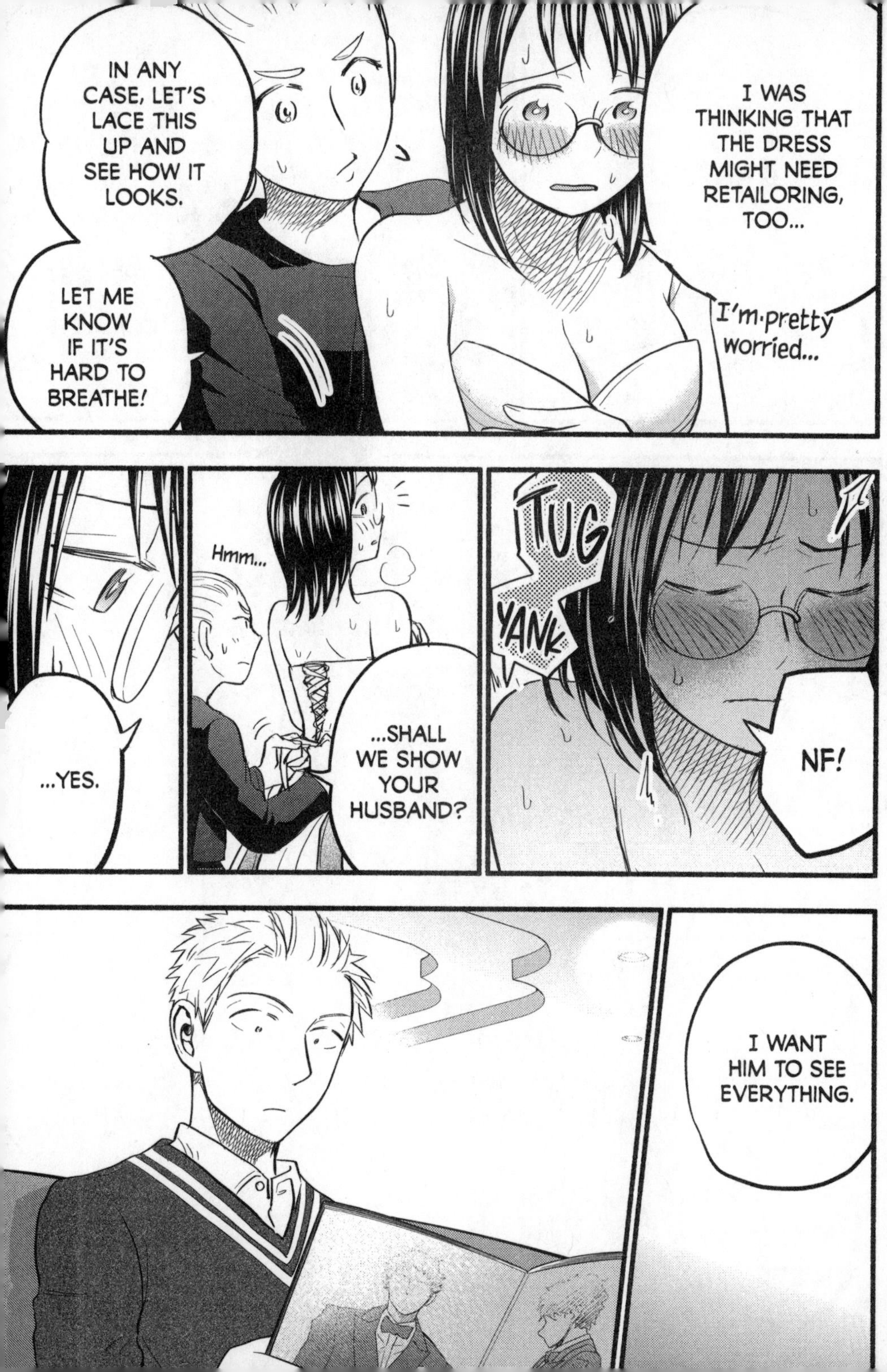
I WAS THINKING THAT THE DRESS MIGHT NEED RETAILORING, TOO...
I'm pretty worried...
IN ANY CASE, LET'S LACE THIS UP AND SEE HOW IT LOOKS.
LET ME KNOW IF IT'S HARD TO BREATHE!
TUG
YANK
NF!
Hmm...
...SHALL WE SHOW YOUR HUSBAND?
...YES.
I WANT HIM TO SEE EVERYTHING.

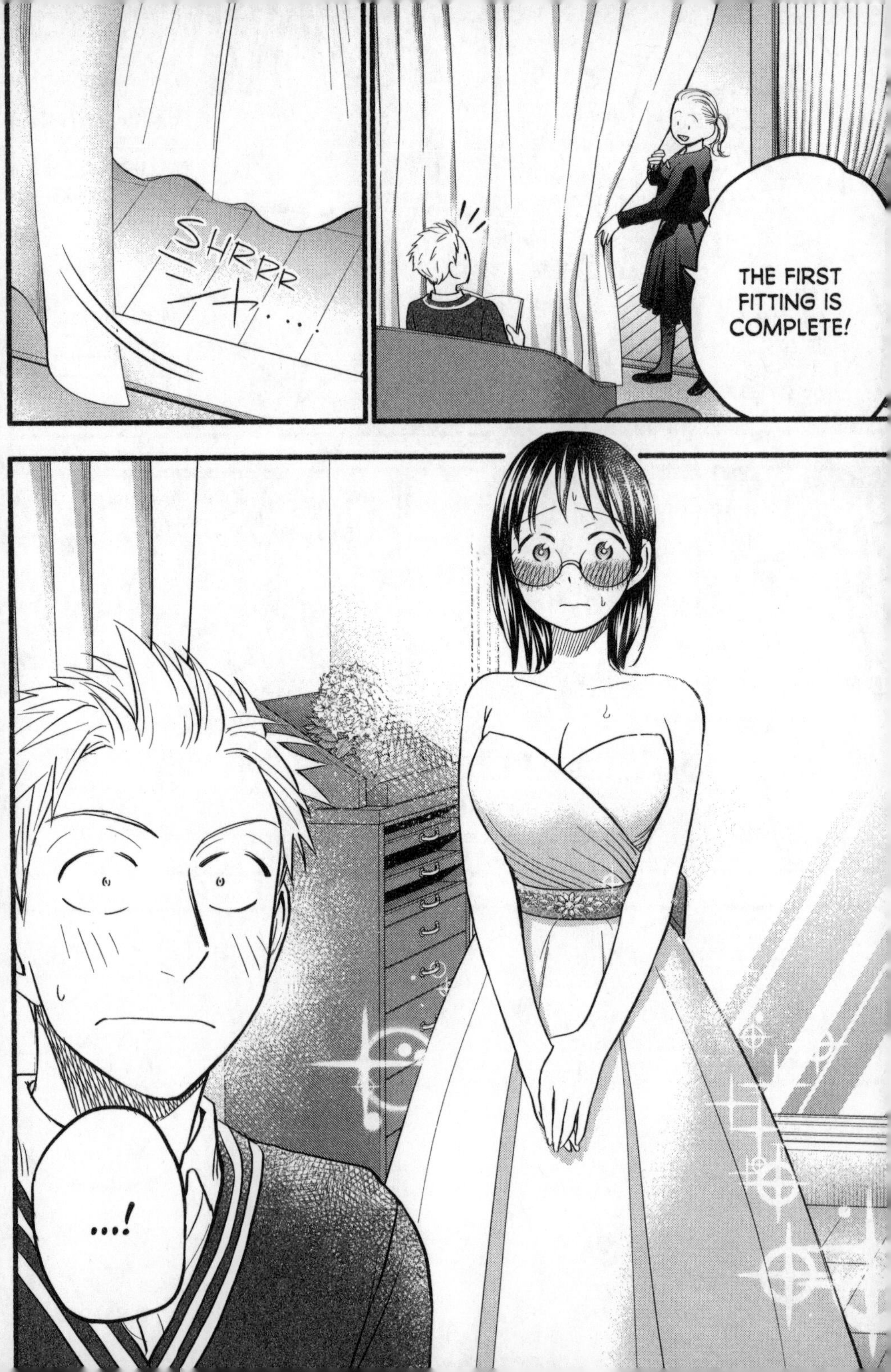
THE FIRST FITTING IS COMPLETE!
SHRRR
...!

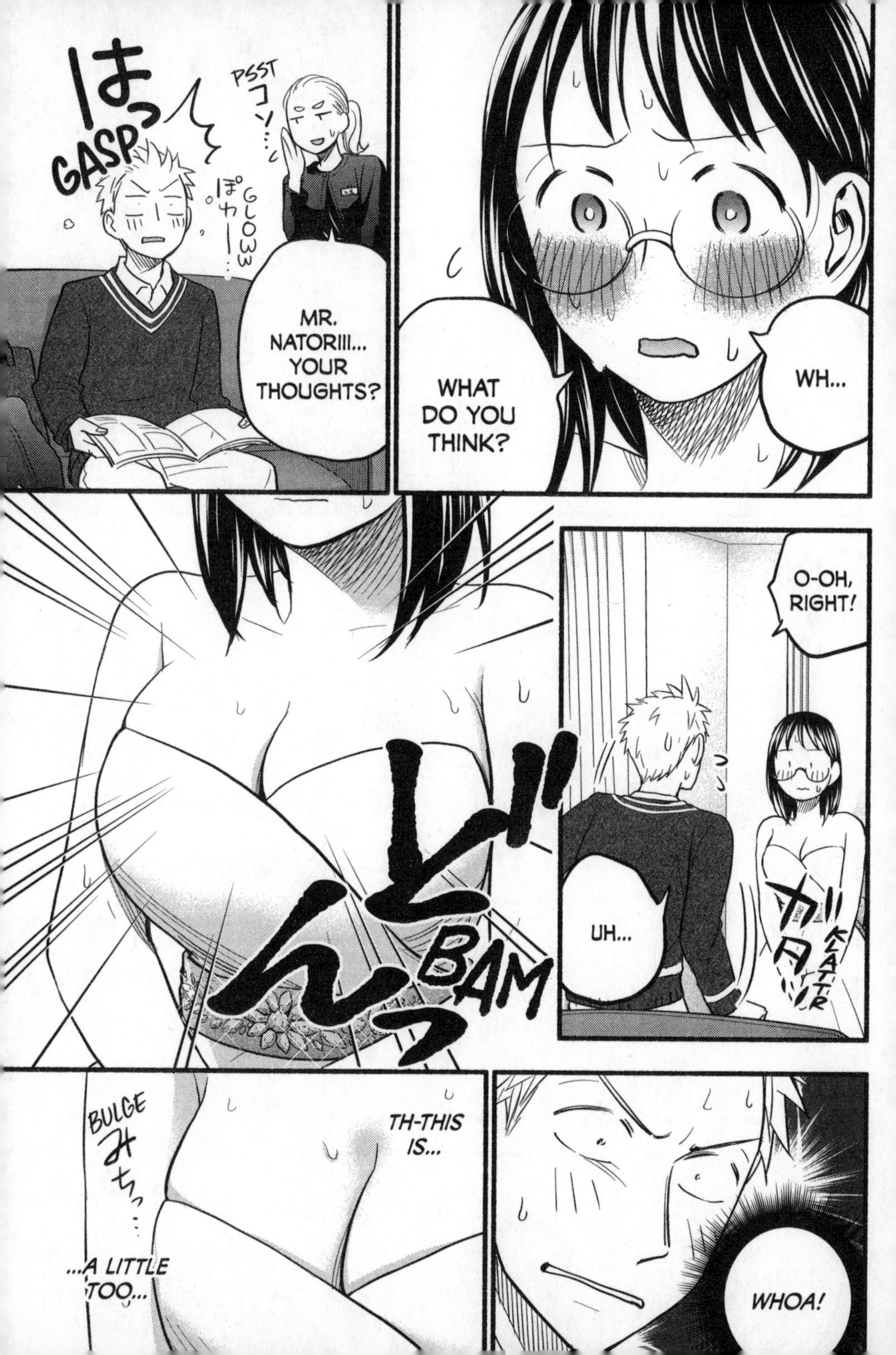
WH...
WHAT DO YOU THINK?
PSST
コソ…
はっ
GASP
ぽかー…
GLOWW
MR. NATORIII... YOUR THOUGHTS?
O-OH, RIGHT!
ガタ
KLATTR
UH...
どんっ
BAM
WHOA!
TH-THIS IS...
BULGE
みちっ…
...A LITTLE TOO...

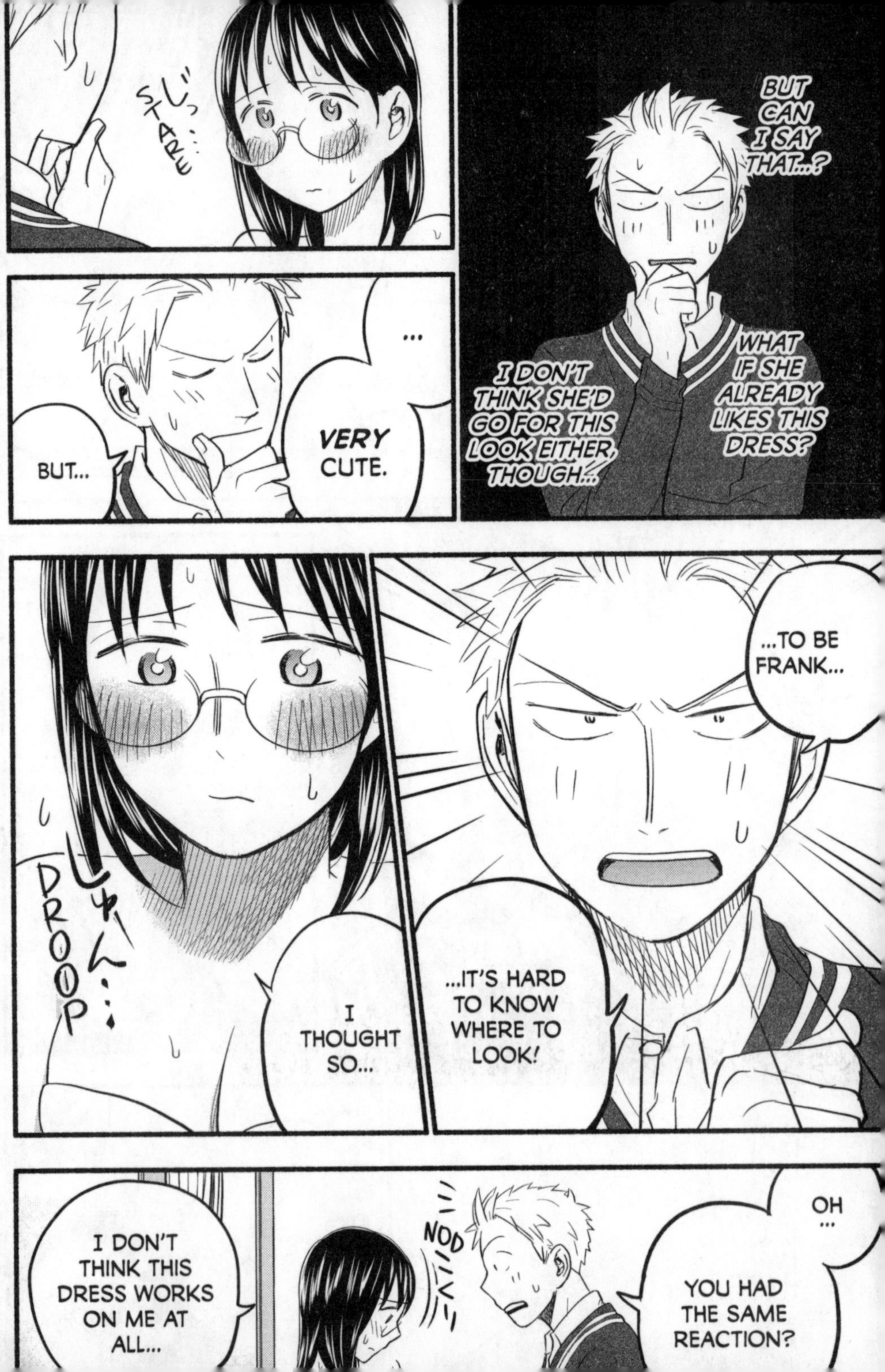
BUT CAN I SAY THAT...?
WHAT IF SHE ALREADY LIKES THIS DRESS?
I DON'T THINK SHE'D GO FOR THIS LOOK EITHER, THOUGH...
STARE
...
VERY CUTE.
BUT...
...TO BE FRANK...
...IT'S HARD TO KNOW WHERE TO LOOK!
I THOUGHT SO...
DROOP
OH ...
YOU HAD THE SAME REACTION?
NOD
I DON'T THINK THIS DRESS WORKS ON ME AT ALL...

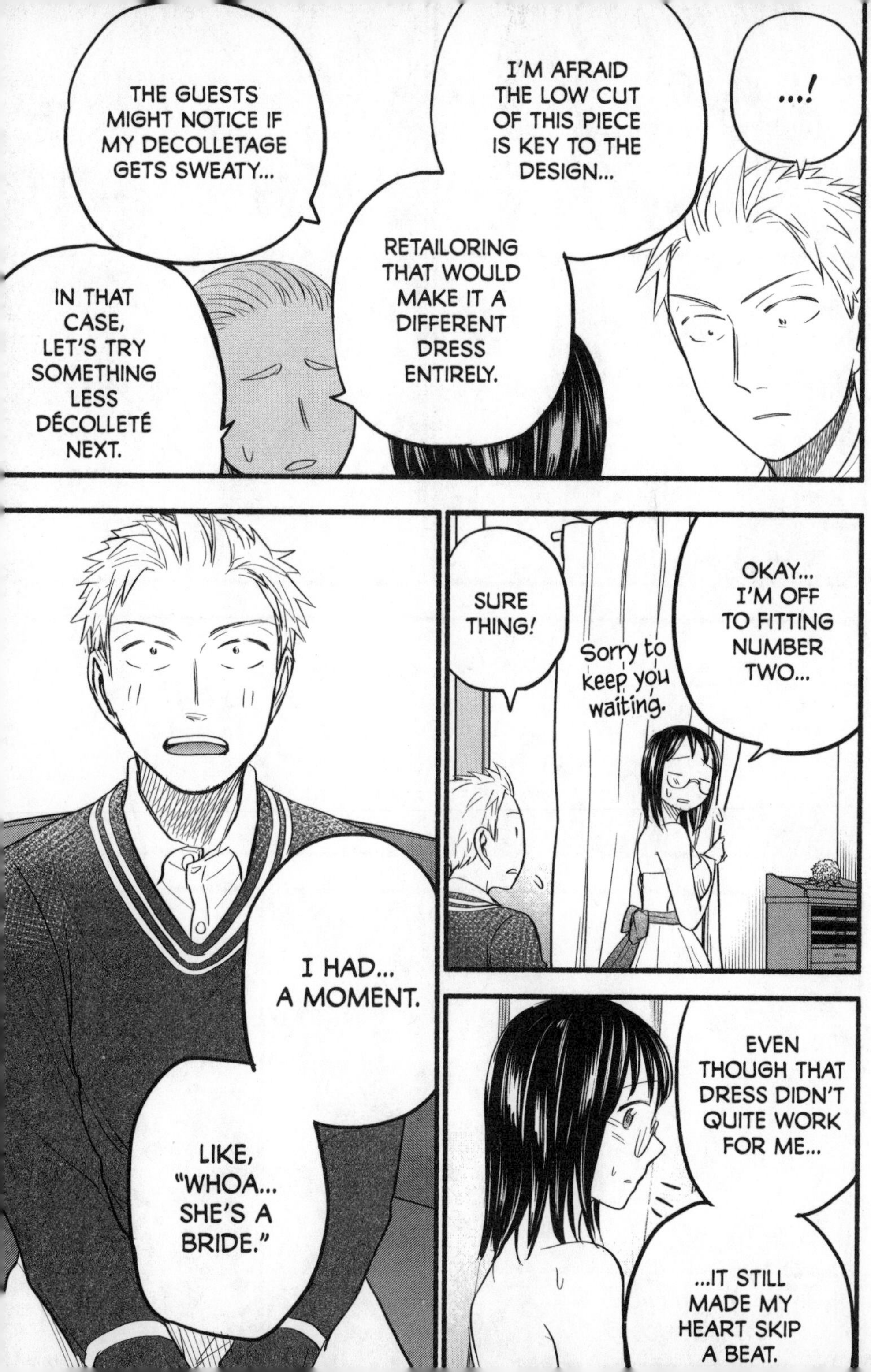
...!
I'M AFRAID THE LOW CUT OF THIS PIECE IS KEY TO THE DESIGN...
THE GUESTS MIGHT NOTICE IF MY DECOLLETAGE GETS SWEATY...
RETAILORING THAT WOULD MAKE IT A DIFFERENT DRESS ENTIRELY.
IN THAT CASE, LET'S TRY SOMETHING LESS DÉCOLLETÉ NEXT.
OKAY... I'M OFF TO FITTING NUMBER TWO...
Sorry to keep you waiting.
SURE THING!
EVEN THOUGH THAT DRESS DIDN'T QUITE WORK FOR ME...
...IT STILL MADE MY HEART SKIP A BEAT.
I HAD... A MOMENT.
LIKE, "WHOA... SHE'S A BRIDE."

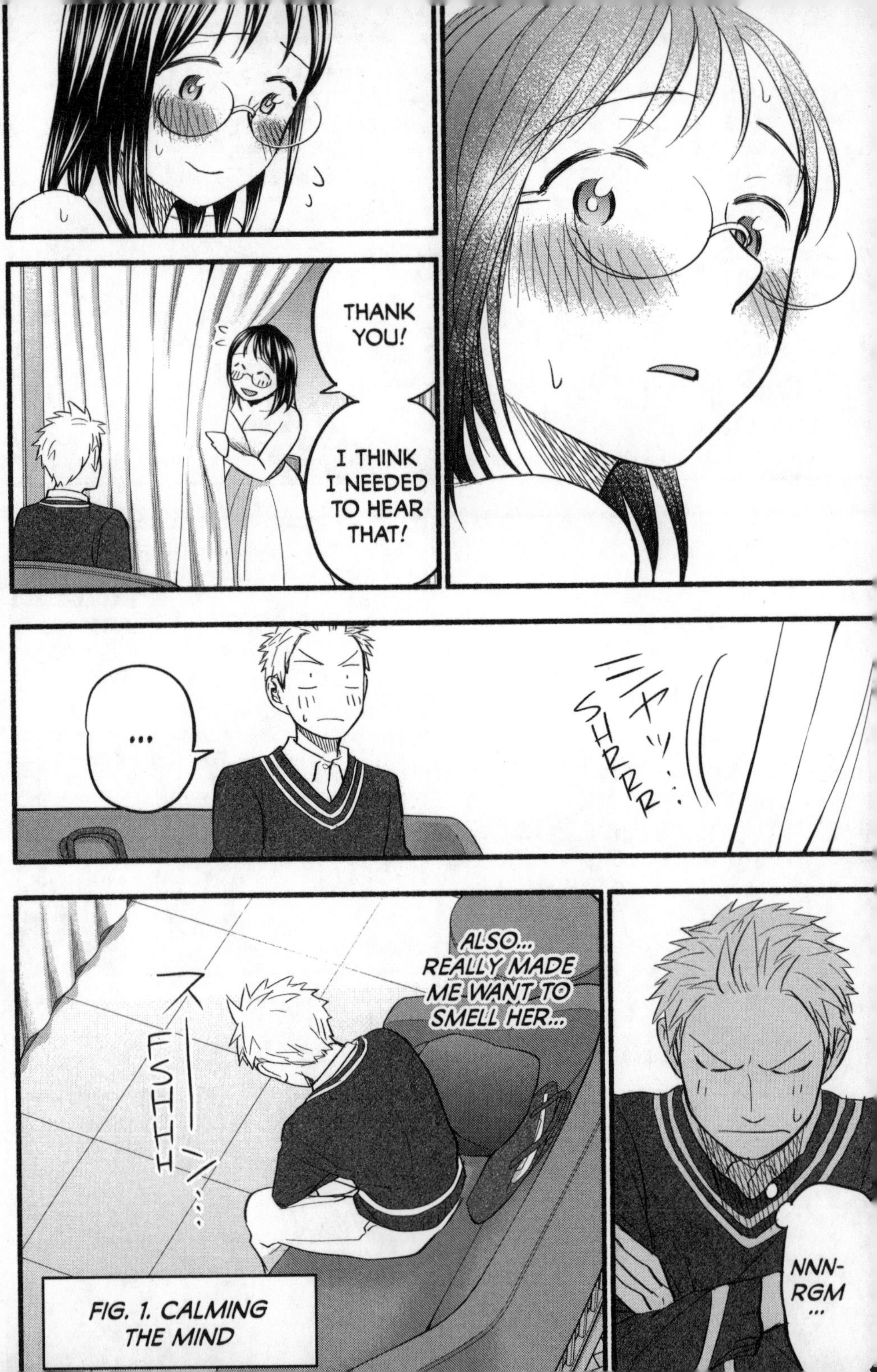
THANK YOU!
I THINK I NEEDED TO HEAR THAT!
SHRRR
...
NNN-RGM...
ALSO... REALLY MADE ME WANT TO SMELL HER...
FSHHH
FIG. 1. CALMING THE MIND

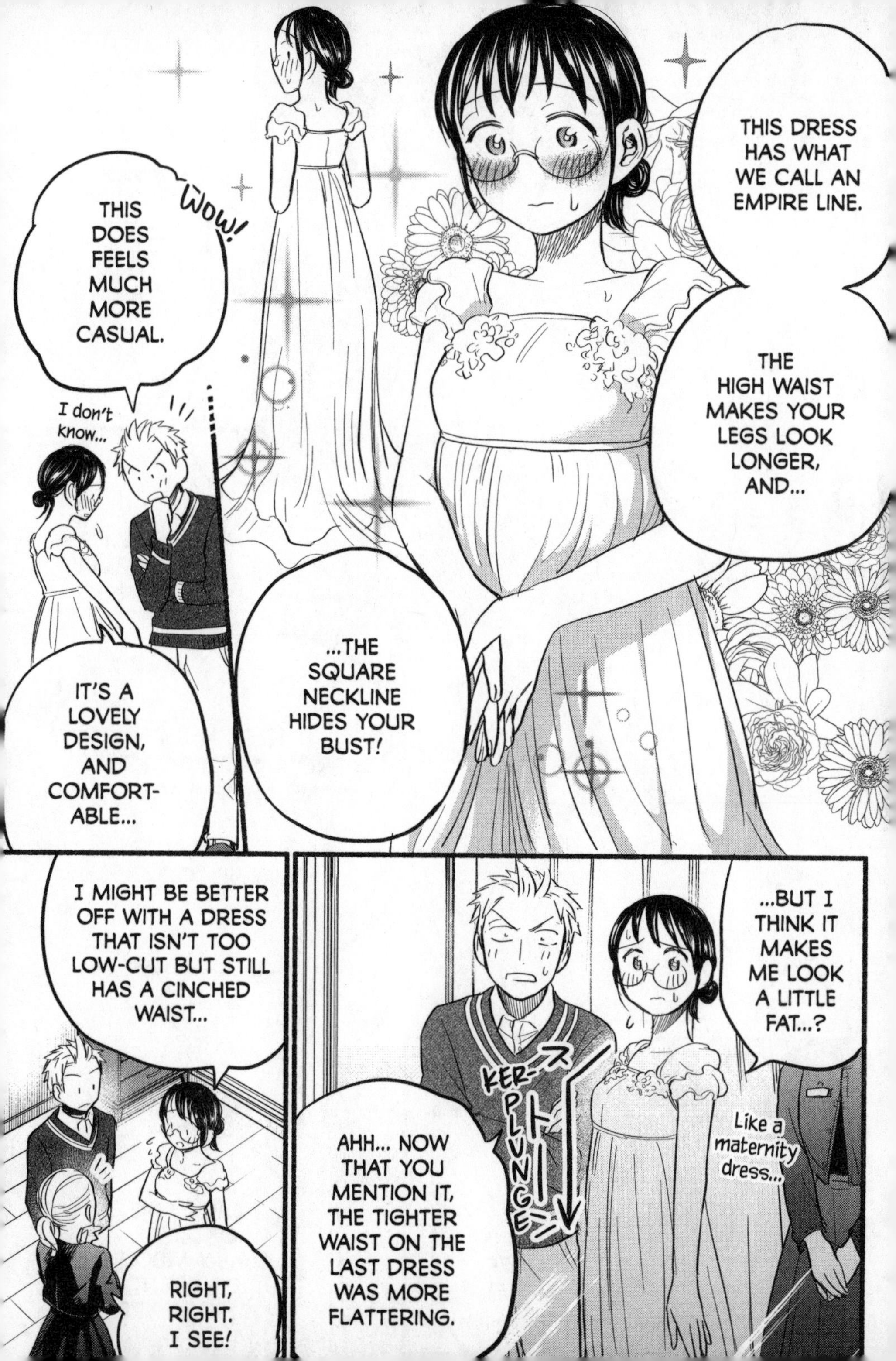
THIS DRESS HAS WHAT WE CALL AN EMPIRE LINE.
THE HIGH WAIST MAKES YOUR LEGS LOOK LONGER, AND...
...THE SQUARE NECKLINE HIDES YOUR BUST!
WOW!
THIS DOES FEELS MUCH MORE CASUAL.
I don't know...
IT'S A LOVELY DESIGN, AND COMFORT-ABLE...
...BUT I THINK IT MAKES ME LOOK A LITTLE FAT...?
Like a maternity dress...
KER-PLUNGE
AHH... NOW THAT YOU MENTION IT, THE TIGHTER WAIST ON THE LAST DRESS WAS MORE FLATTERING.
I MIGHT BE BETTER OFF WITH A DRESS THAT ISN'T TOO LOW-CUT BUT STILL HAS A CINCHED WAIST...
RIGHT, RIGHT. I SEE!

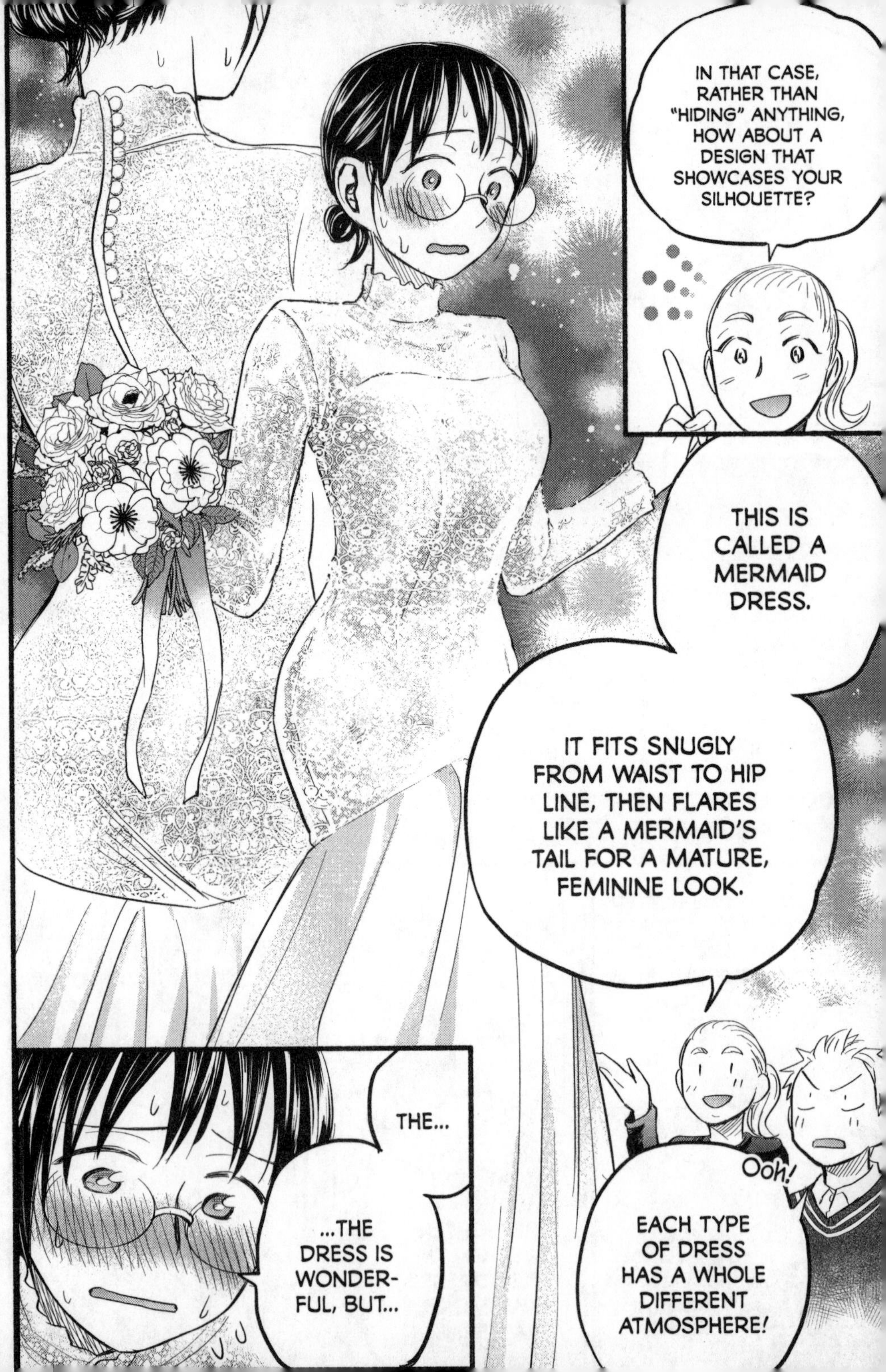
IN THAT CASE, RATHER THAN "HIDING" ANYTHING, HOW ABOUT A DESIGN THAT SHOWCASES YOUR SILHOUETTE?
THIS IS CALLED A MERMAID DRESS.
IT FITS SNUGLY FROM WAIST TO HIP LINE, THEN FLARES LIKE A MERMAID'S TAIL FOR A MATURE, FEMININE LOOK.
Ooh!
EACH TYPE OF DRESS HAS A WHOLE DIFFERENT ATMOSPHERE!
THE...
...THE DRESS IS WONDER-FUL, BUT...

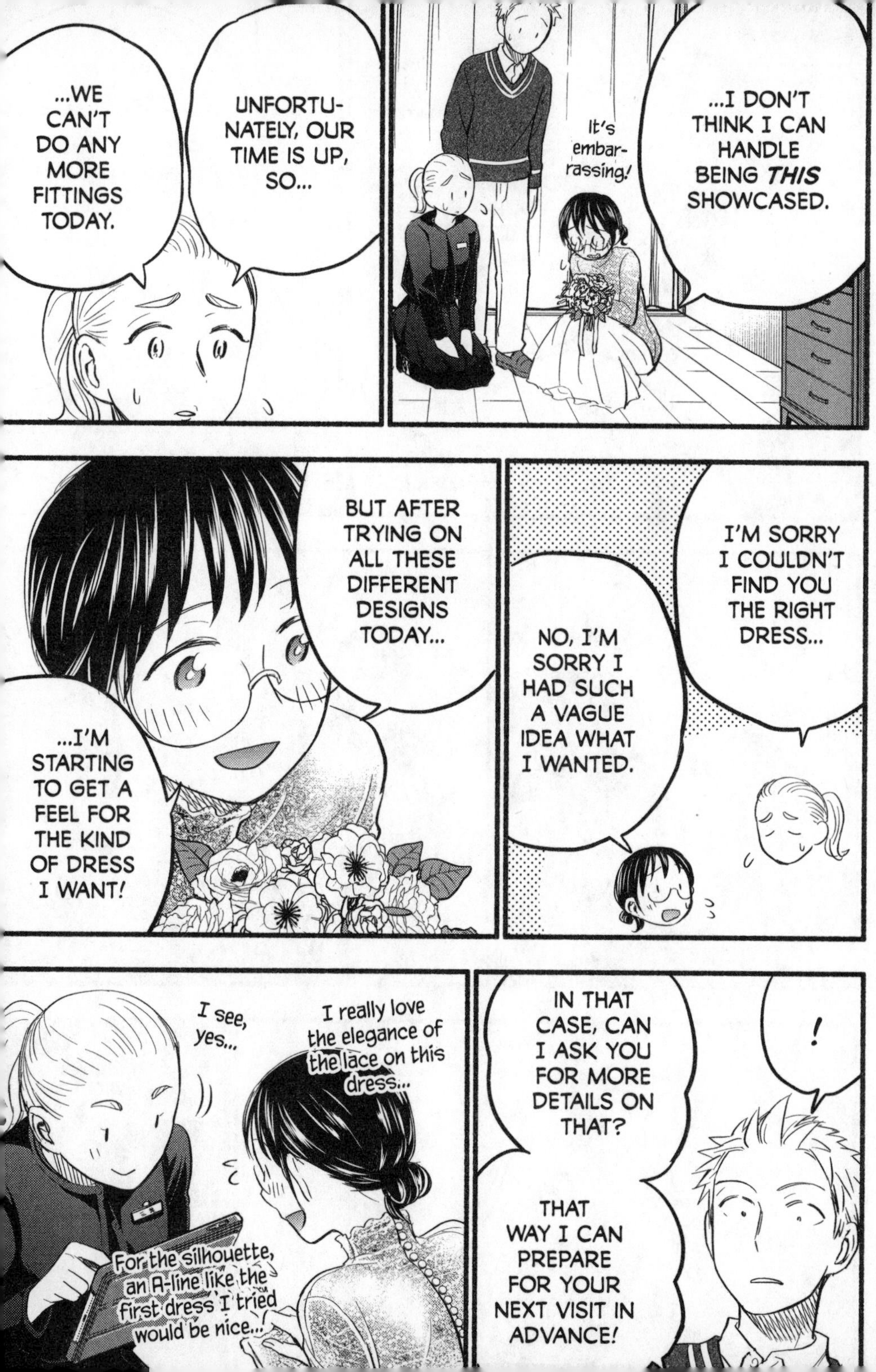
...I DON'T THINK I CAN HANDLE BEING *THIS* SHOWCASED.
It's embarrassing!
UNFORTU-NATELY, OUR TIME IS UP, SO...
...WE CAN'T DO ANY MORE FITTINGS TODAY.
I'M SORRY I COULDN'T FIND YOU THE RIGHT DRESS...
NO, I'M SORRY I HAD SUCH A VAGUE IDEA WHAT I WANTED.
BUT AFTER TRYING ON ALL THESE DIFFERENT DESIGNS TODAY...
...I'M STARTING TO GET A FEEL FOR THE KIND OF DRESS I WANT!
!
IN THAT CASE, CAN I ASK YOU FOR MORE DETAILS ON THAT?
THAT WAY I CAN PREPARE FOR YOUR NEXT VISIT IN ADVANCE!
I really love the elegance of the lace on this dress...
I see, yes...
For the silhouette, an A-line like the first dress I tried would be nice...!

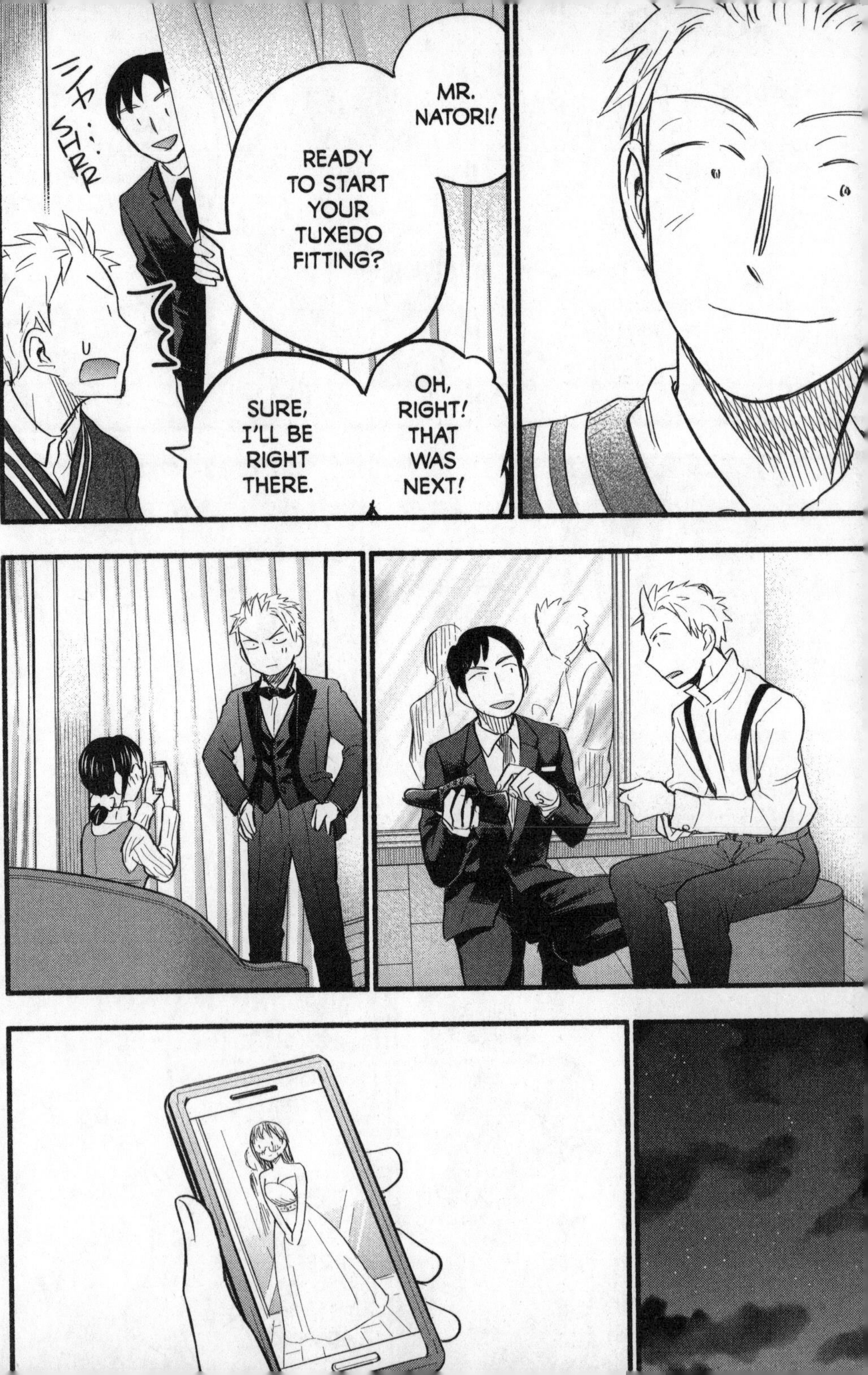
シャ… SHRR
MR. NATORI!
READY TO START YOUR TUXEDO FITTING?
OH, RIGHT! THAT WAS NEXT!
SURE, I'LL BE RIGHT THERE.

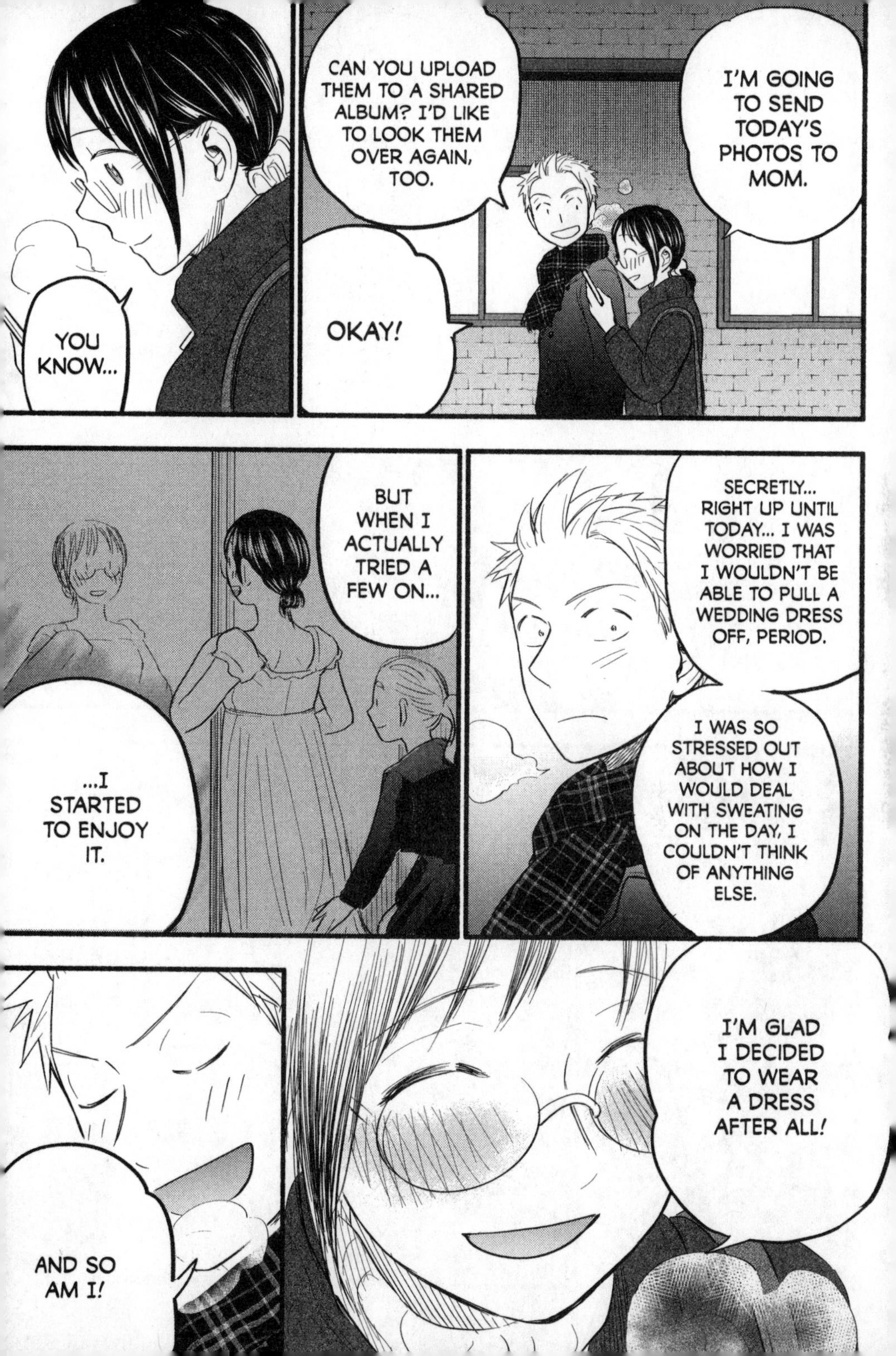
I'M GOING TO SEND TODAY'S PHOTOS TO MOM.
CAN YOU UPLOAD THEM TO A SHARED ALBUM? I'D LIKE TO LOOK THEM OVER AGAIN, TOO.
OKAY!
YOU KNOW...
SECRETLY... RIGHT UP UNTIL TODAY... I WAS WORRIED THAT I WOULDN'T BE ABLE TO PULL A WEDDING DRESS OFF, PERIOD.
I WAS SO STRESSED OUT ABOUT HOW I WOULD DEAL WITH SWEATING ON THE DAY, I COULDN'T THINK OF ANYTHING ELSE.
BUT WHEN I ACTUALLY TRIED A FEW ON...
...I STARTED TO ENJOY IT.
I'M GLAD I DECIDED TO WEAR A DRESS AFTER ALL!
AND SO AM I!

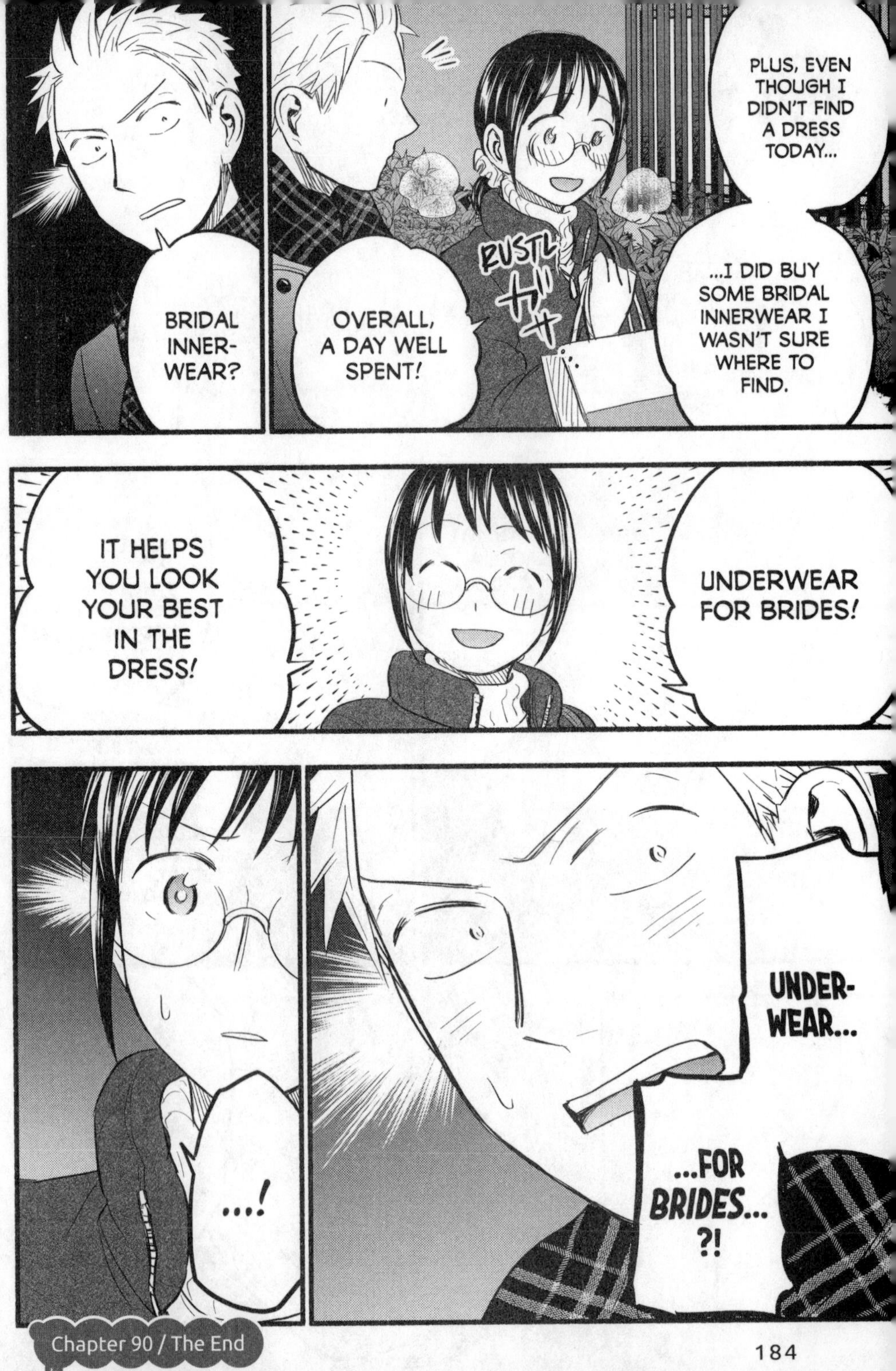
PLUS, EVEN THOUGH I DIDN'T FIND A DRESS TODAY...
...I DID BUY SOME BRIDAL INNERWEAR I WASN'T SURE WHERE TO FIND.
RUSTL
OVERALL, A DAY WELL SPENT!
BRIDAL INNER-WEAR?
UNDERWEAR FOR BRIDES!
IT HELPS YOU LOOK YOUR BEST IN THE DRESS!
UNDER-WEAR...
...FOR BRIDES...?!
...!

THE MAKING OF A *SWEAT AND SOAP* CHAPTER

THIS TIME I'D LIKE TO INTRODUCE SOMETHING I HADN'T GOT AROUND TO COVERING YET: MY MANGA-DRAWING PROCESS.

FIRST, THE BASIC OUTLINE:

DISCUSSION WITH EDITOR ... A PHONE MEETING WITH MY EDITOR ABOUT WHAT I'M PLANNING FOR THE NEXT CHAPTER.

↓

STORYBOARD ("NAME") ... I SPEND 2 OR 3 DAYS THINKING UP THE STORY.

↓

MANUSCRIPT ... I START DRAWING THE ACTUAL MANUSCRIPT. MY STAFF JOIN ME TO ADD BACKGROUNDS AND FINISHING TOUCHES. THIS PROCESS TAKES 4 TO 5 DAYS.

(1) STORYBOARD ("NAME")

MAKING GYOZA
IS THAT ENOUGH...
...TO MAKE US "FAMILY"?
PARDON ME FOR INTER-RUPTING EVERYONE'S MEAL...
N
...BUT I HAPPEN TO HAVE THIS MARRIAGE REGISTRATION FORM WITH ME...
15

FROM CHAPTER 85: "THE DAY WE BECOME FAMILY (1)"

I WORK OUT THE STRUCTURE OF THE CHAPTER BY DRAWING STORYBOARDS ON MY IPAD IN THE STYLE SEEN AT LEFT.

IF THERE ARE PLACES THAT MAKE ME THINK "KIND OF DIALOGUE-HEAVY HERE" OR "THIS PANEL NEEDS TO BE BIGGER," I MAKE THE NECESSARY ADJUSTMENTS OR WHATEVER WHEN DRAWING THE ROUGH DRAFT.

AS A SIDE NOTE, THE ORIGINAL STORYBOARD FOR THE PAGE SEEN ON THE LEFT WAS APPARENTLY MORE LIKE THE ONE BELOW. (I'D FORGOTTEN.)

I PROBABLY WANTED TO ADD MORE EMPHASIS TO THE "IS THAT ENOUGH TO MAKE US FAMILY?" PANEL.

IT'S A STRANGE FEELING.
THE WHOLE FAMILY, OUT TOGETHER...
FOOD
...HAVING DINNER WITH ANOTHER FAMILY.
DOES THIS MEAN THAT, AS OF TODAY...
...WE'RE ALL FAMILY TOGETHER?
WE'VE SAT DOWN TO EAT AT THE SAME TABLE...
...AND INTRODUCED OURSELVES TO EACH OTHER...
...BUT IS THAT ENOUGH...
...TO MAKE US FAMILY?
14
SO, KEITA...
A
IS THE FOOD OKAY?
YEAH
IT'S DELICIOUS.
N
PARDON ME FOR INTER-RUPTING EVERYONE'S MEAL...
...BUT I HAPPEN TO HAVE THIS MARRIAGE REGISTRATION FORM WITH ME...
15

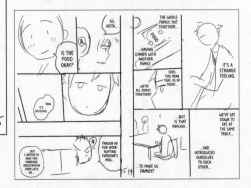

② ROUGH DRAFT (CHARACTER OUTLINES AND INSTRUCTIONS FOR STAFF)

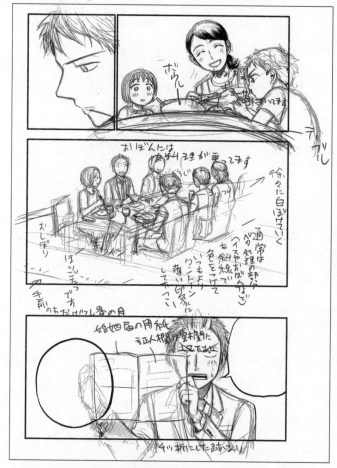

Left to right:
"Bowl",
"Finished Gyoza (on bowl)",
"Table"

Clockwise, from the top:
"Meat course on serving dishes",
"Toothpick holder",
"Cup",
"Gradually fades to white",
"For the parts that would normally be solid-filled (chairs, dishes, etc.), please color with diagonal lines to create an impression one tone lighter",
"tatami mat pattern in the foreground only",
"*horigotatsu* (pit) seating",
"red wine"
"damp washcloth"

Top to bottom:
"On the wedding registration form, please leave the 'witness' boxes blank",
"Creases from being folded in four"

I USE MANGA PRODUCTION SOFTWARE CALLED CLIP STUDIO TO DO PENCILS AND INKING DIRECTLY ON A COMPUTER.

THE IMAGE ABOVE MIGHT BE HARD TO FOLLOW, BUT THE GRAY LINES ARE MY PENCILS, AND THERE ARE DIRECTIONS FOR MY STAFF IN THE BACKGROUND HERE AND THERE.

IN THE ACTUAL PRODUCTION FILES, THE DIRECTIONS ARE IN A SEPARATE, DIFFERENTLY COLORED LAYER, WHICH MAKES THEM EASIER TO TELL APART FROM THE REST. I ALSO SEND MY STAFF REFERENCE PHOTOS AND COMPLETED SAMPLES OF OTHER PAGES (TO ENSURE CONSISTENCY IN MOOD, DETAILS OF THINGS LIKE FOOD ON THE TABLE, ETC.). EVERYONE WORKS REMOTELY.

3. FINAL TOUCHES

...BUT IS THAT ENOUGH...
...TO MAKE US FAMILY?
PARDON ME FOR INTER-RUPTING EVERYONE'S MEAL...
TA-DAH!
...BUT I HAPPEN TO HAVE THIS *MARRIAGE REGISTRATION FORM* WITH ME...

SERIOUSLY, ARE MY STAFF AMAZING OR WHAT?!

MY STAFF HAVE BEEN WORKING REMOTELY SINCE "SWEAT AND SOAP" BEGAN. I HAVEN'T EVEN MET MOST OF THEM FACE-TO-FACE.

BUT WE HAVE IN-DEPTH CONVERSATIONS OVER SKYPE, AND THEY'RE ALL SO DILIGENT AND CONSCIENTIOUS ABOUT THEIR WORK THAT I'VE NEVER FELT ANXIOUS ABOUT IT. I REALLY GOT LUCKY...

I'M DESPERATELY TRYING TO HOLD ONTO MY CURRENT STAFF FOR THE NEXT CHANCE I GET TO DRAW A MANGA.

AFTERWORD

KINTETSU YAMADA

WE HAVE REACHED VOLUME 10 OF "SWEAT AND SOAP"! THANK YOU SO MUCH—I REALLY MEAN THAT!
FLAG: "THANK YOU"

AS I WROTE IN THE LAST VOLUME, "10 VOLUMES" WAS THE SECRET GOAL I HAD SET FOR MYSELF.

WHEN THIS SERIES FIRST STARTED, I WOULD THINK TO MYSELF, "IT MIGHT END TWO VOLUMES IN..." OR "I'LL BE HAPPY IF IT REACHES VOLUME 5..." SO I'M ABSOLUTELY OVERJOYED TO REACH THIS MILESTONE.

AND NOT JUST BECAUSE VOLUME 10 MEANS REACHING DOUBLE DIGITS! THERE ARE SO MANY OTHER REASONS: THE SENSE OF ACHIEVEMENT, AND THE JOY OF KNOWING THAT GETTING THIS FAR INTO THE STORY LET ME DRAW EVERYTHING I WANTED TO. I COULDN'T HAVE COME THIS FAR THIS ON MY OWN.

THANK YOU SO MUCH FOR ALL YOUR SUPPORT.

"STUFF THAT RULES" CORNER PART 10

HOT POT (NABE)

WINTER IS HOT POT SEASON, RIGHT? WHEN I'M NOT IN CRUNCH MODE I HAVE IT ABOUT FOUR TIMES A WEEK.

SPECIAL THANKS

STAFF
SHIJIMA, NONOKO NATSUKI, MAI SETA, SHINPEI SEKI, RAKUTARO SENJU

EDITOR:
RUITO SUZUKI

OFFICIAL TWITTER:
@ASETOSEKKEN

ARTIST TWITTER:
@KINTETSUYMD

SEE YOU NEXT VOLUME!

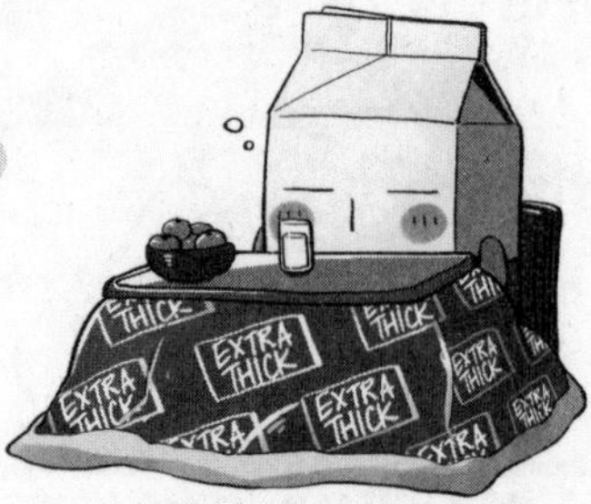
EXTRA THICK
EXTRA THICK
EXTRA THICK
EXTRA THICK
EXTRA THICK
EXTRA THICK
EXTRA THICK

kintetsu yamada

Volume 10 at last! By my rough calculations, that means I've drawn about 2,000 pages of manga… That's astonishing enough, but the best part is that, with your support, I've come this far while having a blast the whooole time. Thank you so much! Please enjoy Volume 10!

ALTHOUGH I DID PUSH IT A BIT WITH A FEW CRUNCH-MODE
DISHES, THIS RECIPE SERIES HAS NOW **MADE IT TO VOLUME 10**...
THERE'S STILL ONE VOLUME TO GO, BUT IT'S MOVING TO THINK
ABOUT ALL THE SAME. UNFORTUNATELY, THERE ISN'T MUCH
COOKING IN THIS VOLUME... OR SO I THOUGHT, BEFORE I
REMEMBERED THE ONE EXCEPTION!

THE
NINJIN SHIRISHIRI
THAT OUR HEROES ATE WITH BREAKFAST
IN CHAPTER 82

INGREDIENTS

- CARROT 1
- EGG 1
- SESAME OIL .... 1 TBSP
- TUNA (DRAIN OIL) .... 1 CAN
- NOODLE SOUP BASE.................... 1 TO 1.5 TBSP

OR SUBSTITUTE → (*MEN TSUYU*) (TRIPLE CONCENTRATED)
WITH DASHI
POWDER + SOY   • TOASTED SESAME SEEDS .... TO TASTE
SAUCE, ETC.

① JULIENNE THE CARROT. CRACK THE
EGG INTO A BOWL AND WHISK THE
YOLK INTO THE WHITE.

② HEAT THE SESAME OIL IN A FRYING PAN, THEN
ADD THE CARROT AND SAUTÉ UNTIL SOFT.

③ ADD THE TUNA. SAUTÉ, THEN ADD THE NOODLE
SOUP BASE TO FLAVOR.

④ ADD THE EGG FROM STEP 1 AND QUICKLY SAUTÉ
SOME MORE. FINALLY, SPRINKLE WITH TOASTED
SESAME SEEDS, SAUTÉ TO STIR THEM IN, AND SERVE!

ALSO DELICIOUS COLD!
GOES GREAT WITH
DRINKS!

WHAT HAPPENED AFTER CHAPTER 82

PLEASE READ THIS AFTER READING CHAPTER 82.
-KINTETSU YAMADA

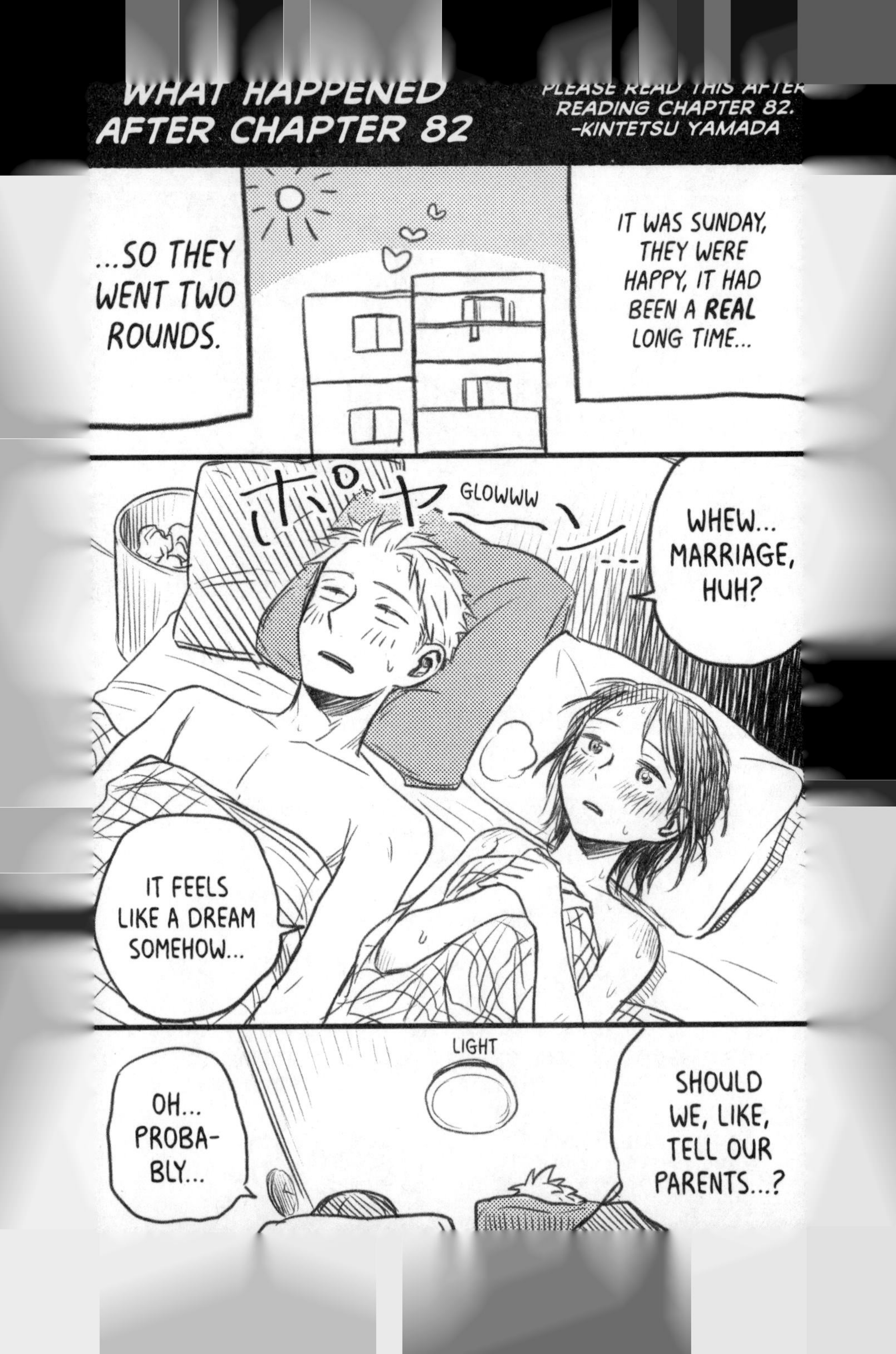
IT WAS SUNDAY, THEY WERE HAPPY, IT HAD BEEN A **REAL** LONG TIME...
...SO THEY WENT TWO ROUNDS.
GLOWWW
WHEW... MARRIAGE, HUH?
IT FEELS LIKE A DREAM SOMEHOW...
SHOULD WE, LIKE, TELL OUR PARENTS...?
LIGHT
OH... PROBA-BLY...

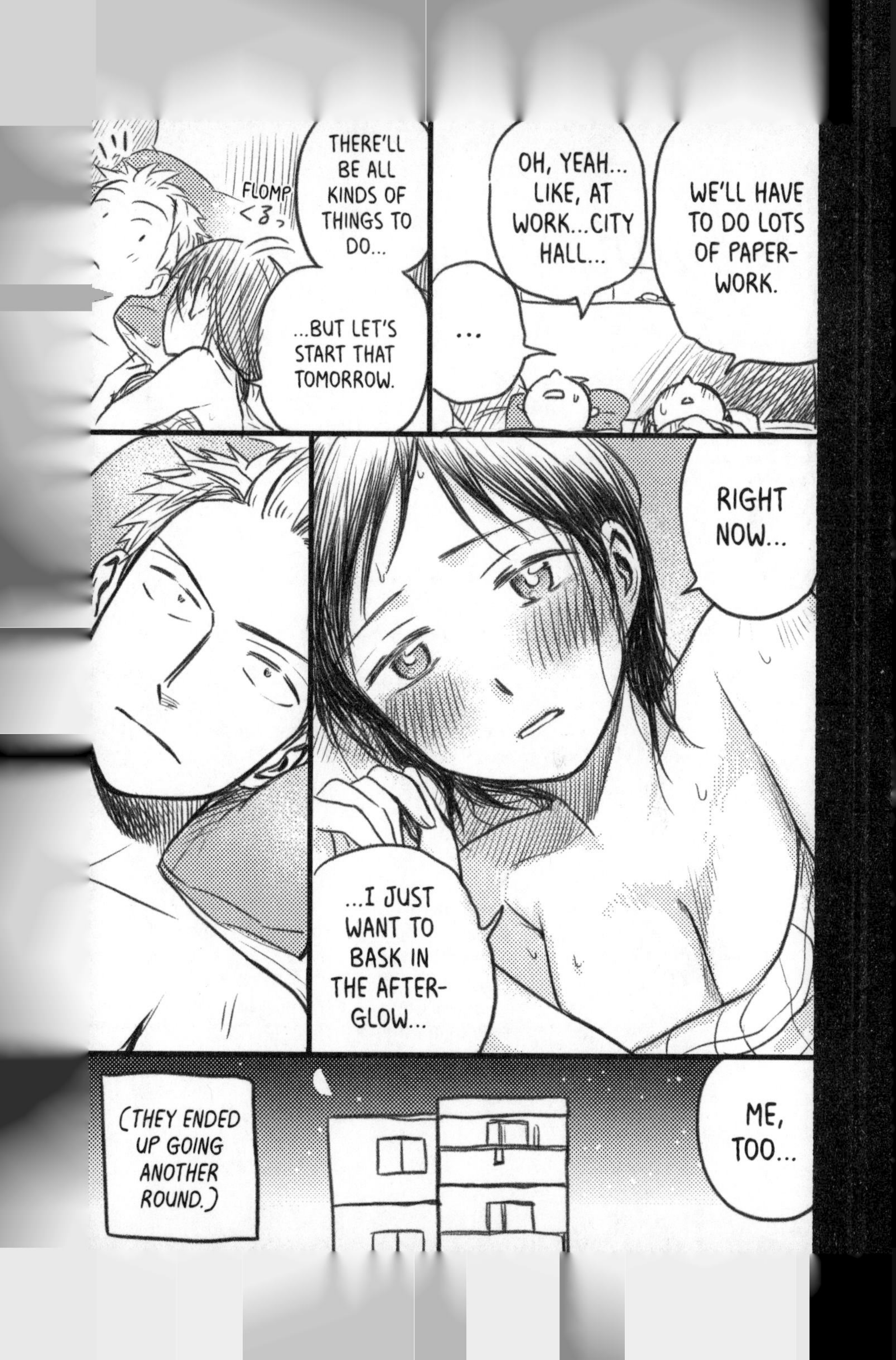
WE'LL HAVE TO DO LOTS OF PAPER-WORK.
OH, YEAH... LIKE, AT WORK...CITY HALL...
...
THERE'LL BE ALL KINDS OF THINGS TO DO...
FLOMP
くるっ
...BUT LET'S START THAT TOMORROW.
RIGHT NOW...
...I JUST WANT TO BASK IN THE AFTER-GLOW...
ME, TOO...
(THEY ENDED UP GOING ANOTHER ROUND.)

Translation Notes

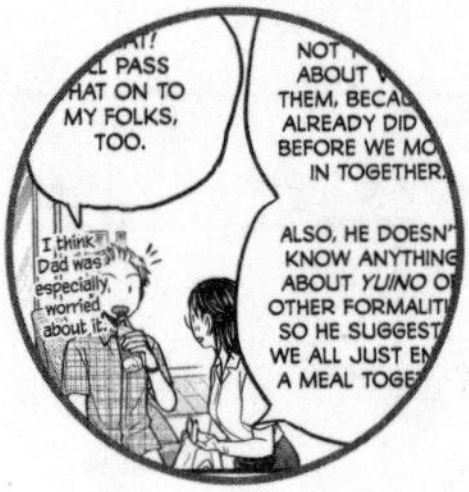
I think Dad was especially worried about it.

***Yuino*, page 51**
Yuino is a formal betrothal ceremony where the families of the bride and groom exchange traditional gifts.

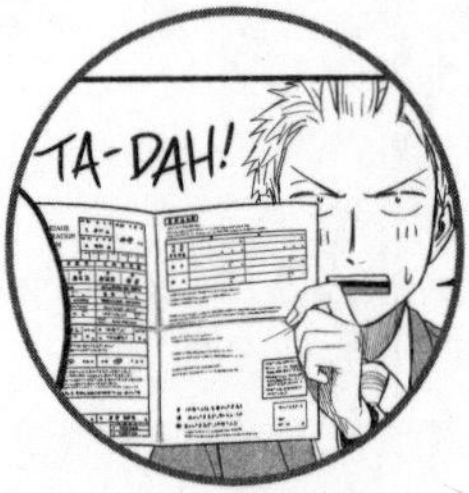
TA-DAH!

I happen to have this marriage registration form with me, page 91
Administratively speaking, marriage in Japan is just a matter of lodging the right form at city hall. Many couples do this months or even years before they hold an actual wedding ceremony—if they have a ceremony at all.

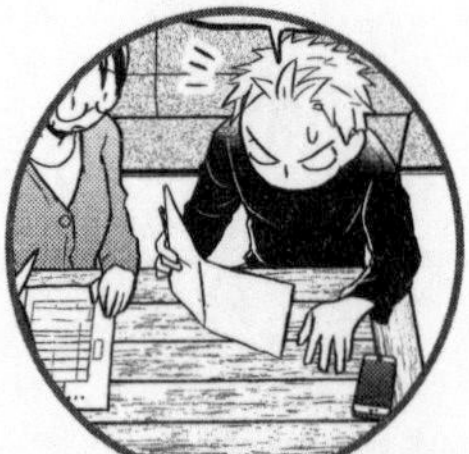

Pencil board, page 110
A pencil board (*shitajiki*) is a plastic board laid under papers to be written on, to create a smooth surface even on rough desks. Elementary school students are taught to use them, so they're a fairly standard stationery item in Japan.

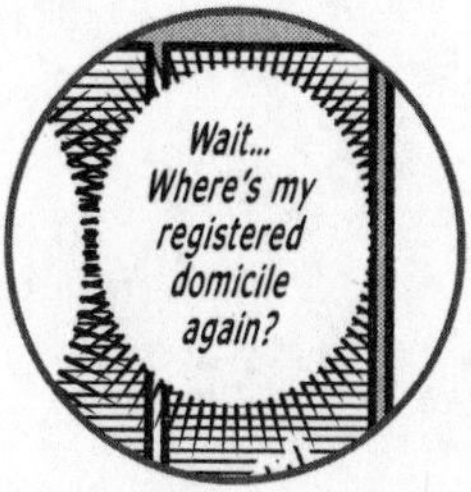
Wait... Where's my registered domicile again?

Where's my registered domicile again?, page 110
In Japan, your registered domicile (*honseki*) isn't necessarily your address, or even your parents' address. It doesn't come up much in everyday life, so it's fairly common for people to need to double-check when asked to provide it.

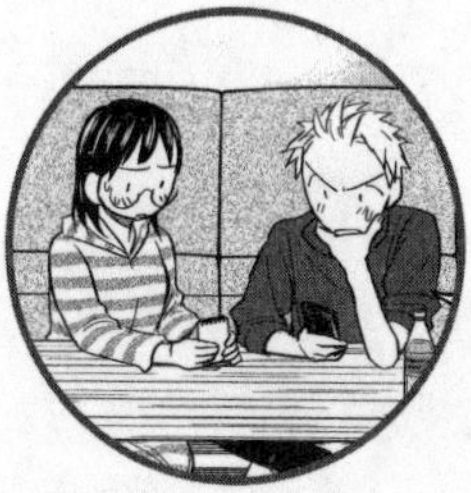

November 22 is "Good Couple" day, page 113
November 22 can be written "11/22," which can be pronounced *ii fufu* or "good (married) couple" in Japanese.

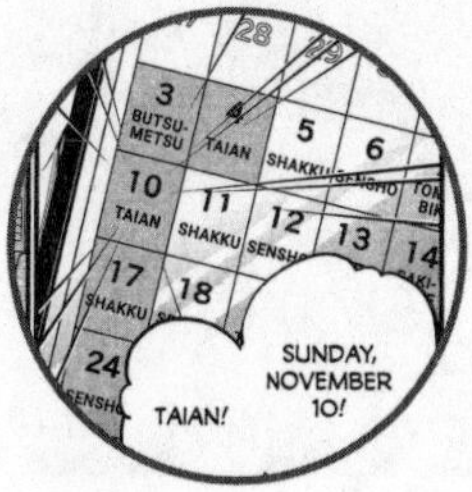
SUNDAY, NOVEMBER 10!
TAIAN!
BUTSU-METSU
TAIAN
SHAKKU
SENSHO
TAIAN
SHAKKU
SHAKKU

Taian, page 114
Taian, meaning "Great Peace," is the most auspicious day in the traditional "six-day" (*rokuyo*) cycle used to choose dates for big events like weddings. (The other days in the cycle are Sensho, Tomobiki, Senbu, Butsumetsu, and Shakku, some of which can be seen on the calendar.)

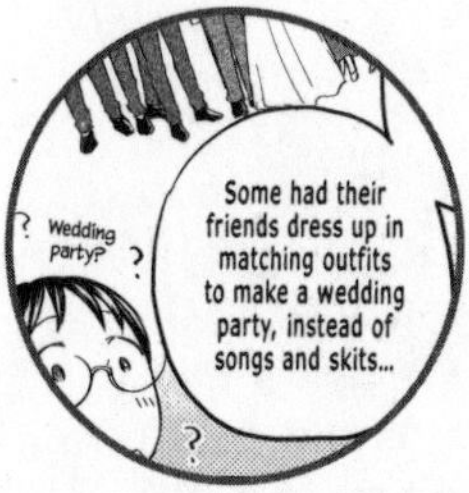
Some had their friends dress up in matching outfits to make a wedding party, instead of songs and skits...
Wedding party?

A wedding party, instead of songs and skits, page 145
Having a wedding party of groomsmen and bridesmaids is still relatively rare in Japan. More common is for groups of guests (for example, friends from school, colleagues, etc.) to put on little skits or musical performances during the reception.

CLAMP

Chobits 1
20TH ANNIVERSARY EDITION

Chobits © CLAMP·ShigatsuTsuitachi CO.,LTD./Kodansha Ltd.

Poor college student Hideki is down on his luck. All he wants is a good job, a girlfriend, and his very own "persocom"—the latest and greatest in humanoid computer technology. Hideki's luck changes one night when he finds Chi—a persocom thrown out in a pile of trash. But Hideki soon discovers that there's much more to his cute new persocom than meets the eye.

KC
KODANSHA
COMICS

THE WORLD OF CLAMP!

Cardcaptor Sakura Collector's Edition

Cardcaptor Sakura: Clear Card

Magic Knight Rayearth 25th Anniversary Box Set

Chobits

TSUBASA Omnibus

TSUBASA WoRLD CHRoNiCLE

xxxHOLiC Omnibus

xxxHOLiC Rei

CLOVER Collector's Edition

Kodansha Comics welcomes you to explore the expansive world of CLAMP, the all-female artist collective that has produced some of the most acclaimed manga of the century. Our growing catalog includes icons like *Cardcaptor Sakura* and *Magic Knight Rayearth*, each crafted with CLAMP's one-of-a-kind style and characters!

The art-deco cyberpunk classic from the creators of *xxxHOLiC* and *Cardcaptor Sakura*!

"Starred Review.
This experimental
sci-fi work from
CLAMP reads like a
romantic version of
AKIRA."
—Publishers Weekly

CLOVER © CLAMP·ShigatsuTsuitachi CO.,LTD./Kodansha Ltd.

Su was born into a bleak future, where the government keeps tight control over children with magical powers—codenamed "Clovers." With Su being the only "four-leaf" Clover in the world, she has been kept isolated nearly her whole life. Can ex-military agent Kazuhiko deliver her to the happiness she seeks? Experience the complete series in this hardcover edition, which also includes over twenty pages of ravishing color art!

KC
KODANSHA
COMICS

Knight of the ICE

Yayoi Ogawa

Knight of the Ice ©Yayoi Ogawa/Kodansha Ltd.

SKATING THRILLS AND ICY CHILLS WITH THIS NEW TINGLY ROMANCE SERIES!

A rom-com on ice, perfect for fans of *Princess Jellyfish* and *Wotakoi*. Kokoro is the talk of the figure-skating world, winning trophies and hearts. But little do they know... he's actually a huge nerd! From the beloved creator of *You're My Pet* (*Tramps Like Us*).

Chitose is a serious young woman, working for the health magazine *SASSO*. Or at least, she would be, if she wasn't constantly getting distracted by her childhood friend, international figure skating star Kokoro Kijinami! In the public eye and on the ice, Kokoro is a gallant, flawless knight, but behind his glittery costumes and breathtaking spins lies a secret: He's actually a hopelessly romantic otaku, who can only land his quad jumps when Chitose is on hand to recite a spell from his favorite magical girl anime!

A SMART, NEW ROMANTIC COMEDY FOR FANS OF *SHORTCAKE CAKE* AND *TERRACE HOUSE!*

A romance manga starring high school girl Meeko, who learns to live on her own in a boarding house whose living room is home to the odd (but handsome) Matsunaga-san. She begins to adjust to her new life away from her parents, but Meeko soon learns that no matter how far away from home she is, she's still a young girl at heart — especially when she finds herself falling for Matsunaga-san.

Young characters and steampunk setting, like *Howl's Moving Castle* and *Battle Angel Alita*

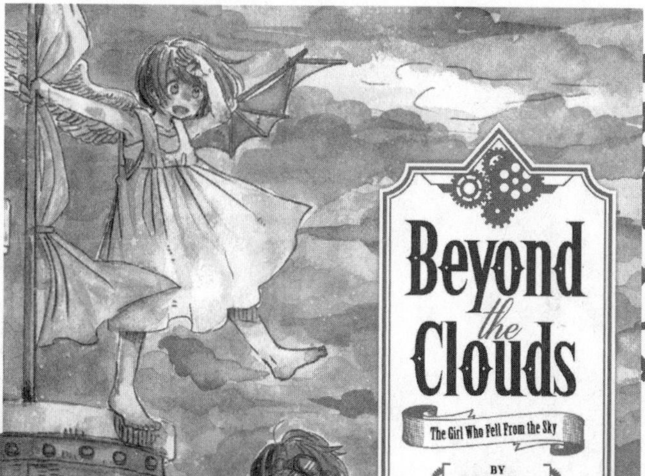
Beyond the Clouds
The Girl Who Fell From the Sky
BY
Nicke
VOLUME
01

A boy with a talent for machines and a mysterious girl whose wings he's fixed will take you beyond the clouds! In the tradition of the high-flying, resonant adventure stories of Studio Ghibli comes a gorgeous tale about the longing of young hearts for adventure and friendship!

PERFECT WORLD
Rie Aruga

A TOUCHING NEW SERIES ABOUT LOVE AND COPING WITH DISABILITY

An office party reunites Tsugumi with her high school crush Itsuki. He's realized his dream of becoming an architect, but along the way, he experienced a spinal injury that put him in a wheelchair. Now Tsugumi's rekindled feelings will butt up against prejudices she never considered — and Itsuki will have to decide if he's ready to let someone into his heart...

"Depicts with great delicacy and courage the difficulties some with disabilities experience getting involved in romantic relationships... Rie Aruga refuses to romanticize, pushing her heroine to face the reality of disability. She invites her readers to the same tasks of empathy, knowledge and recognition."
—Slate.fr

"An important entry [in manga romance]... The emotional core of both plot and characters indicates thoughtfulness... [Aruga's] research is readily apparent in the text and artwork, making this feel like a real story."
—Anime News Network

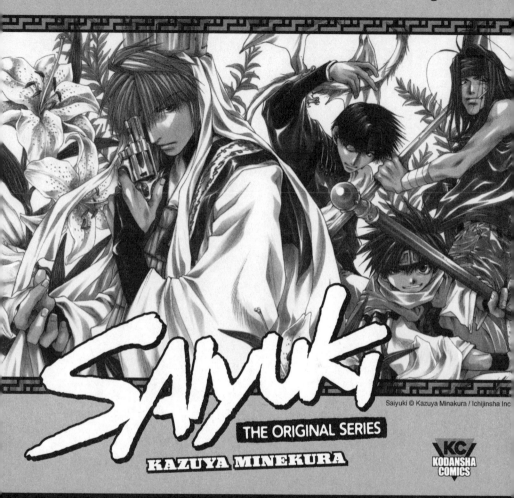

CUTE ANIMALS AND LIFE LESSONS, PERFECT FOR ASPIRING PET VETS OF ALL AGES!

YUZU THE PET VET

1

BY
MINGO ITO

In collaboration with
NIPPON COLUMBIA CO., LTD.

Yuzu the Pet Vet © Mingo Ito / NIPPON COLUMBIA CO., LTD./ Kodansha Ltd.

For an 11-year-old, Yuzu has a lot on her plate. When her mom gets sick and has to be hospitalized, Yuzu goes to live with her uncle who runs the local veterinary clinic. Yuzu's always been scared of animals, but she tries to help out. Through all the tough moments in her life, Yuzu realizes that she can help make things all right with a little help from her animal pals, peers, and kind grown-ups.

Every new patient is a furry friend in the making!

The beloved characters from *Cardcaptor Sakura* return in a brand new, reimagined fantasy adventure!

"[*Tsubasa*] takes readers on a fantastic ride that only gets more exhilarating with each successive chapter." —Anime News Network

In the Kingdom of Clow, an archaeological dig unleashes an incredible power, causing Princess Sakura to lose her memories. To save her, her childhood friend Syaoran must follow the orders of the Dimension Witch and travel alongside Kurogane, an unrivaled warrior; Fai, a powerful magician; and Mokona, a curiously strange creature, to retrieve Sakura's dispersed memories!

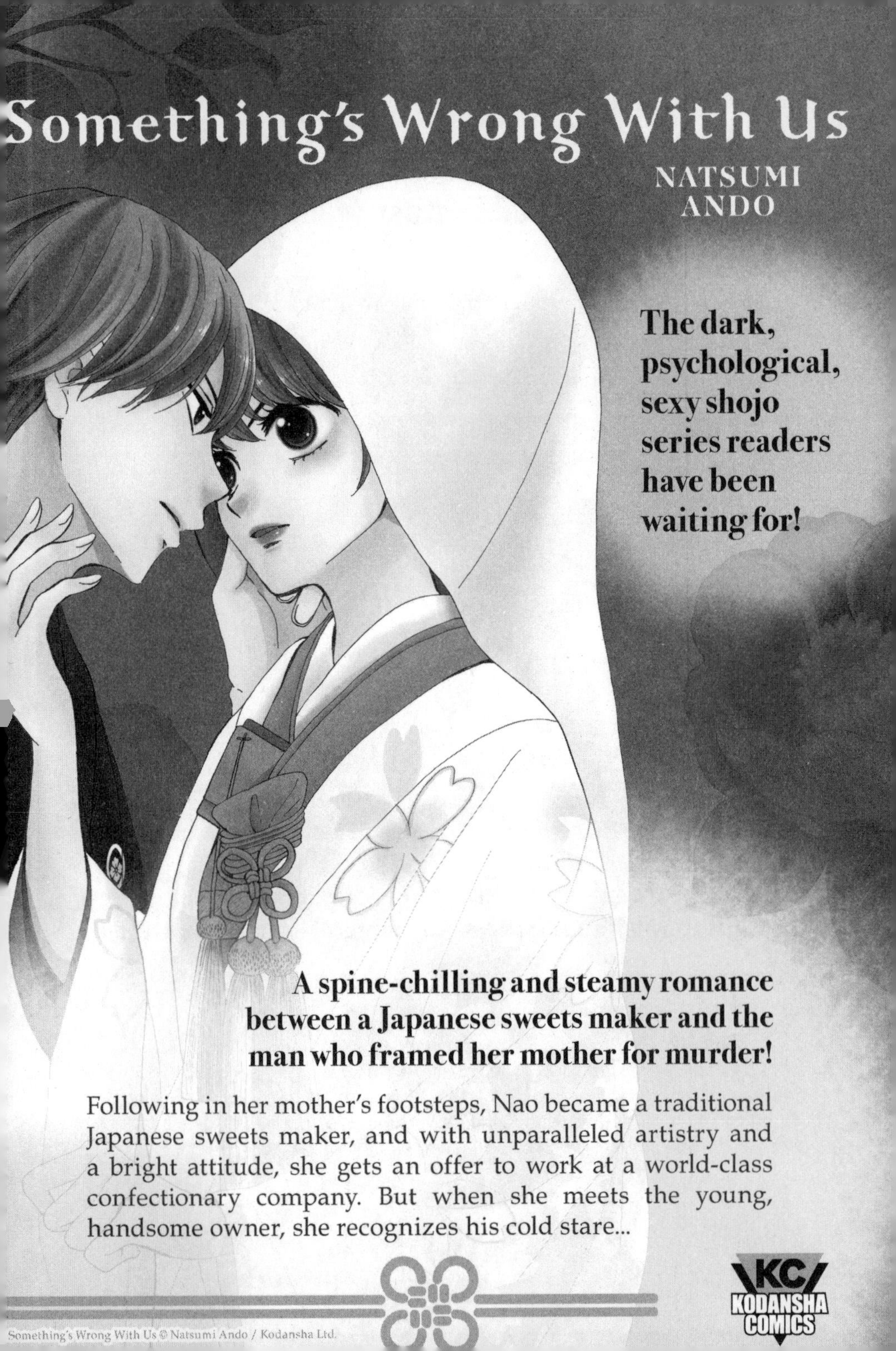
Something's Wrong With Us
NATSUMI ANDO
The dark, psychological, sexy shojo series readers have been waiting for!
A spine-chilling and steamy romance between a Japanese sweets maker and the man who framed her mother for murder!
Following in her mother's footsteps, Nao became a traditional Japanese sweets maker, and with unparalleled artistry and a bright attitude, she gets an offer to work at a world-class confectionary company. But when she meets the young, handsome owner, she recognizes his cold stare...
KC KODANSHA COMICS
Something's Wrong With Us © Natsumi Ando / Kodansha Ltd.

The adorable new odd-couple cat comedy manga from the creator of the beloved *Chi's Sweet Home*, in full color!

Praise for *Chi's Sweet Home*

"Nearly impossible to turn away... a true all-ages title that anyone, young or old, cat lover or not, will enjoy. The stories will bring a smile to your face and warm your heart."

—*School Library Journal*

Sue & Tai-chan

Konami Kanata

Sue is an aging housecat who's looking forward to living out her life in peace... but her plans change when the mischievous black tomcat Tai-chan enters the picture! Hey! Sue never signed up to be a catsitter! *Sue & Tai-chan* is the latest from the reigning meow-narch of cute kitty comics, Konami Kanata.

KC KODANSHA COMICS

A Kodansha Comics Trade Paperback Original
Sweat and Soap 10 copyright © 2021 Kintetsu Yamada
English translation copyright © 2021 Kintetsu Yamada

Published in the United States by Kodansha Comics, an imprint of Kodansha USA Publishing, LLC, New York.

Publication rights for this English edition arranged through Kodansha Ltd., Tokyo.

First published in Japan in 2021 by Kodansha Ltd., Tokyo as Ase to Sekken volume 10.

ISBN 978-1-64651-296-6

Printed in the United States of America.

www.kodansha.us

1st Printing
Translation: Matt Treyvaud
Lettering: Sara Linsley
Editing: Kristin Osani
Kodansha Comics edition cover design by Phil Balsman

Publisher: Kiichiro Sugawara

Director of publishing services: Ben Applegate
Associate director of operations: Stephen Pakula
Publishing services managing editorial: Madison Salters, Alanna Ruse
Production Managers: Emi Lotto, Angela Zurlo